SORCERERS

S

HAMBURG // LONDON // LOS ANGELES // TOKYO

Sorcerers & Secretaries Vol.2
Created by Amy Kim Ganter

Lettering - Star Print Brokers and Lucas Rivera
Cover Design - Anne Marie Horne

Editor - Lillian Diaz-Przybyl
Digital Imaging Manager - Chris Buford
Pre-Production Supervisor - Erika Terriquez
Art Director - Anne Marie Horne
Production Manager - Elisabeth Brizzi
Managing Editor - Vy Nguyen
VP of Production - Ron Klamert
Editor-in-Chief - Rob Tokar
Publisher - Mike Kiley
President and C.O.O. - John Parker
C.E.O. and Chief Creative Officer - Stuart Levy

A  Manga

TOKYOPOP and  are trademarks or registered trademarks of TOKYOPOP Inc.

TOKYOPOP Inc.
5900 Wilshire Blvd. Suite 2000
Los Angeles, CA 90036

E-mail: info@TOKYOPOP.com
Come visit us online at www.TOKYOPOP.com

ISBN: 978-1-59816-410-7

First TOKYOPOP printing: June 2007
10 9 8 7 6 5 4 3 2 1
Printed in the USA

contents

Chapter One

Has A Confession

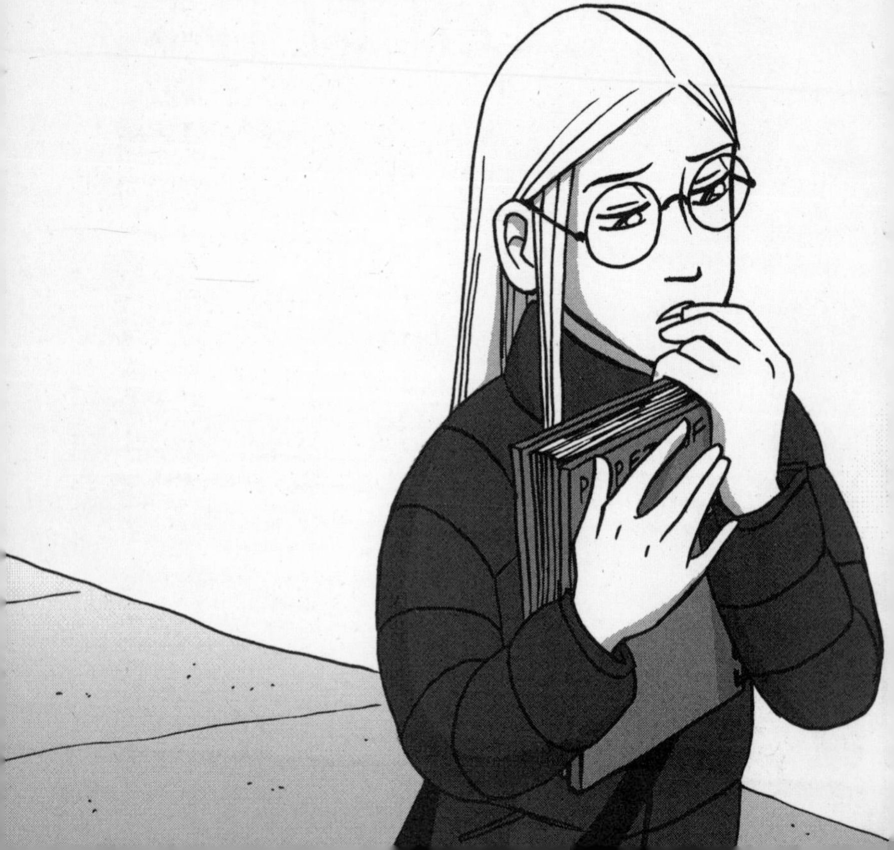

I asked you not to contact me again.

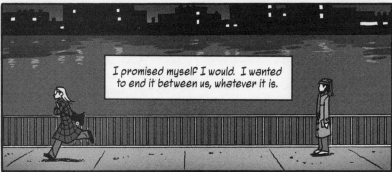

I promised myself I would. I wanted to end it between us, whatever it is.

But I wasn't expecting it to feel like this.

hFF hFF

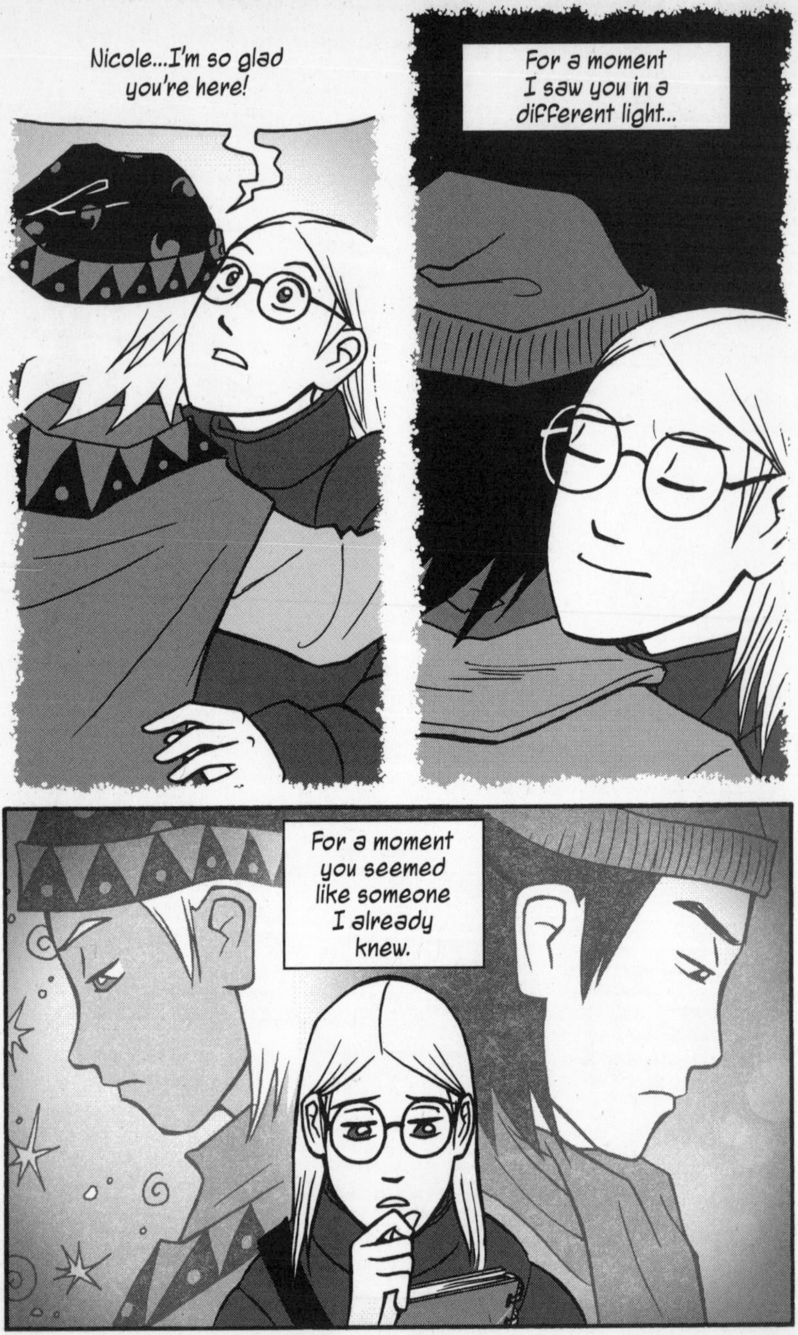
Nicole...I'm so glad you're here!
For a moment I saw you in a different light...
For a moment you seemed like someone I already knew.

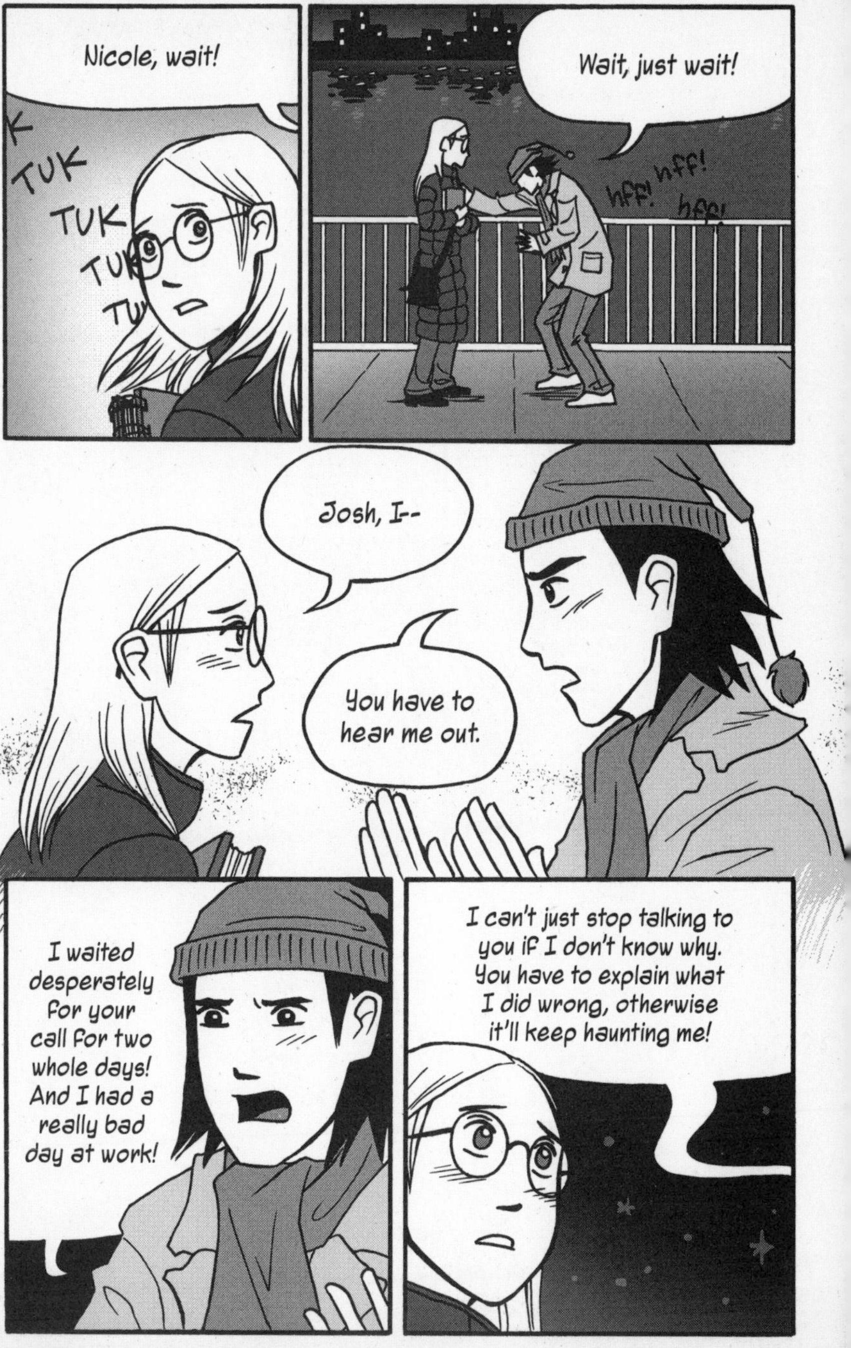
Nicole, wait!
TUK
TUK
TUK
TUK
Wait, just wait!
hff! hff!
hff!
Josh, I--
You have to hear me out.
I waited desperately for your call for two whole days! And I had a really bad day at work!
I can't just stop talking to you if I don't know why. You have to explain what I did wrong, otherwise it'll keep haunting me!

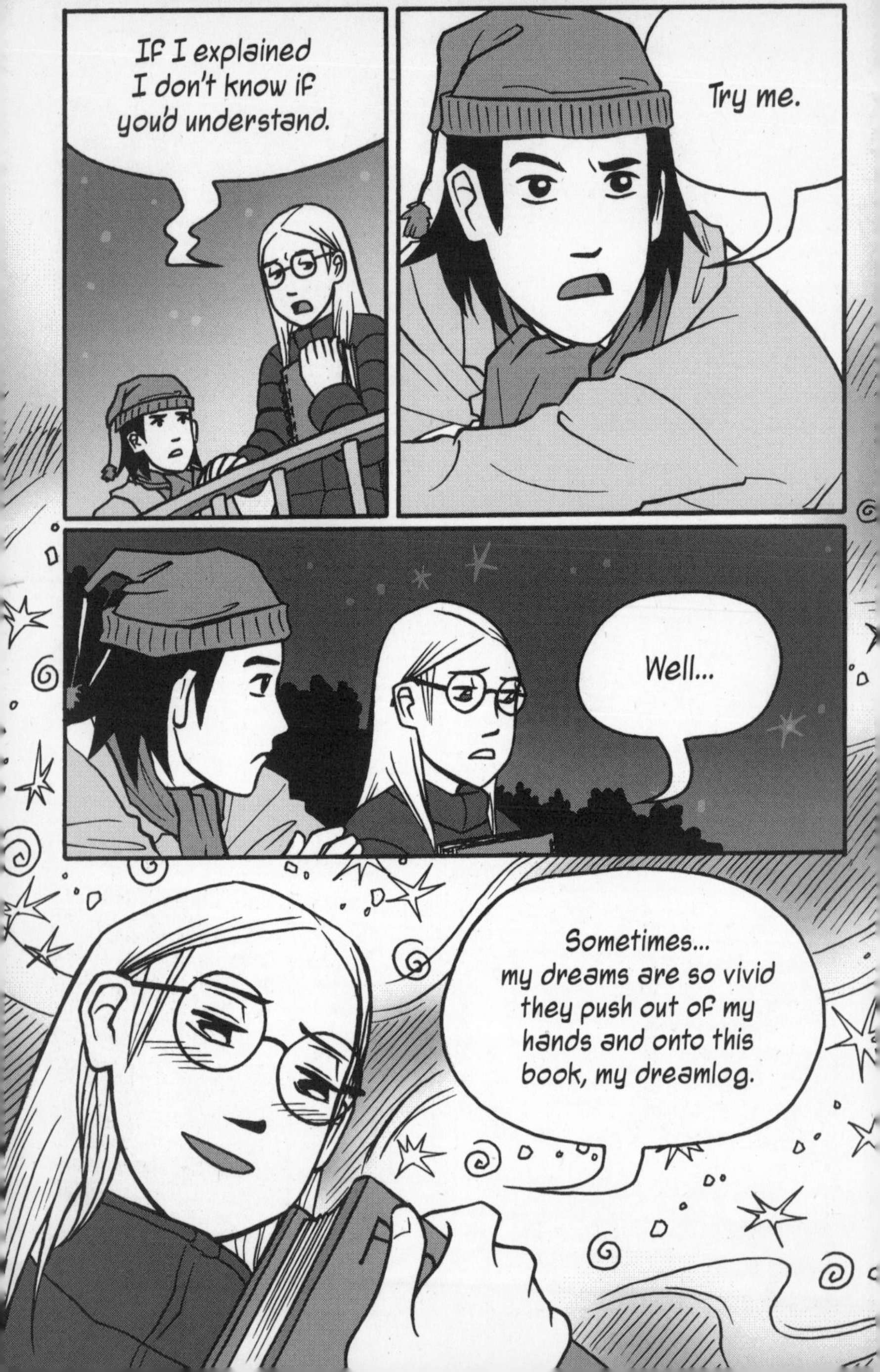
If I explained I don't know if you'd understand.
Try me.
Well...
Sometimes... my dreams are so vivid they push out of my hands and onto this book, my dreamlog.

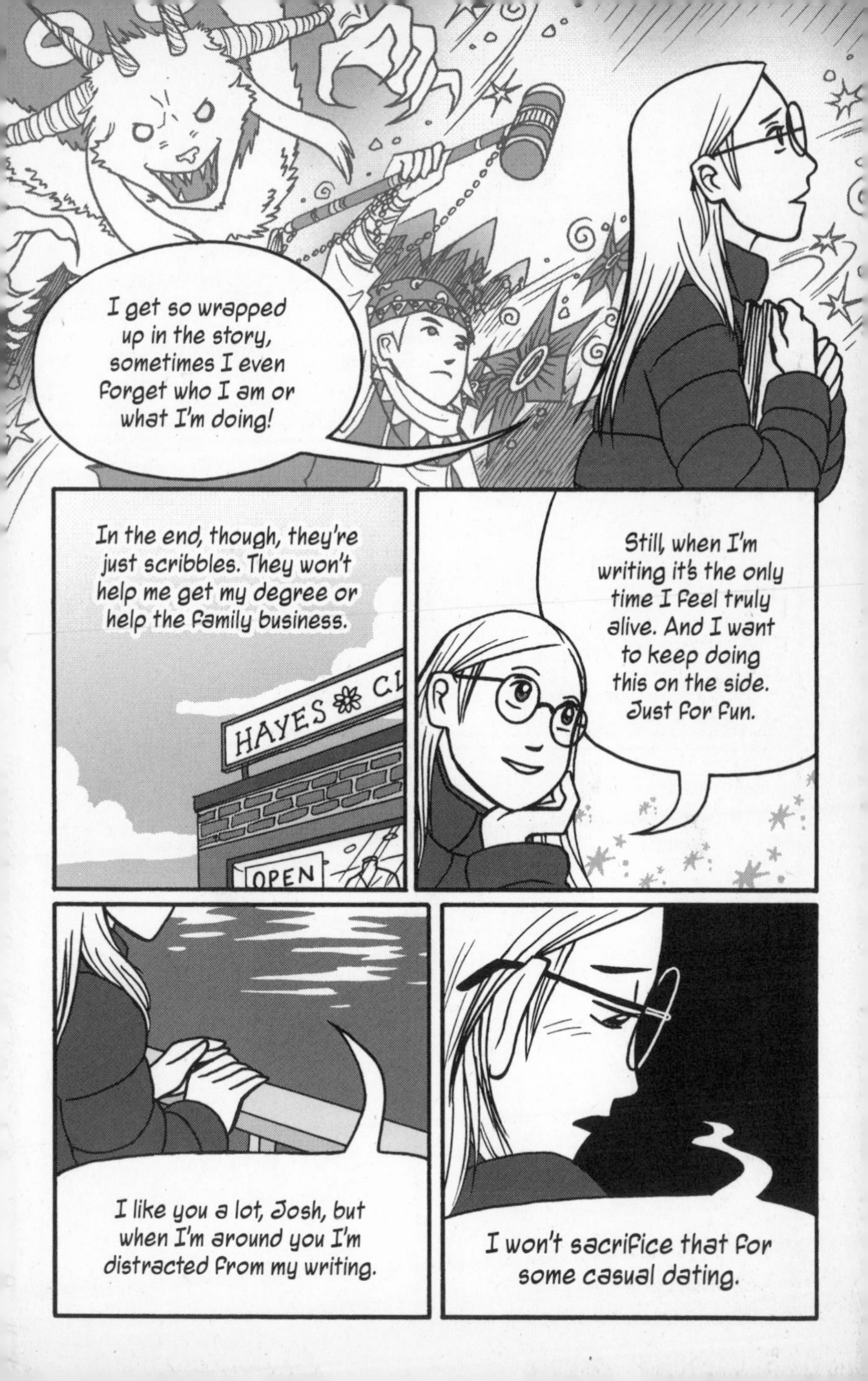
I get so wrapped up in the story, sometimes I even forget who I am or what I'm doing!
In the end, though, they're just scribbles. They won't help me get my degree or help the family business.
HAYES ✿ CL
OPEN
Still, when I'm writing it's the only time I feel truly alive. And I want to keep doing this on the side. Just for fun.
I like you a lot, Josh, but when I'm around you I'm distracted from my writing.
I won't sacrifice that for some casual dating.

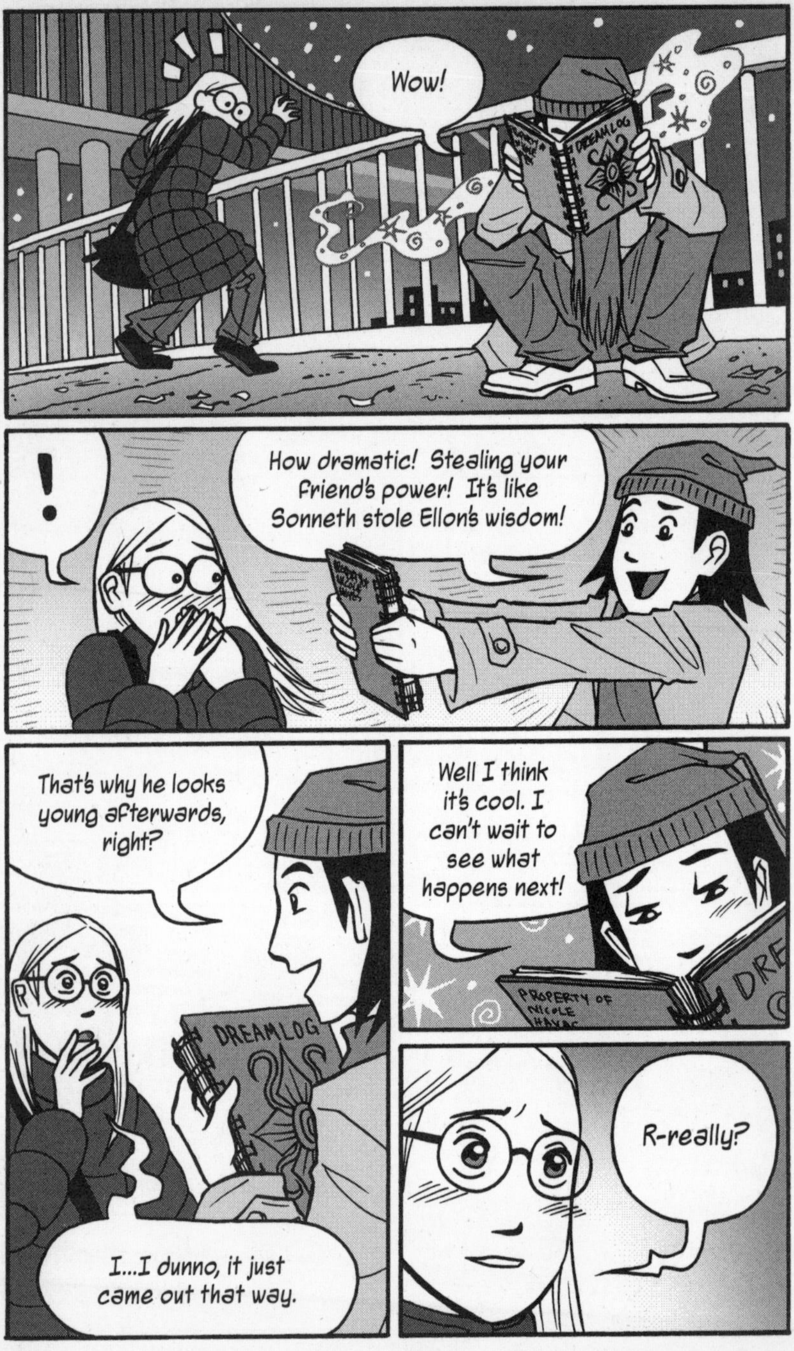
Wow!
!
How dramatic! Stealing your friend's power! It's like Sonneth stole Ellon's wisdom!
That's why he looks young afterwards, right?
DREAMLOG
I...I dunno, it just came out that way.
Well I think it's cool. I can't wait to see what happens next!
R-really?

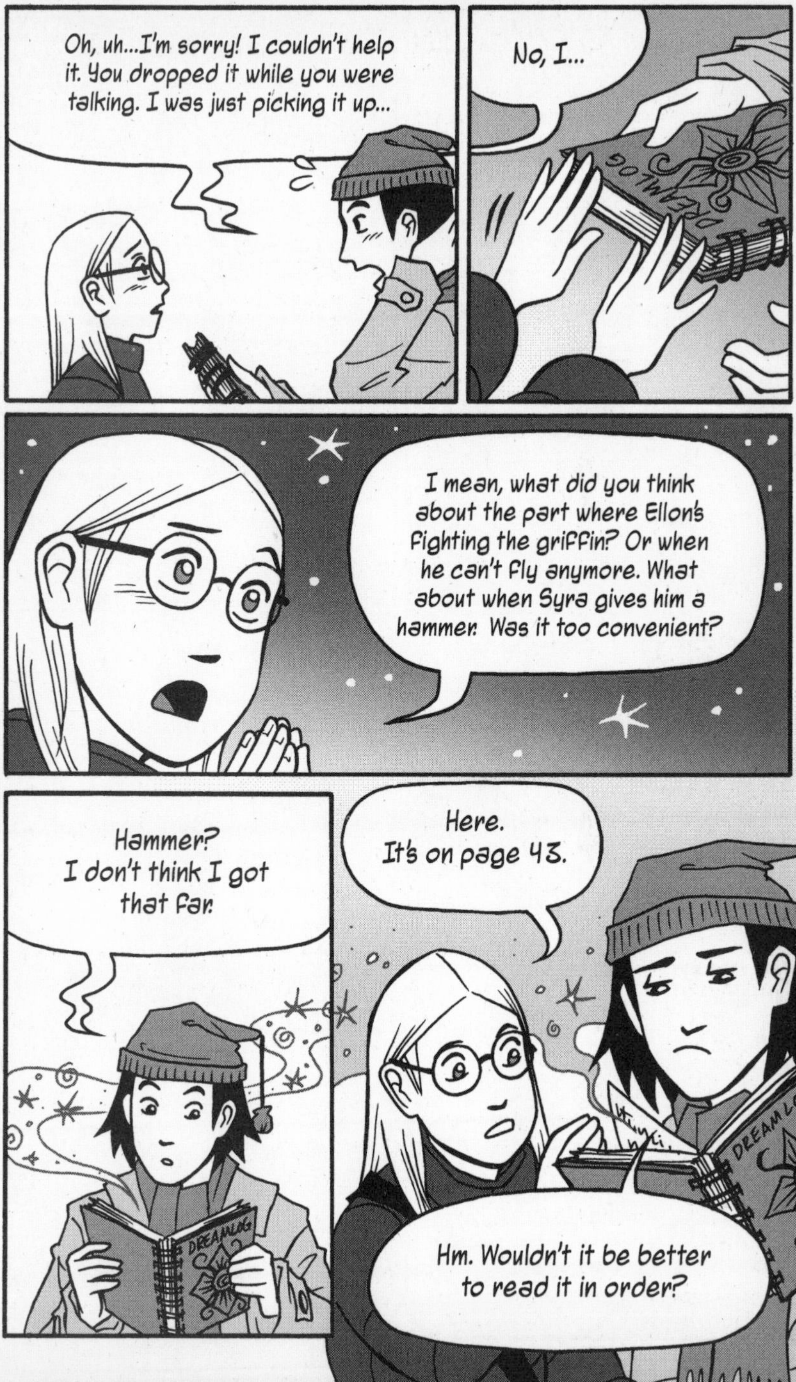
Oh, uh...I'm sorry! I couldn't help it. You dropped it while you were talking. I was just picking it up...
No, I...
I mean, what did you think about the part where Ellon's fighting the griffin? Or when he can't fly anymore. What about when Syra gives him a hammer. Was it too convenient?
Hammer? I don't think I got that far.
DREAMLOG
Here. It's on page 43.
DREAM LOG
Hm. Wouldn't it be better to read it in order?

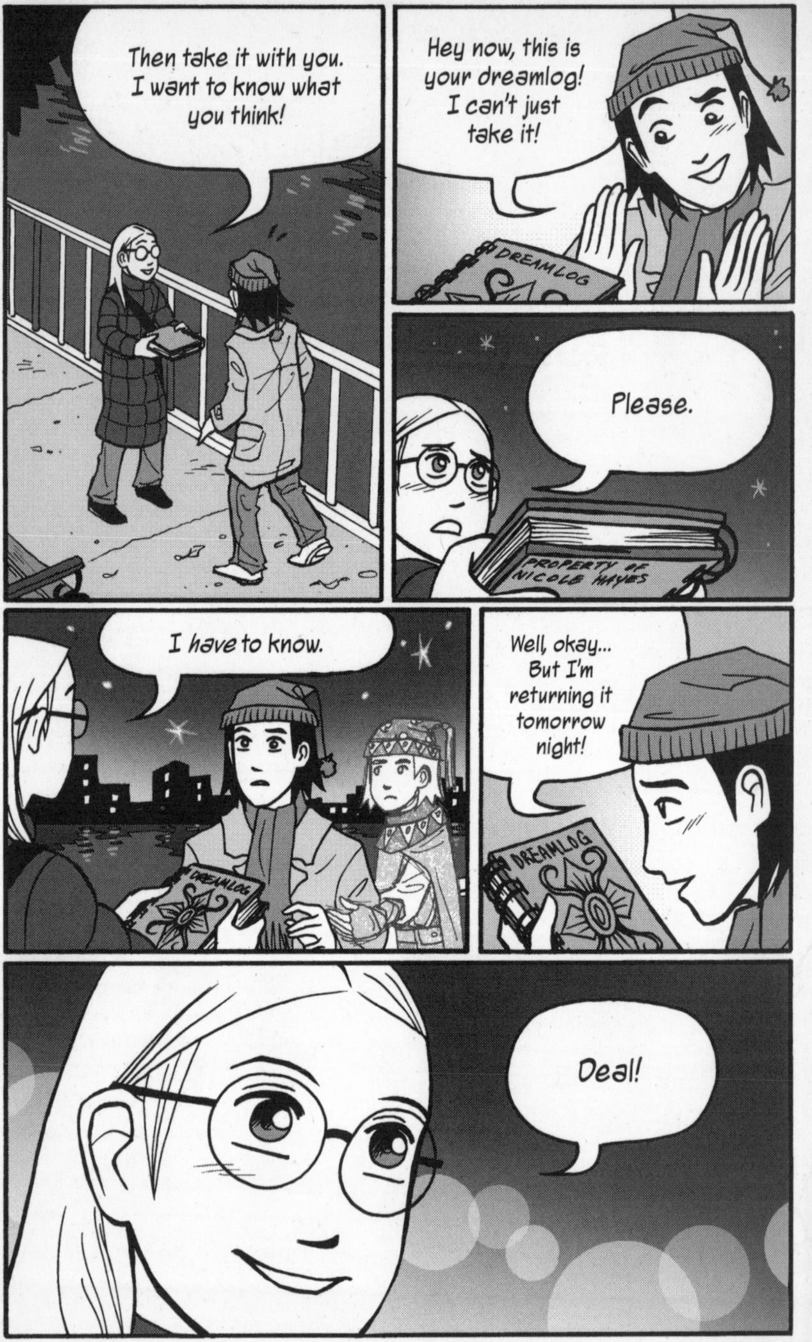
Then take it with you. I want to know what you think!
Hey now, this is your dreamlog! I can't just take it!
DREAMLOG
Please.
PROPERTY OF NICOLE HAYES
I *have* to know.
DREAMLOG
Well, okay... But I'm returning it tomorrow night!
DREAMLOG
Deal!

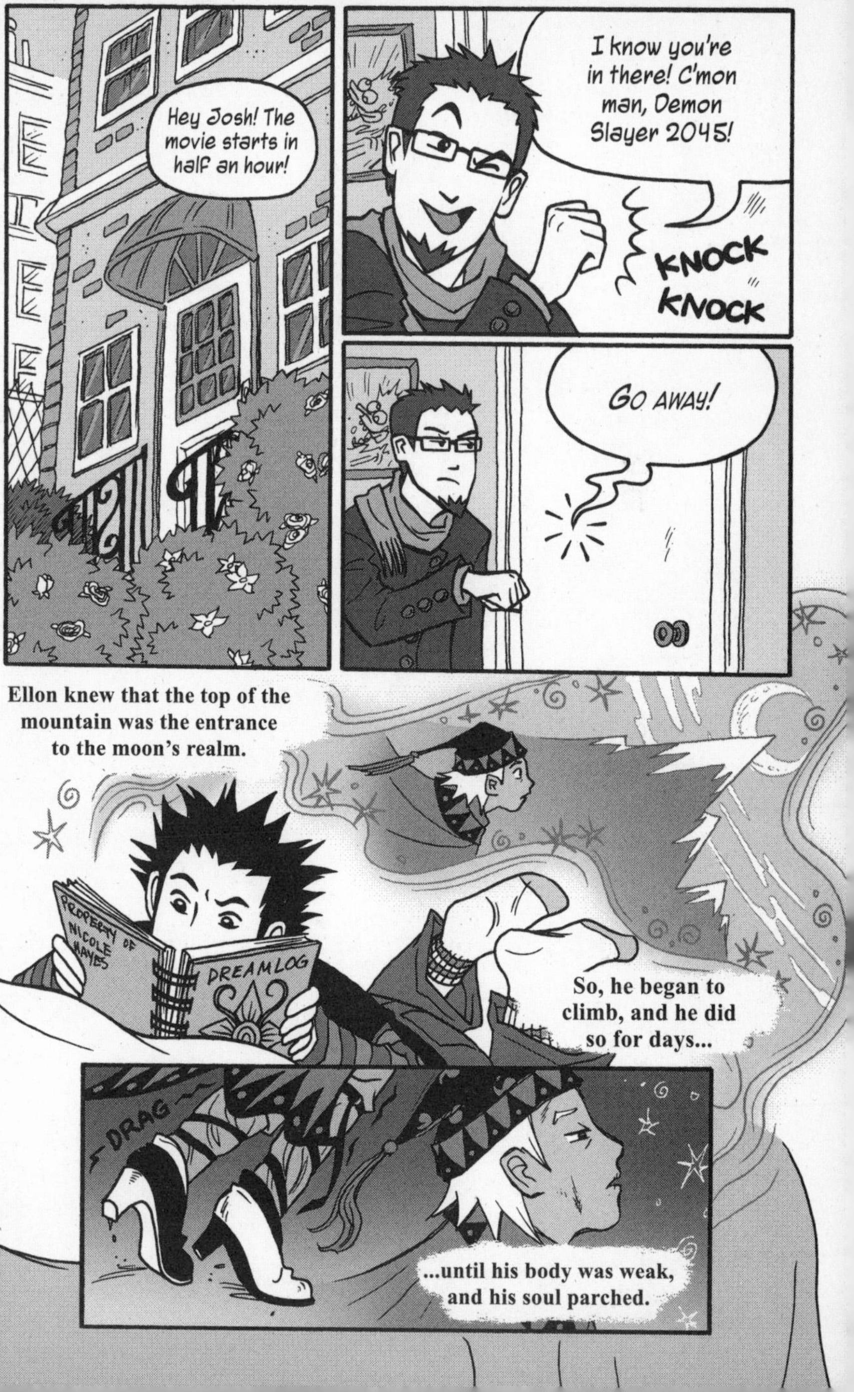
Hey Josh! The movie starts in half an hour!
I know you're in there! C'mon man, Demon Slayer 2045!
KNOCK KNOCK
GO AWAY!
Ellon knew that the top of the mountain was the entrance to the moon's realm.
PROPERTY OF NICOLE HAYES
DREAMLOG
So, he began to climb, and he did so for days...
DRAG
...until his body was weak, and his soul parched.

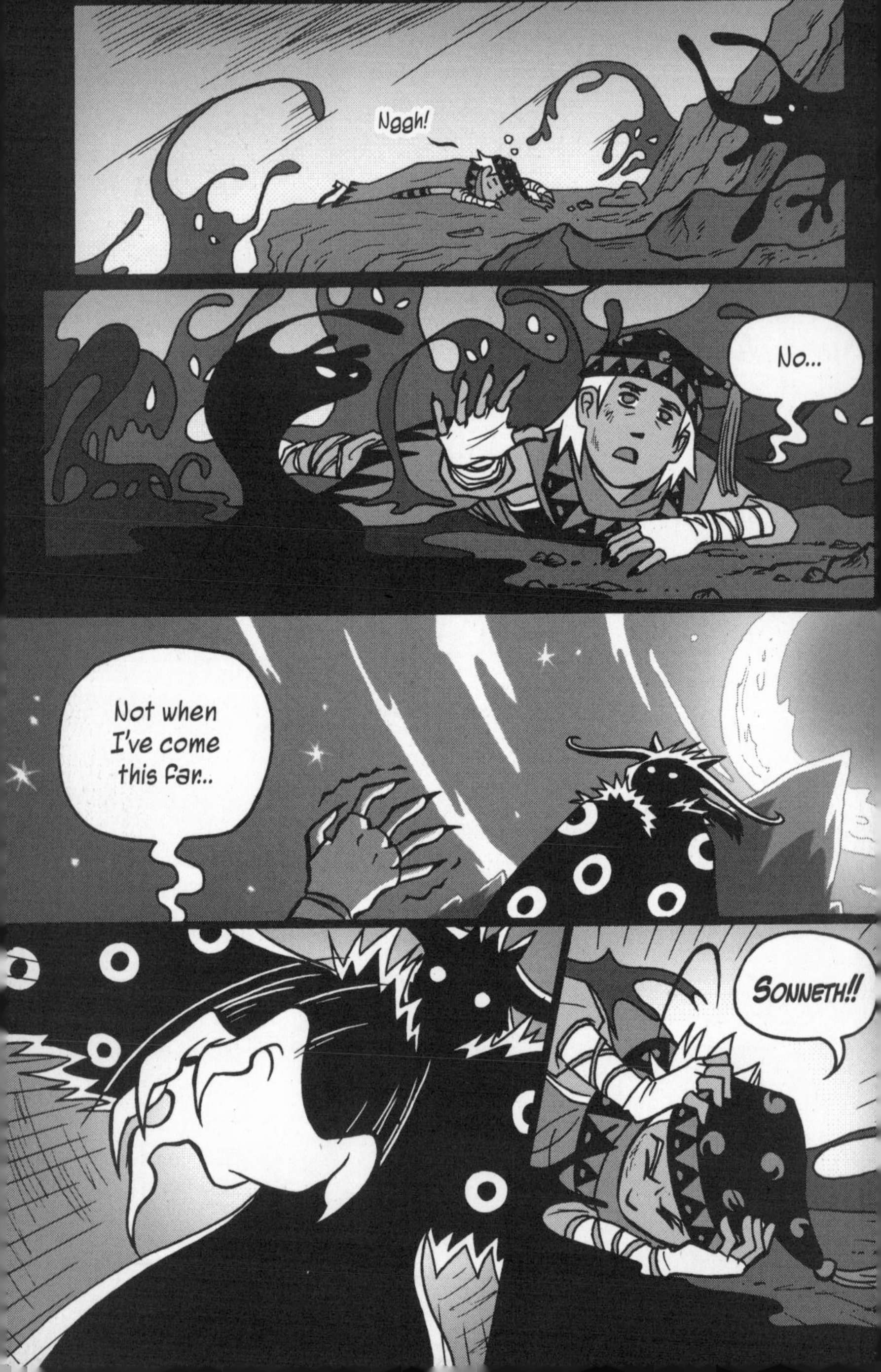
Nggh!
No...
Not when I've come this far...
SONNETH!!

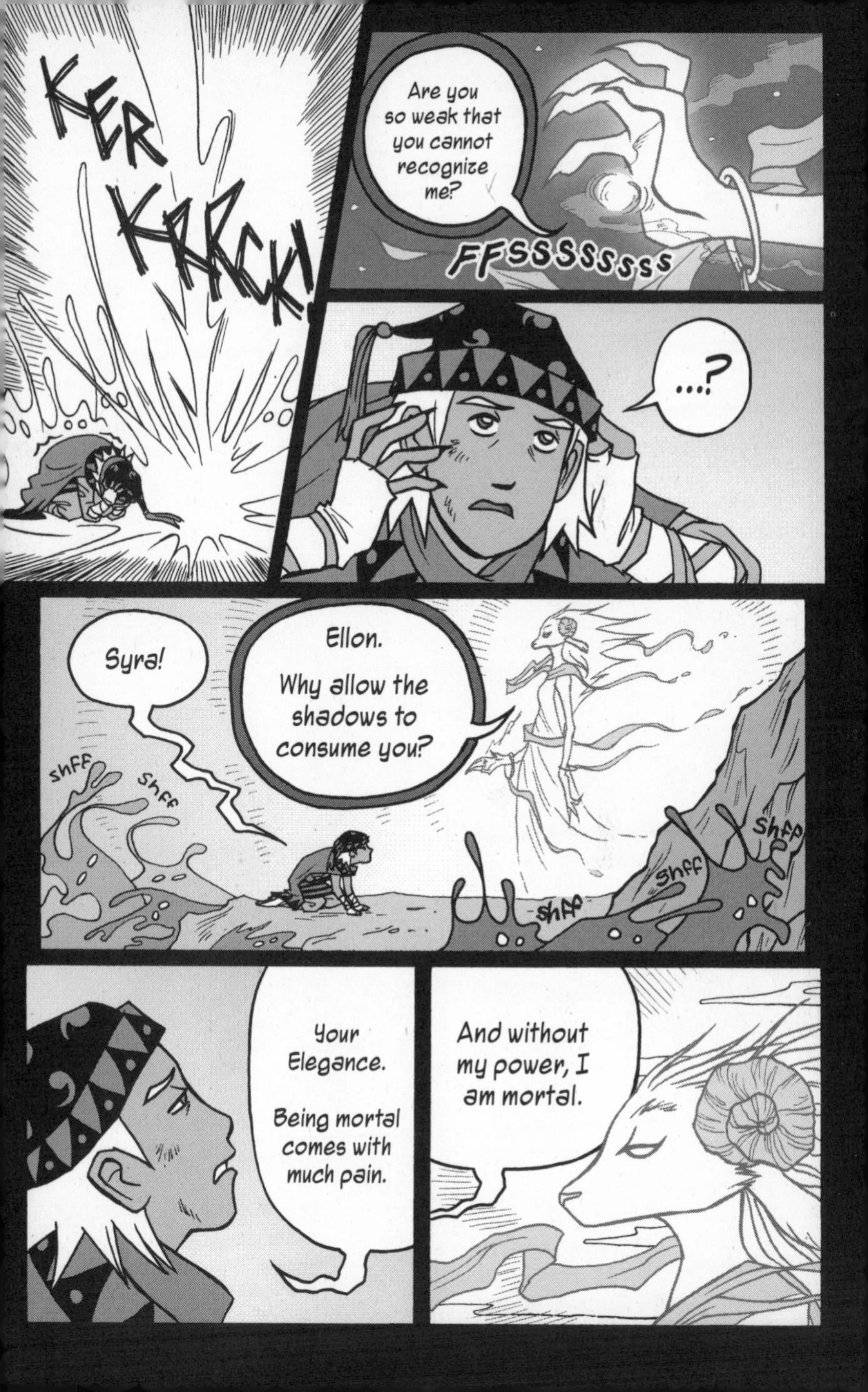
KER KRRCK!
Are you so weak that you cannot recognize me?
FFSSSSSSSSS
...?
Syra!
Ellon. Why allow the shadows to consume you?
shff
shff
shff
shff
shff
Your Elegance. Being mortal comes with much pain.
And without my power, I am mortal.

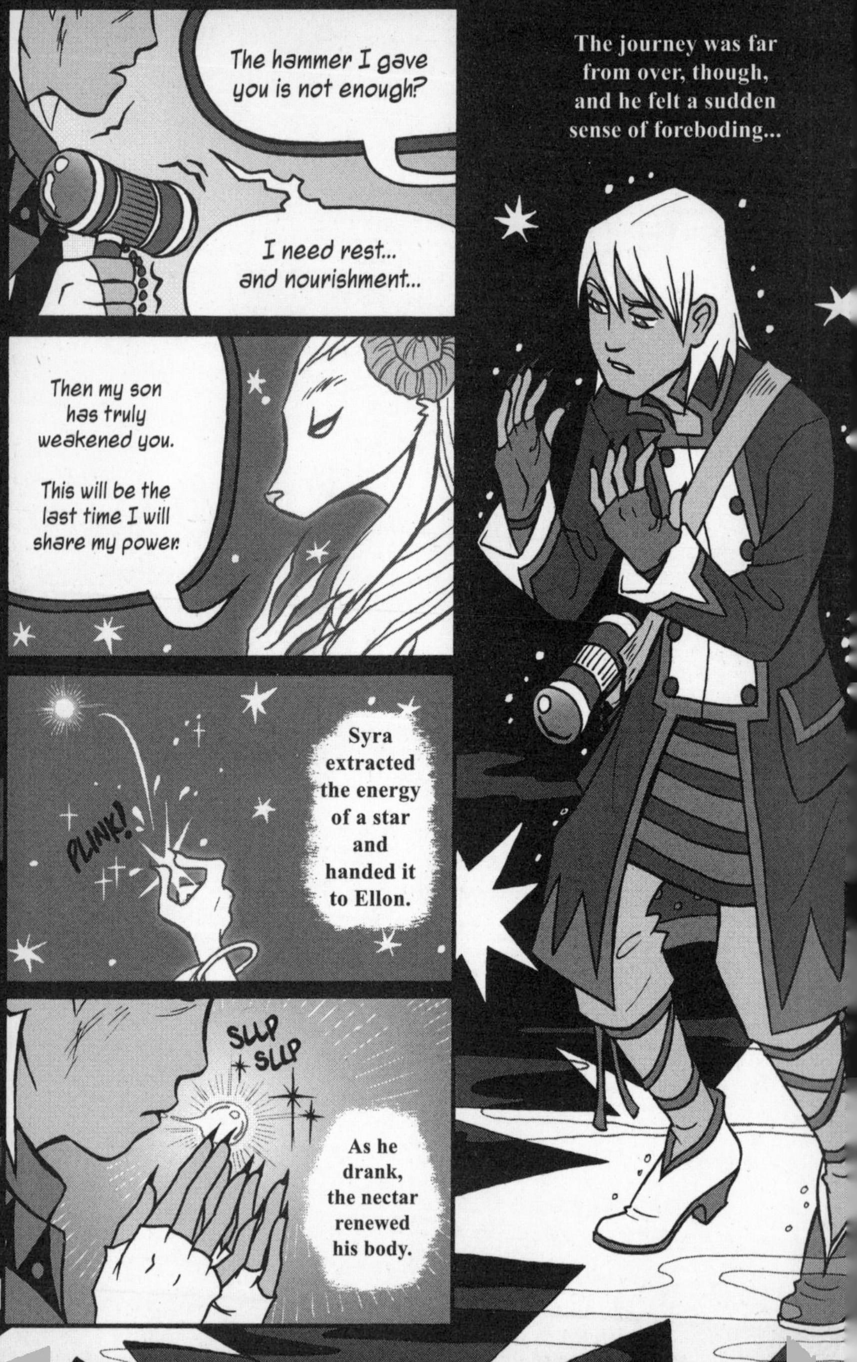
The hammer I gave you is not enough?
I need rest... and nourishment...
Then my son has truly weakened you.
This will be the last time I will share my power.
Syra extracted the energy of a star and handed it to Ellon.
PLINK!
SLLP SLLP
As he drank, the nectar renewed his body.
The journey was far from over, though, and he felt a sudden sense of foreboding...

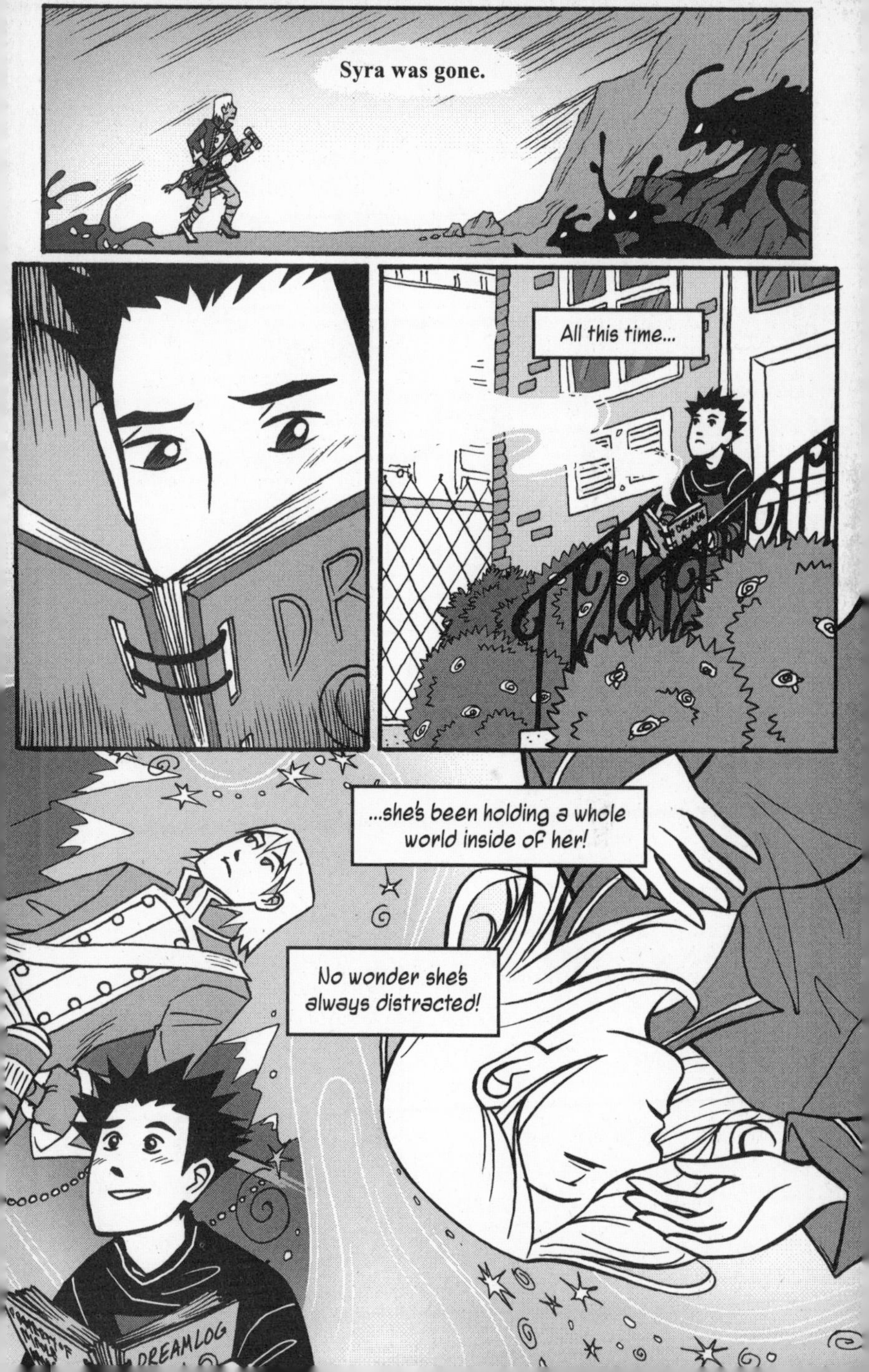
Syra was gone.
All this time...
...she's been holding a whole world inside of her!
No wonder she's always distracted!
DREAMLOG

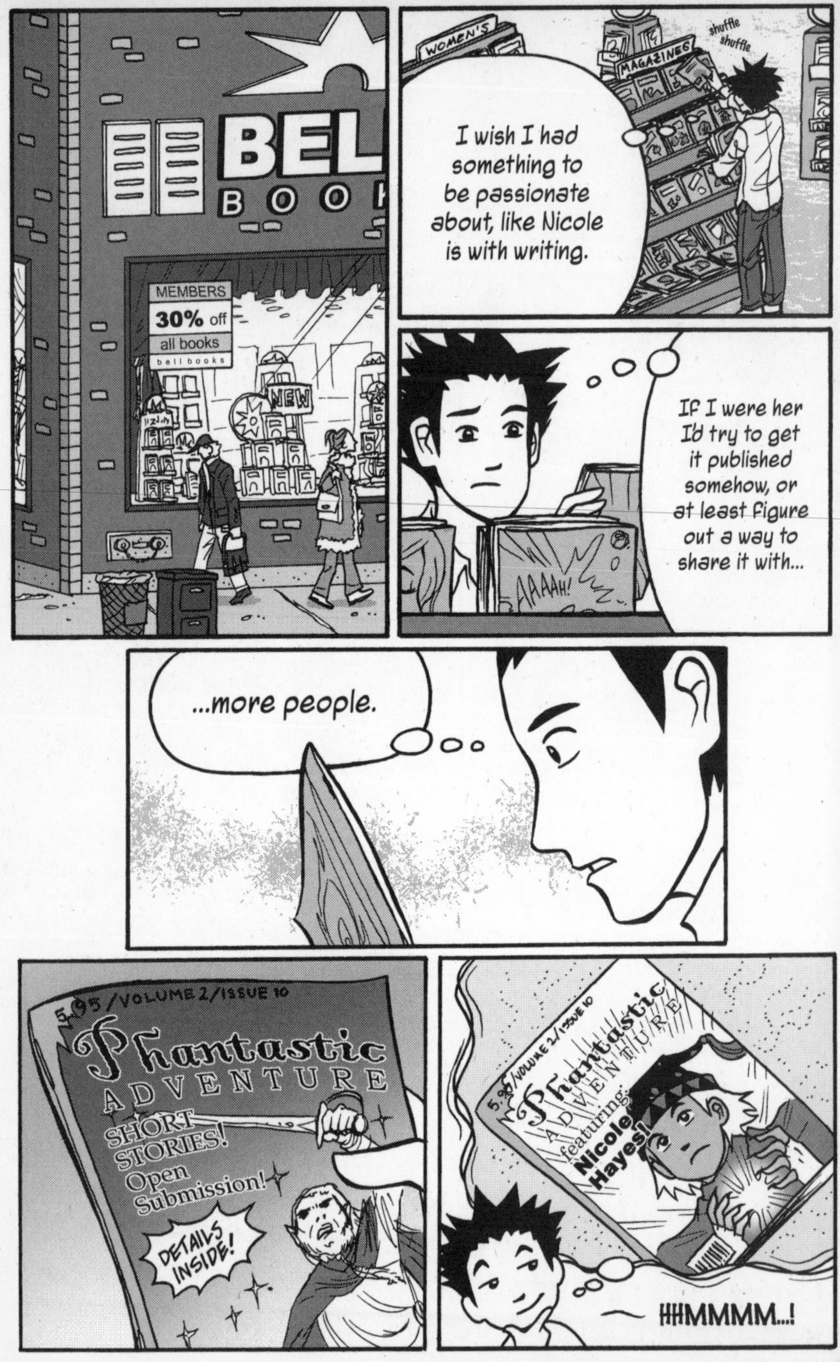
BEL
B O O
MEMBERS
30% off
all books
bell books
NEW
WOMEN'S
MAGAZINES
shuffle
shuffle
I wish I had something to be passionate about, like Nicole is with writing.
If I were her I'd try to get it published somehow, or at least figure out a way to share it with...
AAAAH!
...more people.
5.95/VOLUME 2/ISSUE 10
Phantastic
ADVENTURE
SHORT STORIES!
Open Submission!
DETAILS INSIDE!
5.95/VOLUME 2/ISSUE 10
Phantastic
ADVENTURE
featuring:
Nicole Hayes!
HHMMMM...!

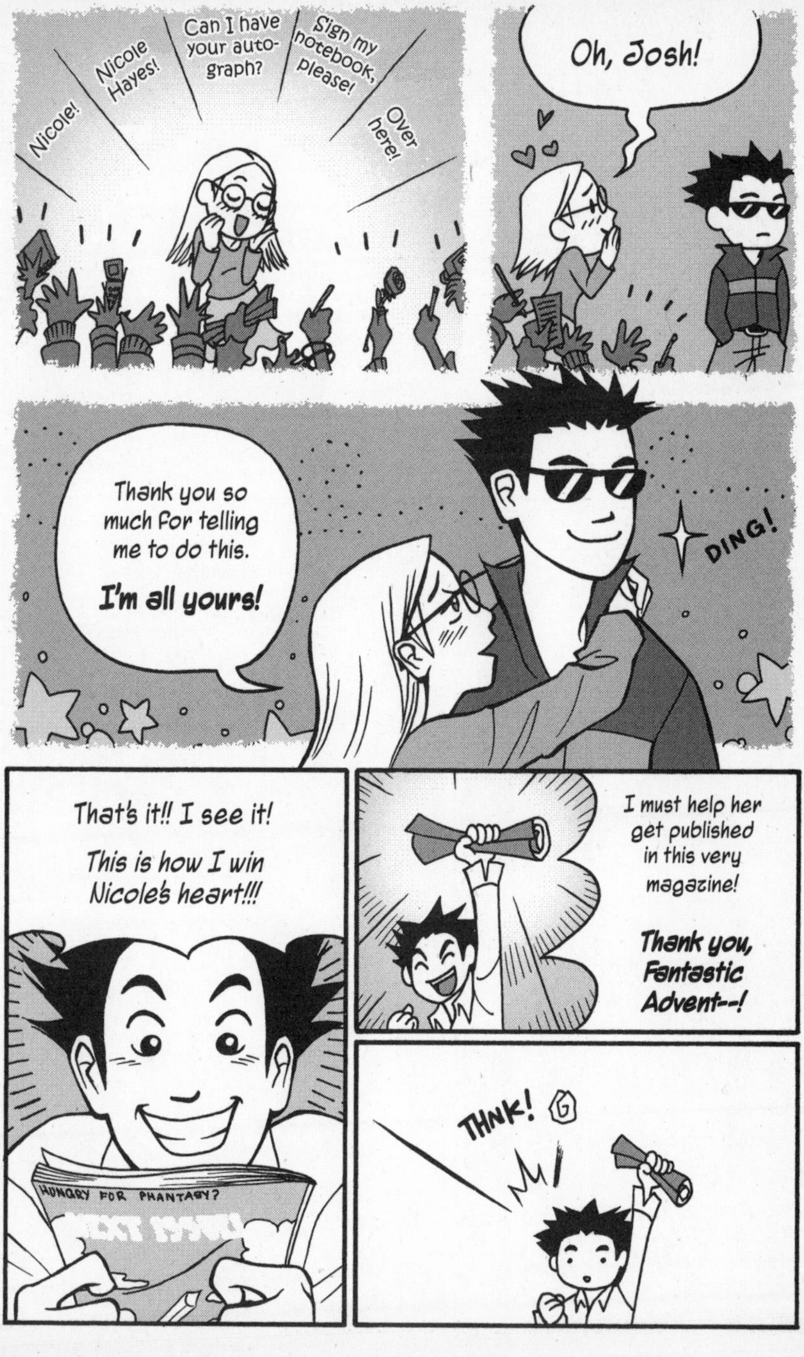
Nicole!
Nicole Hayes!
Can I have your autograph?
Sign my notebook, please!
Over here!
Oh, Josh!
Thank you so much for telling me to do this.
I'm all yours!
DING!
That's it!! I see it!
This is how I win Nicole's heart!!!
HUNGRY FOR PHANTASY?
I must help her get published in this very magazine!
Thank you, Fantastic Advent--!
THNK!

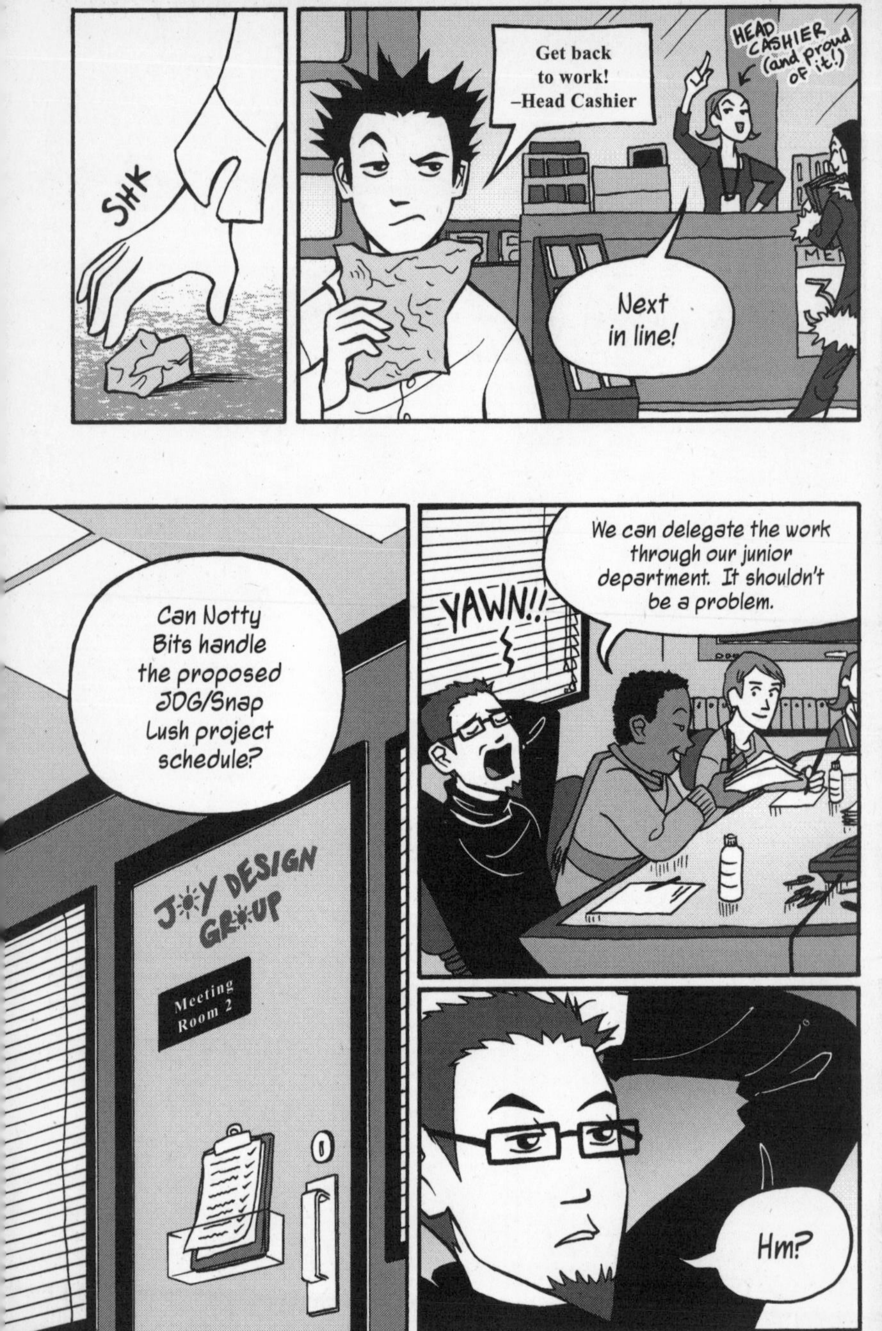
SHK
Get back to work! –Head Cashier
HEAD CASHIER (and proud of it!)
Next in line!
Can Notty Bits handle the proposed JOG/Snap Lush project schedule?
JOY DESIGN GROUP
Meeting Room 2
YAWN!!
We can delegate the work through our junior department. It shouldn't be a problem.
Hm?

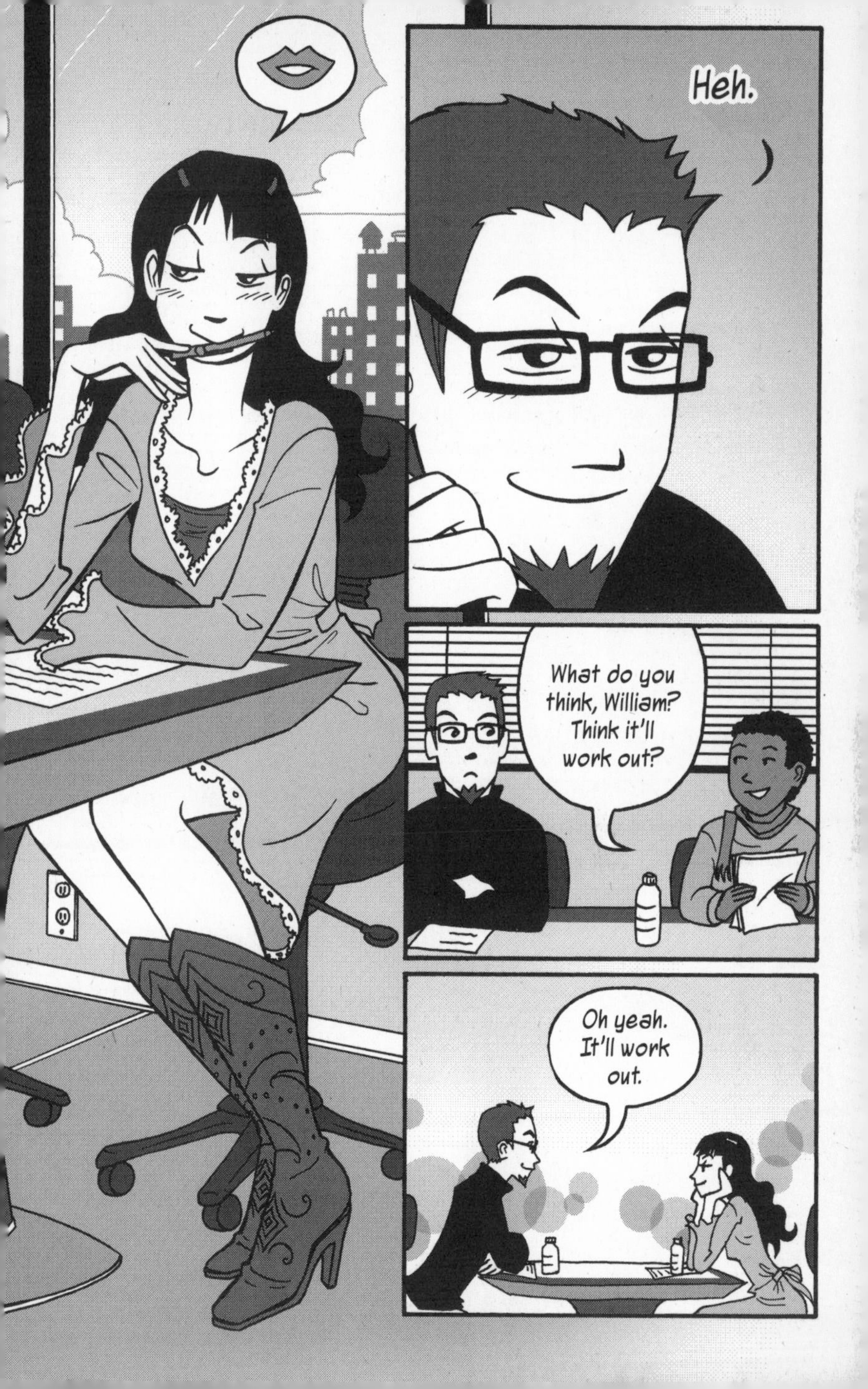
Heh.
What do you think, William? Think it'll work out?
Oh yeah. It'll work out.

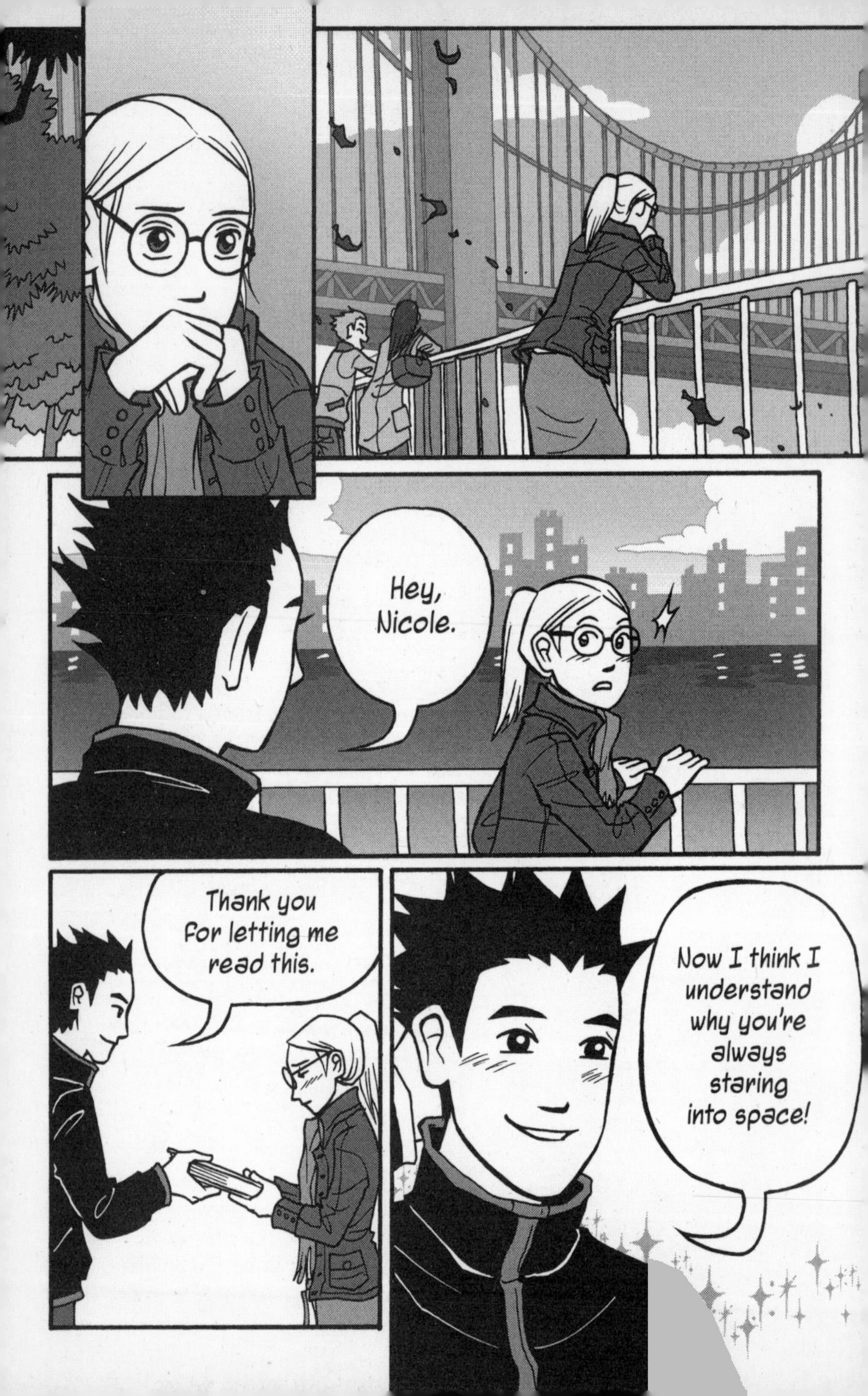
Hey, Nicole.
Thank you for letting me read this.
Now I think I understand why you're always staring into space!

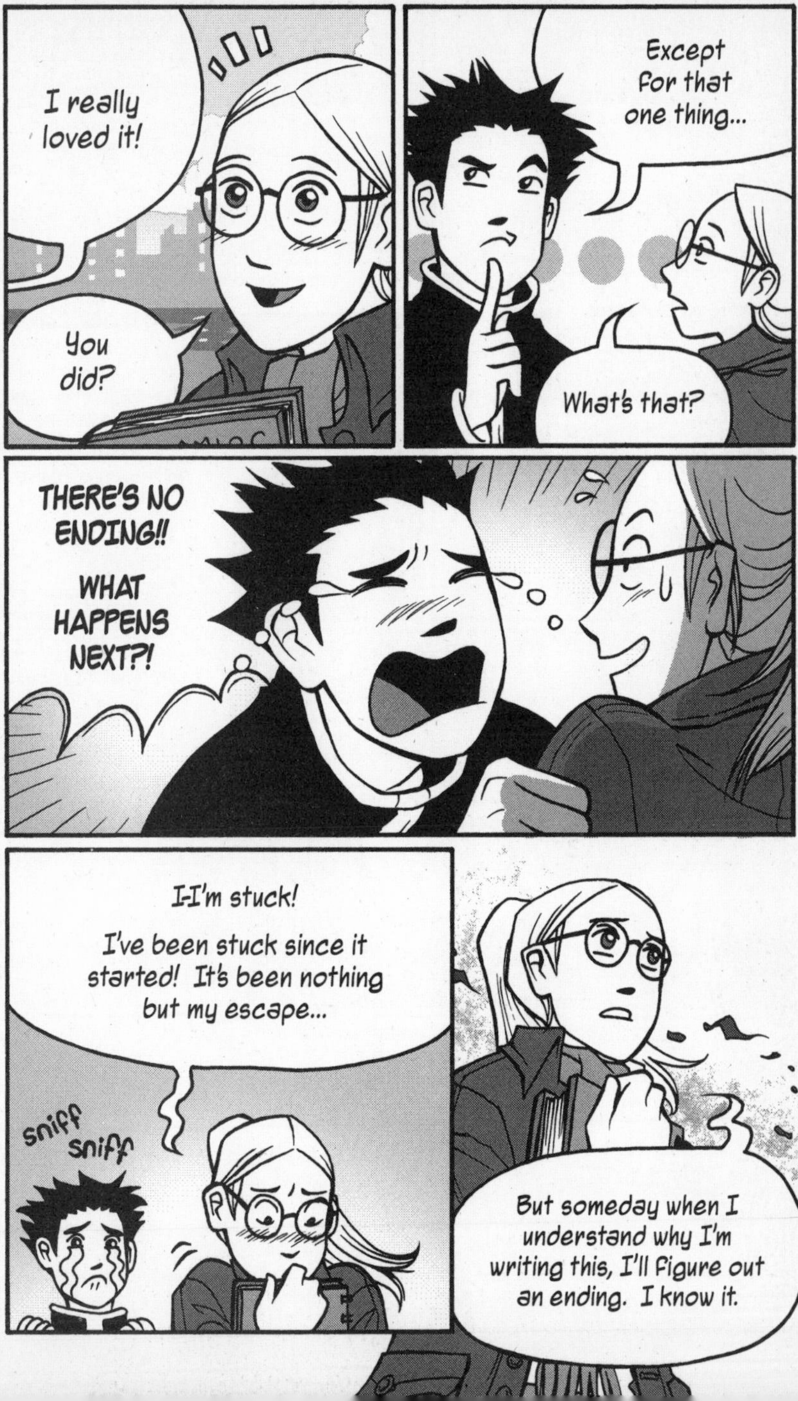
I really loved it!
You did?
Except for that one thing...
What's that?
THERE'S NO ENDING!! WHAT HAPPENS NEXT?!
I-I'm stuck!
I've been stuck since it started! It's been nothing but my escape...
sniff sniff
But someday when I understand why I'm writing this, I'll figure out an ending. I know it.

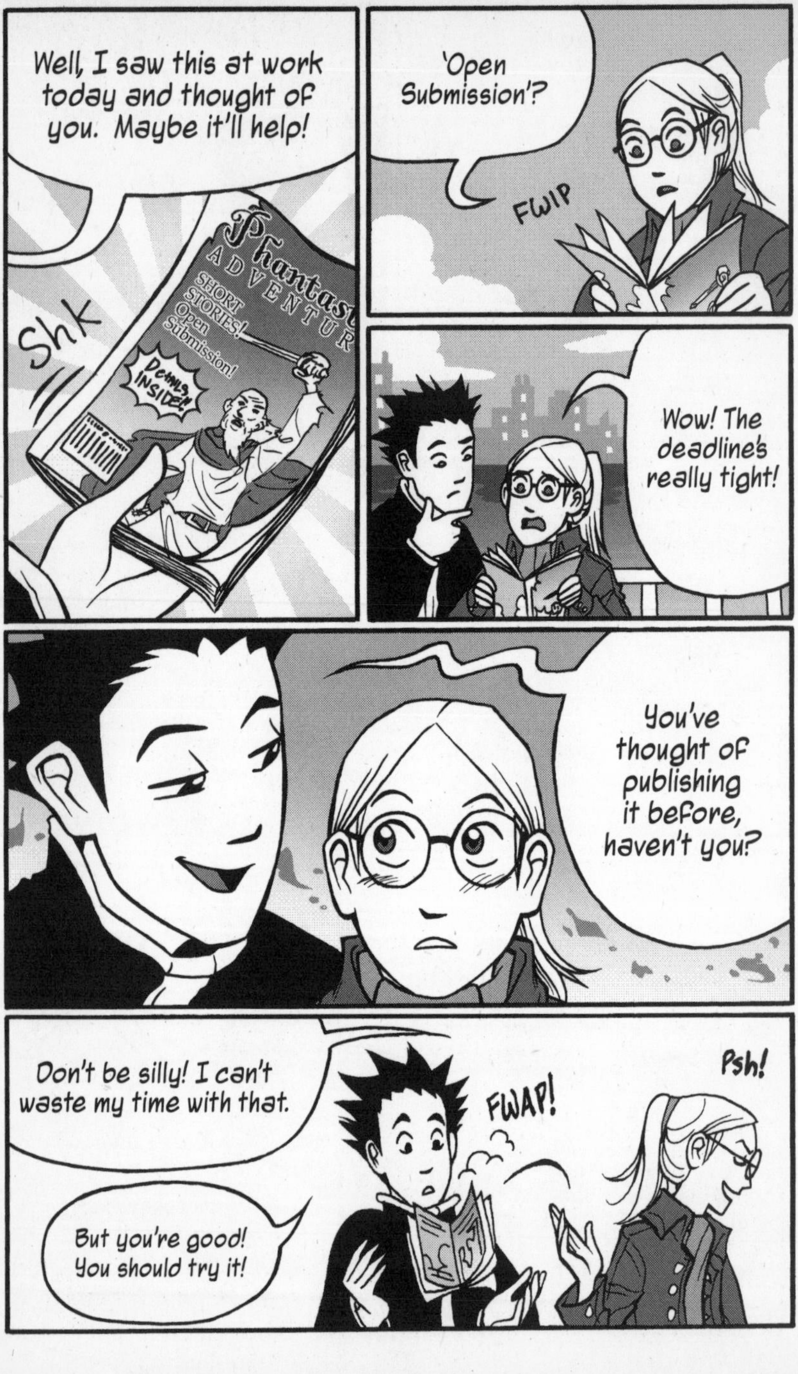
Well, I saw this at work today and thought of you. Maybe it'll help!
Shk
Phantast
ADVENTUR
SHORT STORIES! Open Submission!
DETAILS INSIDE!!
'Open Submission'?
FWIP
Wow! The deadline's really tight!
You've thought of publishing it before, haven't you?
Don't be silly! I can't waste my time with that.
FWAP!
Psh!
But you're good! You should try it!

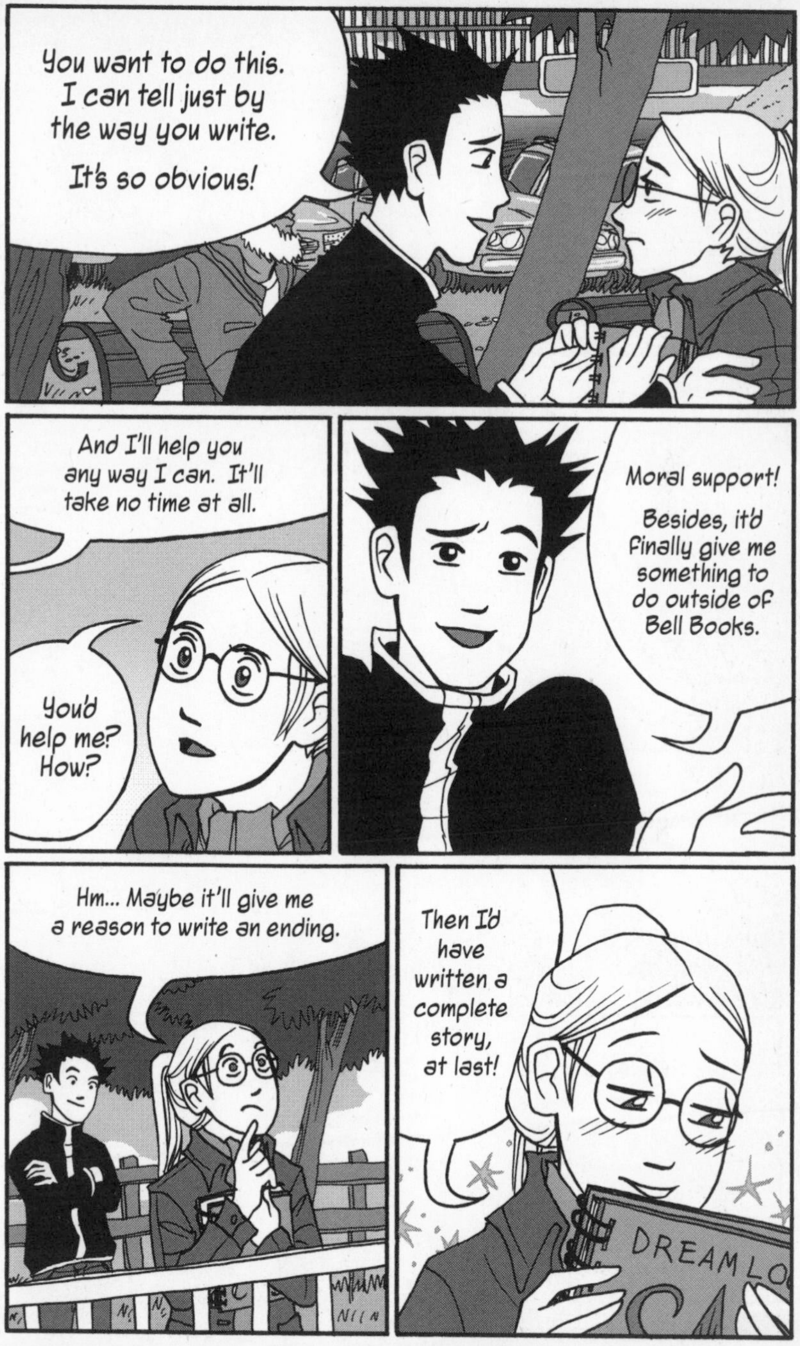
You want to do this. I can tell just by the way you write.
It's so obvious!
And I'll help you any way I can. It'll take no time at all.
You'd help me? How?
Moral support!
Besides, it'd finally give me something to do outside of Bell Books.
Hm... Maybe it'll give me a reason to write an ending.
Then I'd have written a complete story, at last!
DREAM LO

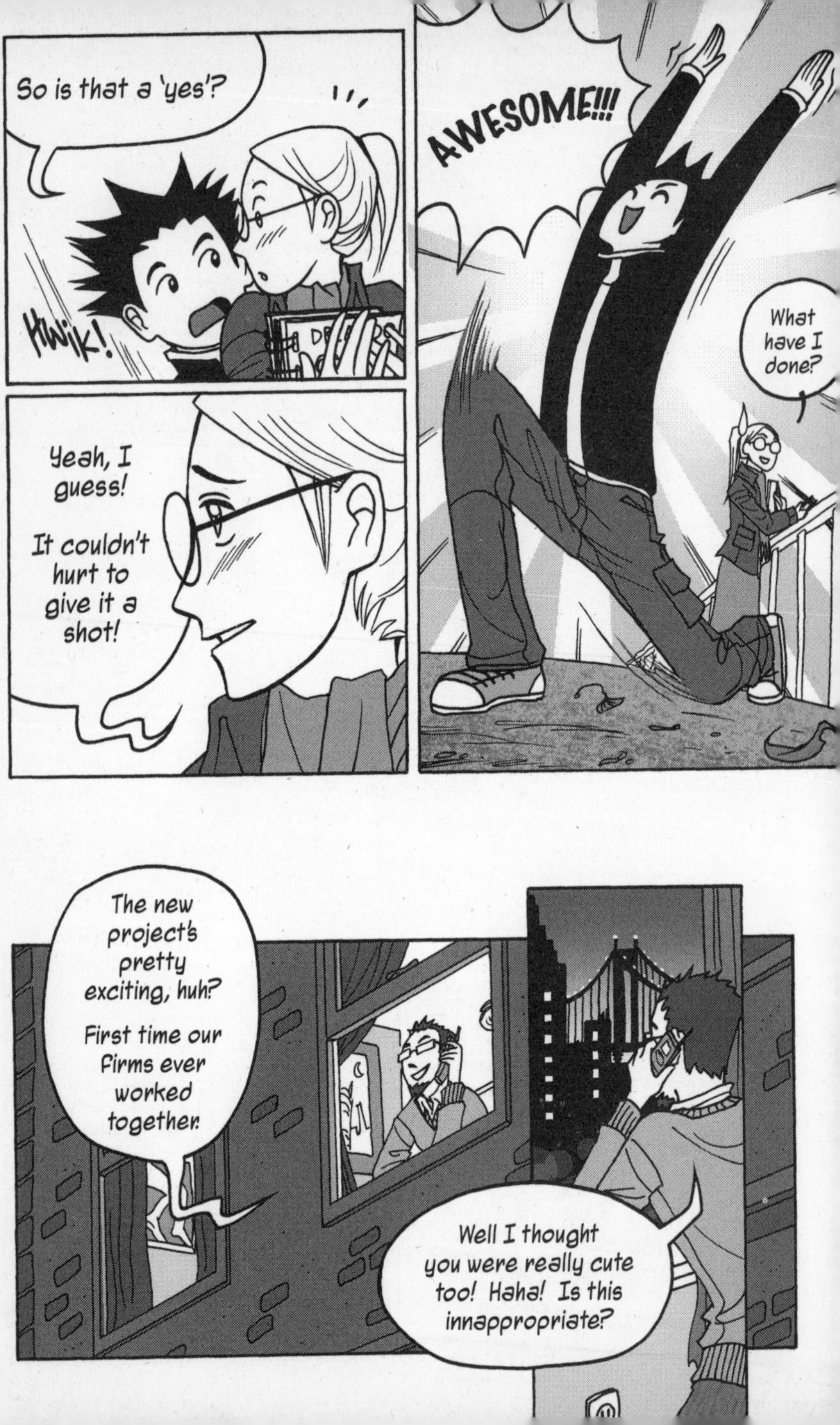
So is that a 'yes'?
HWIK!
Yeah, I guess! It couldn't hurt to give it a shot!
AWESOME!!!
What have I done?
The new project's pretty exciting, huh? First time our firms ever worked together.
Well I thought you were really cute too! Haha! Is this innappropriate?

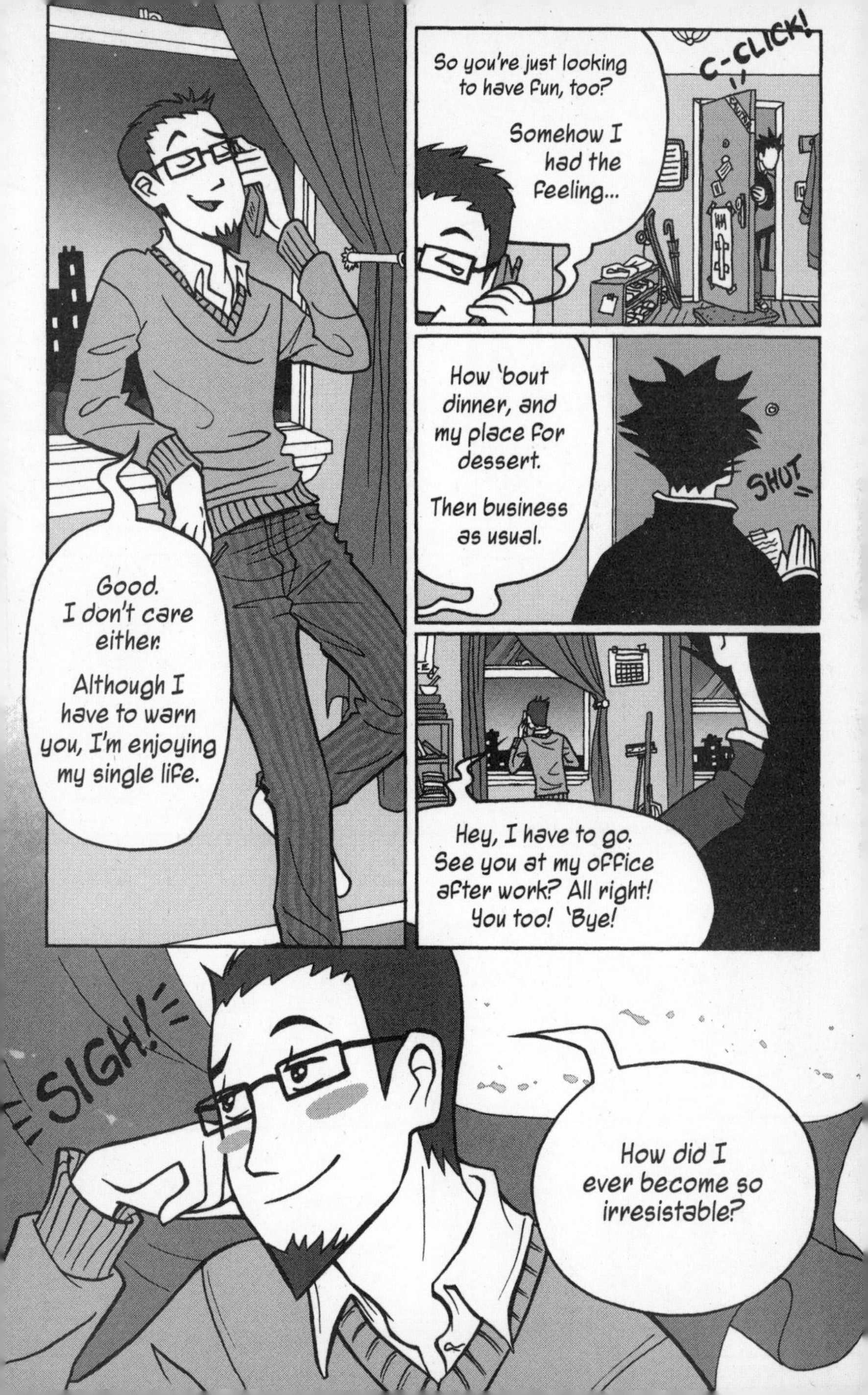
Good. I don't care either.
Although I have to warn you, I'm enjoying my single life.
So you're just looking to have fun, too?
Somehow I had the feeling...
C-CLICK!
How 'bout dinner, and my place for dessert.
Then business as usual.
SHUT
Hey, I have to go. See you at my office after work? All right! You too! 'Bye!
SIGH!
How did I ever become so irresistable?

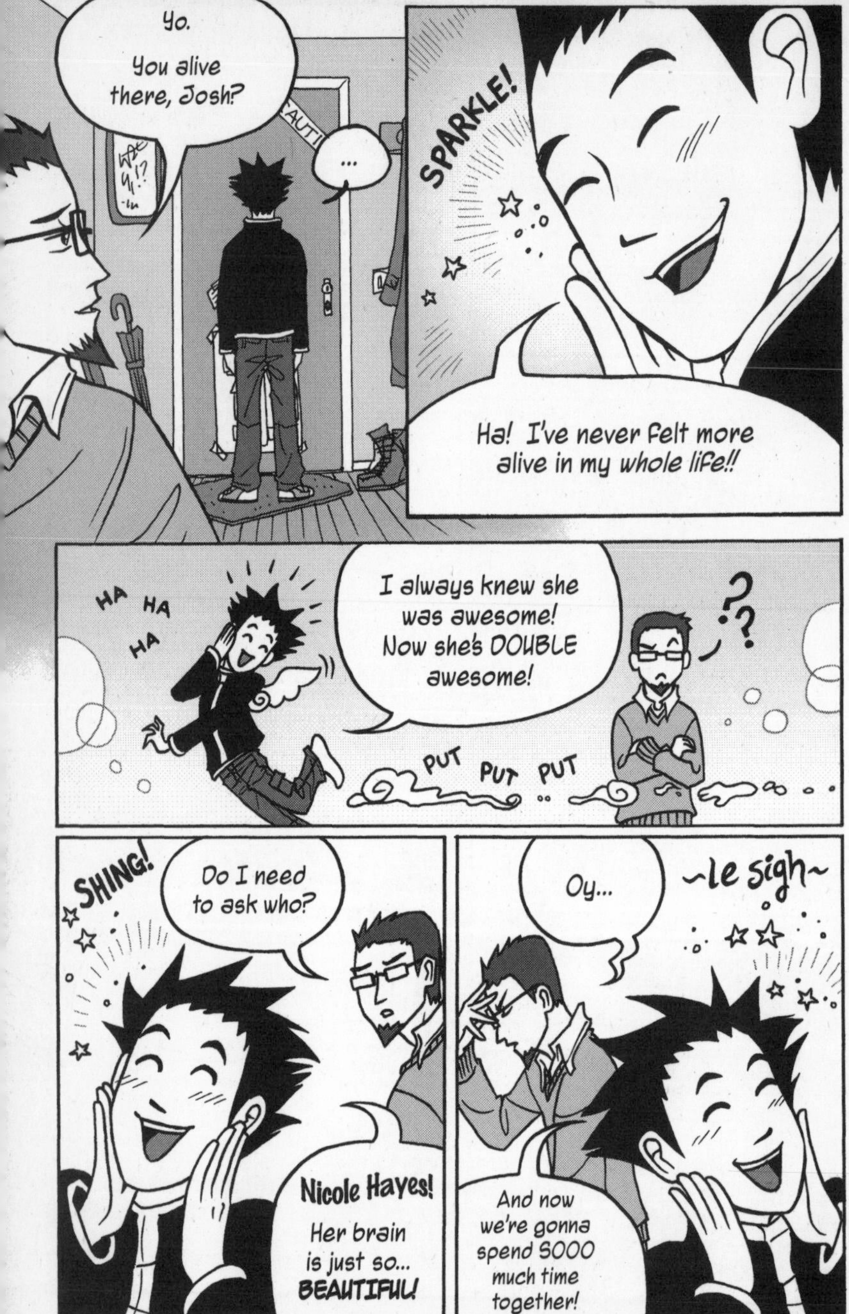
Yo.
You alive there, Josh?
...
SPARKLE!
Ha! I've never felt more alive in my whole life!!
HA HA HA
I always knew she was awesome! Now she's DOUBLE awesome!
??
PUT PUT PUT
SHING!
Do I need to ask who?
Nicole Hayes! Her brain is just so... BEAUTIFUL!
Oy...
~le sigh~
And now we're gonna spend SOOO much time together!

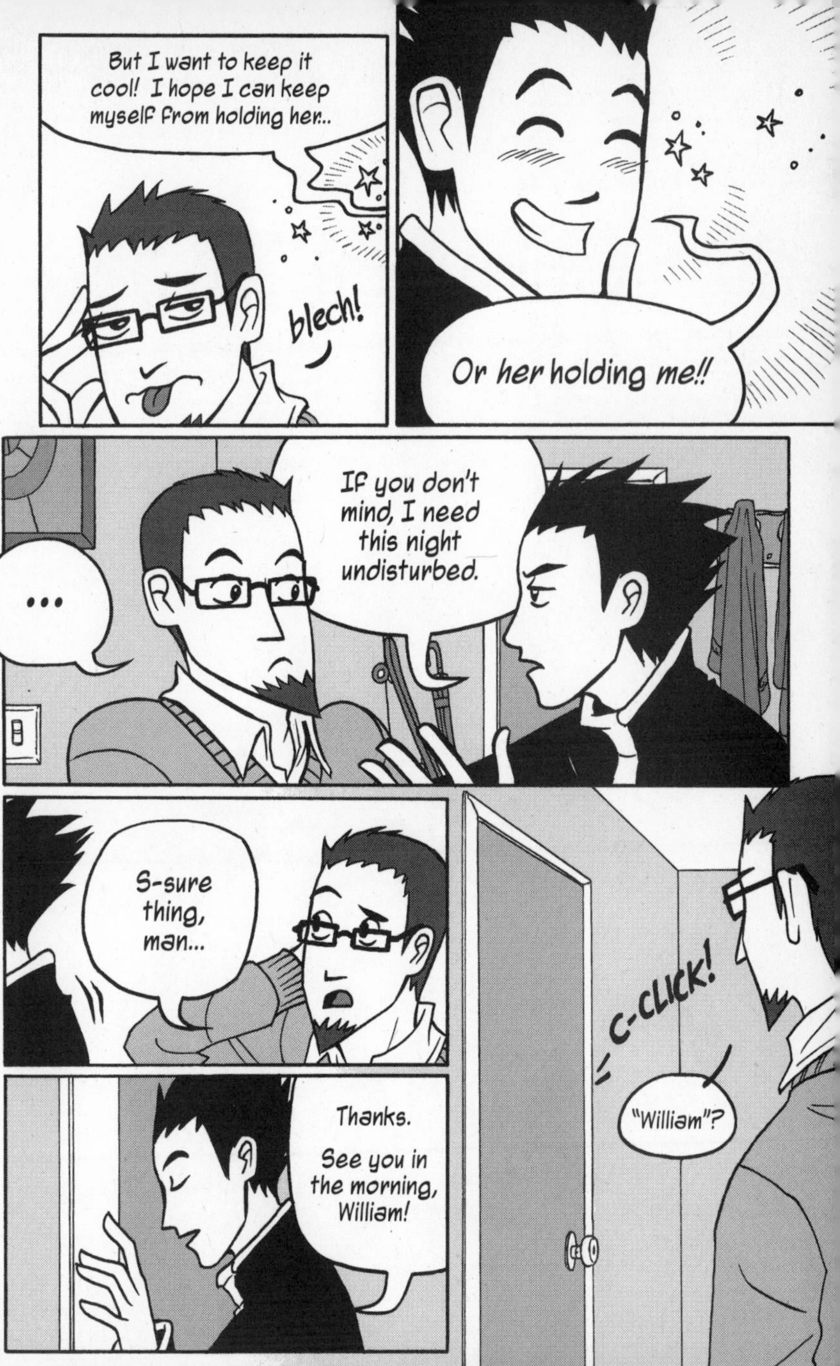
But I want to keep it cool! I hope I can keep myself from holding her...
blech!
Or her holding me!!
...
If you don't mind, I need this night undisturbed.
S-sure thing, man...
Thanks.
See you in the morning, William!
C-CLICK!
"William"?

Chapter Two

Makes Things Awkward

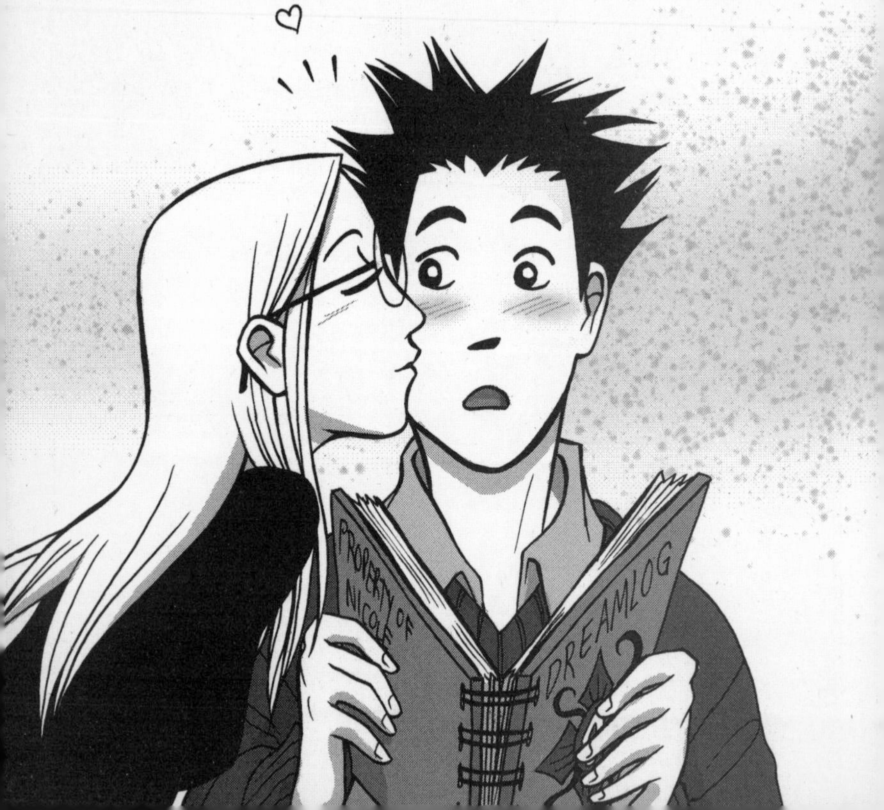
PROPERTY OF NICOLE
DREAMLOG

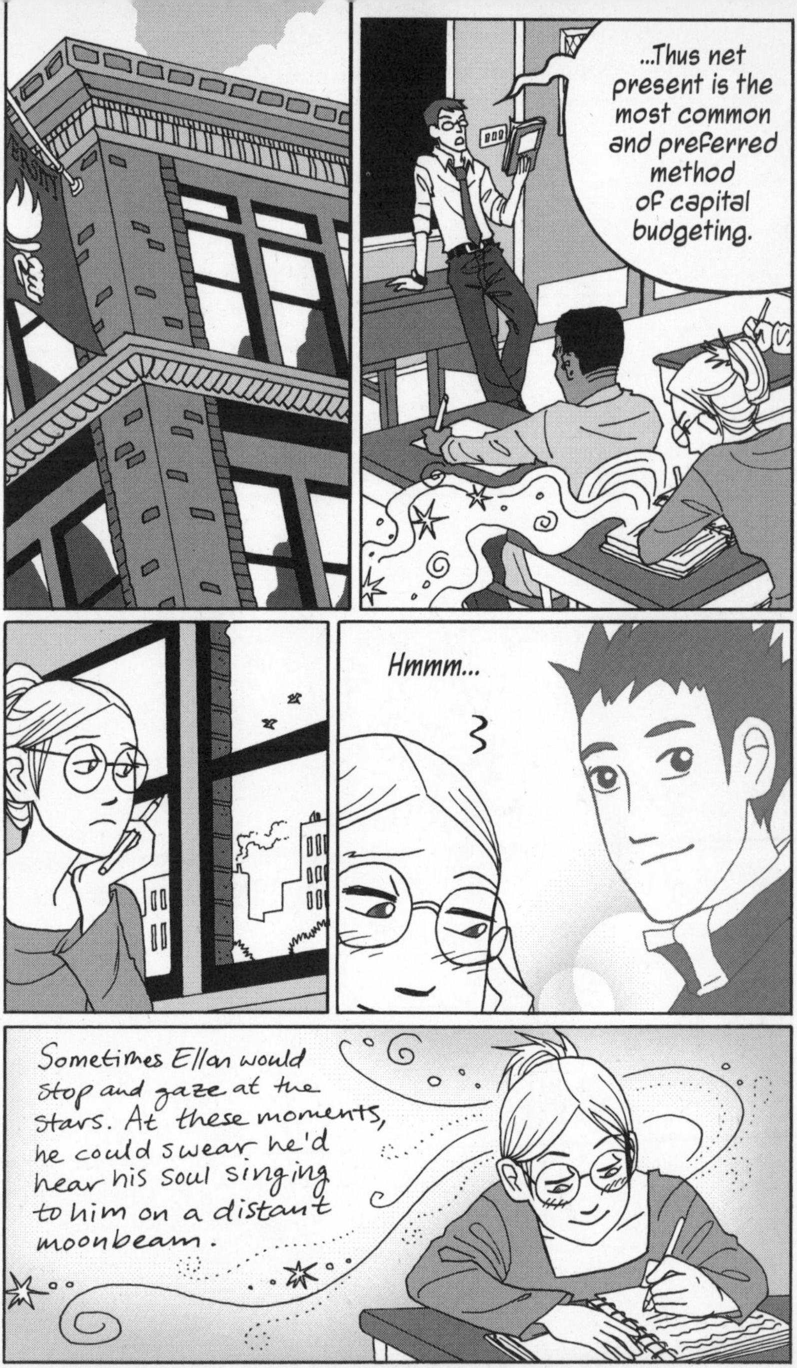
...Thus net present is the most common and preferred method of capital budgeting.
Hmmm...
Sometimes Ellan would stop and gaze at the stars. At these moments, he could swear he'd hear his soul singing to him on a distant moonbeam.

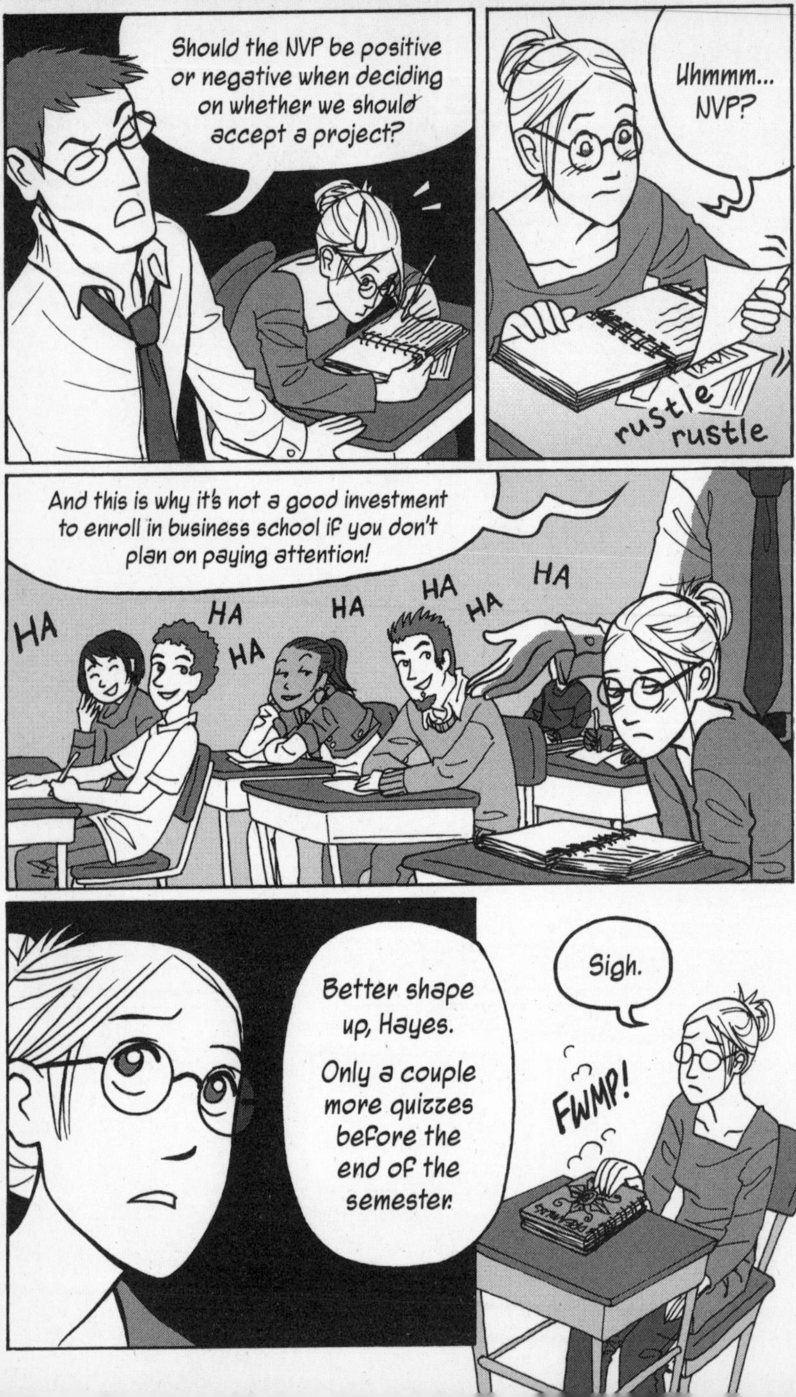
Should the NVP be positive or negative when deciding on whether we should accept a project?
Uhmmm... NVP?
rustle rustle
And this is why it's not a good investment to enroll in business school if you don't plan on paying attention!
HA HA HA HA HA HA HA
Better shape up, Hayes.
Only a couple more quizzes before the end of the semester.
Sigh.
FWMP!

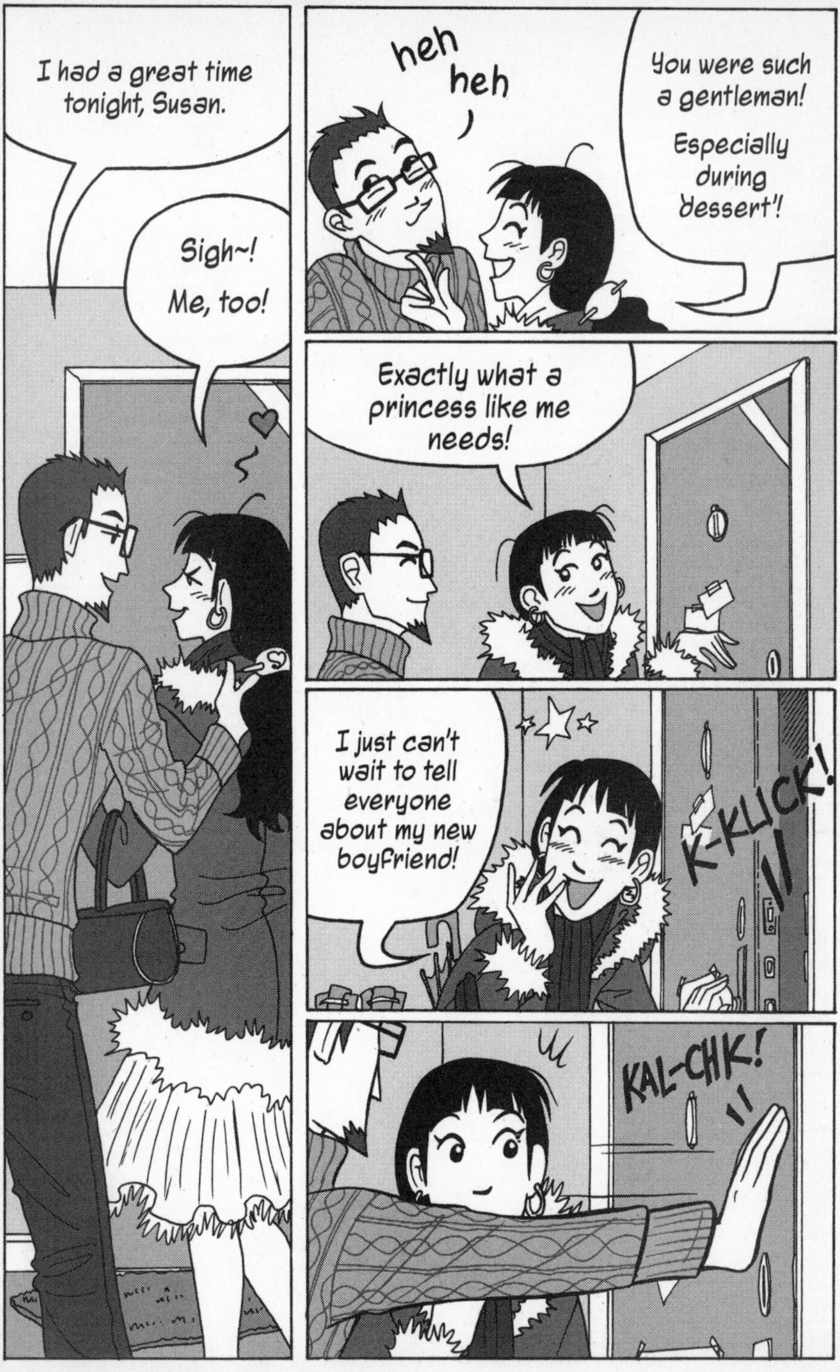
I had a great time tonight, Susan.
Sigh~! Me, too!
heh heh
You were such a gentleman! Especially during dessert'!
Exactly what a princess like me needs!
I just can't wait to tell everyone about my new boyfriend!
K-KLICK!
KAL-CHK!

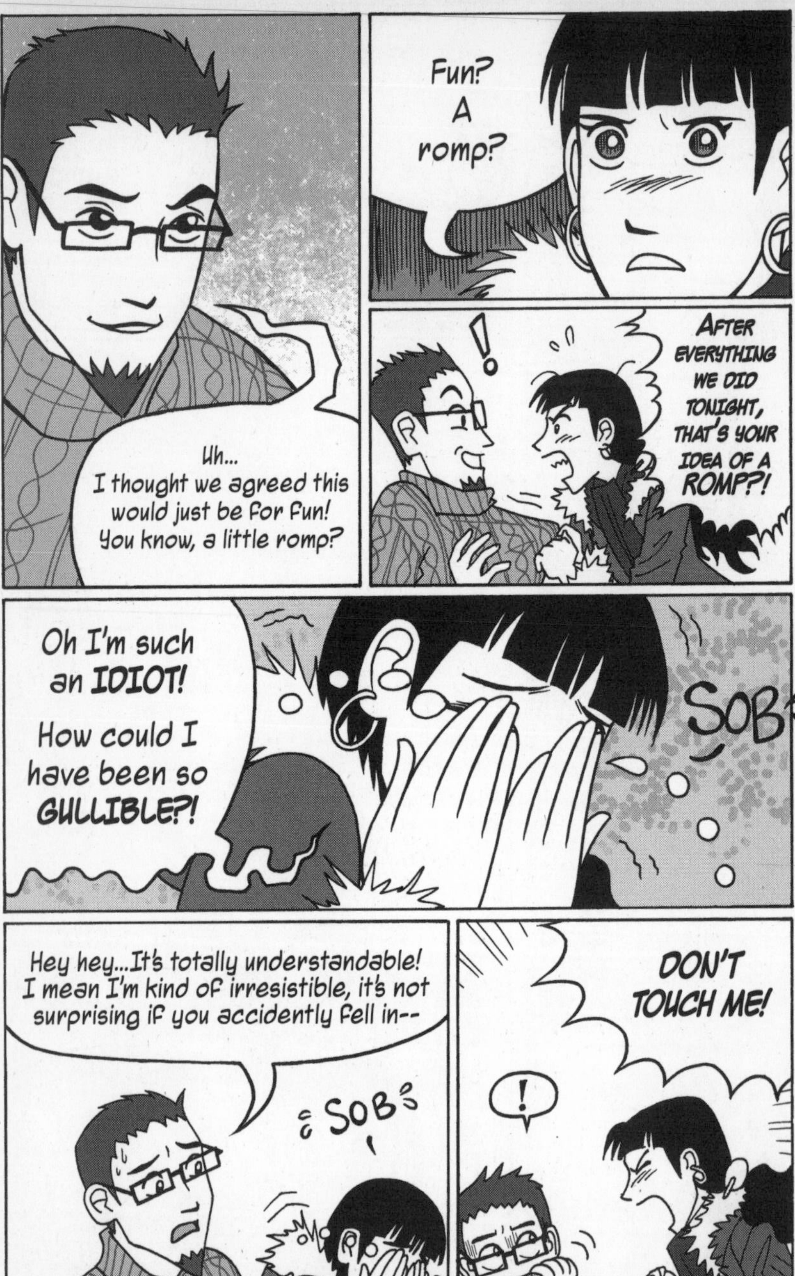
Uh...
I thought we agreed this would just be for fun! You know, a little romp?
Fun? A romp?
!
After everything we did tonight, that's your idea of a ROMP?!
Oh I'm such an IDIOT!
How could I have been so GULLIBLE?!
SOB
Hey hey...It's totally understandable! I mean I'm kind of irresistible, it's not surprising if you accidently fell in--
SOB
!
DON'T TOUCH ME!

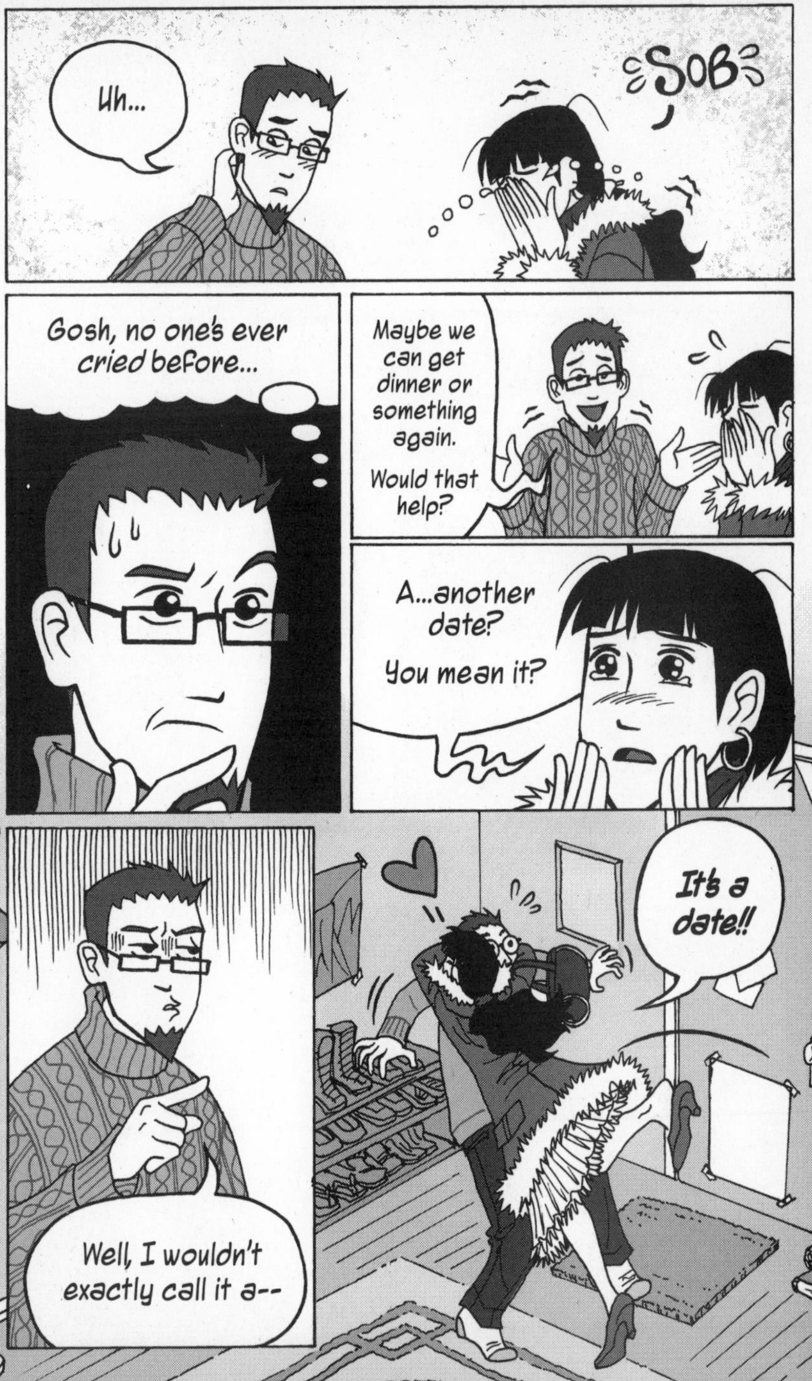
Uh...
SOB
Gosh, no one's ever cried before...
Maybe we can get dinner or something again.
Would that help?
A...another date?
You mean it?
Well, I wouldn't exactly call it a--
It's a date!!

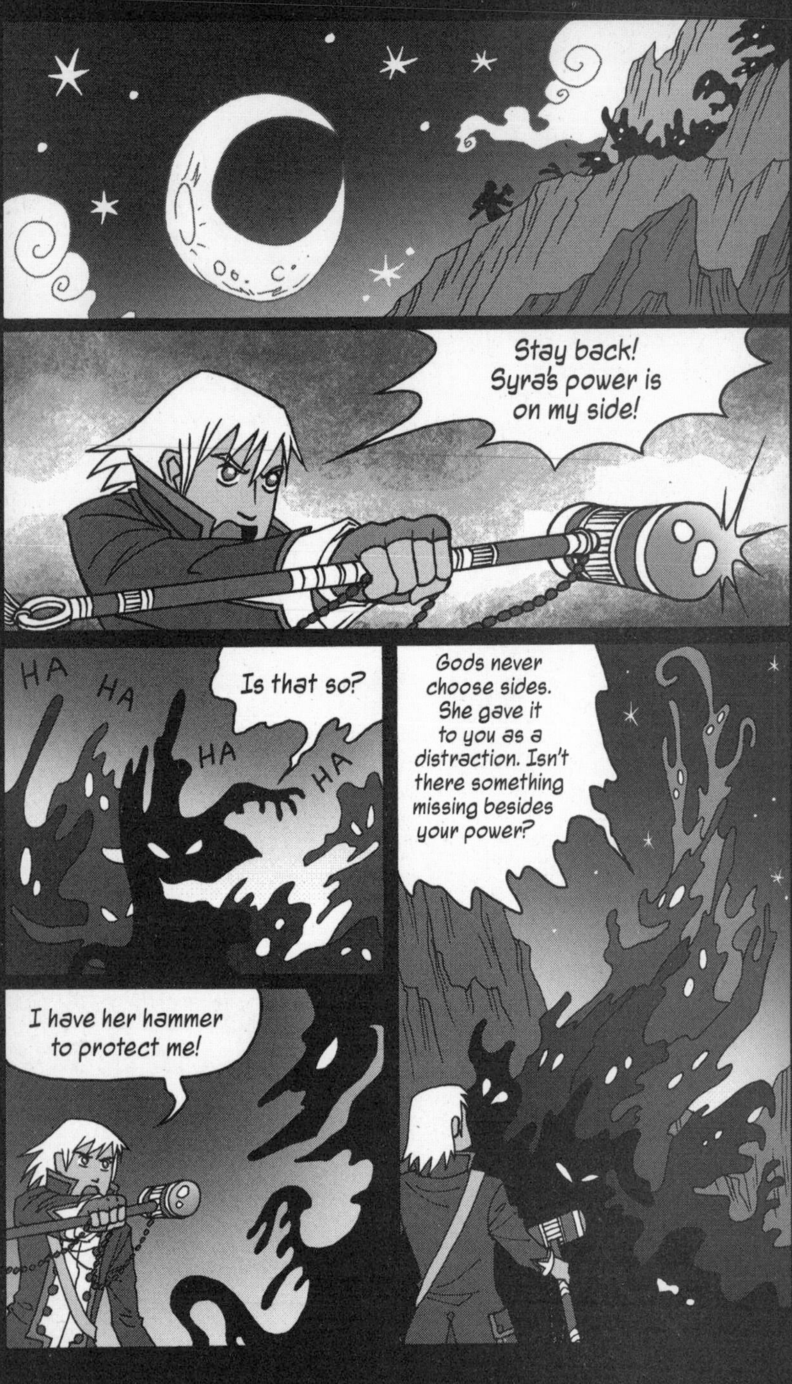
Stay back! Syra's power is on my side!
HA HA HA HA
Is that so?
Gods never choose sides. She gave it to you as a distraction. Isn't there something missing besides your power?
I have her hammer to protect me!

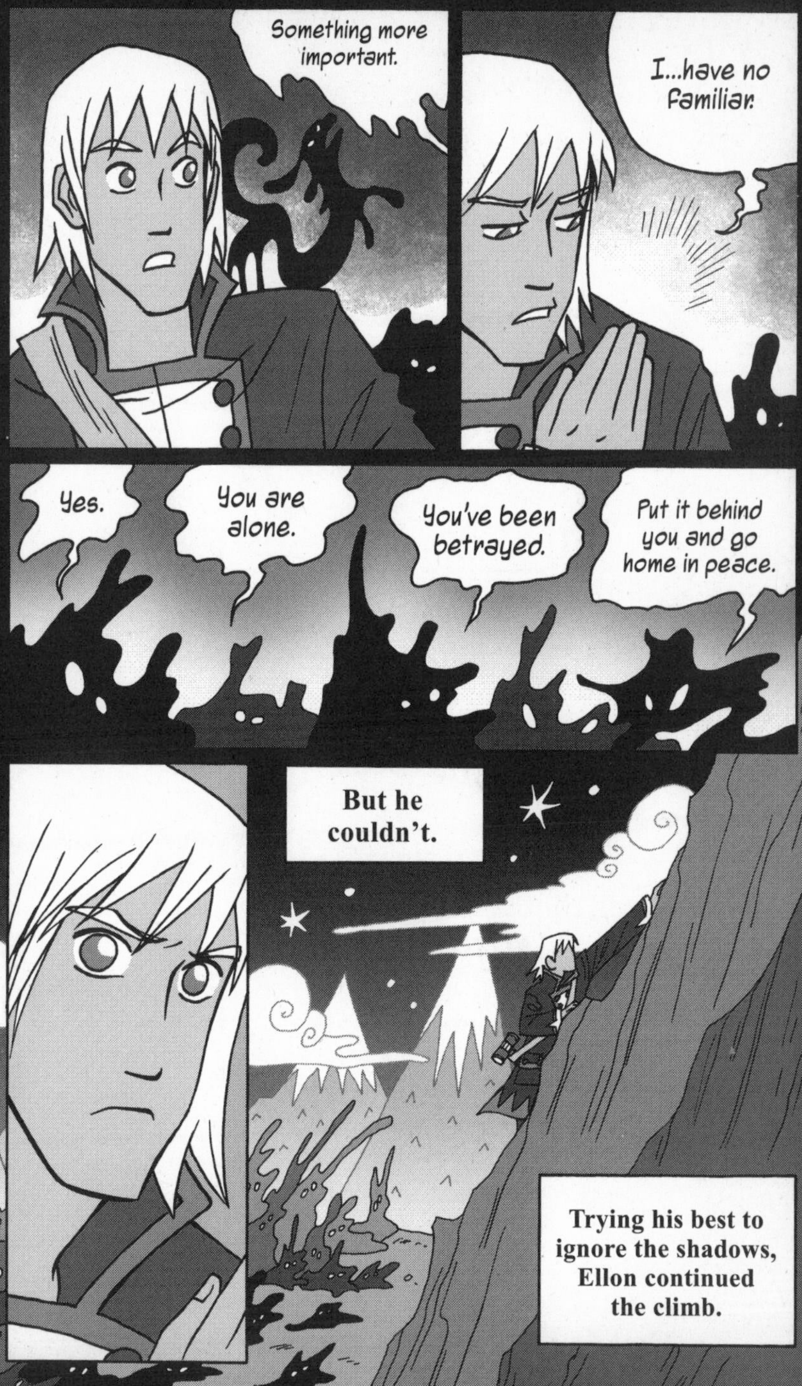
Something more important.
I...have no familiar.
Yes.
You are alone.
You've been betrayed.
Put it behind you and go home in peace.
But he couldn't.
Trying his best to ignore the shadows, Ellon continued the climb.

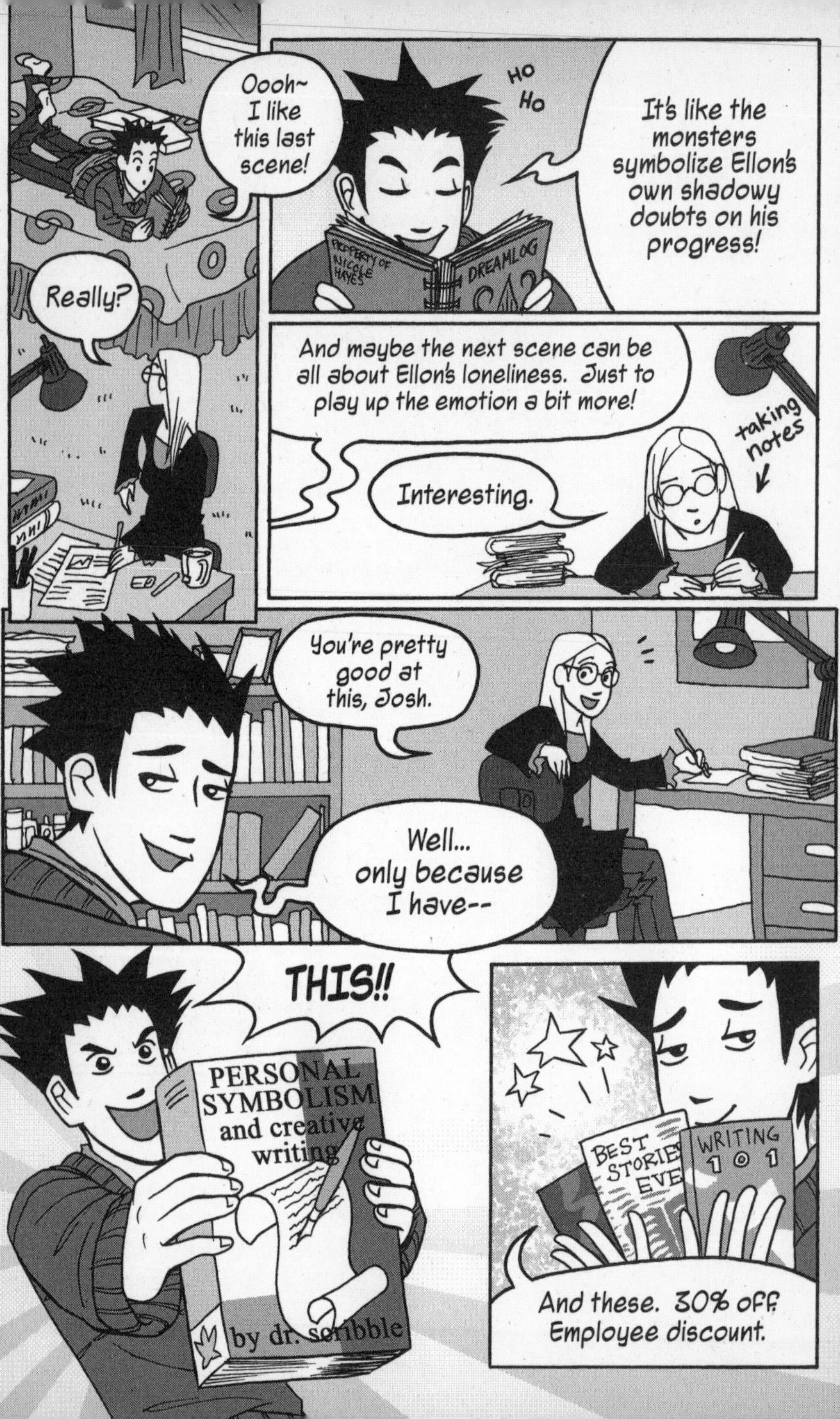
Oooh~ I like this last scene!
Really?
HO HO
It's like the monsters symbolize Ellon's own shadowy doubts on his progress!
PROPERTY OF NICOLE HAYES
DREAMLOG
And maybe the next scene can be all about Ellon's loneliness. Just to play up the emotion a bit more!
Interesting.
taking notes
You're pretty good at this, Josh.
Well... only because I have--
THIS!!
PERSONAL SYMBOLISM and creative writing
by dr. scribble
BEST STORIES EVE
WRITING 101
And these. 30% off. Employee discount.

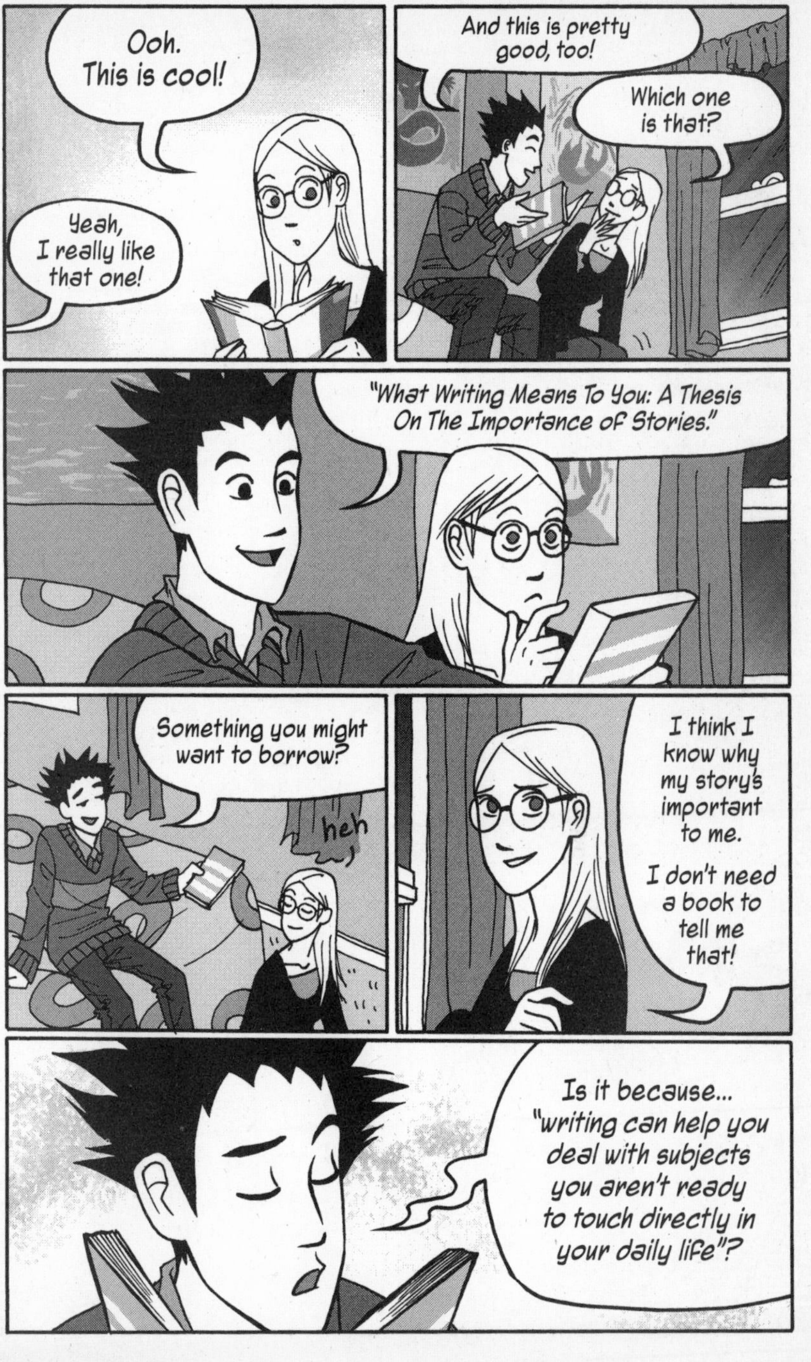
Ooh. This is cool!
Yeah, I really like that one!
And this is pretty good, too!
Which one is that?
"What Writing Means To You: A Thesis On The Importance of Stories."
Something you might want to borrow?
heh
I think I know why my story's important to me.
I don't need a book to tell me that!
Is it because... "writing can help you deal with subjects you aren't ready to touch directly in your daily life"?

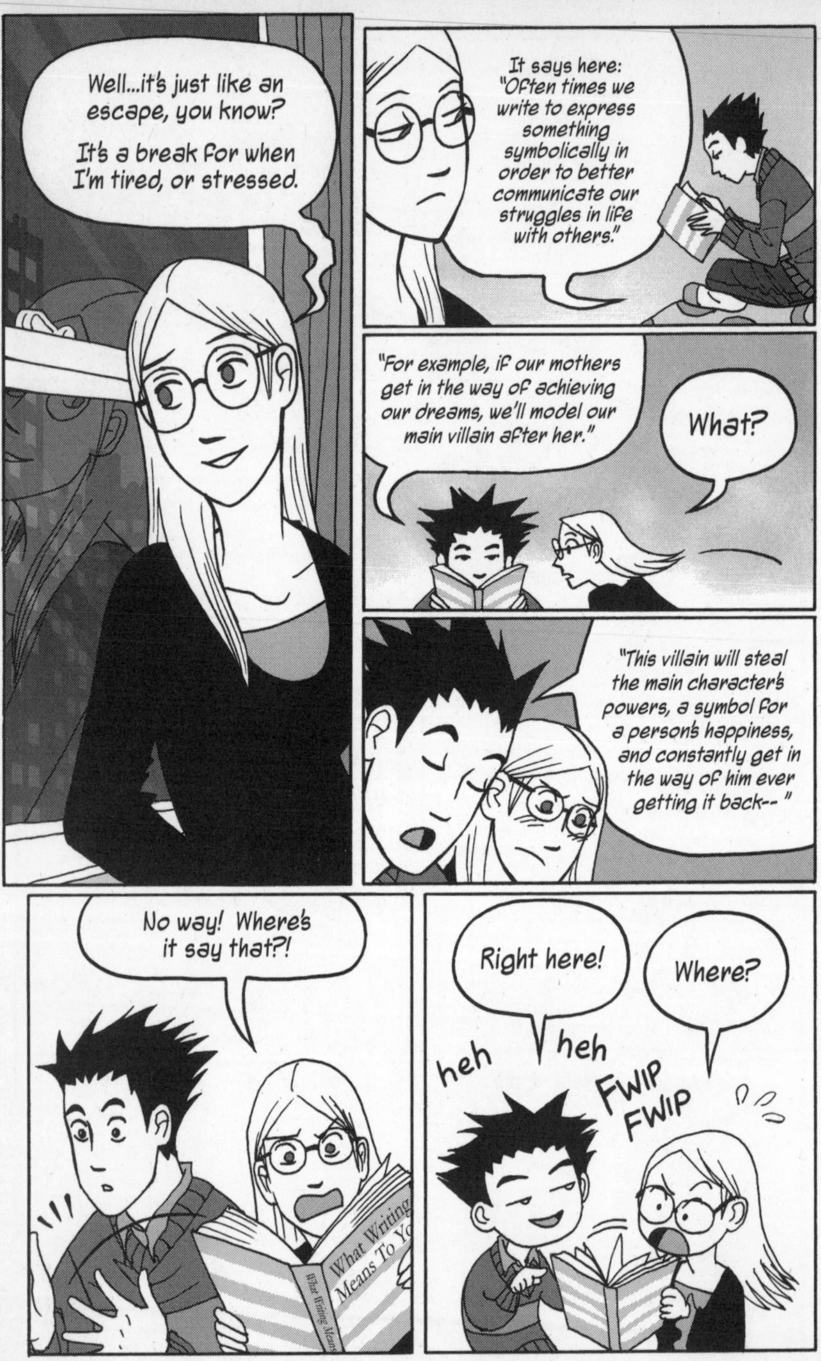
Well...it's just like an escape, you know?
It's a break for when I'm tired, or stressed.
It says here: "Often times we write to express something symbolically in order to better communicate our struggles in life with others."
"For example, if our mothers get in the way of achieving our dreams, we'll model our main villain after her."
What?
"This villain will steal the main character's powers, a symbol for a person's happiness, and constantly get in the way of him ever getting it back-- "
No way! Where's it say that?!
What Writing Means To Yo
What Writing Means
Right here!
Where?
heh
heh
FWIP
FWIP

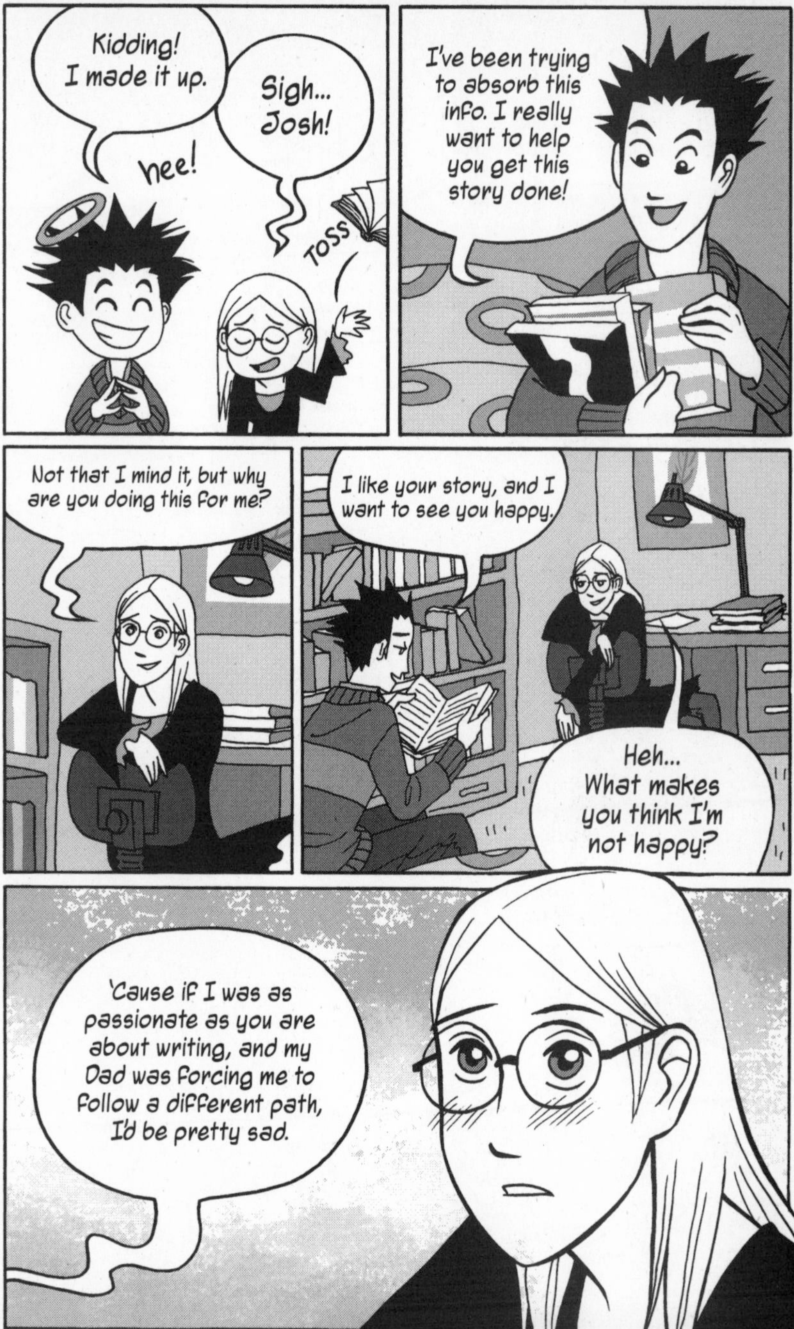
Kidding! I made it up.
hee!
Sigh... Josh!
TOSS
I've been trying to absorb this info. I really want to help you get this story done!
Not that I mind it, but why are you doing this for me?
I like your story, and I want to see you happy.
Heh... What makes you think I'm not happy?
'Cause if I was as passionate as you are about writing, and my Dad was forcing me to follow a different path, I'd be pretty sad.

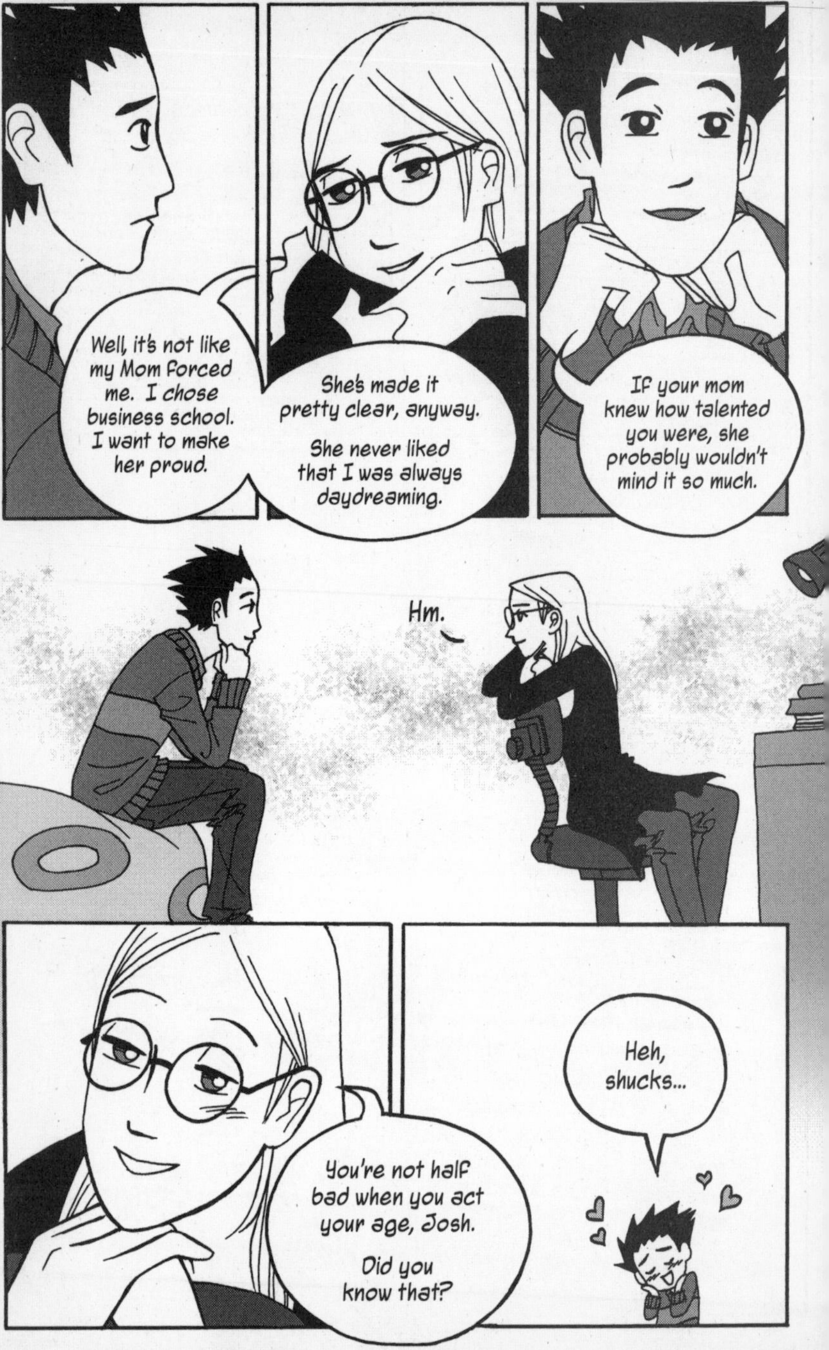
Well, it's not like my Mom forced me. I chose business school. I want to make her proud.
She's made it pretty clear, anyway.
She never liked that I was always daydreaming.
If your mom knew how talented you were, she probably wouldn't mind it so much.
Hm.
You're not half bad when you act your age, Josh.
Did you know that?
Heh, shucks...

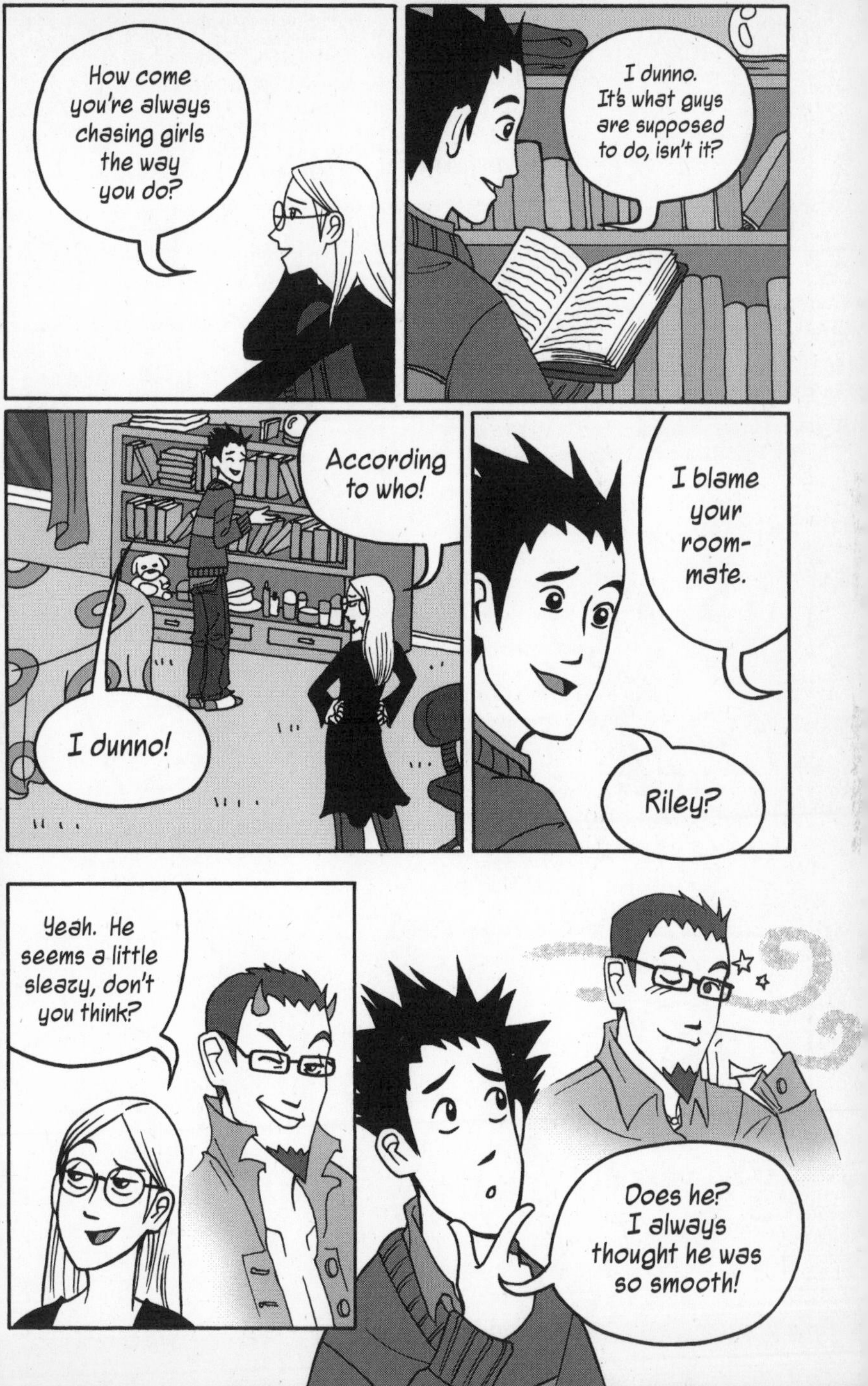
How come you're always chasing girls the way you do?
I dunno. It's what guys are supposed to do, isn't it?
According to who!
I dunno!
I blame your room-mate.
Riley?
Yeah. He seems a little sleazy, don't you think?
Does he? I always thought he was so smooth!

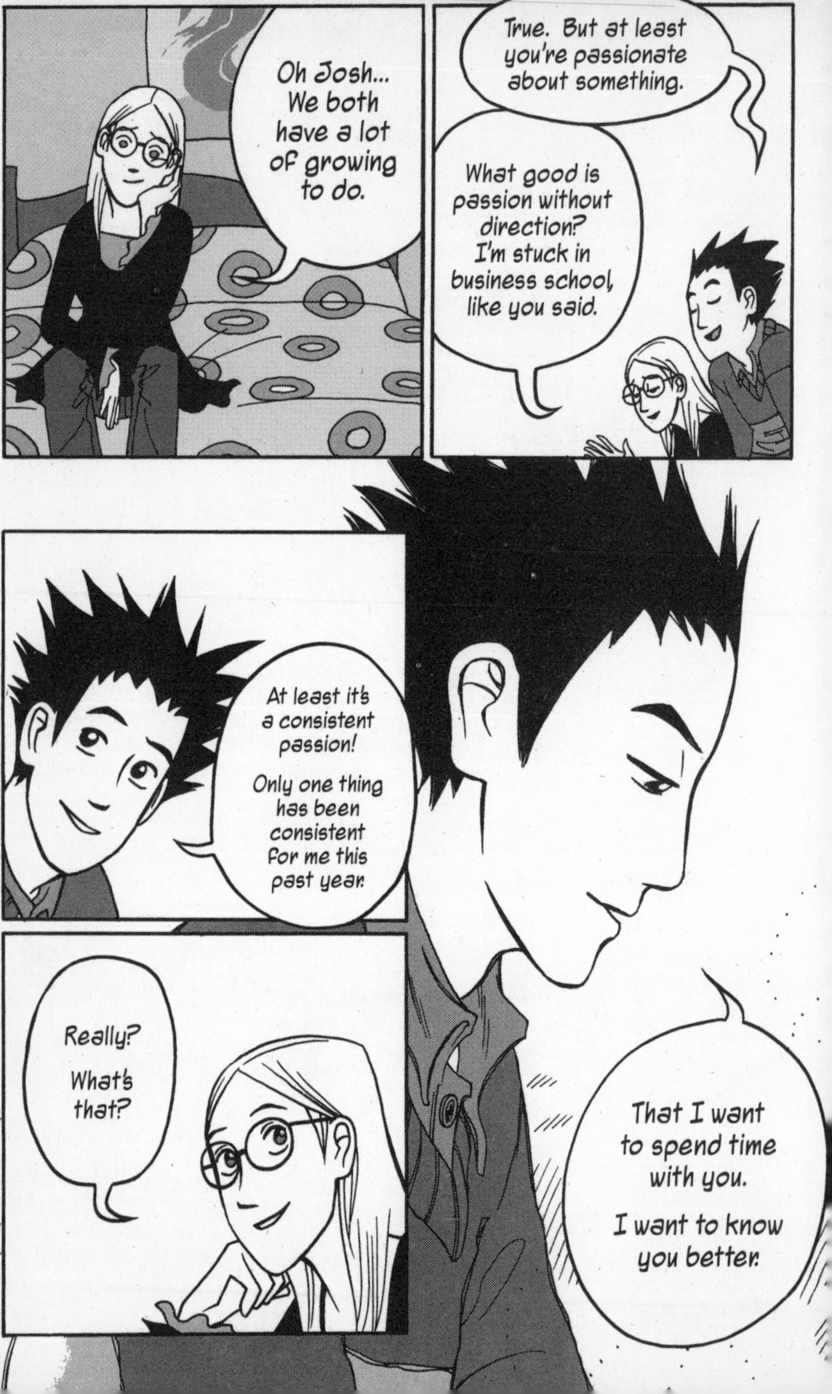
Oh Josh... We both have a lot of growing to do.
True. But at least you're passionate about something.
What good is passion without direction? I'm stuck in business school, like you said.
At least it's a consistent passion!
Only one thing has been consistent for me this past year.
Really?
What's that?
That I want to spend time with you.
I want to know you better.

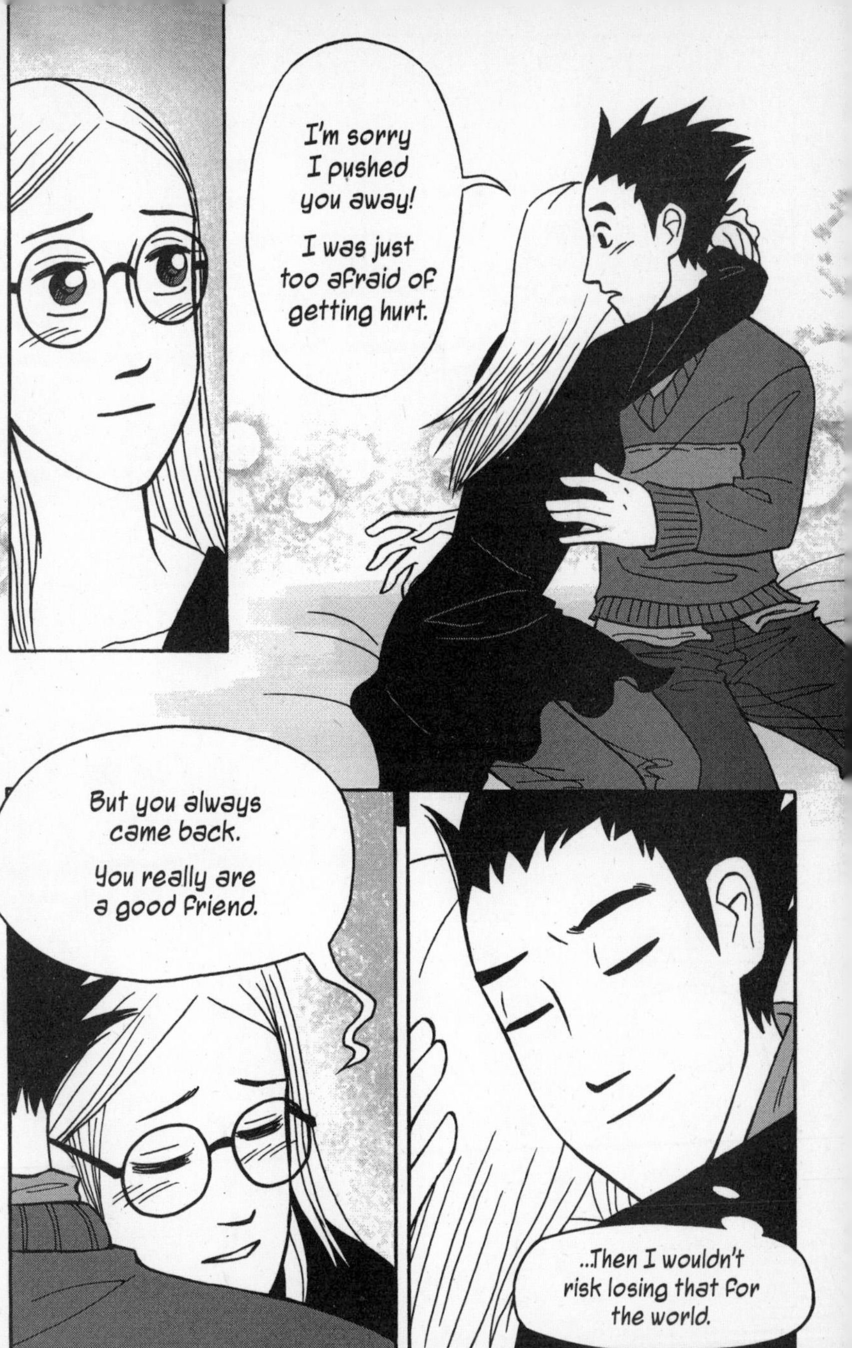
I'm sorry I pushed you away!
I was just too afraid of getting hurt.
But you always came back.
You really are a good friend.
...Then I wouldn't risk losing that for the world.

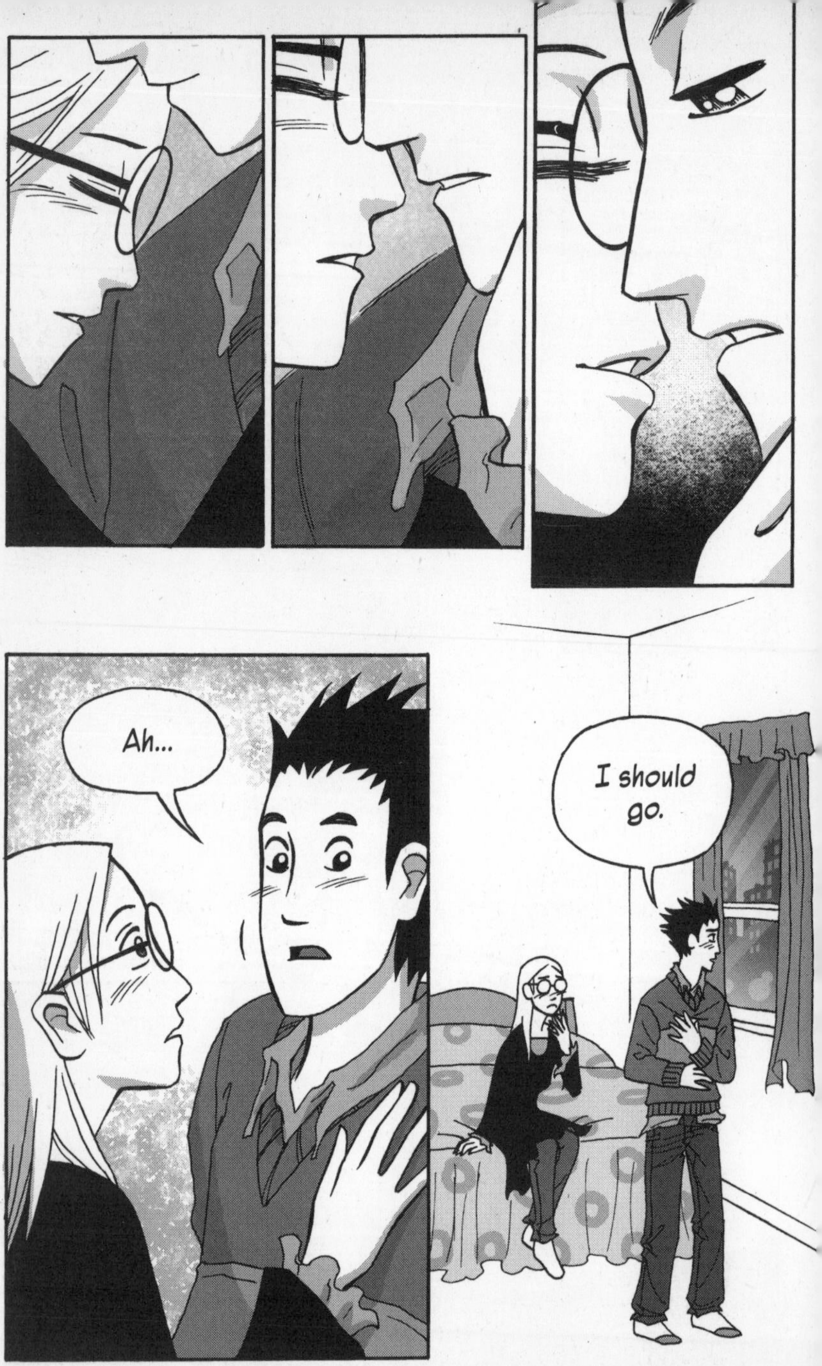
Ah...
I should go.

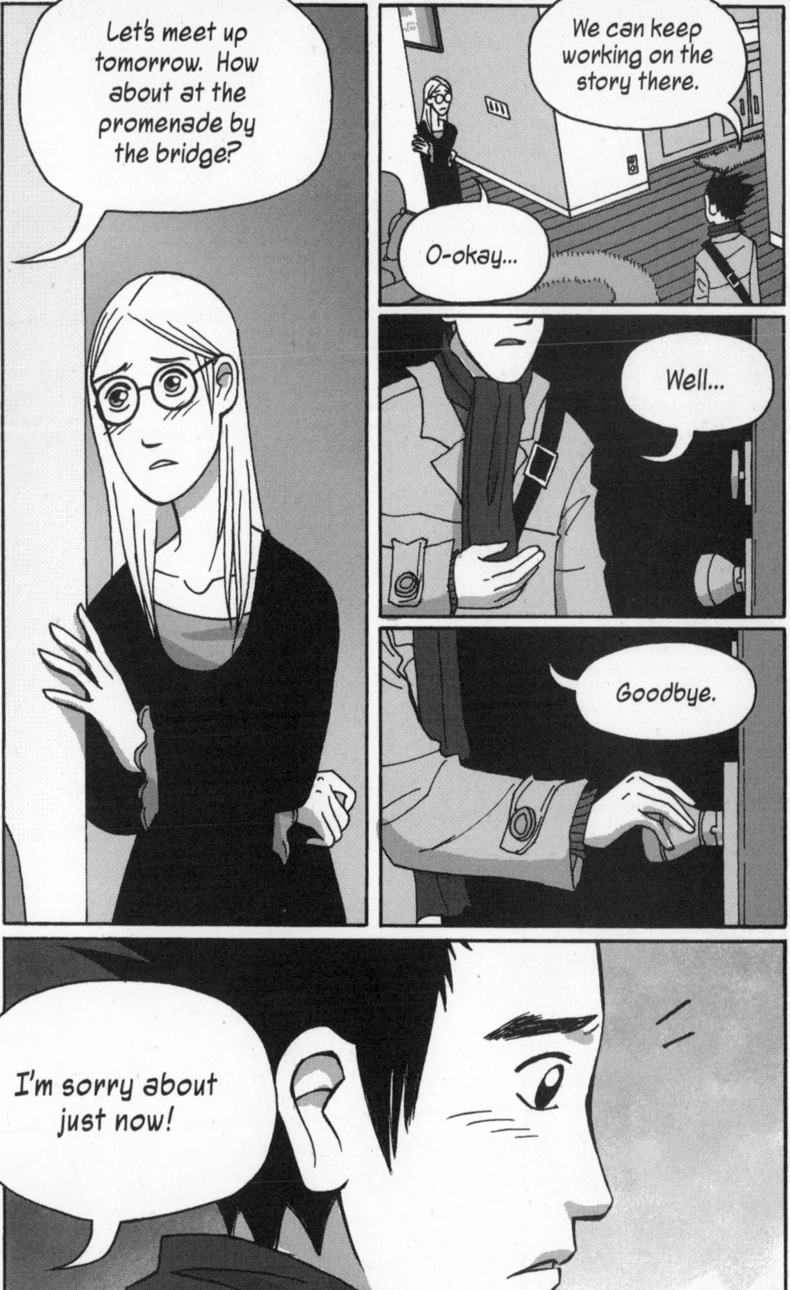
Let's meet up tomorrow. How about at the promenade by the bridge?
We can keep working on the story there.
O-okay...
Well...
Goodbye.
I'm sorry about just now!

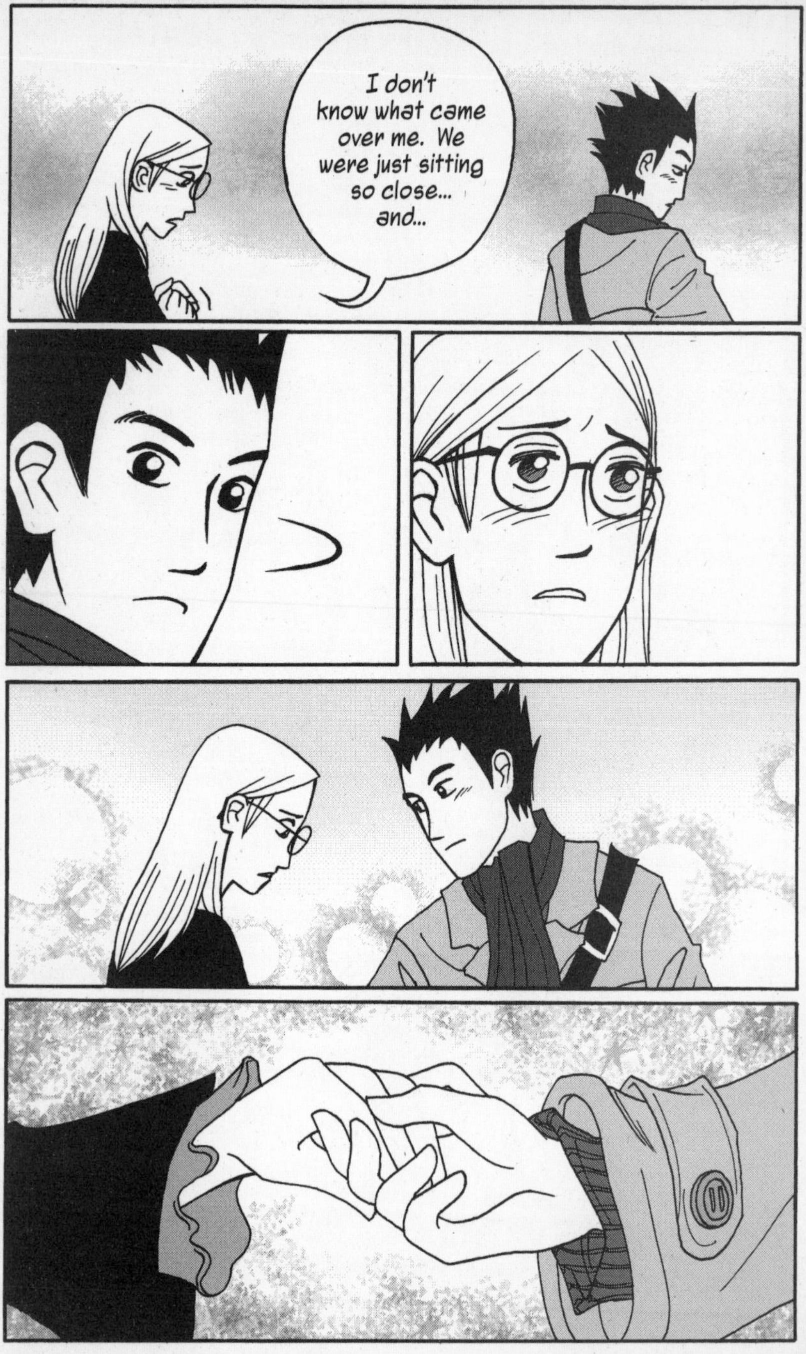
I don't know what came over me. We were just sitting so close... and...

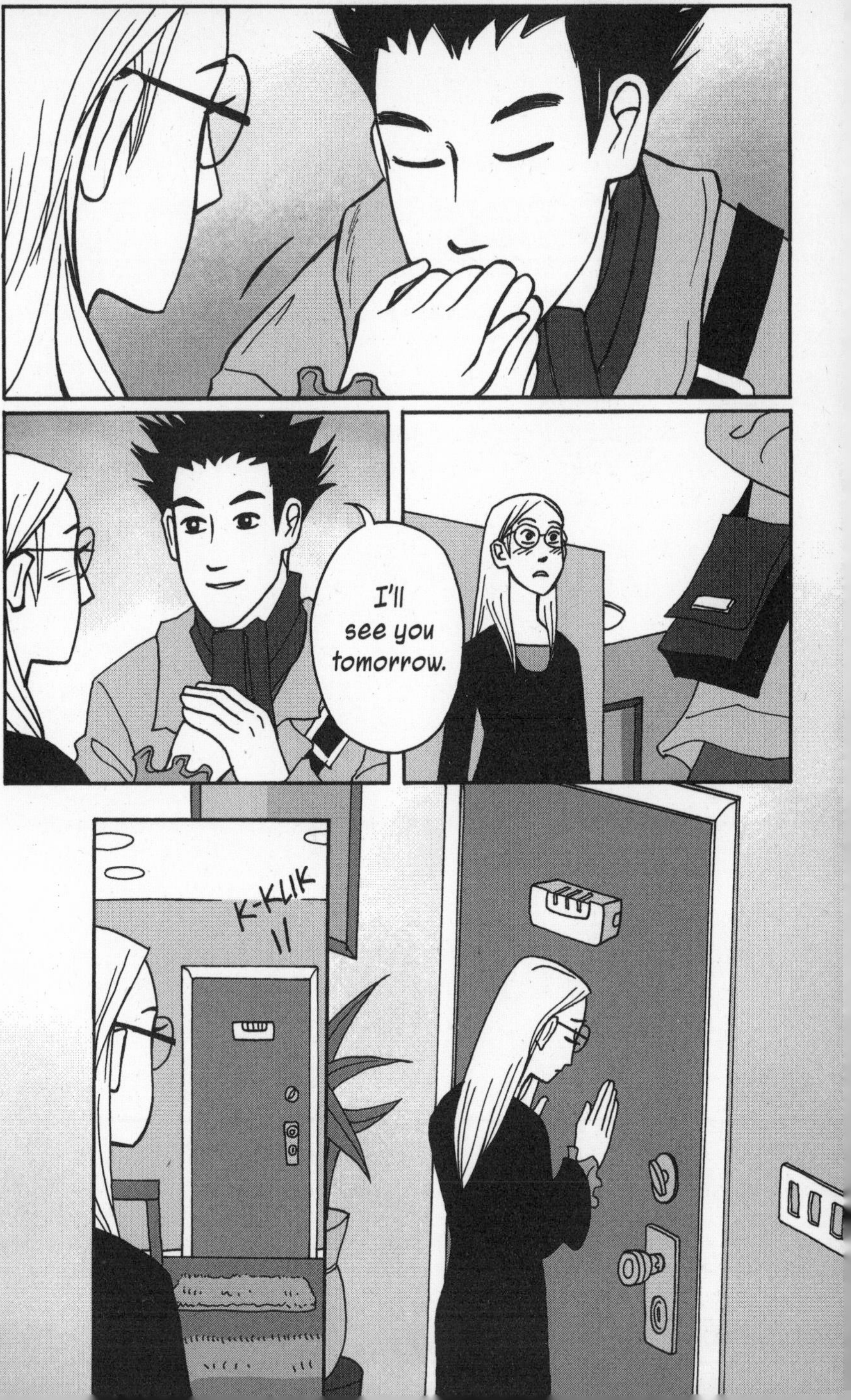
I'll see you tomorrow.
K-KLIK

Chapter Three

is about a new haircut

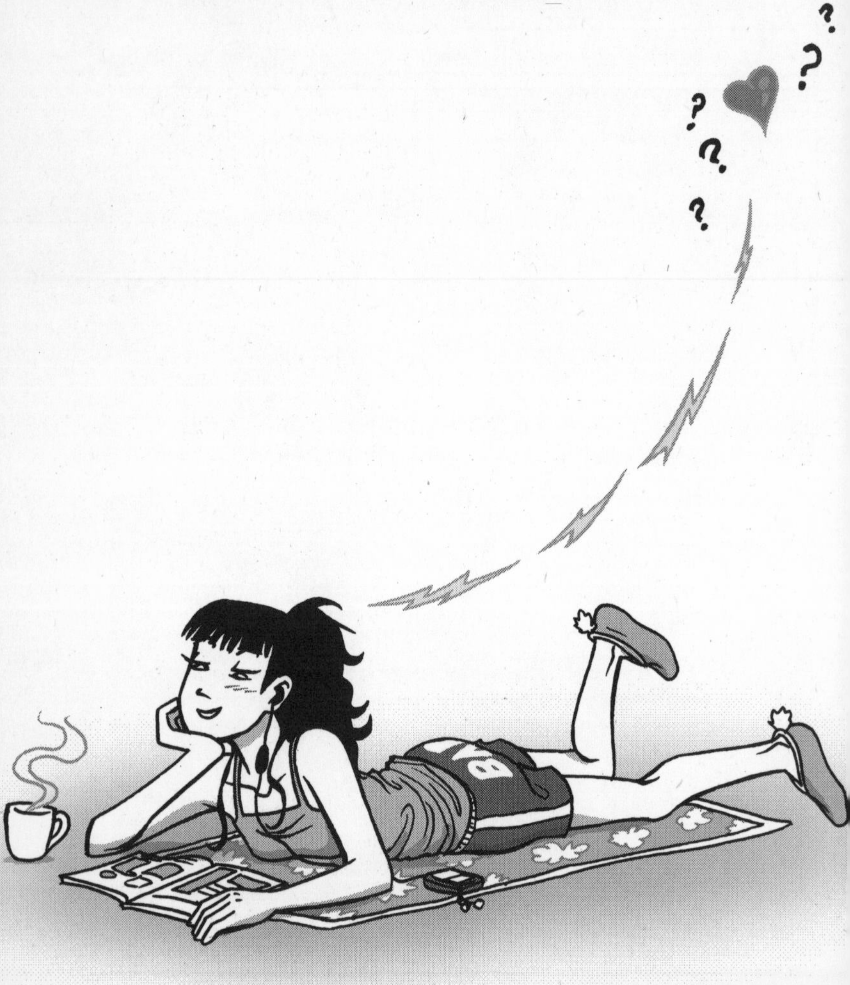

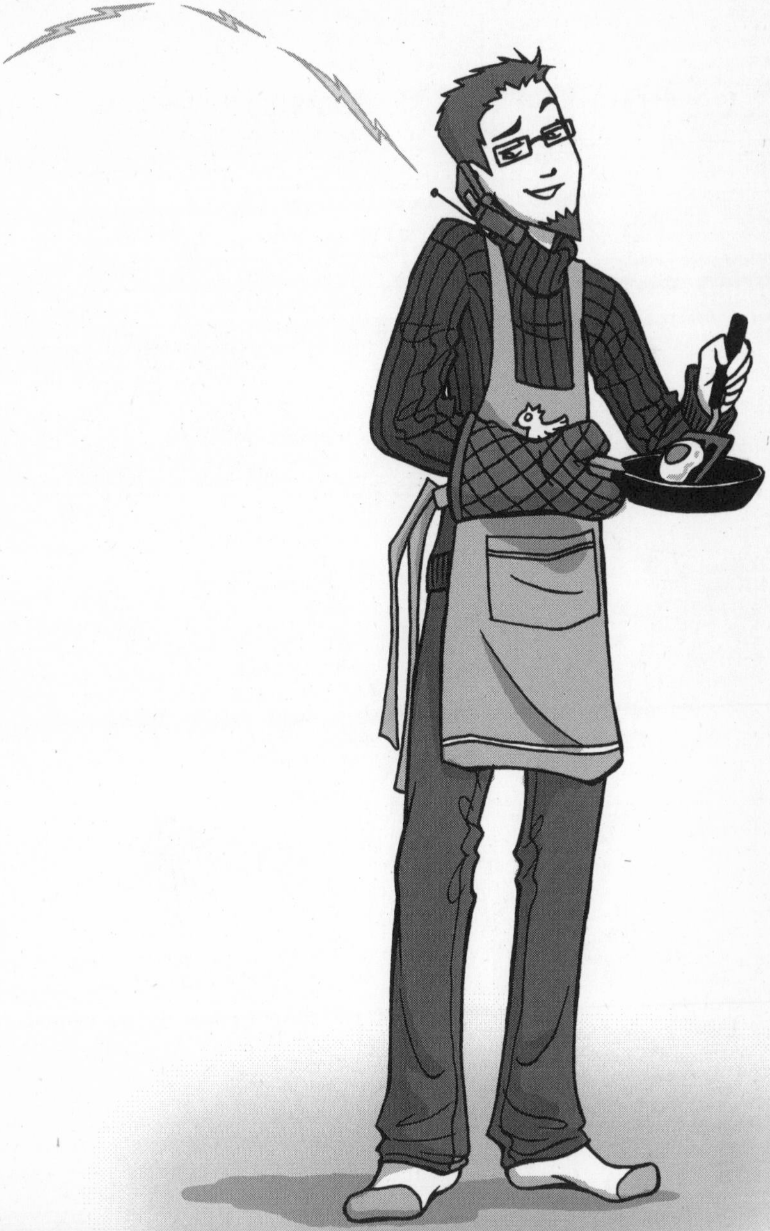

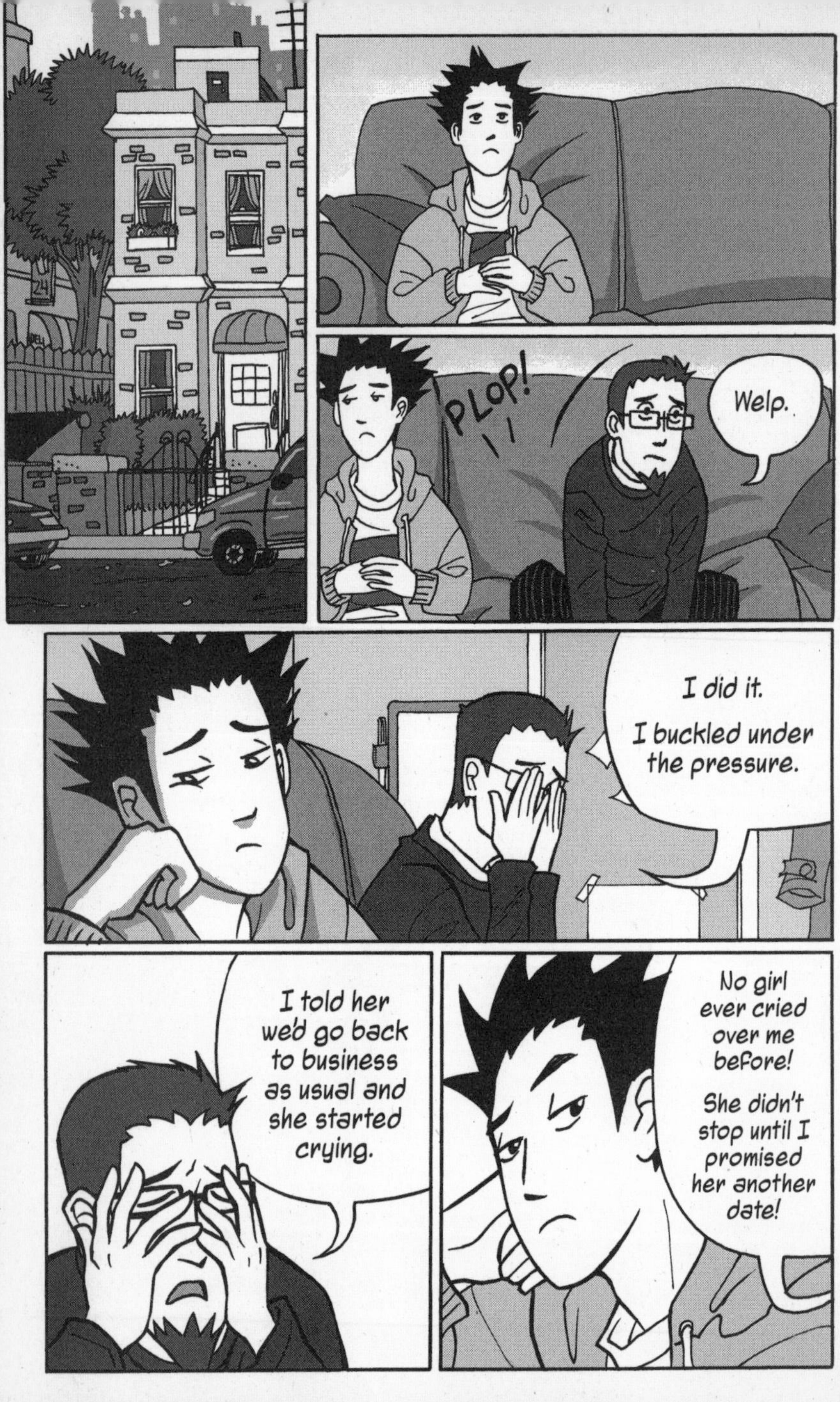

PLOP!
Welp.
I did it.
I buckled under the pressure.
I told her we'd go back to business as usual and she started crying.
No girl ever cried over me before!
She didn't stop until I promised her another date!

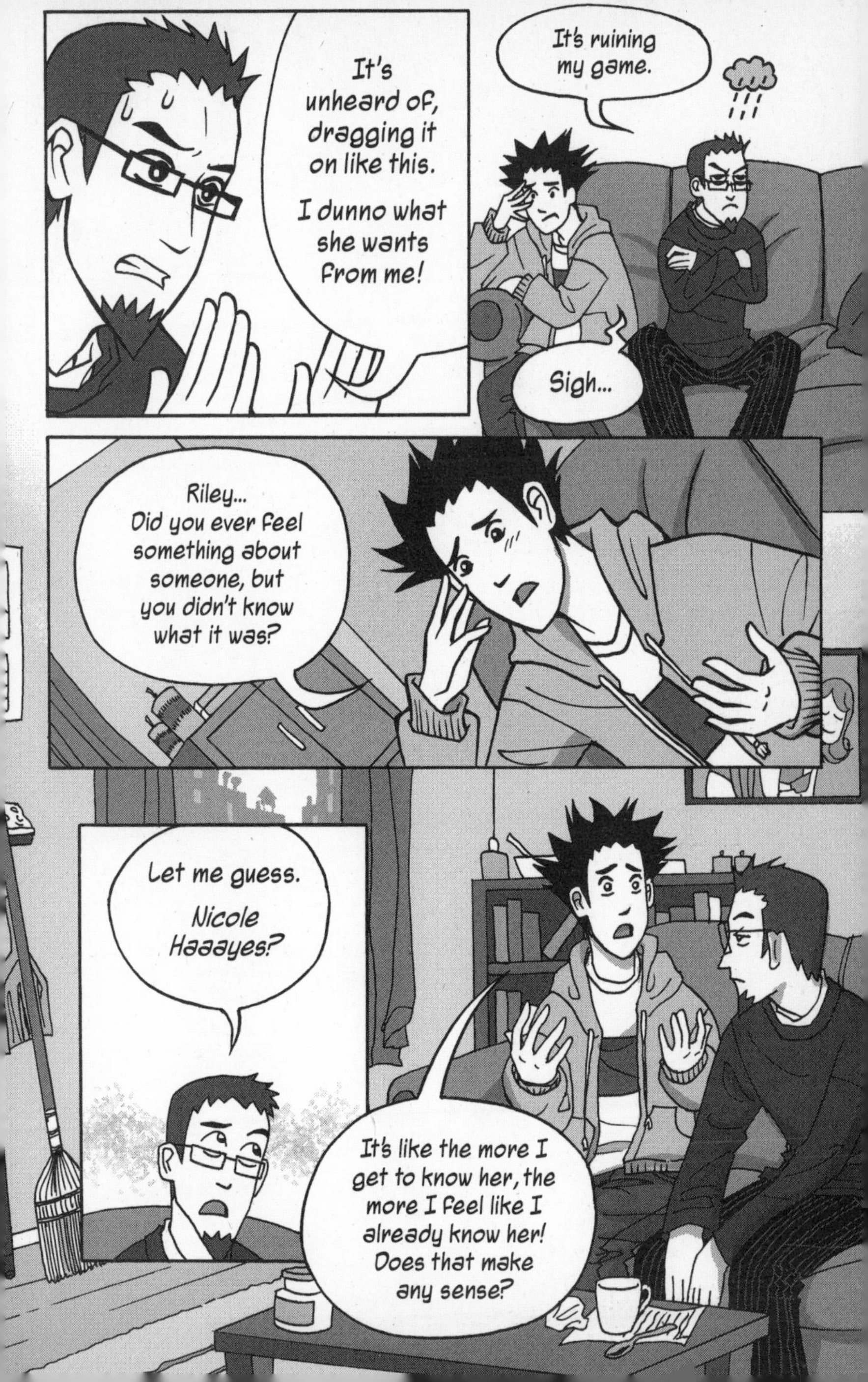
It's unheard of, dragging it on like this.
I dunno what she wants from me!
It's ruining my game.
Sigh...
Riley... Did you ever feel something about someone, but you didn't know what it was?
Let me guess.
Nicole Haaayes?
It's like the more I get to know her, the more I feel like I already know her! Does that make any sense?

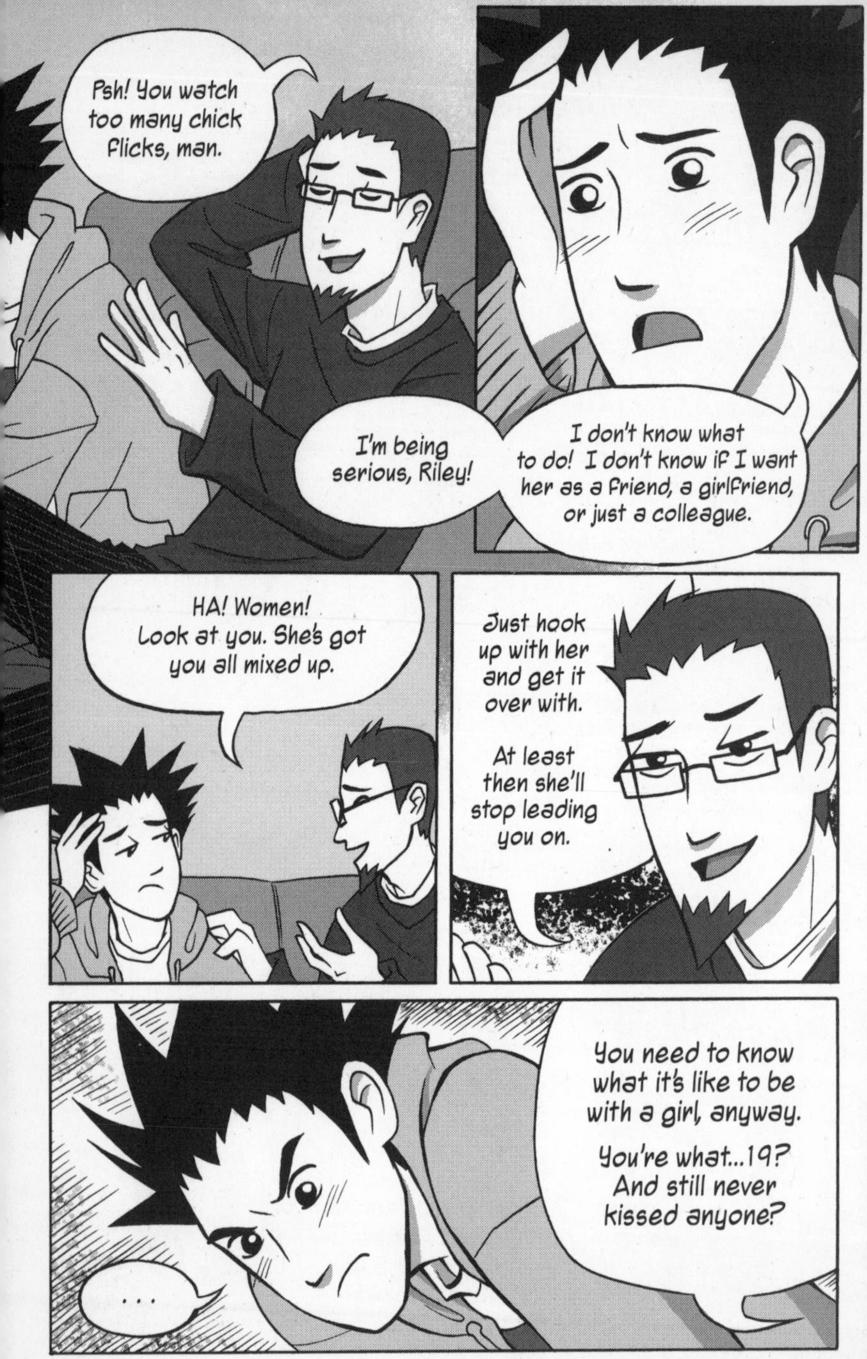
Psh! You watch too many chick flicks, man.
I'm being serious, Riley!
I don't know what to do! I don't know if I want her as a friend, a girlfriend, or just a colleague.
HA! Women! Look at you. She's got you all mixed up.
Just hook up with her and get it over with.
At least then she'll stop leading you on.
You need to know what it's like to be with a girl, anyway.
You're what...19? And still never kissed anyone?
...

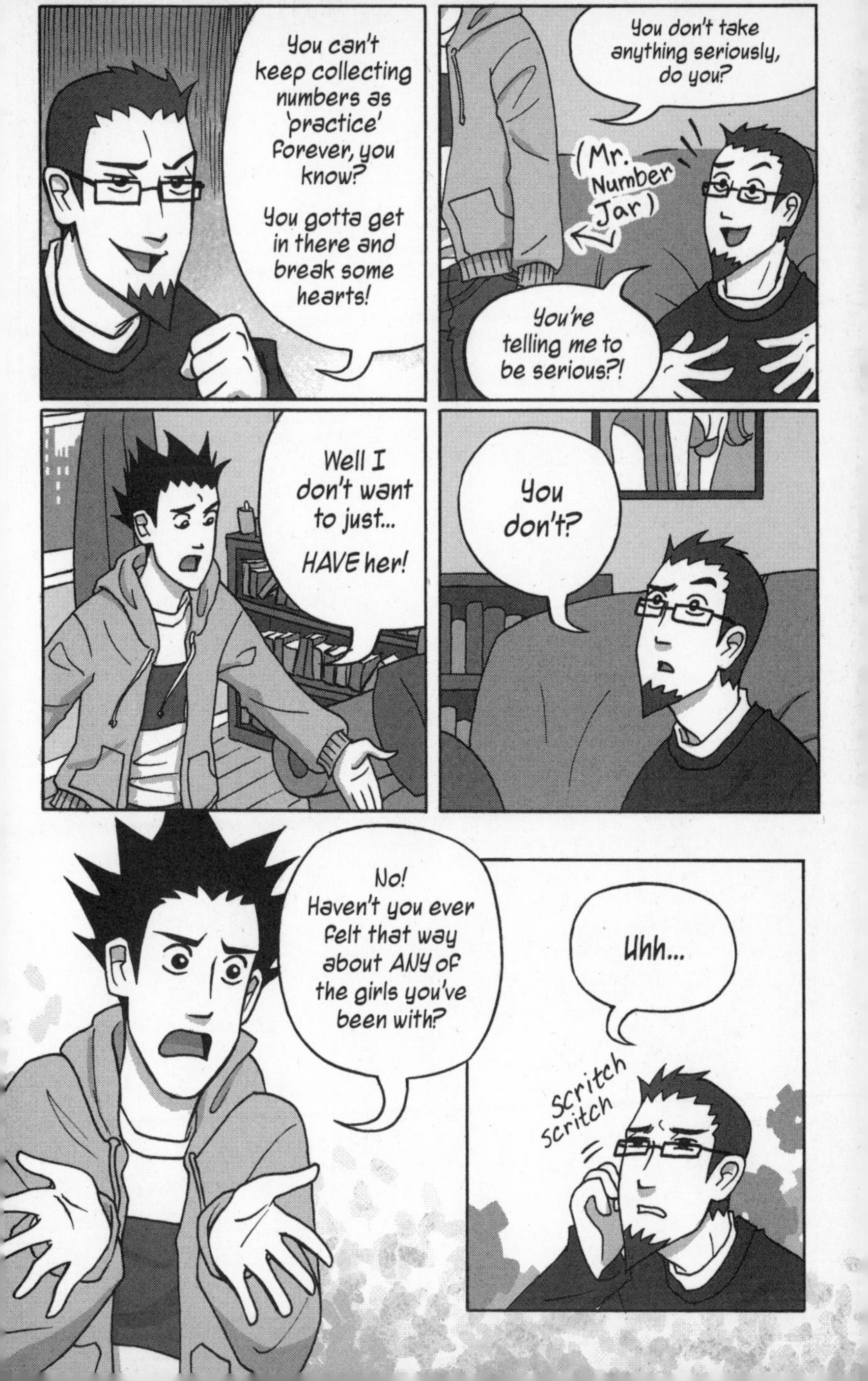
You can't keep collecting numbers as 'practice' forever, you know?
You gotta get in there and break some hearts!
You don't take anything seriously, do you?
(Mr. Number Jar)
You're telling me to be serious?!
Well I don't want to just...
HAVE her!
You don't?
No!
Haven't you ever felt that way about ANY of the girls you've been with?
Uhh...
Scritch scritch

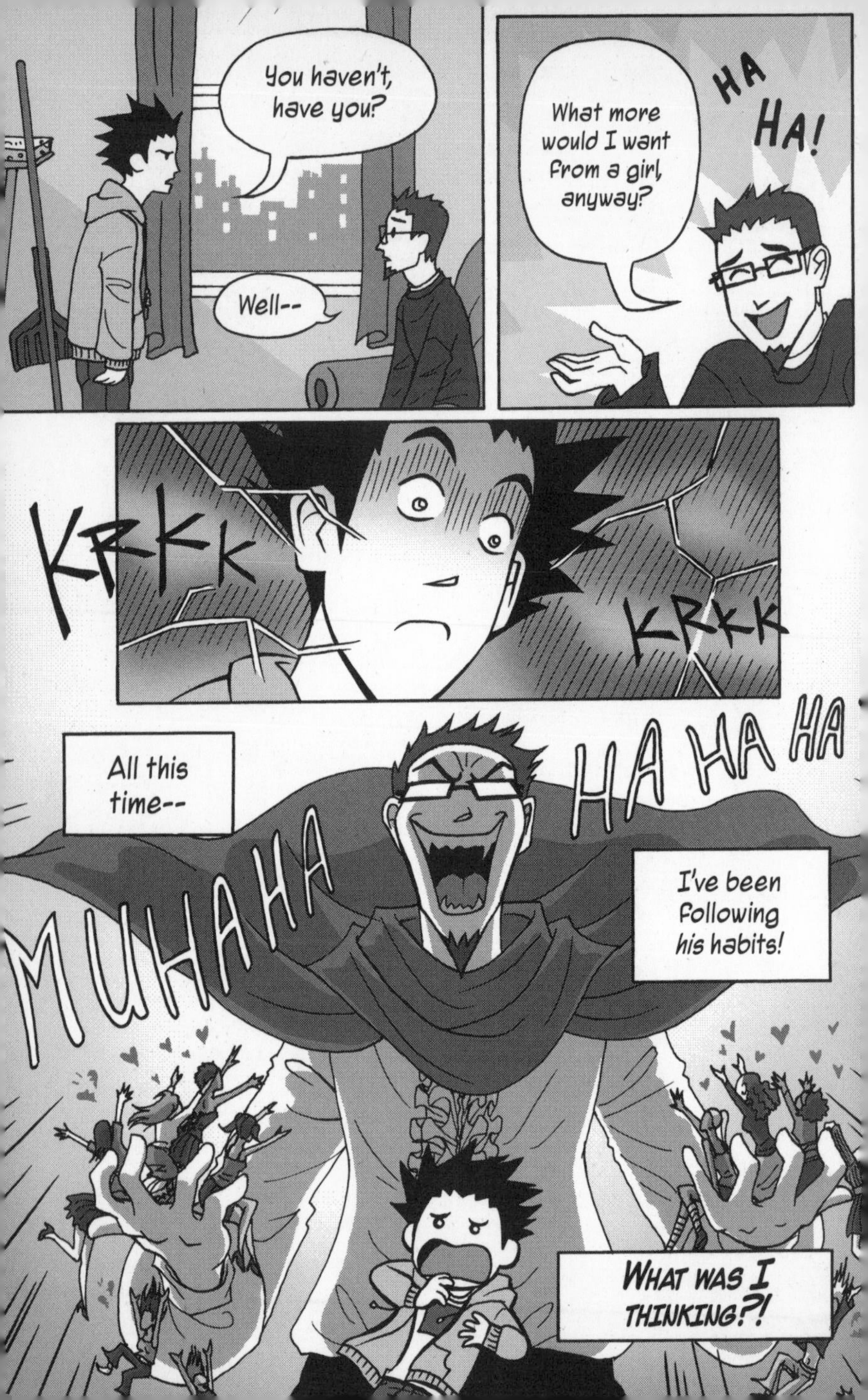
You haven't, have you?
Well--
What more would I want from a girl, anyway?
HA HA!
KRKK
KRKK
All this time--
MUHAHA HA HA HA HA
I've been following his habits!
WHAT WAS I THINKING?!

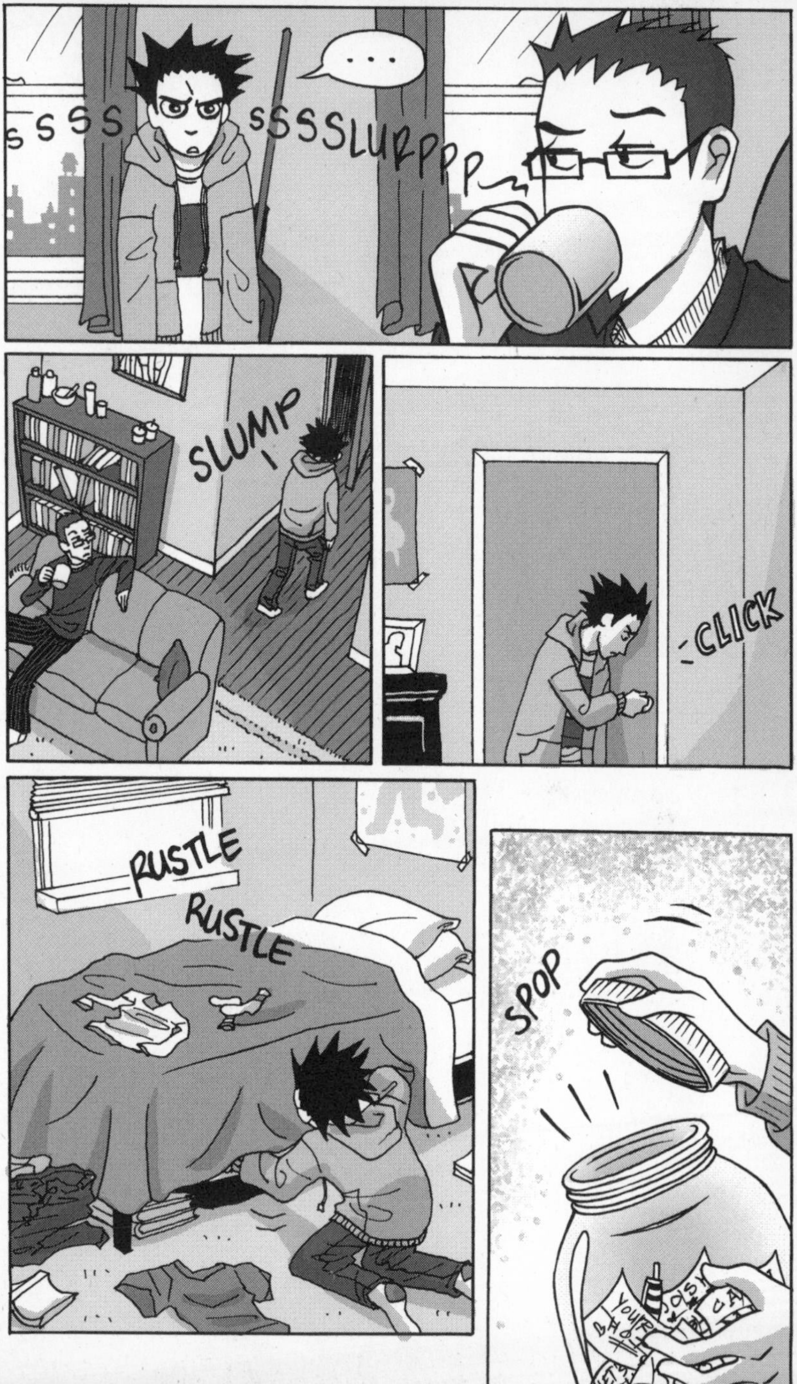

SSSSS
...
SSSSSLURPPPP
SLUMP
CLICK
RUSTLE
RUSTLE
SPOP

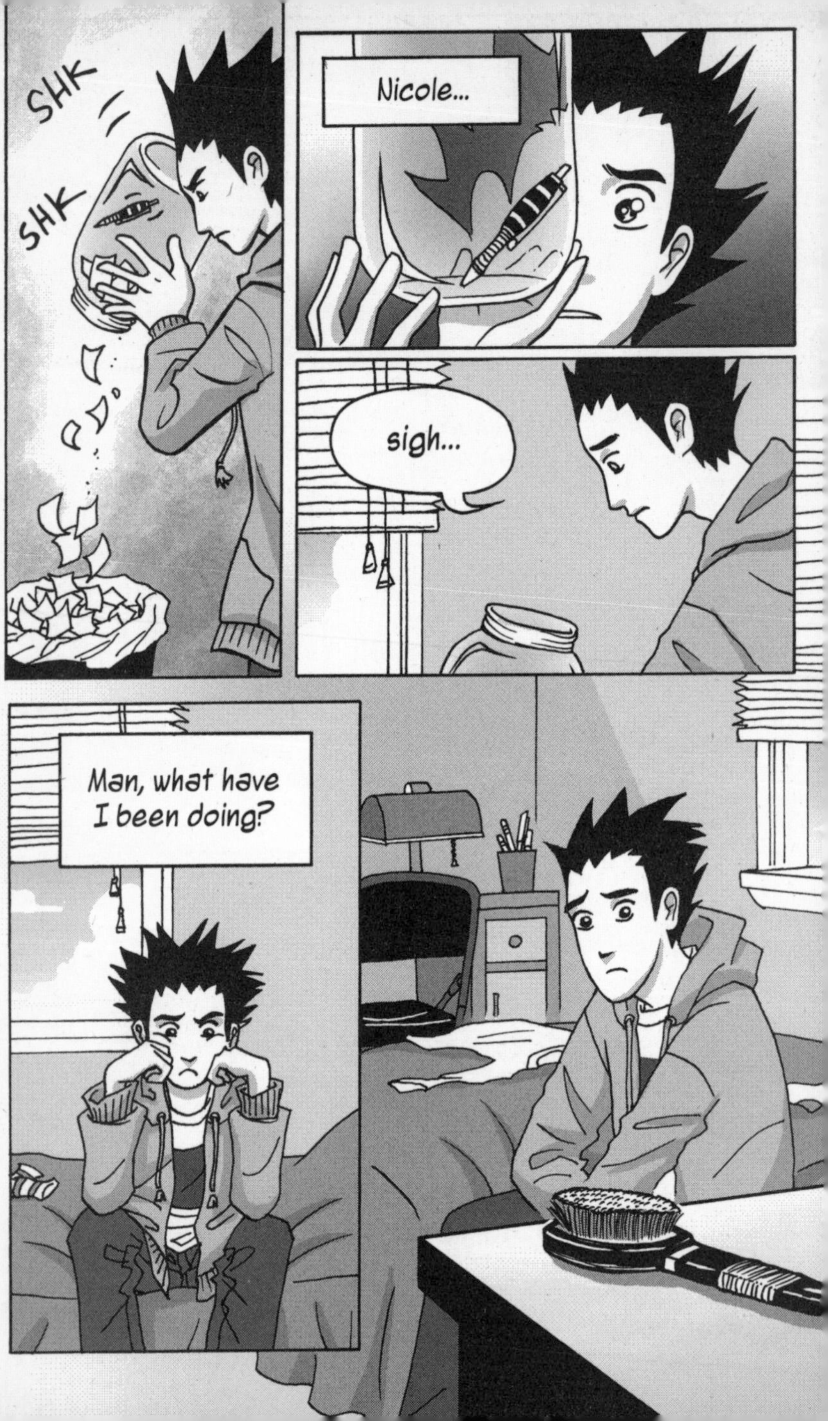
SHK
SHK
Nicole...
sigh...
Man, what have I been doing?

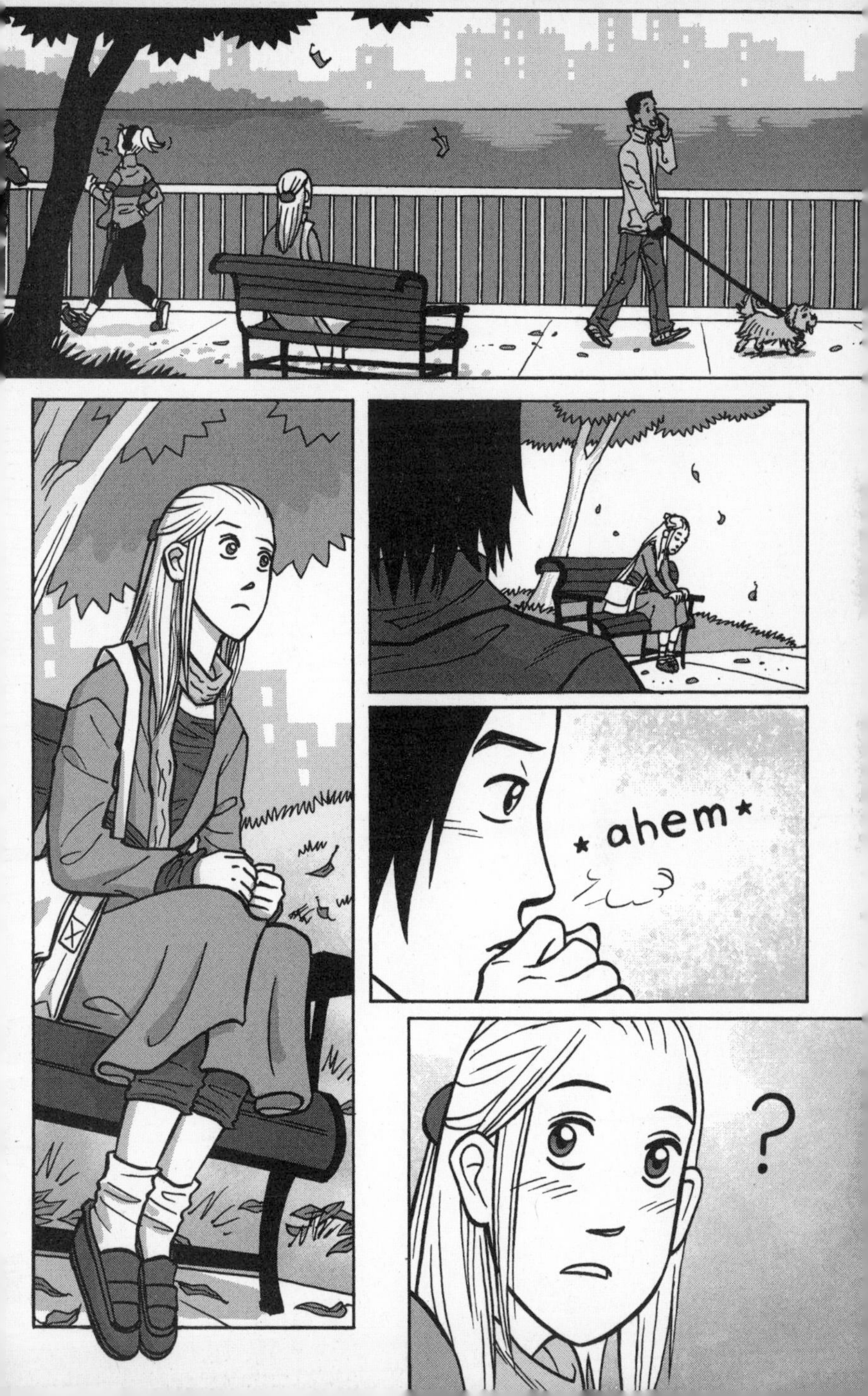
ahem
?

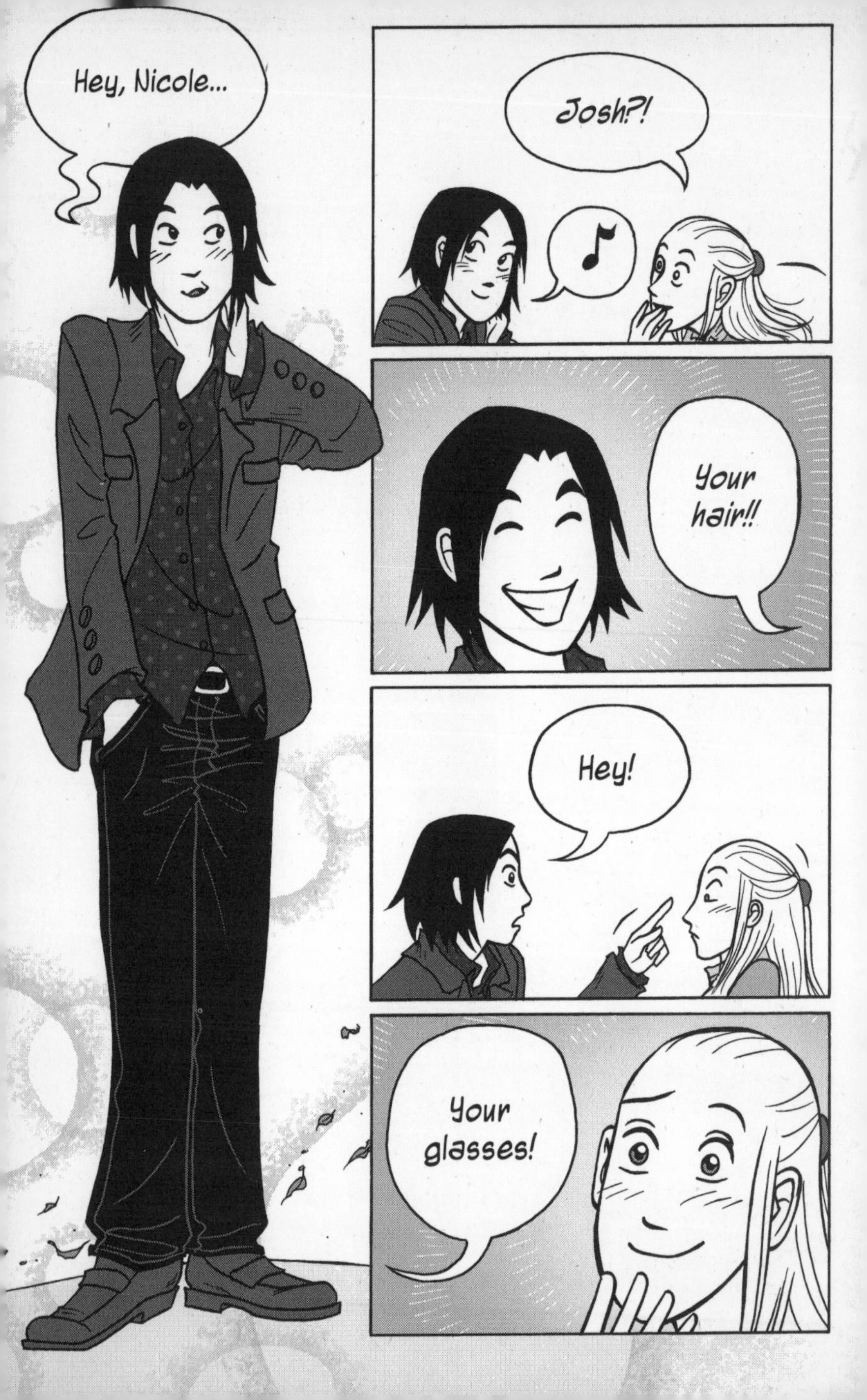
Hey, Nicole...
Josh?!
♪
Your hair!!
Hey!
Your glasses!

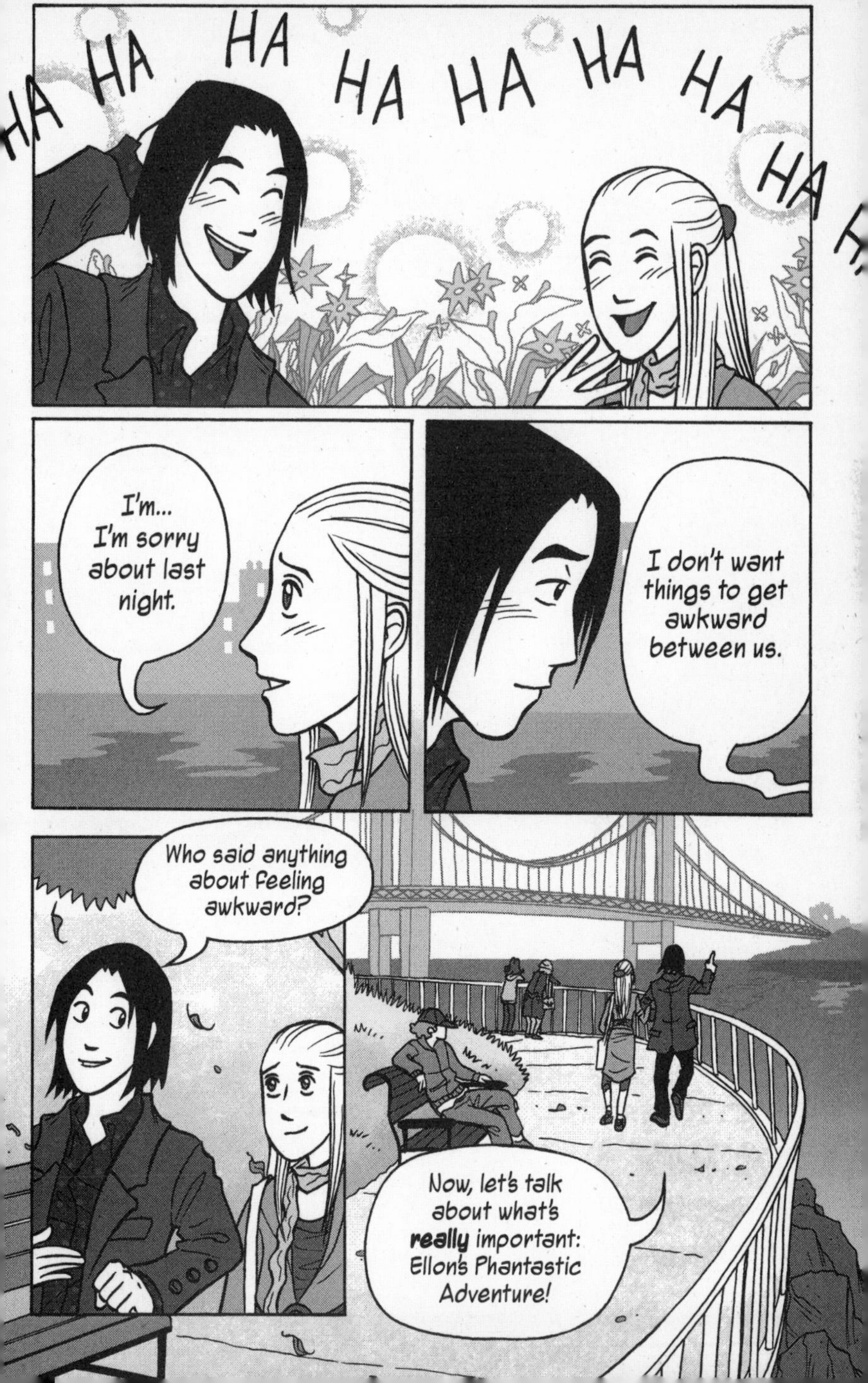
HA HA HA HA HA HA HA HA HA
I'm... I'm sorry about last night.
I don't want things to get awkward between us.
Who said anything about feeling awkward?
Now, let's talk about what's **really** important: Ellon's Phantastic Adventure!

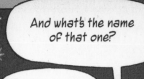

And what's the name of that one?

That is Tridios, where the god of stew sleeps.

And that one, sweet Ellon?

That is Menutu, where the goddess of ink calls home.

You know everything, don't you?

No one can know everything. Even the Gods.

I hope we'll be friends for a long time.

We will be.

I'll make sure of it.

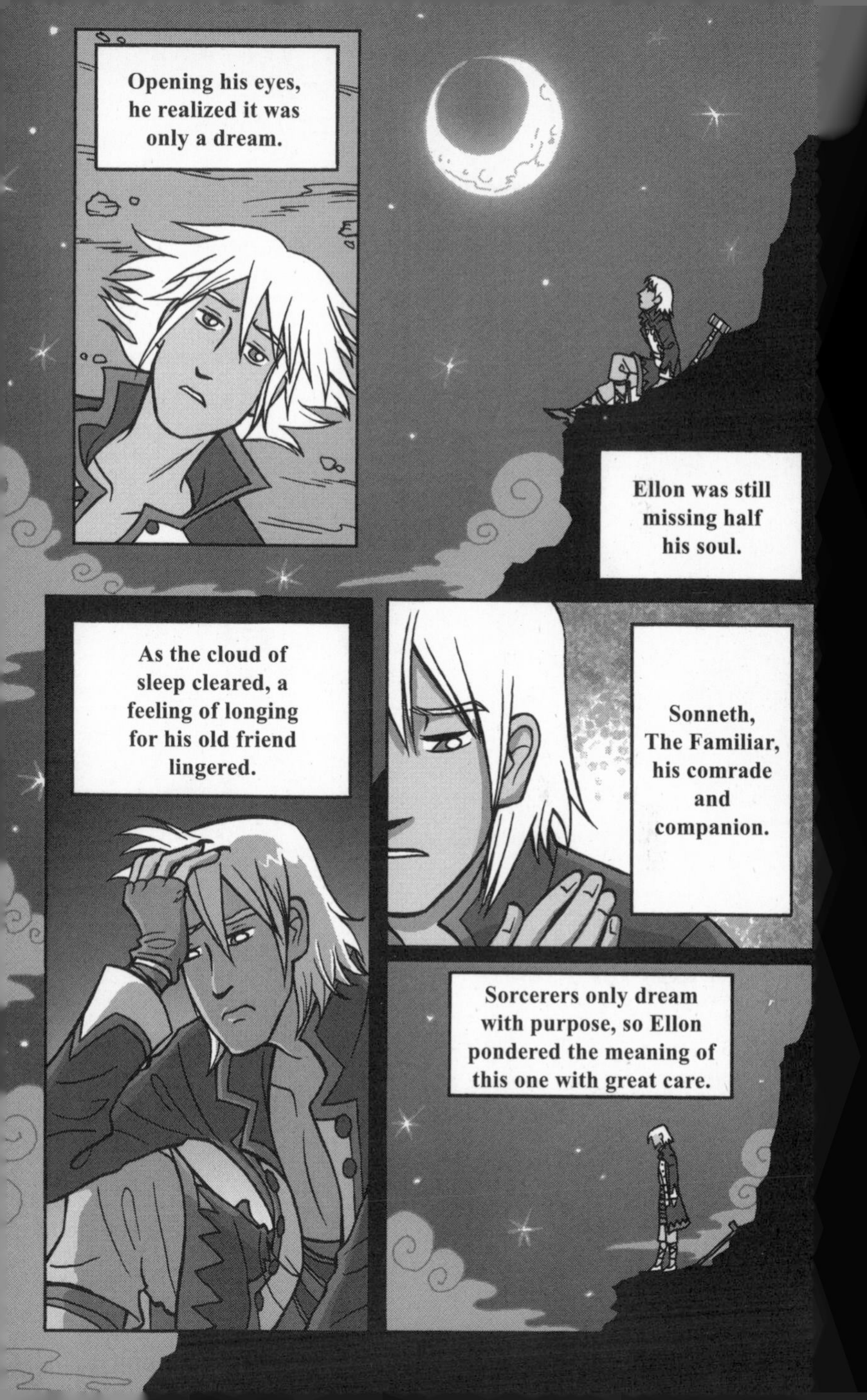
Opening his eyes, he realized it was only a dream.
Ellon was still missing half his soul.
As the cloud of sleep cleared, a feeling of longing for his old friend lingered.
Sonneth, The Familiar, his comrade and companion.
Sorcerers only dream with purpose, so Ellon pondered the meaning of this one with great care.

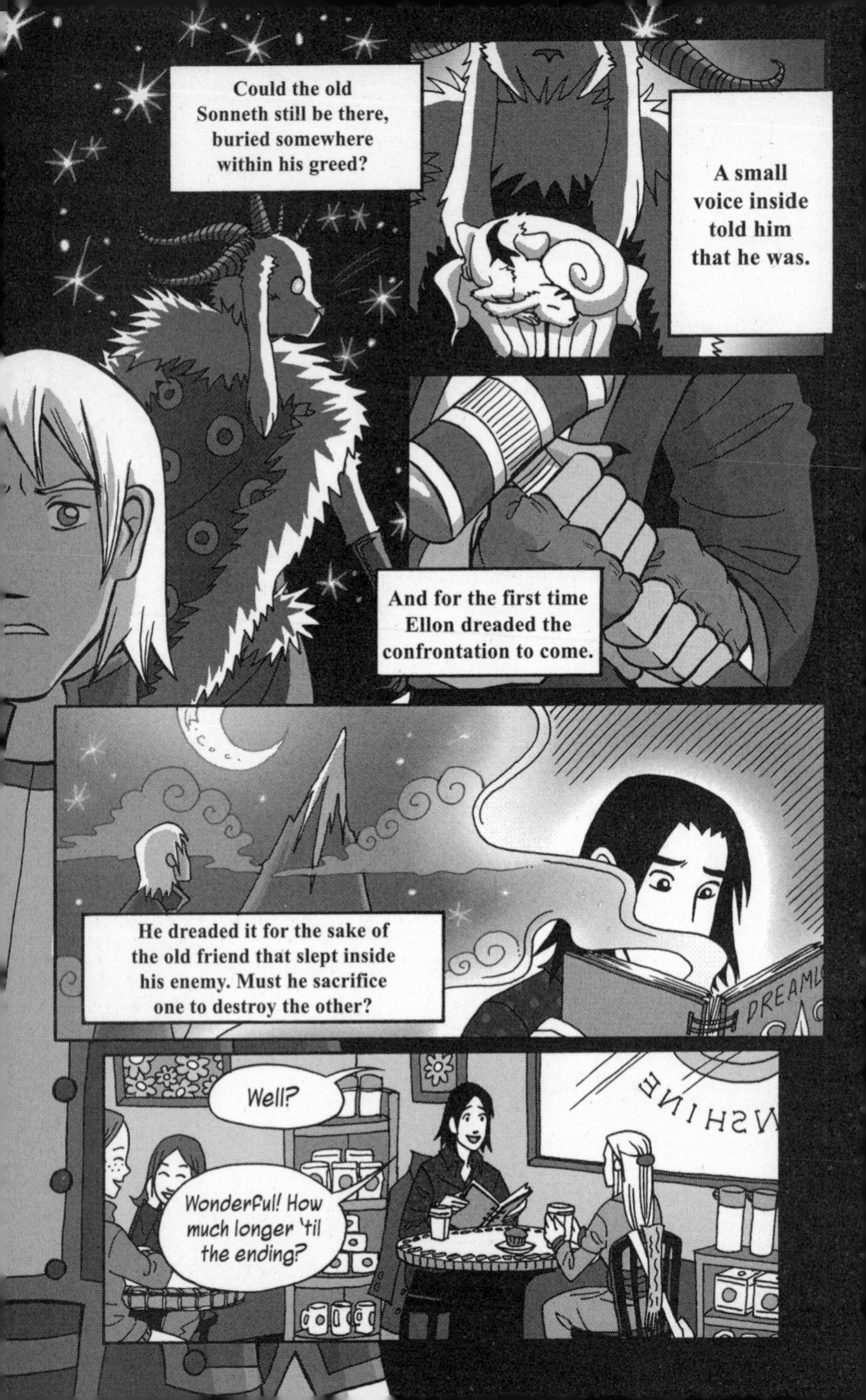
Could the old Sonneth still be there, buried somewhere within his greed?
A small voice inside told him that he was.
And for the first time Ellon dreaded the confrontation to come.
He dreaded it for the sake of the old friend that slept inside his enemy. Must he sacrifice one to destroy the other?
Well?
Wonderful! How much longer 'til the ending?

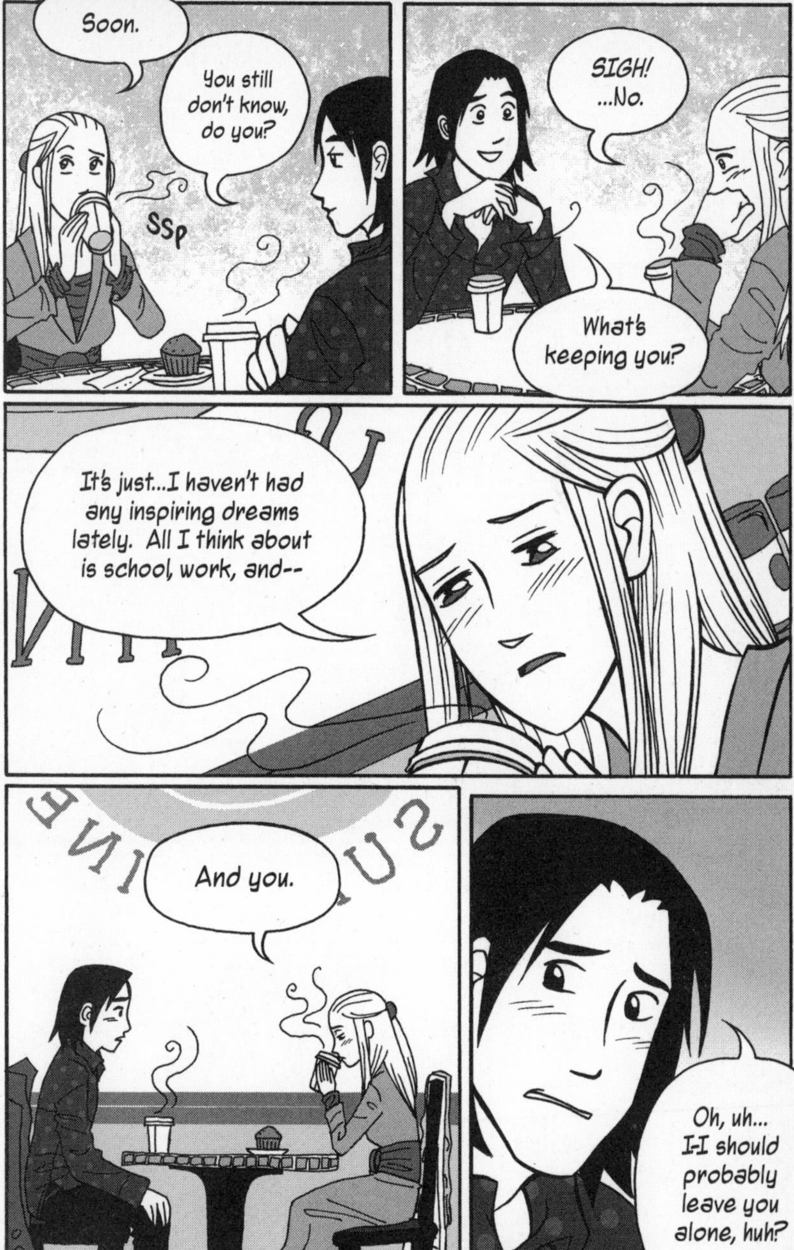
Soon.
You still don't know, do you?
SSP
SIGH! ...No.
What's keeping you?
It's just...I haven't had any inspiring dreams lately. All I think about is school, work, and--
And you.
Oh, uh... I-I should probably leave you alone, huh?

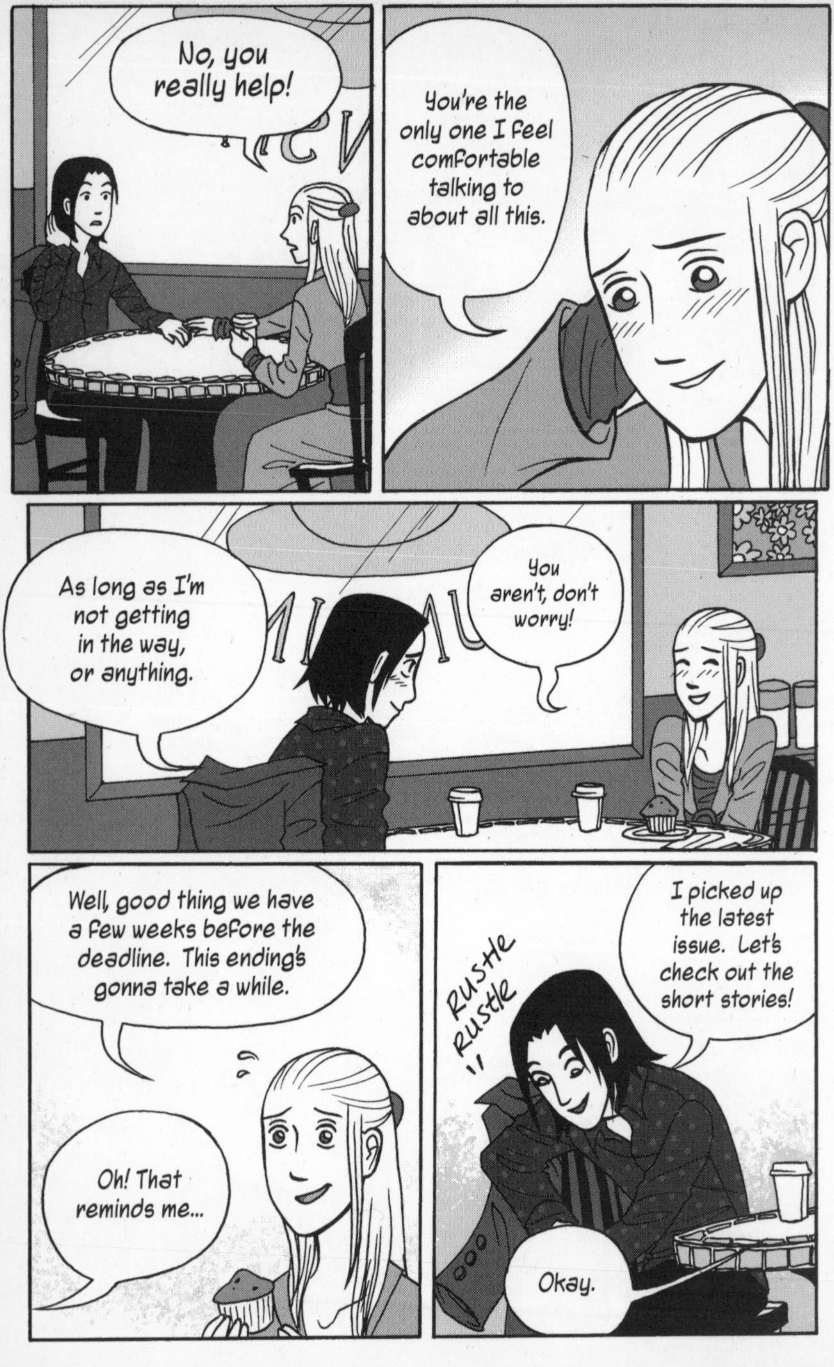
No, you really help!
You're the only one I feel comfortable talking to about all this.
As long as I'm not getting in the way, or anything.
You aren't, don't worry!
Well, good thing we have a few weeks before the deadline. This ending's gonna take a while.
Oh! That reminds me...
Rustle Rustle
I picked up the latest issue. Let's check out the short stories!
Okay.

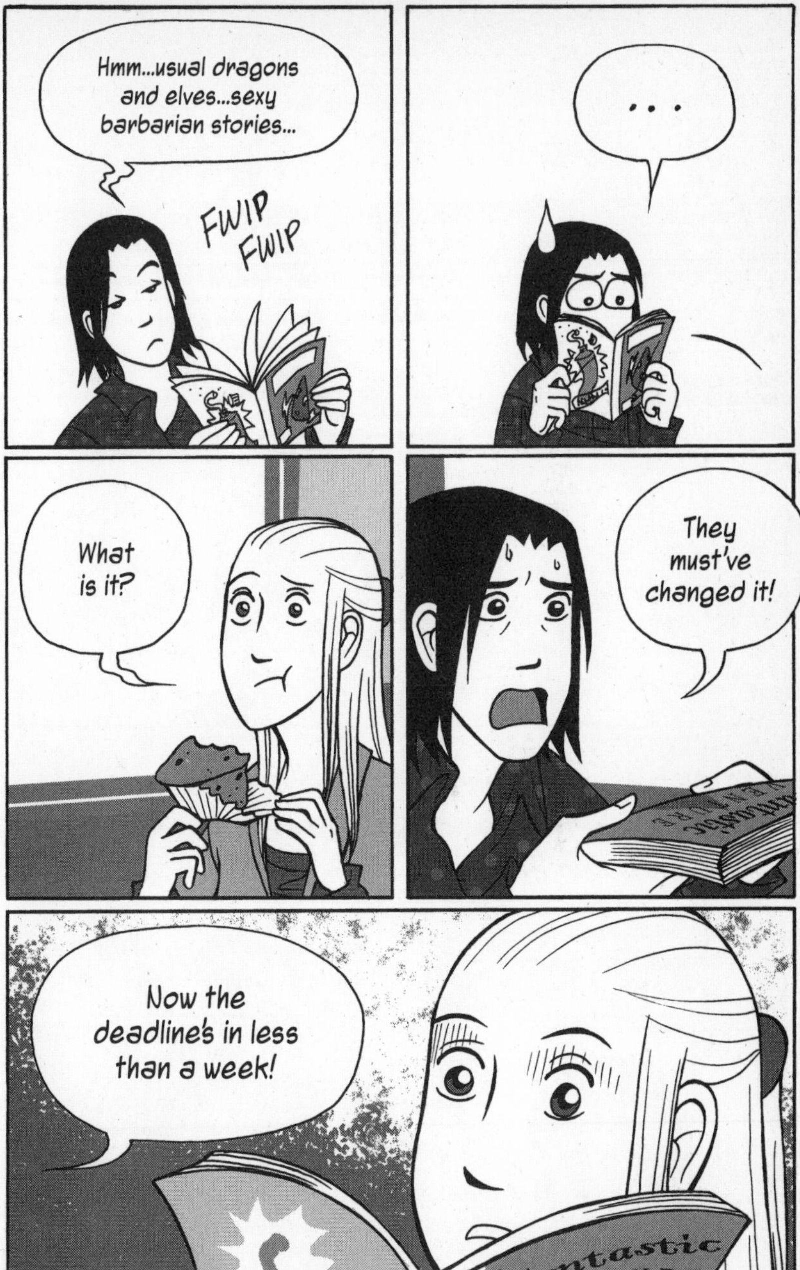
Hmm...usual dragons and elves...sexy barbarian stories...
FWIP FWIP
...
What is it?
They must've changed it!
Now the deadline's in less than a week!
Phantastic ADVENTURE

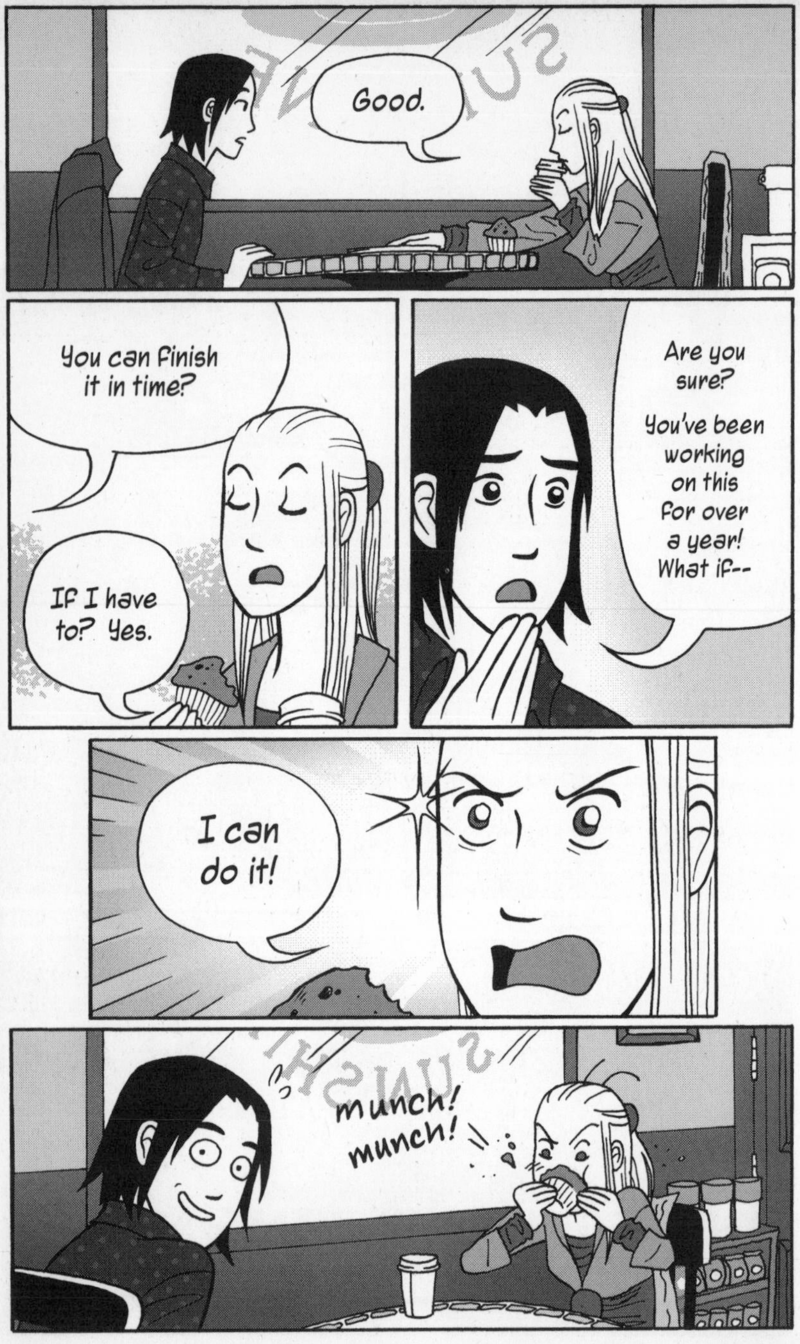
Good.
You can finish it in time?
If I have to? Yes.
Are you sure?
You've been working on this for over a year! What if--
I can do it!
munch! munch!

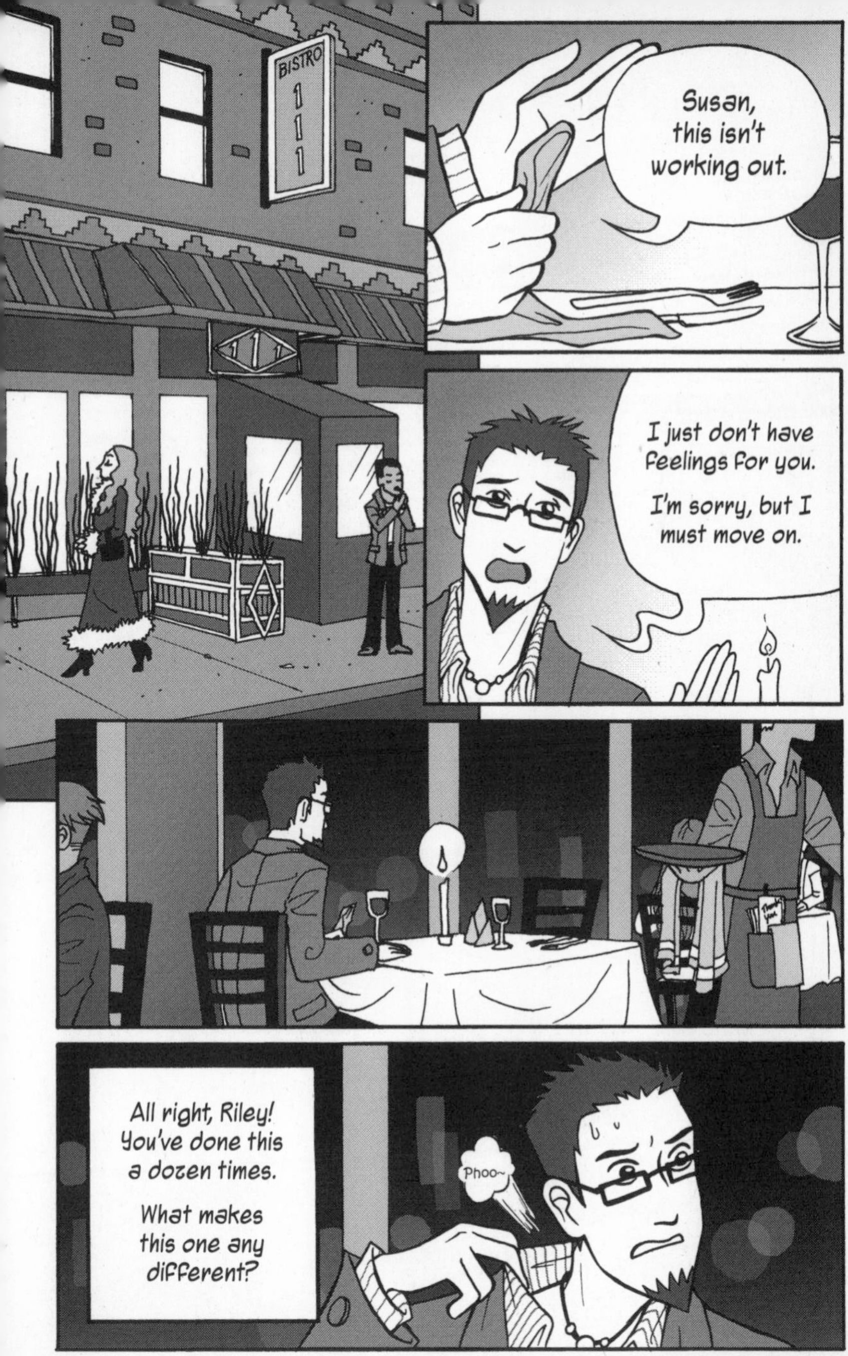
BISTRO 111
111
Susan, this isn't working out.
I just don't have feelings for you.
I'm sorry, but I must move on.
All right, Riley! You've done this a dozen times.
What makes this one any different?
Phoo~

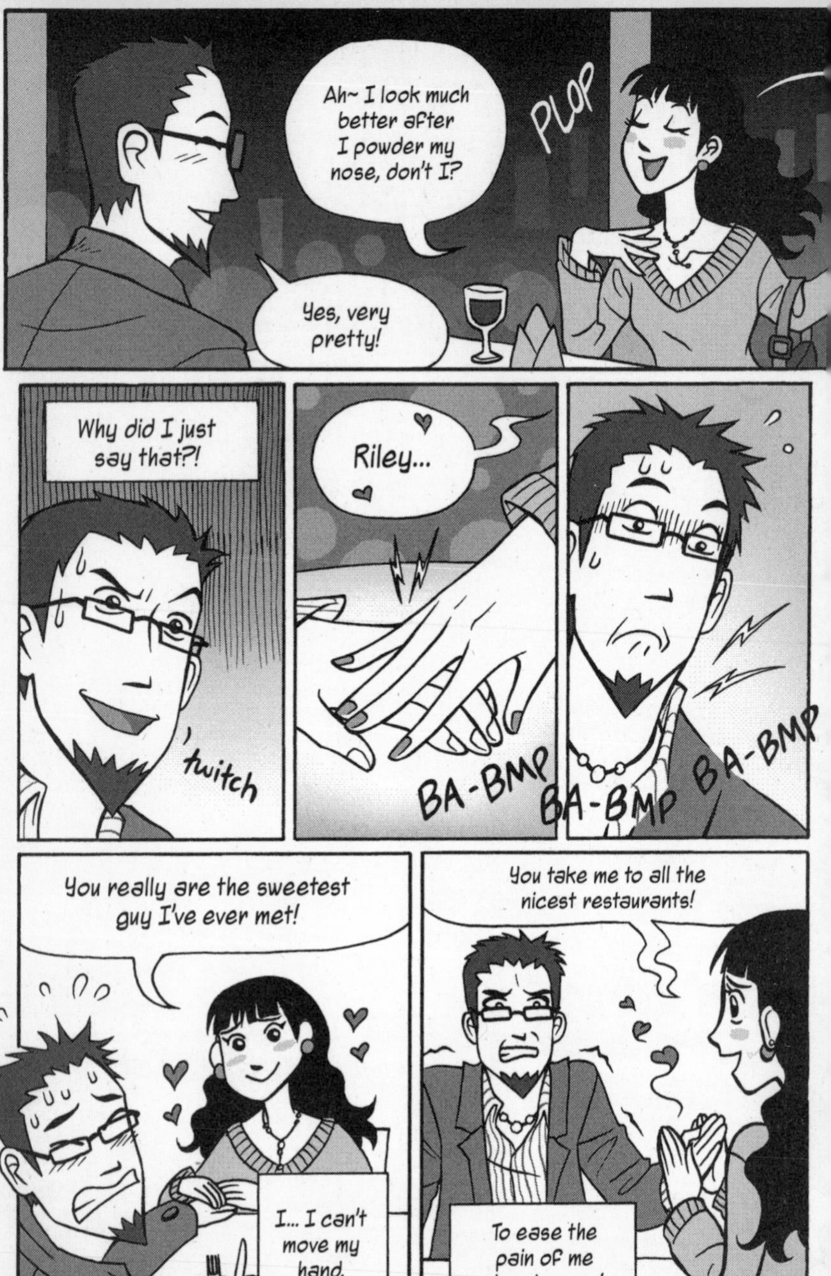
Ah~ I look much better after I powder my nose, don't I?
PLOP
Yes, very pretty!
Why did I just say that?!
twitch
Riley...
BA-BMP
BA-BMP
BA-BMP
You really are the sweetest guy I've ever met!
I... I can't move my hand.
You take me to all the nicest restaurants!
To ease the pain of me dumping you!

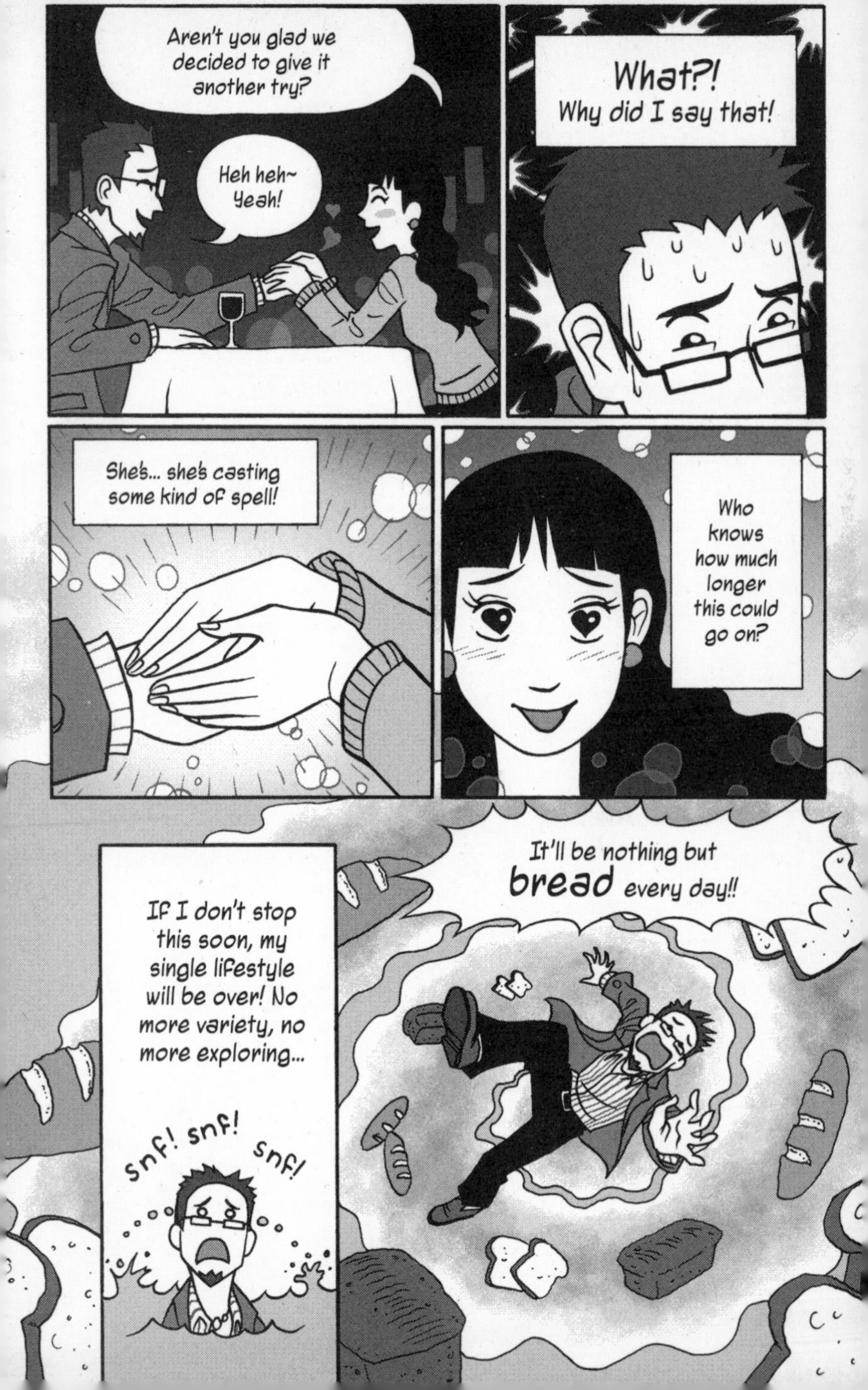
Aren't you glad we decided to give it another try?
Heh heh~ Yeah!
What?! Why did I say that!
She's... she's casting some kind of spell!
Who knows how much longer this could go on?
If I don't stop this soon, my single lifestyle will be over! No more variety, no more exploring...
Snf! snf! snf!
It'll be nothing but bread every day!!

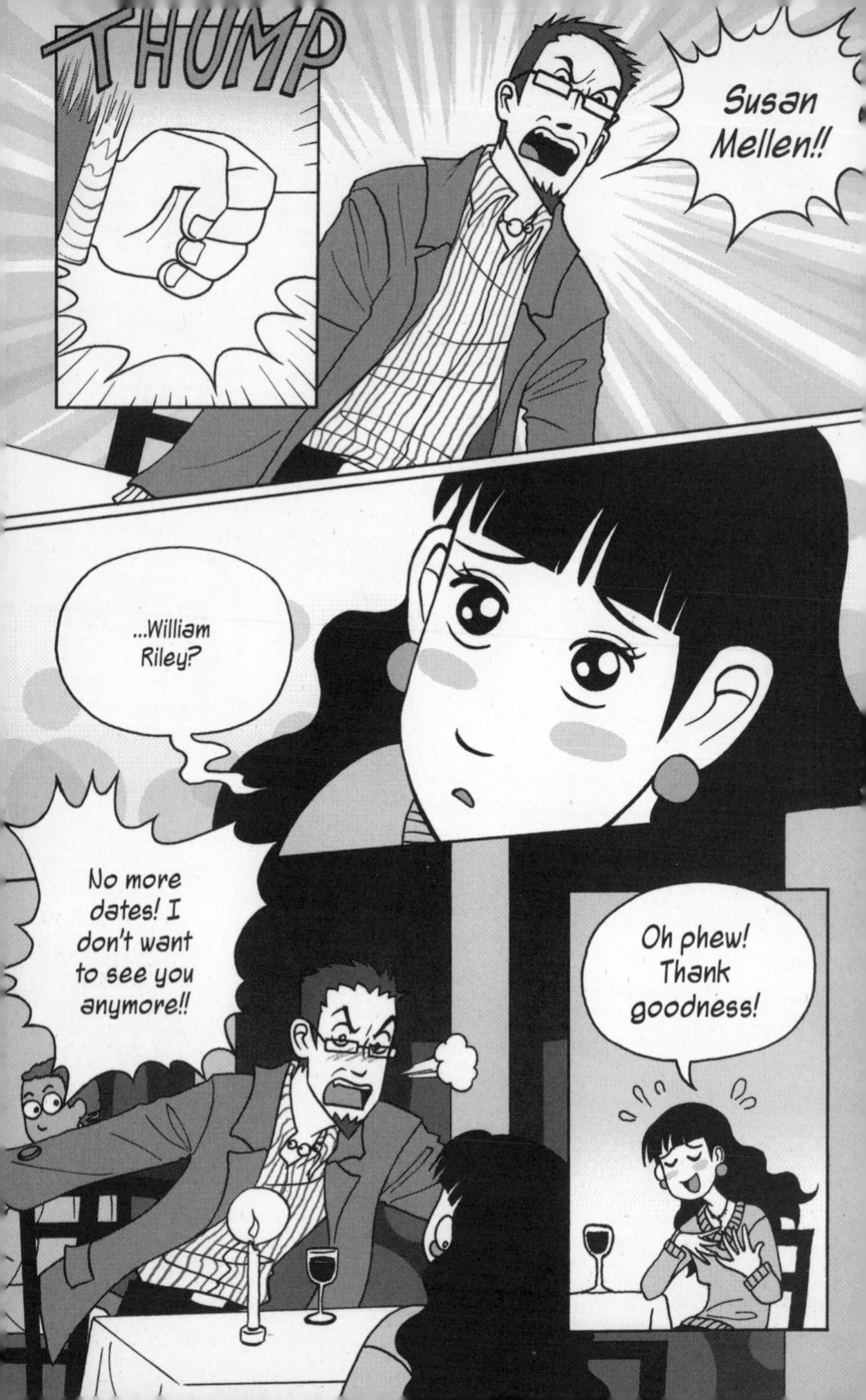
THUMP
Susan Mellen!!
...William Riley?
No more dates! I don't want to see you anymore!!
Oh phew! Thank goodness!

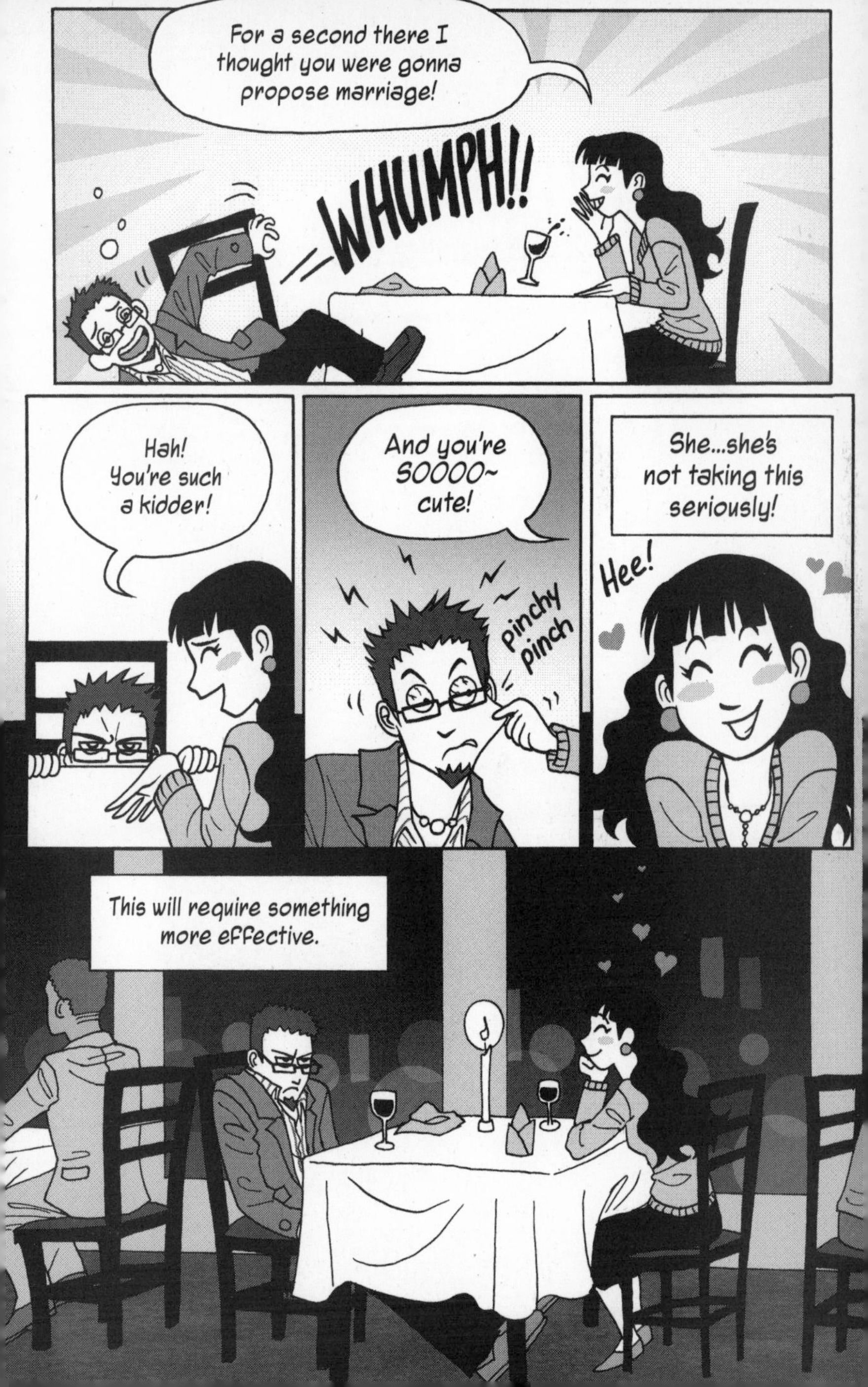

For a second there I thought you were gonna propose marriage!
WHUMPH!!
Hah! You're such a kidder!
And you're SOOOO~ cute!
pinchy pinch
She...she's not taking this seriously!
Hee!
This will require something more effective.

Chapter Four
Stresses Out

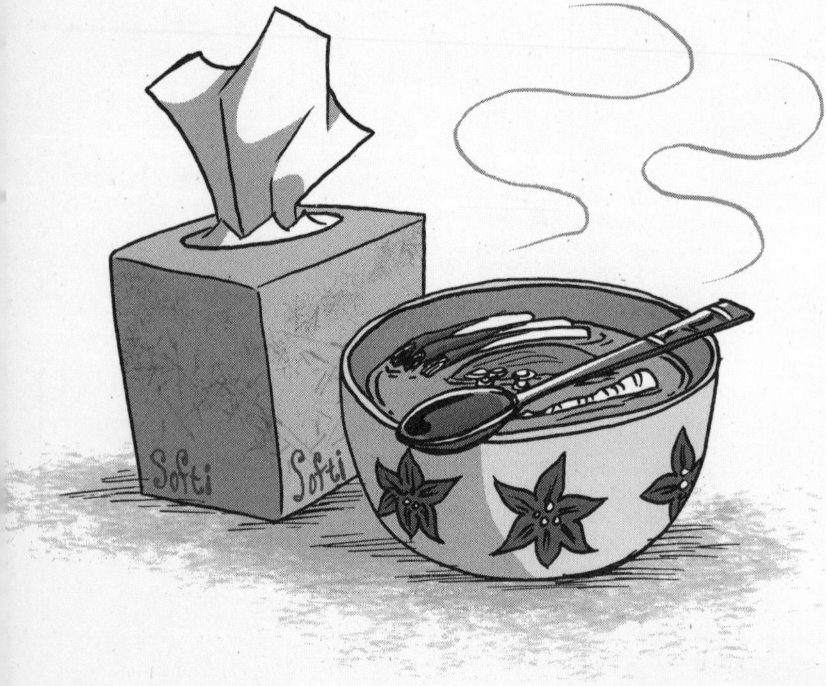
Softi
Softi

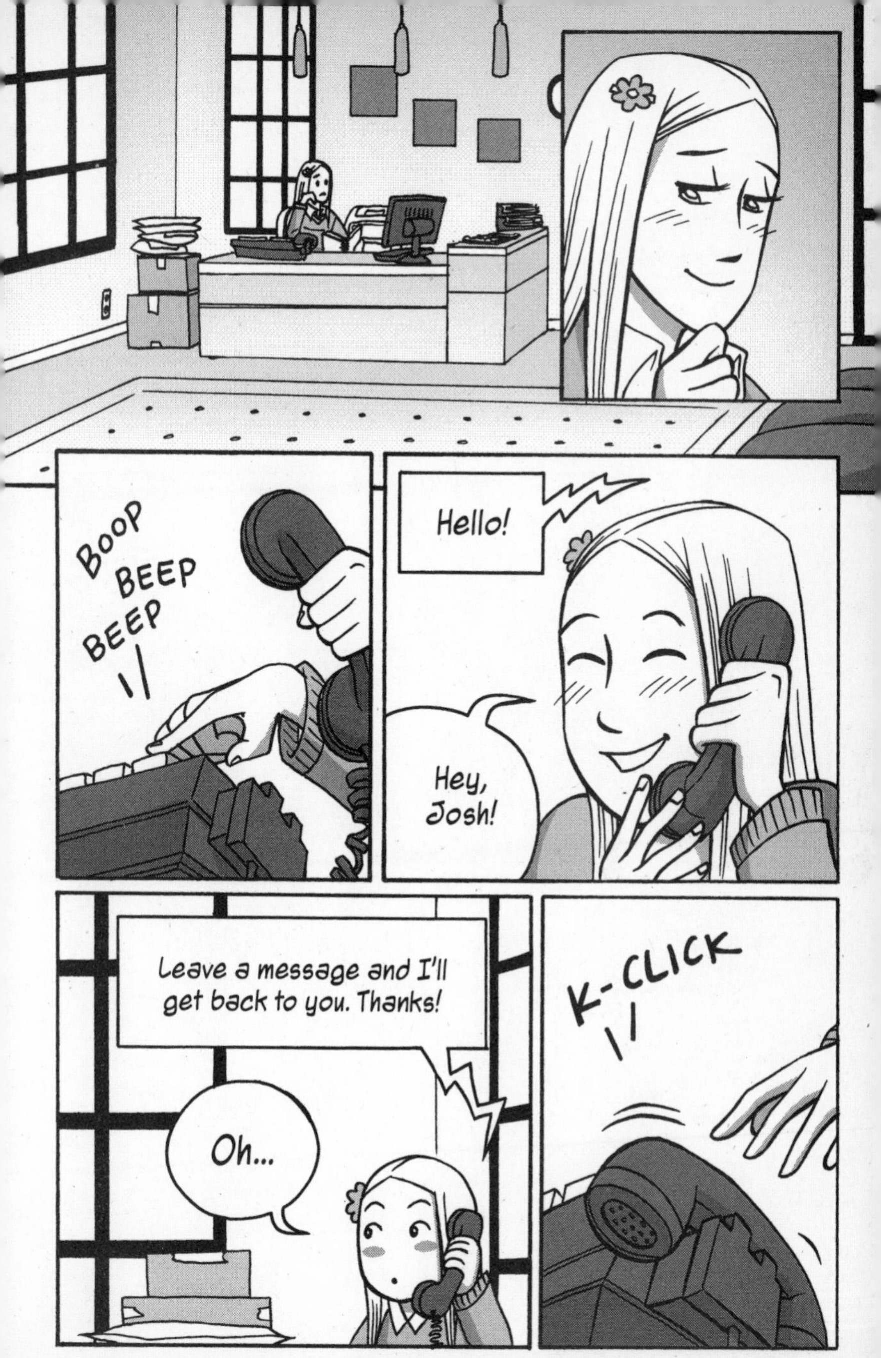
BOOP
BEEP
BEEP
Hello!
Hey, Josh!
Leave a message and I'll get back to you. Thanks!
Oh...
K-CLICK

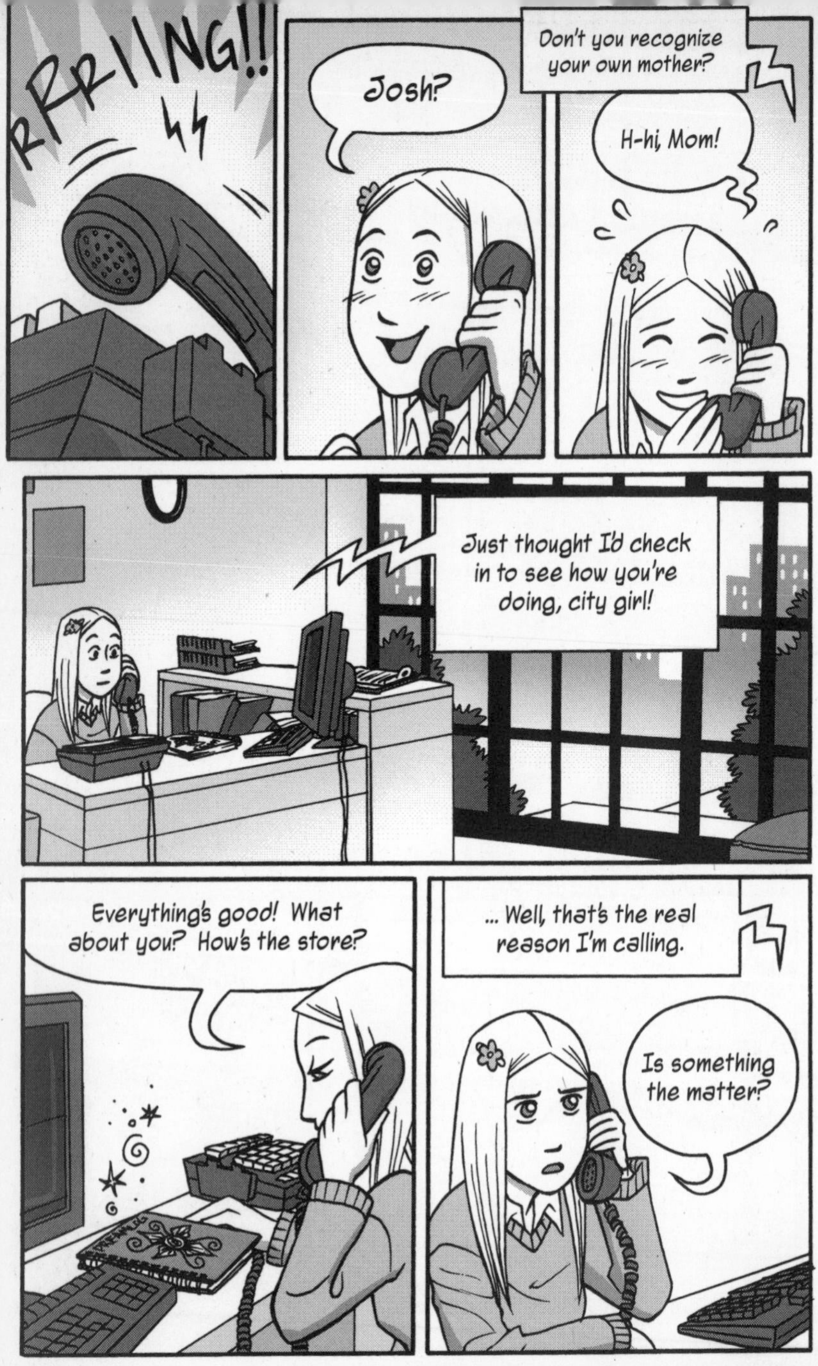
RRRIING!!!
Josh?
Don't you recognize your own mother?
H-hi, Mom!
Just thought I'd check in to see how you're doing, city girl!
Everything's good! What about you? How's the store?
... Well, that's the real reason I'm calling.
Is something the matter?

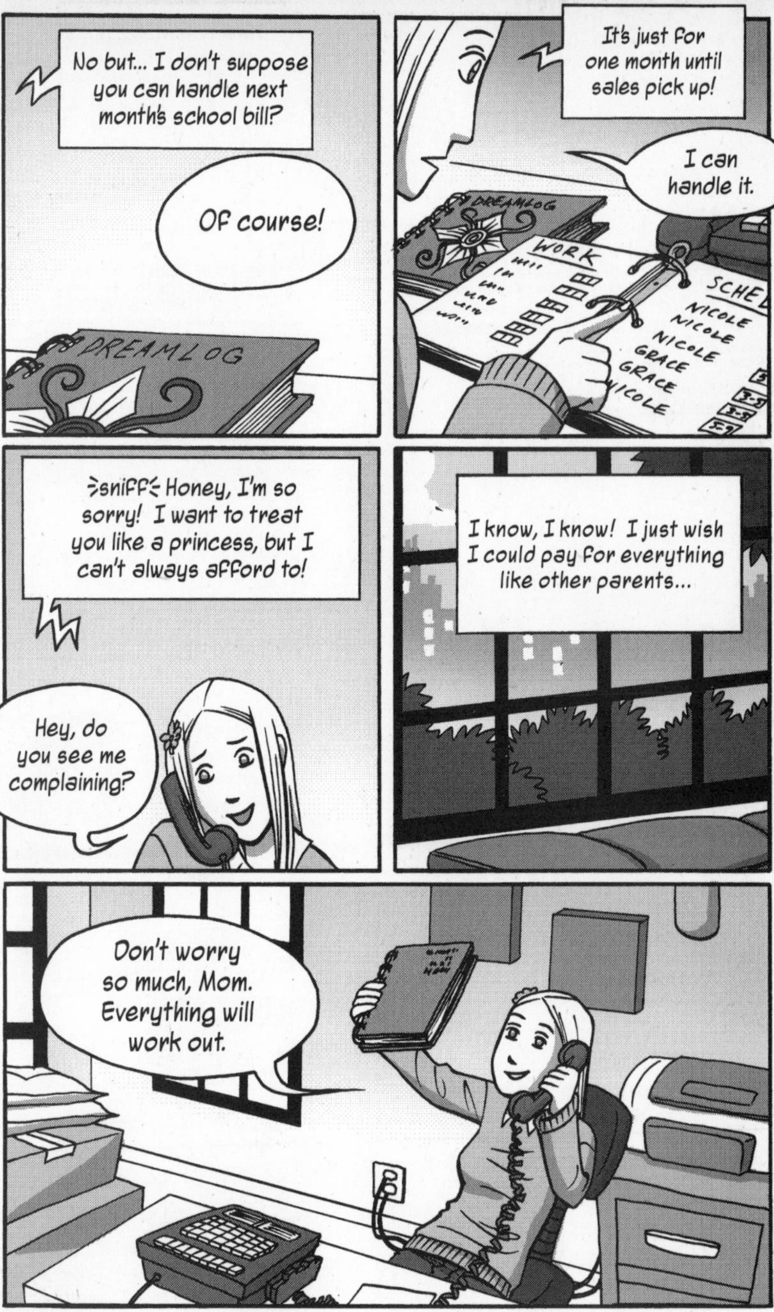
No but... I don't suppose you can handle next month's school bill?
Of course!
DREAMLOG
It's just for one month until sales pick up!
I can handle it.
DREAMLOG
WORK
SCHE
NICOLE
NICOLE
NICOLE
GRACE
GRACE
NICOLE
≥sniff≤ Honey, I'm so sorry! I want to treat you like a princess, but I can't always afford to!
Hey, do you see me complaining?
I know, I know! I just wish I could pay for everything like other parents...
Don't worry so much, Mom. Everything will work out.

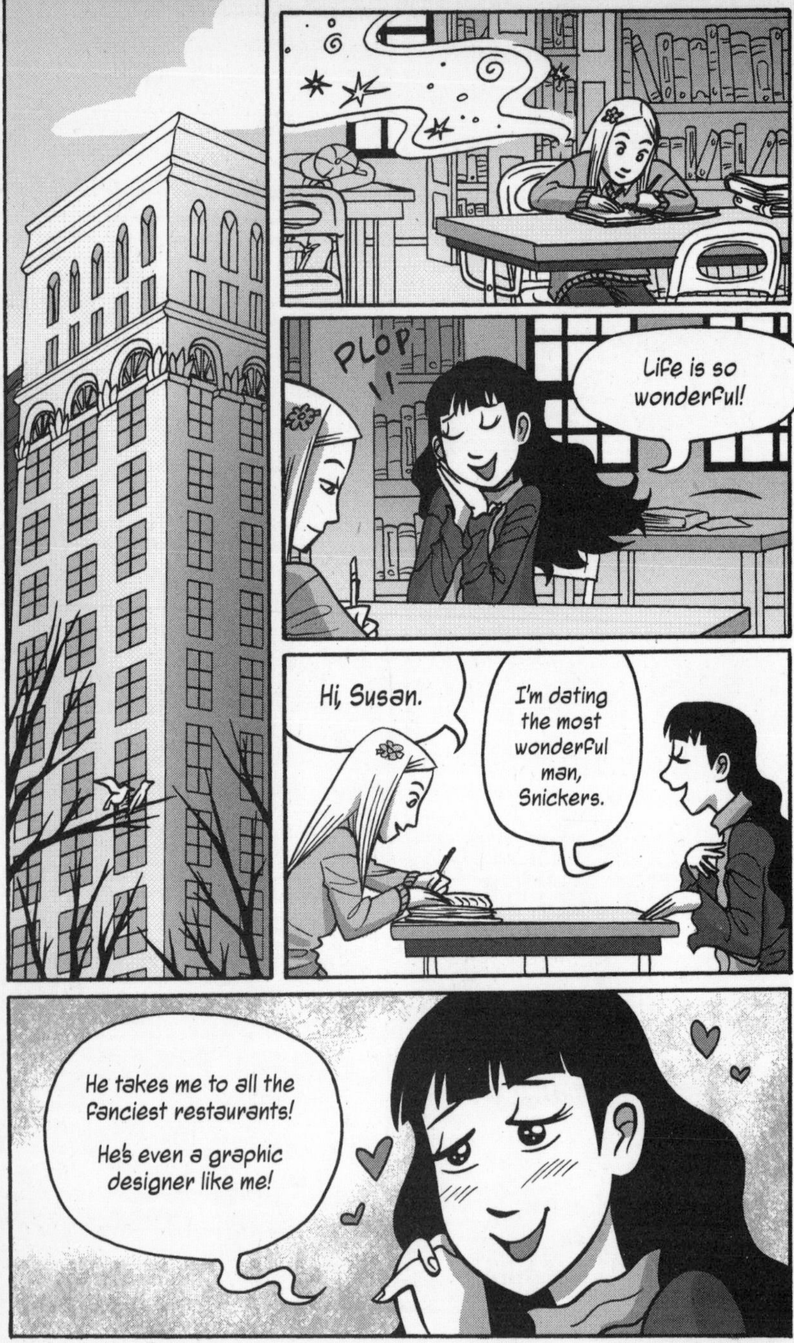
PLOP
Life is so wonderful!
Hi, Susan.
I'm dating the most wonderful man, Snickers.
He takes me to all the fanciest restaurants!
He's even a graphic designer like me!

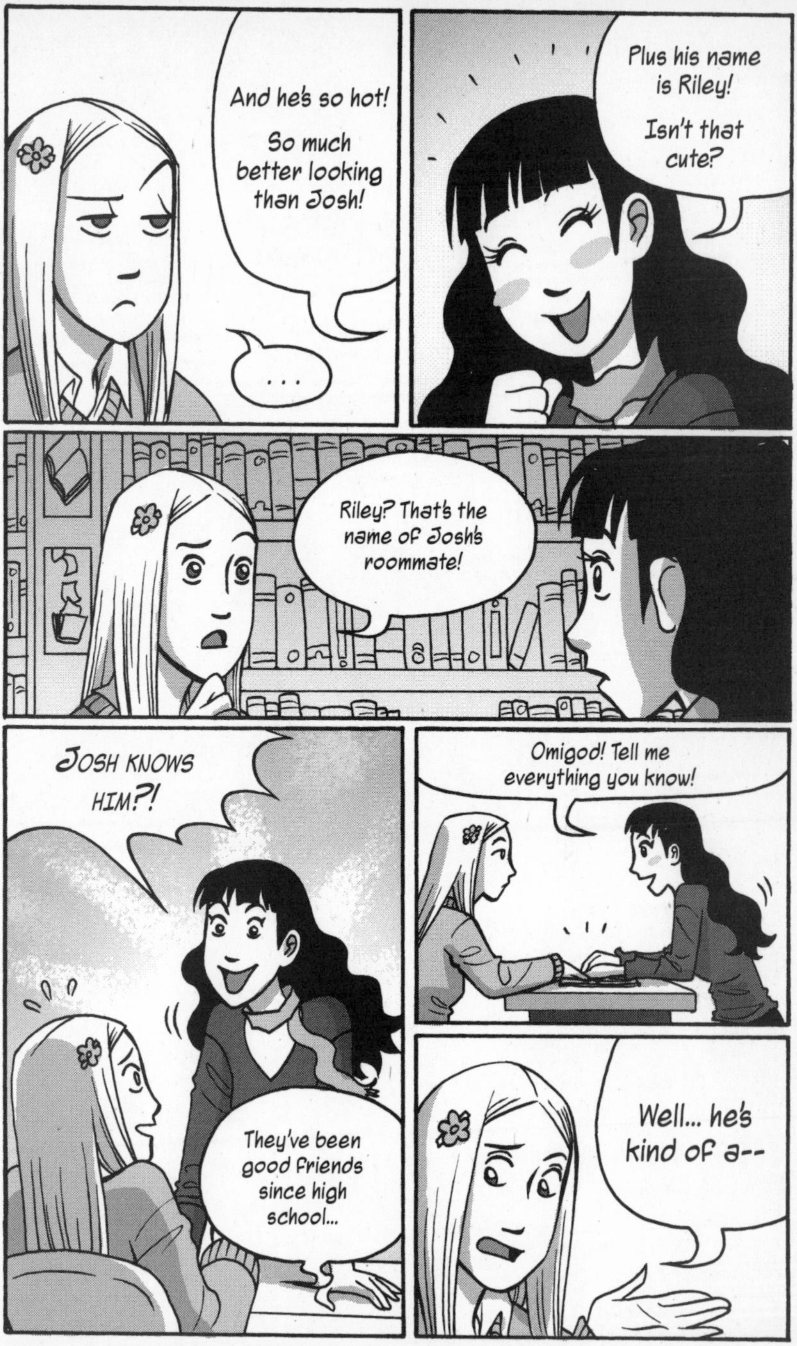
And he's so hot!
So much better looking than Josh!
...
Plus his name is Riley!
Isn't that cute?
Riley? That's the name of Josh's roommate!
JOSH KNOWS HIM?!
They've been good friends since high school...
Omigod! Tell me everything you know!
Well... he's kind of a--

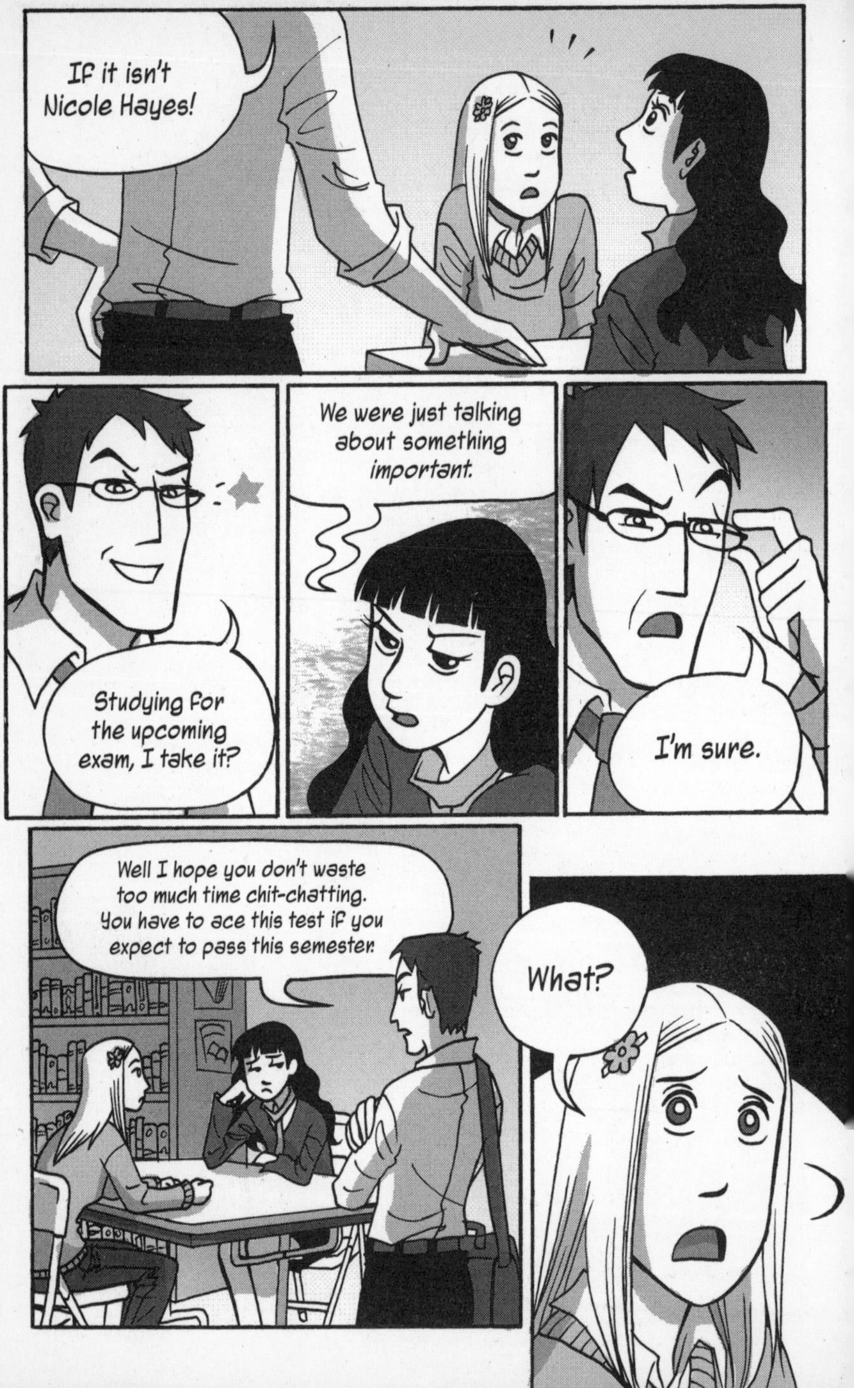
If it isn't Nicole Hayes!
Studying for the upcoming exam, I take it?
We were just talking about something *important*.
I'm sure.
Well I hope you don't waste too much time chit-chatting. You have to ace this test if you expect to pass this semester.
What?

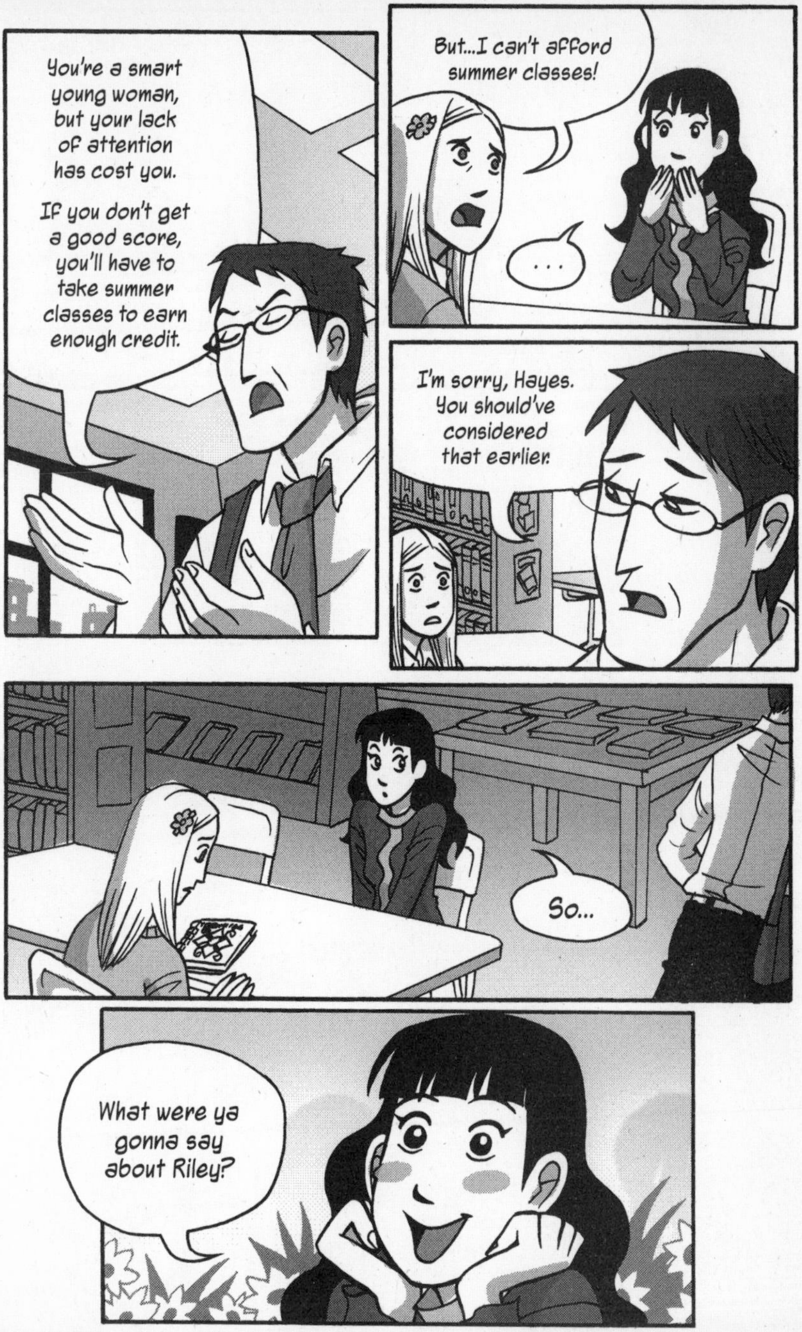
You're a smart young woman, but your lack of attention has cost you.
If you don't get a good score, you'll have to take summer classes to earn enough credit.
But...I can't afford summer classes!
...
I'm sorry, Hayes. You should've considered that earlier.
So...
What were ya gonna say about Riley?

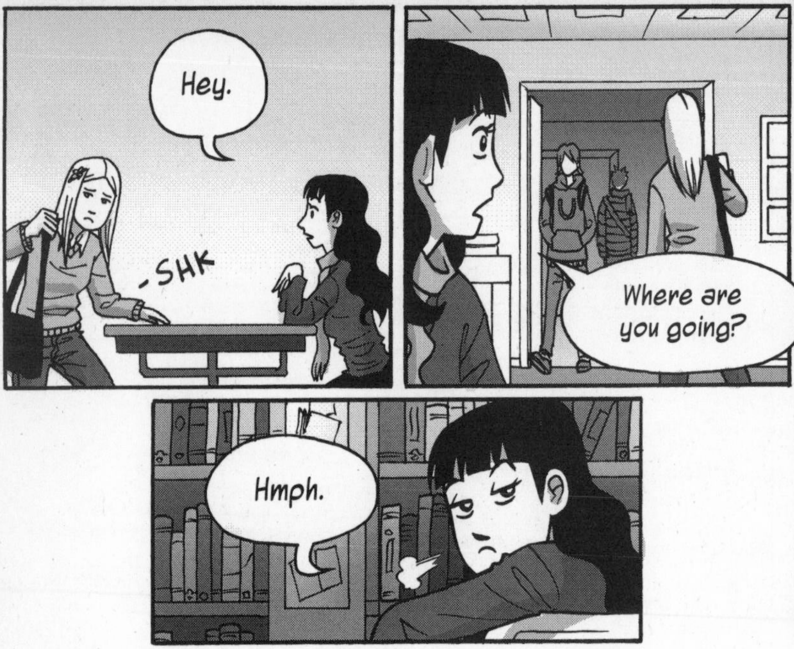
Hey.
-SHK
Where are you going?
Hmph.

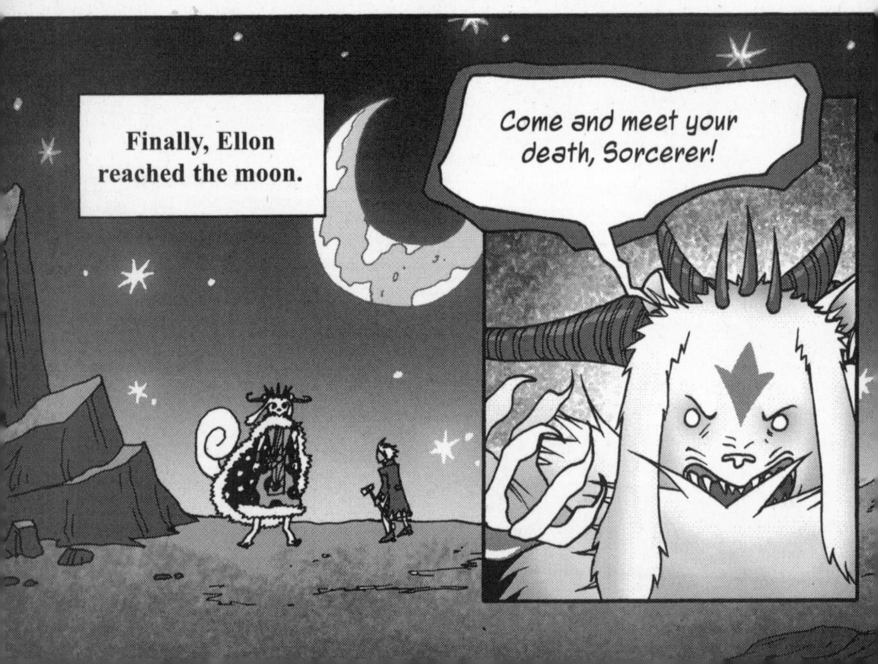
Finally, Ellon reached the moon.
Come and meet your death, Sorcerer!

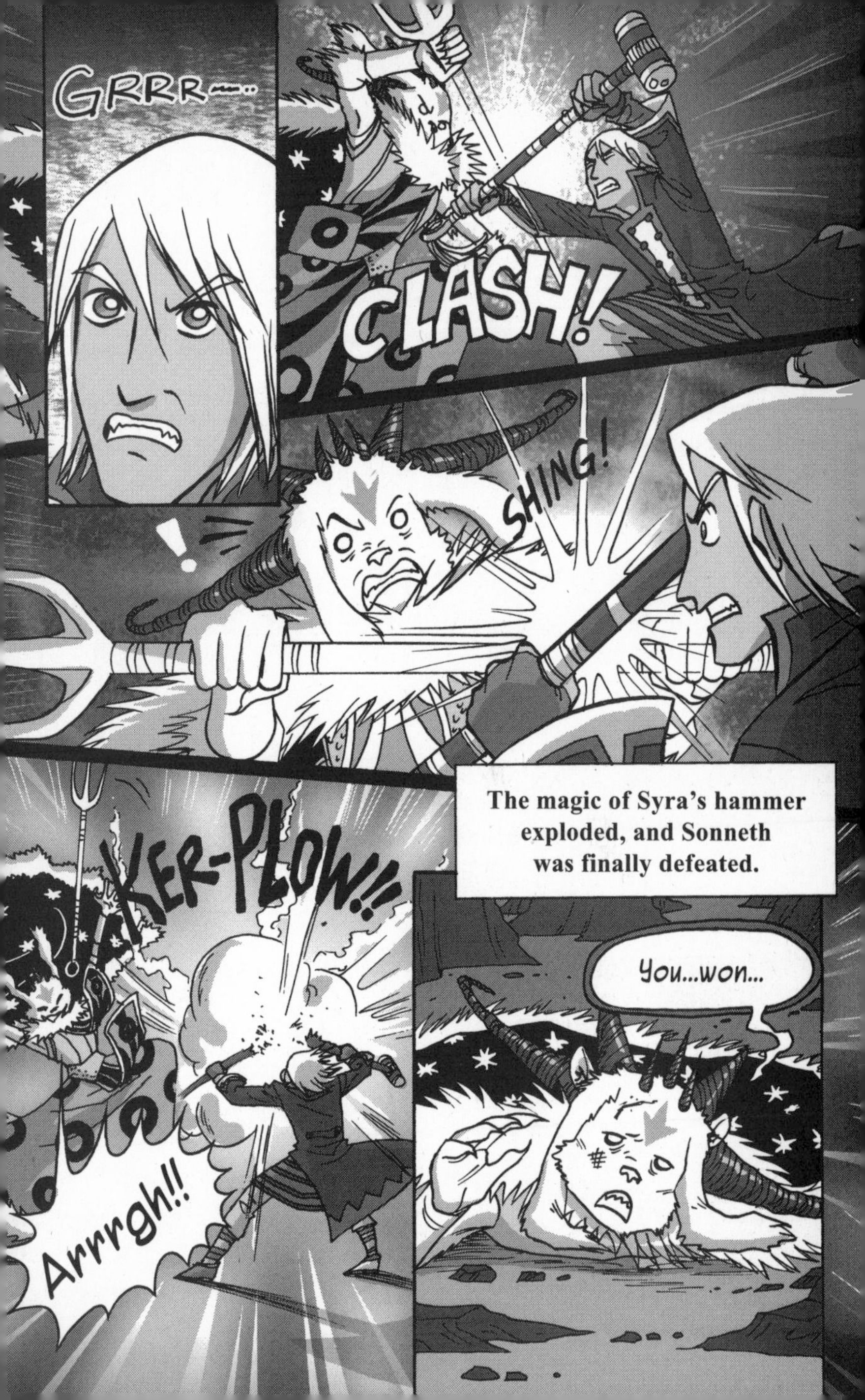

GRRR....
CLASH!
SHING!
!
KER-PLOW!!!
Arrrgh!!
The magic of Syra's hammer exploded, and Sonneth was finally defeated.
You...won...

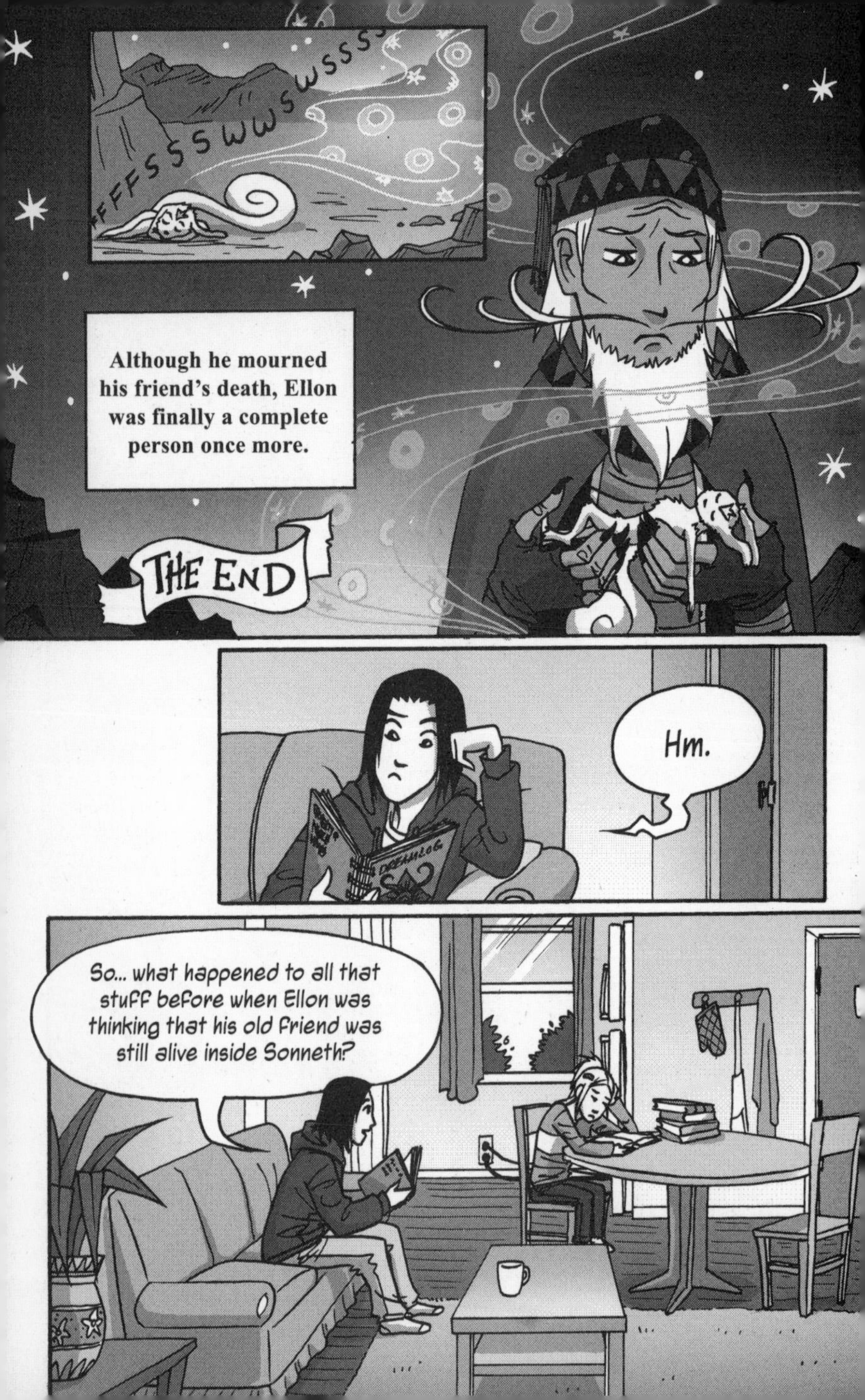
FFFSSSSWWWSWSSSS
Although he mourned his friend's death, Ellon was finally a complete person once more.
THE END
Hm.
So... what happened to all that stuff before when Ellon was thinking that his old friend was still alive inside Sonneth?

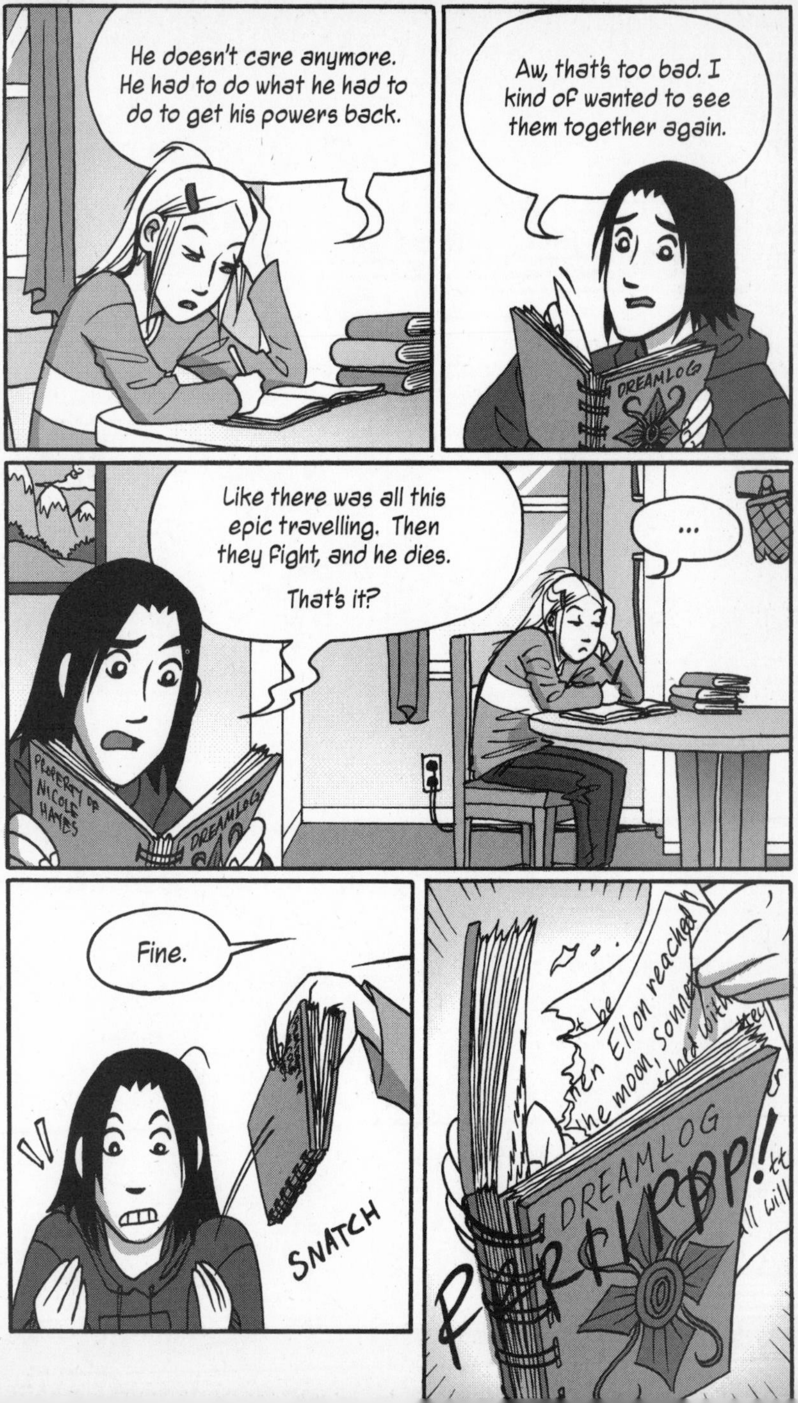
He doesn't care anymore. He had to do what he had to do to get his powers back.
Aw, that's too bad. I kind of wanted to see them together again.
DREAMLOG
Like there was all this epic travelling. Then they fight, and he dies.
That's it?
...
PROPERTY OF NICOLE HAYES
DREAMLOG
Fine.
SNATCH
DREAMLOG
RRRIPPP!

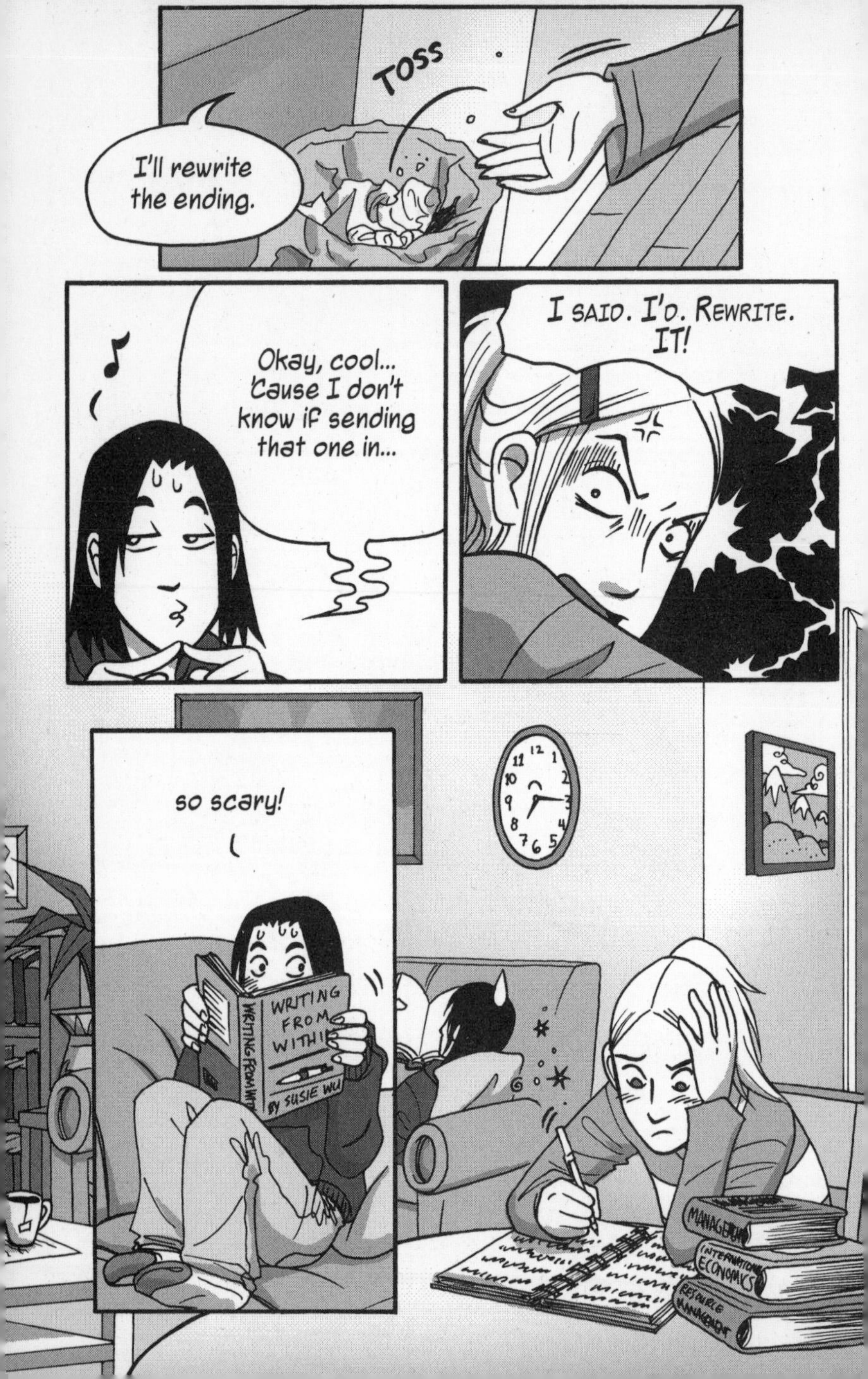
TOSS
I'll rewrite the ending.
Okay, cool... 'Cause I don't know if sending that one in...
I SAID. I'D. REWRITE. IT!
so scary!
WRITING FROM WITHIN
BY SUSIE WU
MANAGEMENT
INTERNATIONAL ECONOMICS
RESOURCE MANAGEMENT

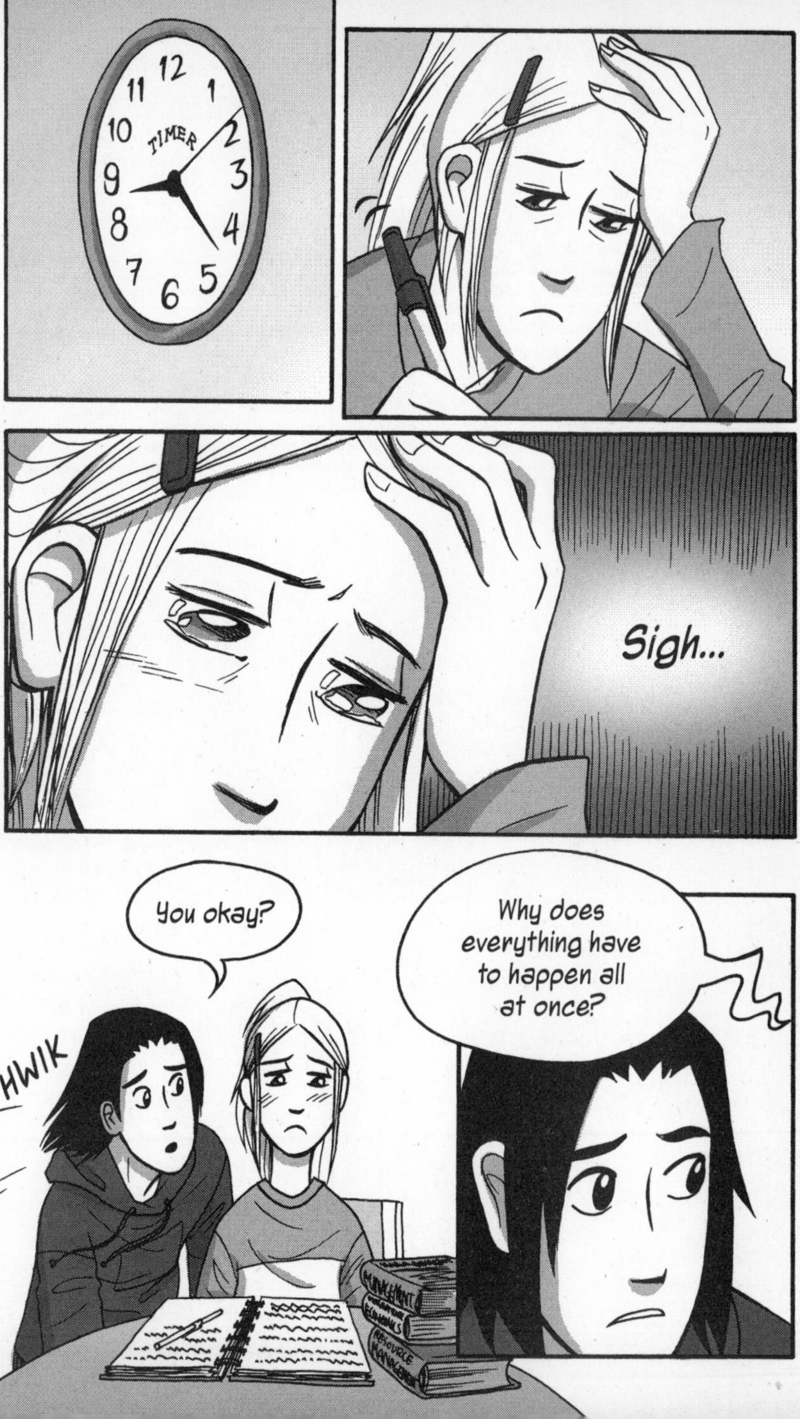
TIMER
Sigh...
You okay?
HWIK
Why does everything have to happen all at once?

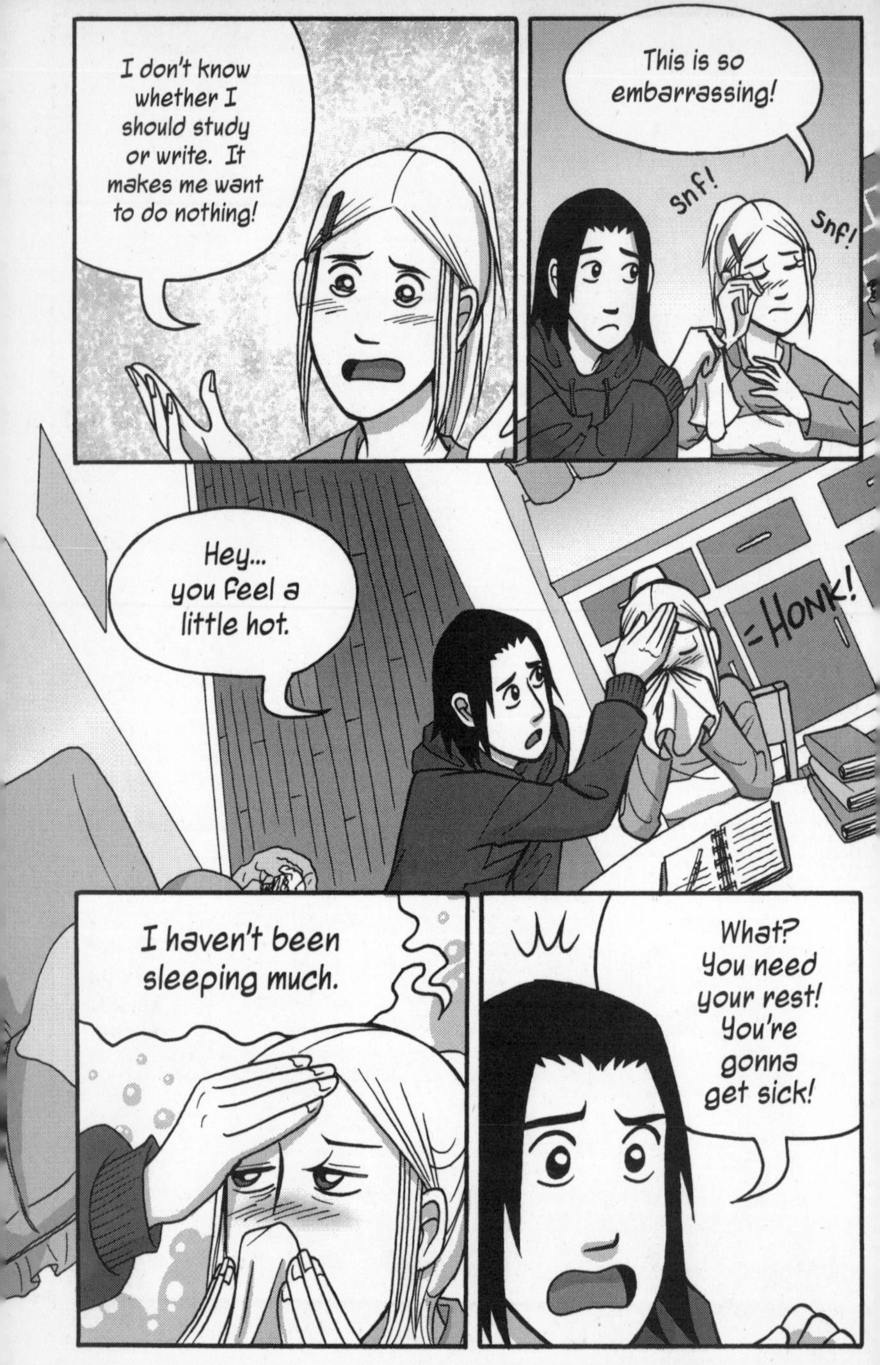
I don't know whether I should study or write. It makes me want to do nothing!
This is so embarrassing!
Snf!
Snf!
Hey... you feel a little hot.
HONK!
I haven't been sleeping much.
What? You need your rest! You're gonna get sick!

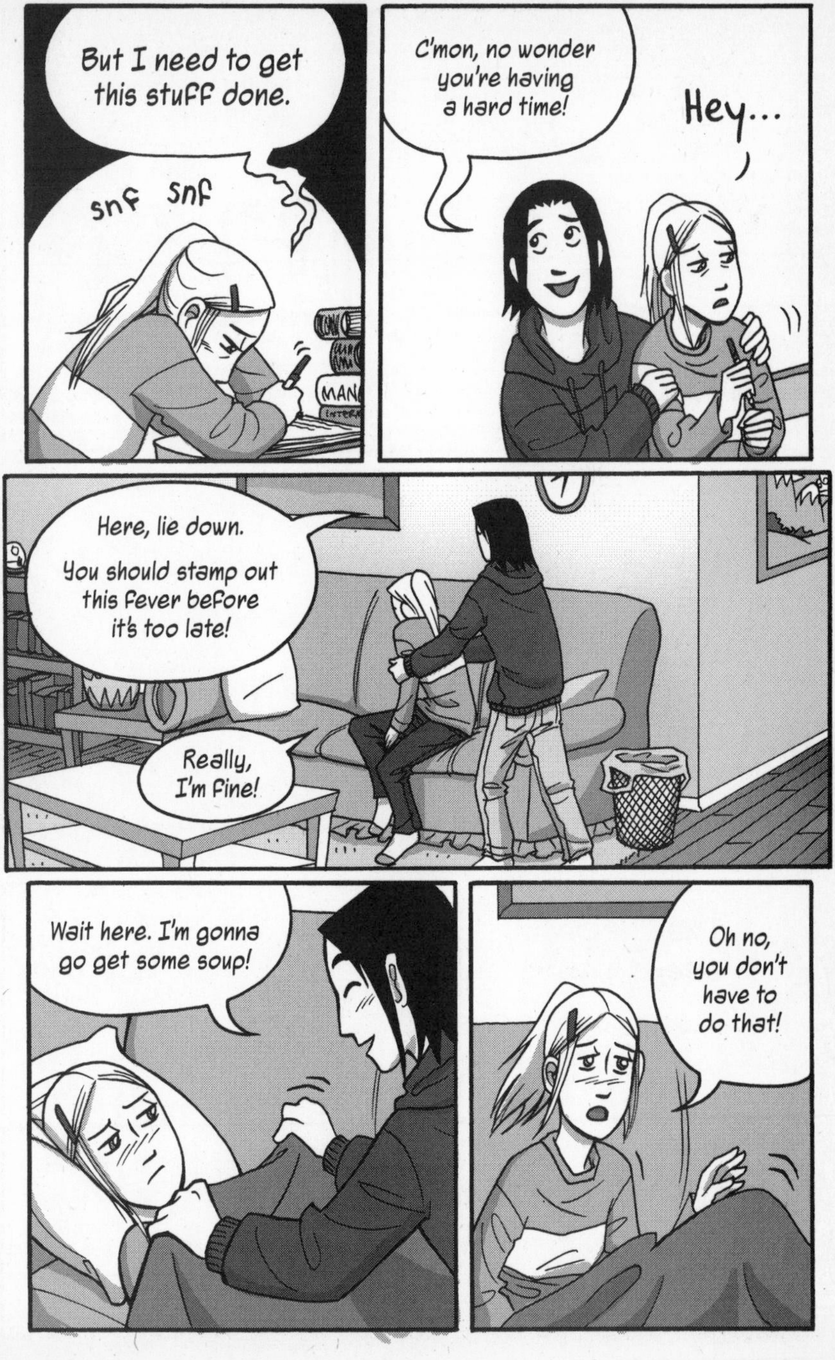
But I need to get this stuff done.
snf snf
C'mon, no wonder you're having a hard time!
Hey...
Here, lie down.
You should stamp out this fever before it's too late!
Really, I'm fine!
Wait here. I'm gonna go get some soup!
Oh no, you don't have to do that!

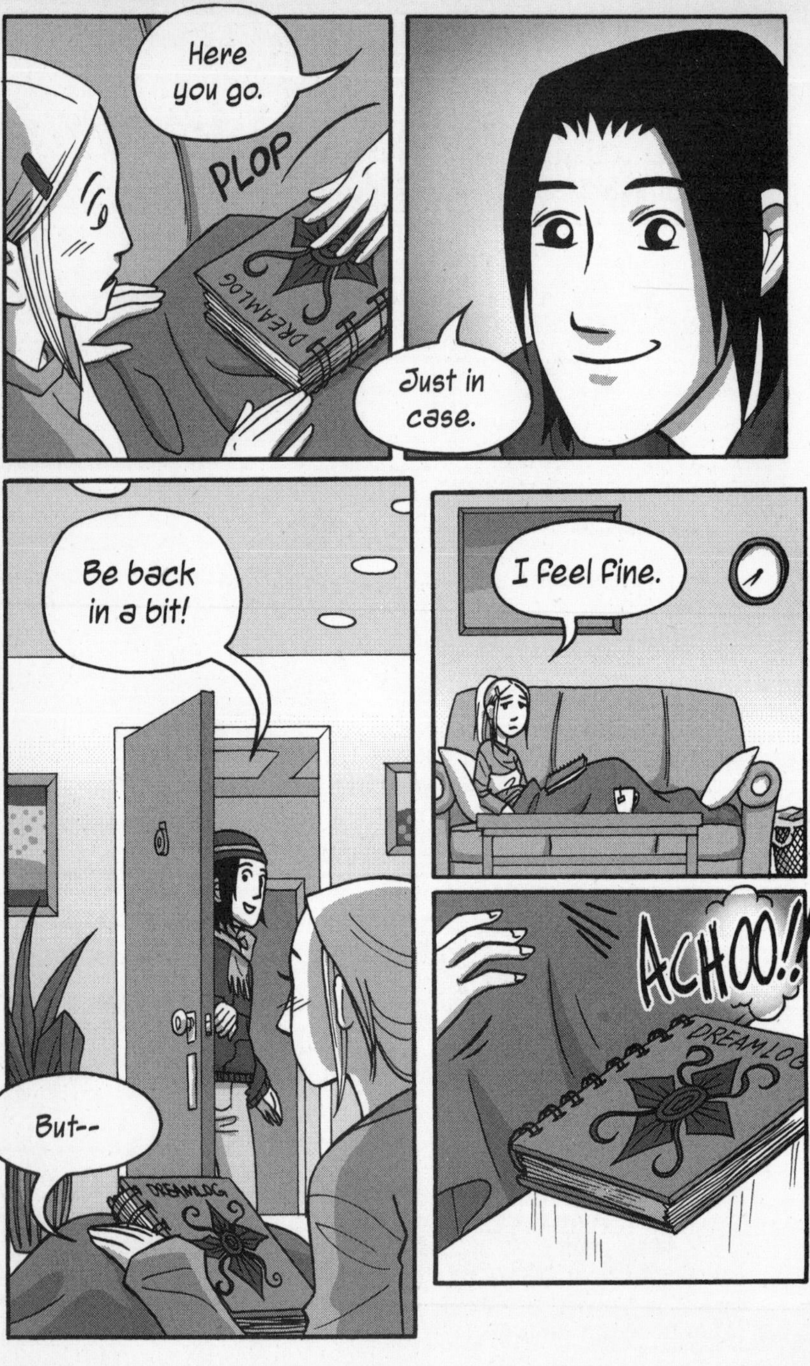
Here you go.
PLOP
DREAMLOG
Just in case.
Be back in a bit!
But--
DREAMLOG
I feel fine.
ACHOO!!
DREAMLOG

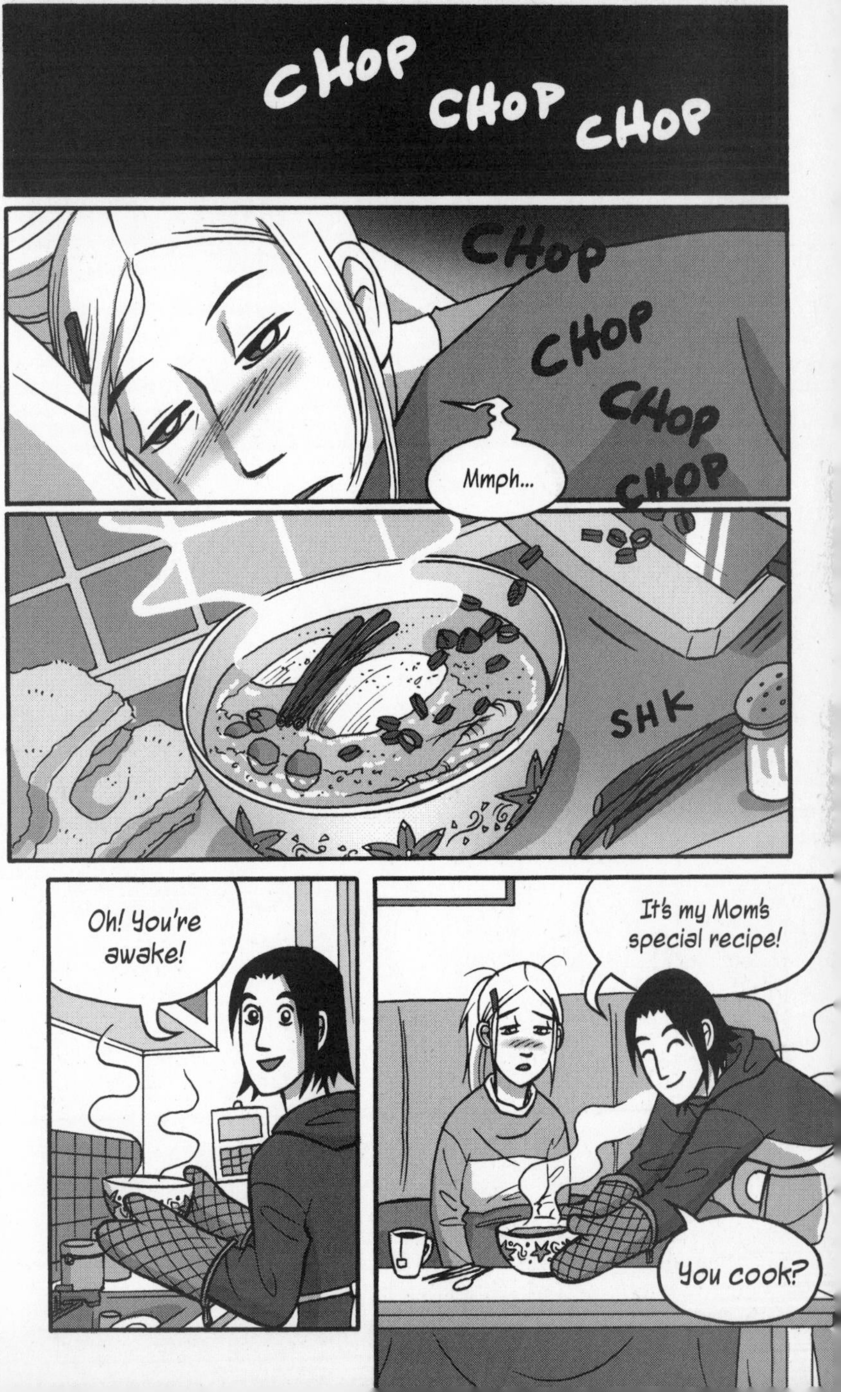
CHOP CHOP CHOP
CHOP CHOP CHOP CHOP
Mmph...
SHK
Oh! You're awake!
It's my Mom's special recipe!
You cook?

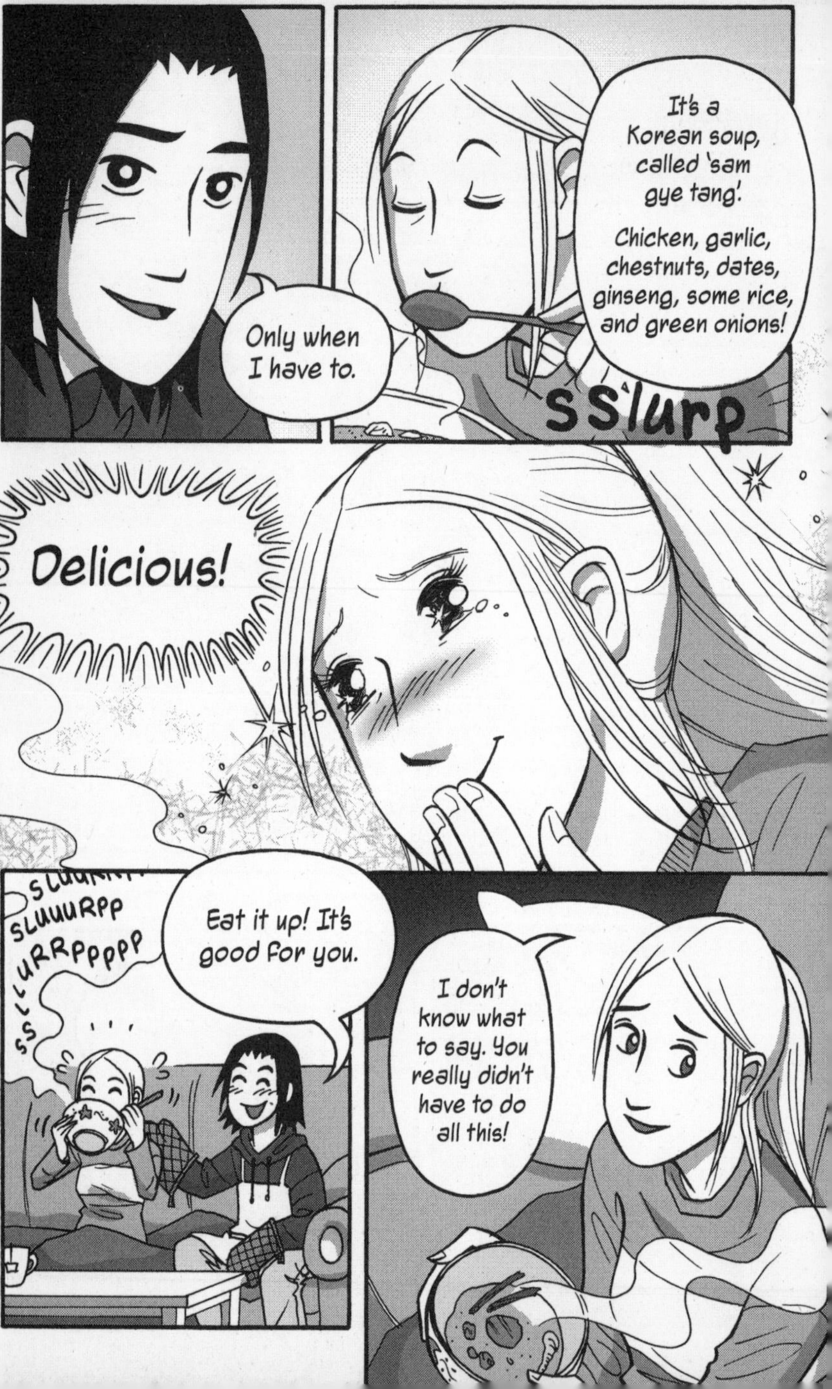
Only when I have to.
It's a Korean soup, called 'sam gye tang.'
Chicken, garlic, chestnuts, dates, ginseng, some rice, and green onions!
SSLURP
Delicious!
SLUUURPP
URRPPPPP
SS
...
Eat it up! It's good for you.
I don't know what to say. You really didn't have to do all this!

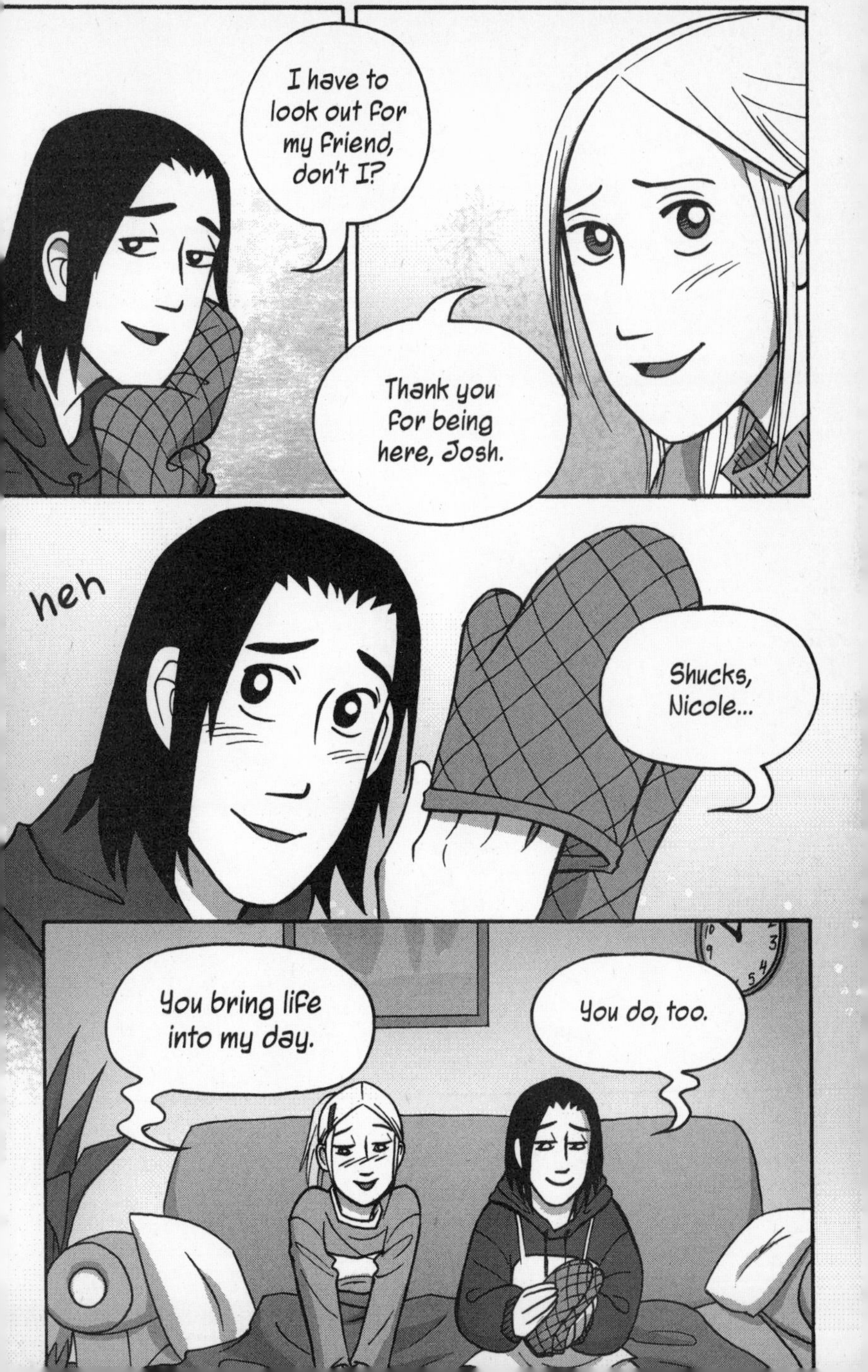
I have to look out for my friend, don't I?
Thank you for being here, Josh.
heh
Shucks, Nicole...
You bring life into my day.
You do, too.

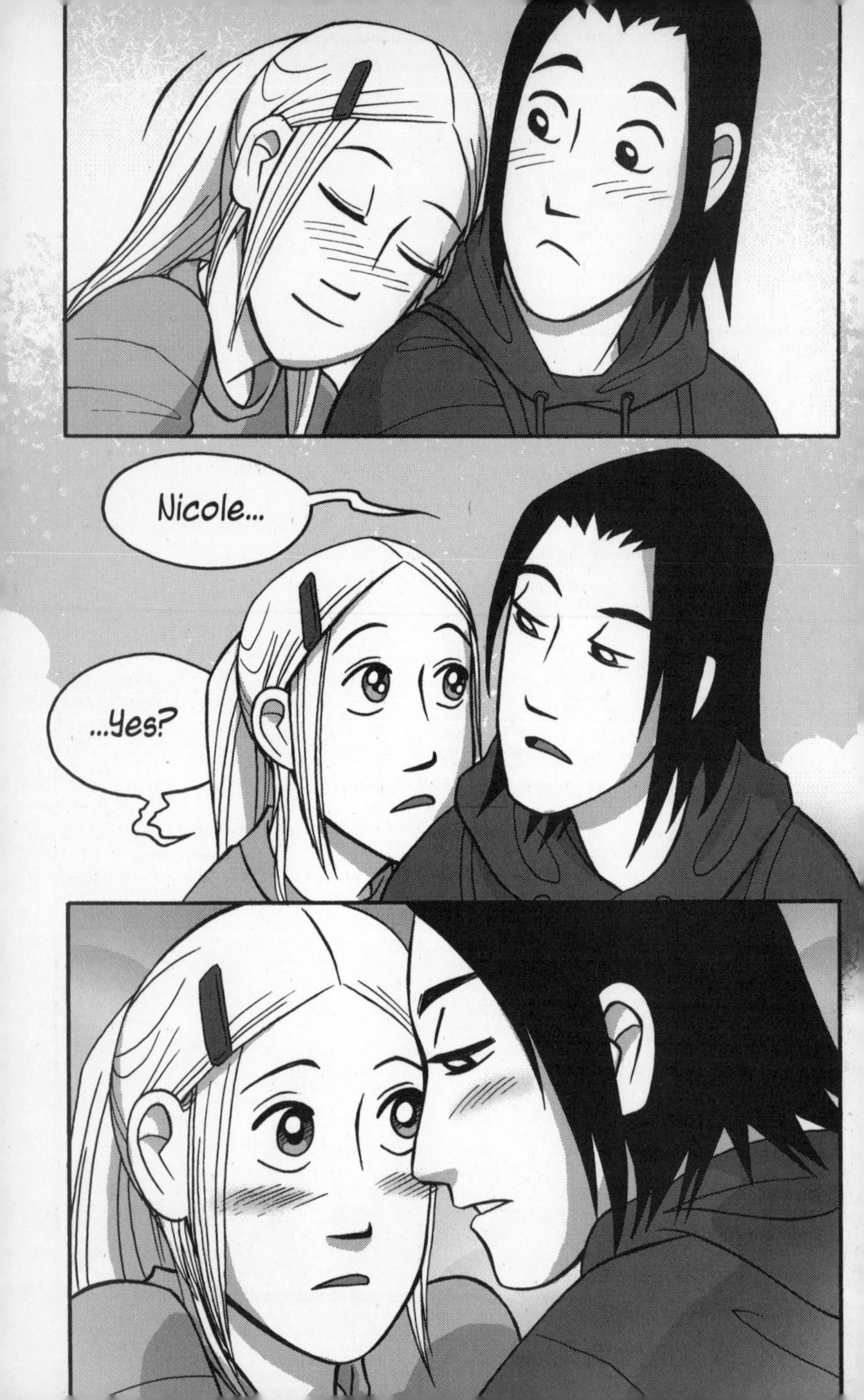
Nicole...
...Yes?

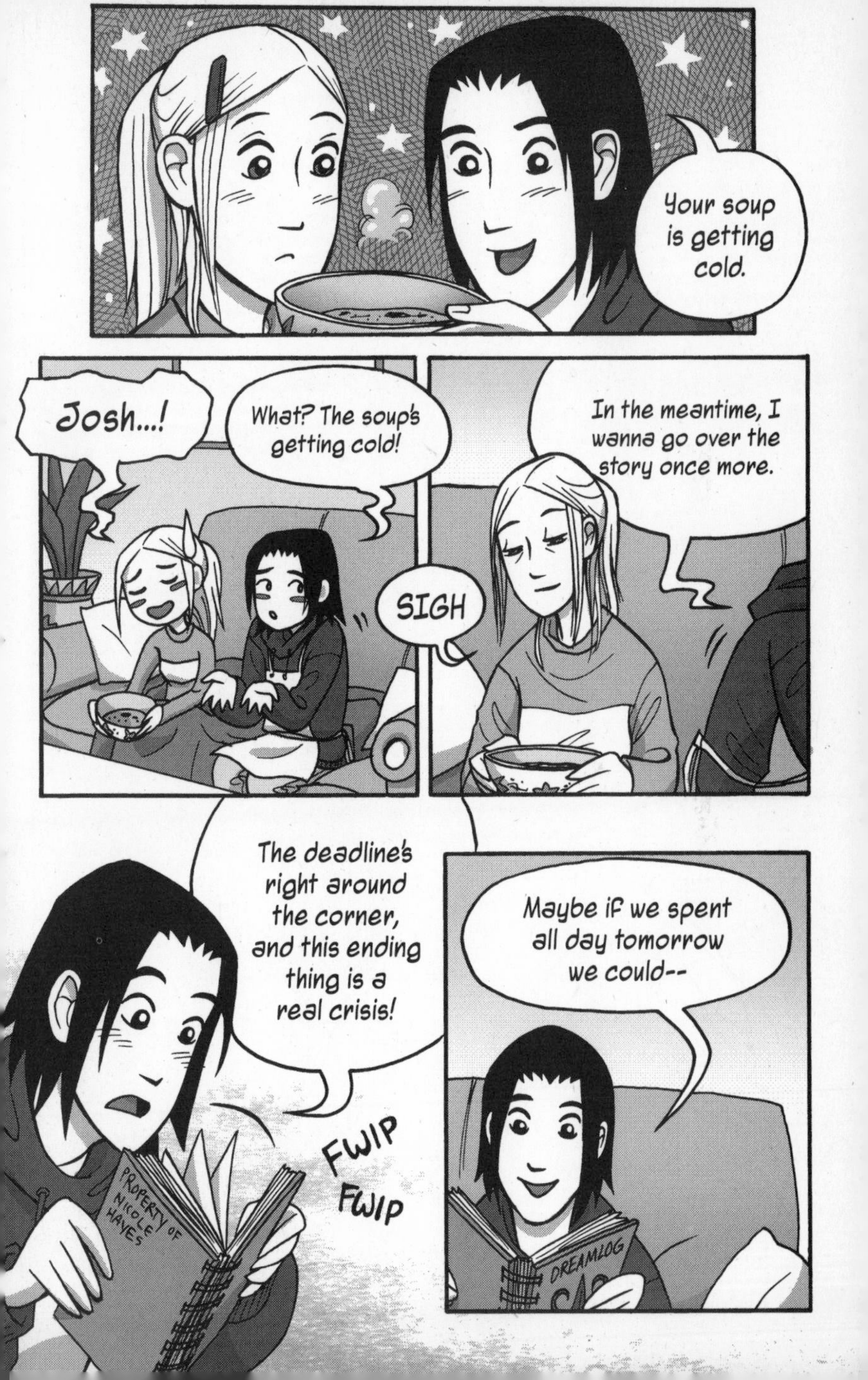
Your soup is getting cold.
Josh...!
What? The soup's getting cold!
SIGH
In the meantime, I wanna go over the story once more.
The deadline's right around the corner, and this ending thing is a real crisis!
FWIP
FWIP
PROPERTY OF NICOLE HAYES
Maybe if we spent all day tomorrow we could--
DREAMLOG

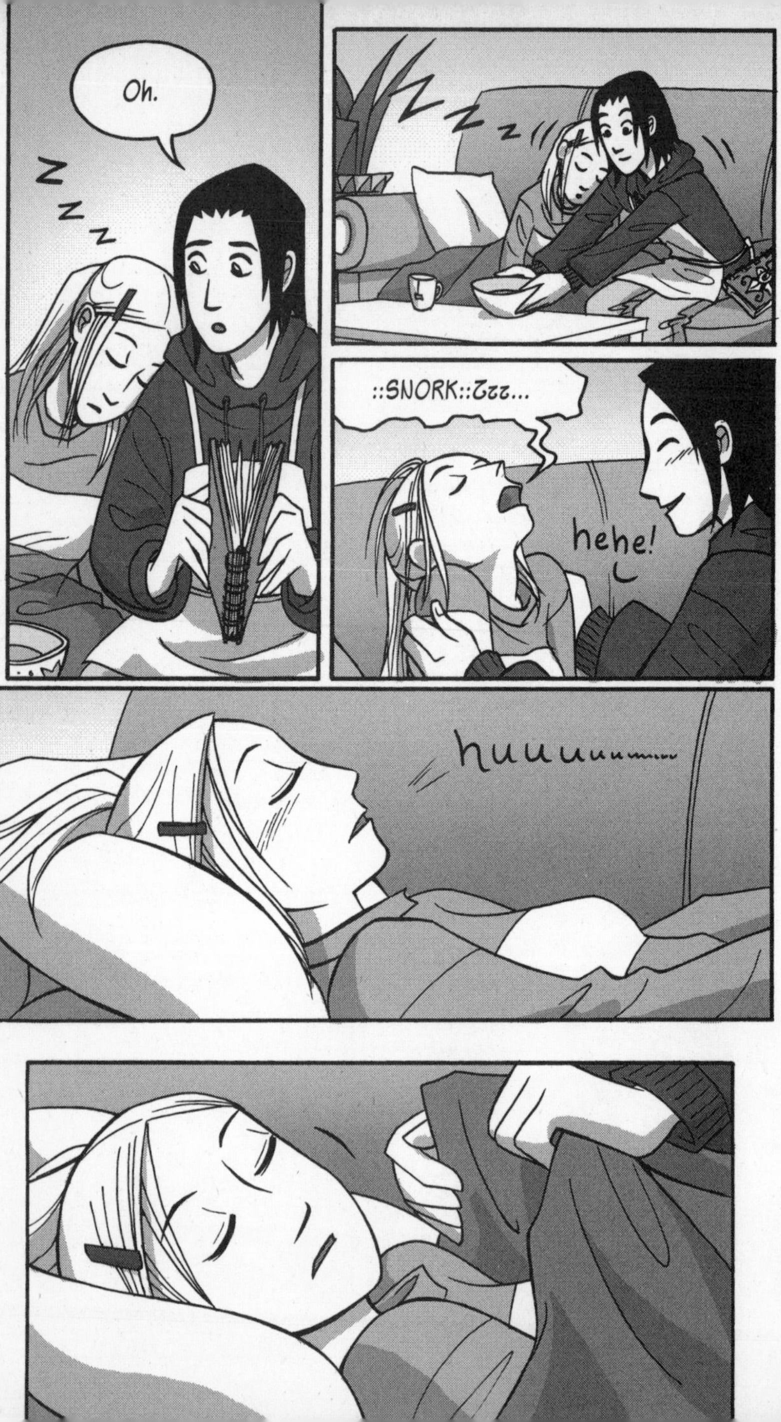
Oh.
Z Z Z
Z Z Z
::SNORK::Zzz...
hehe!
huuuu.........

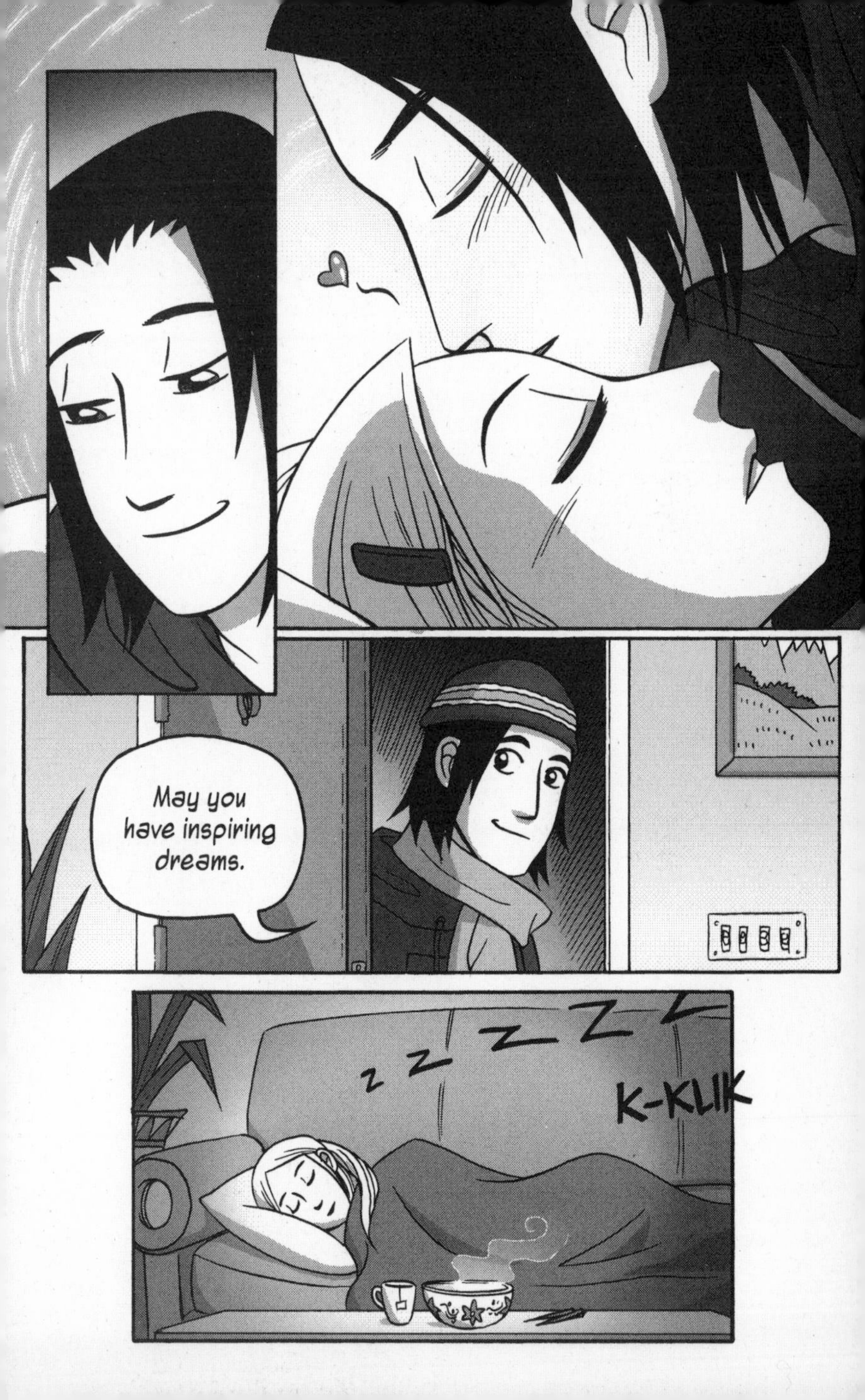
May you have inspiring dreams.
z z Z Z Z
K-KLIK

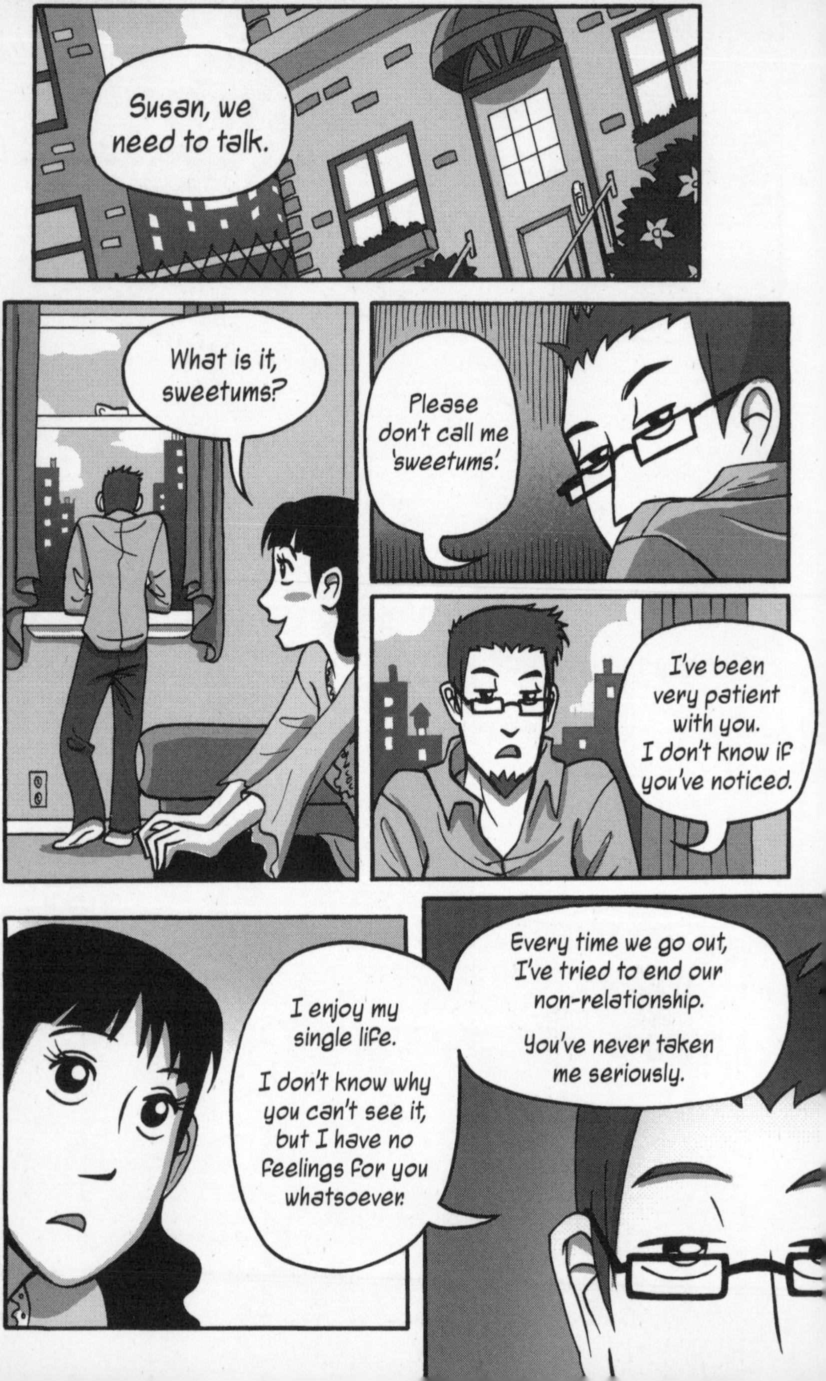
Susan, we need to talk.
What is it, sweetums?
Please don't call me 'sweetums.'
I've been very patient with you. I don't know if you've noticed.
I enjoy my single life.
I don't know why you can't see it, but I have no feelings for you whatsoever.
Every time we go out, I've tried to end our non-relationship.
You've never taken me seriously.

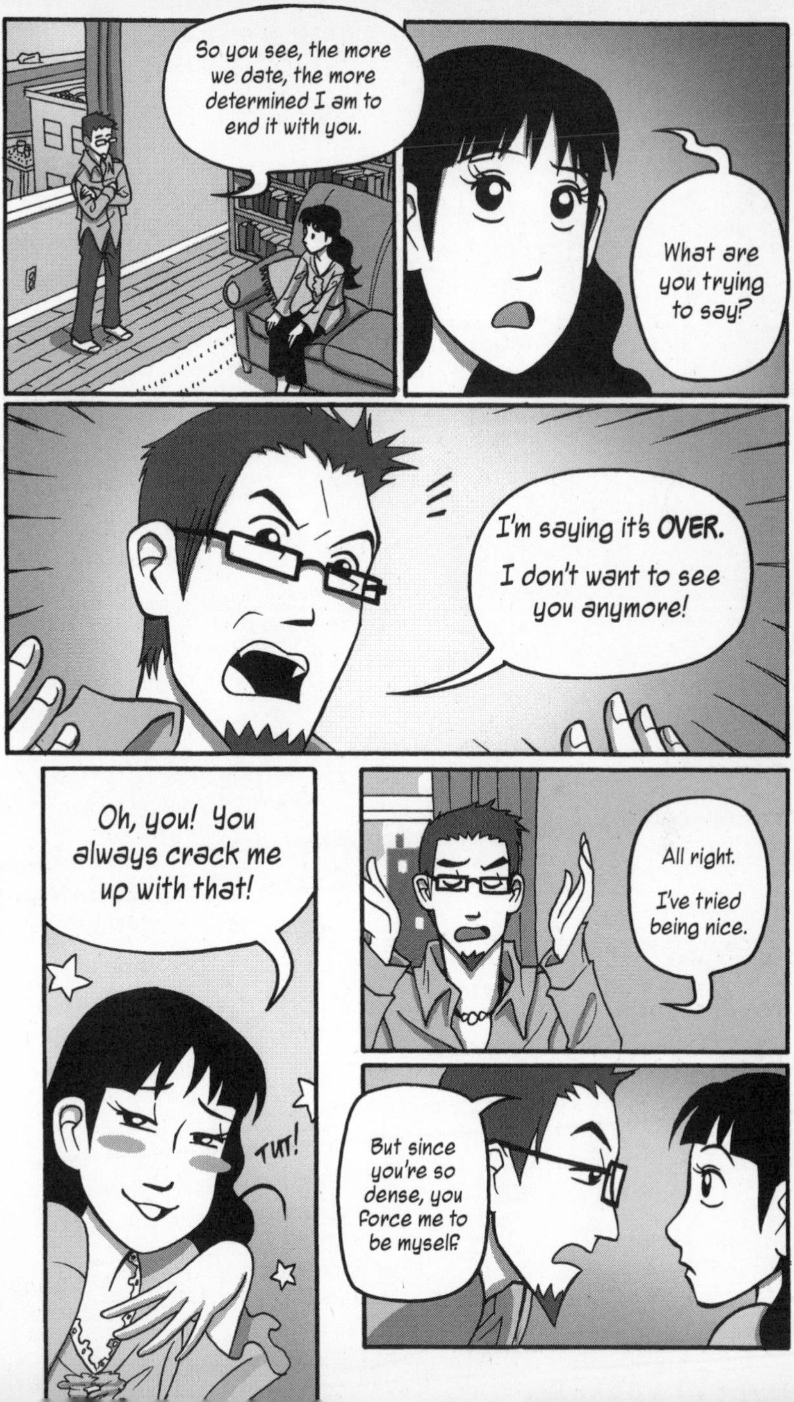
So you see, the more we date, the more determined I am to end it with you.
What are you trying to say?
I'm saying it's OVER.
I don't want to see you anymore!
Oh, you! You always crack me up with that!
TUT!
All right.
I've tried being nice.
But since you're so dense, you force me to be myself.

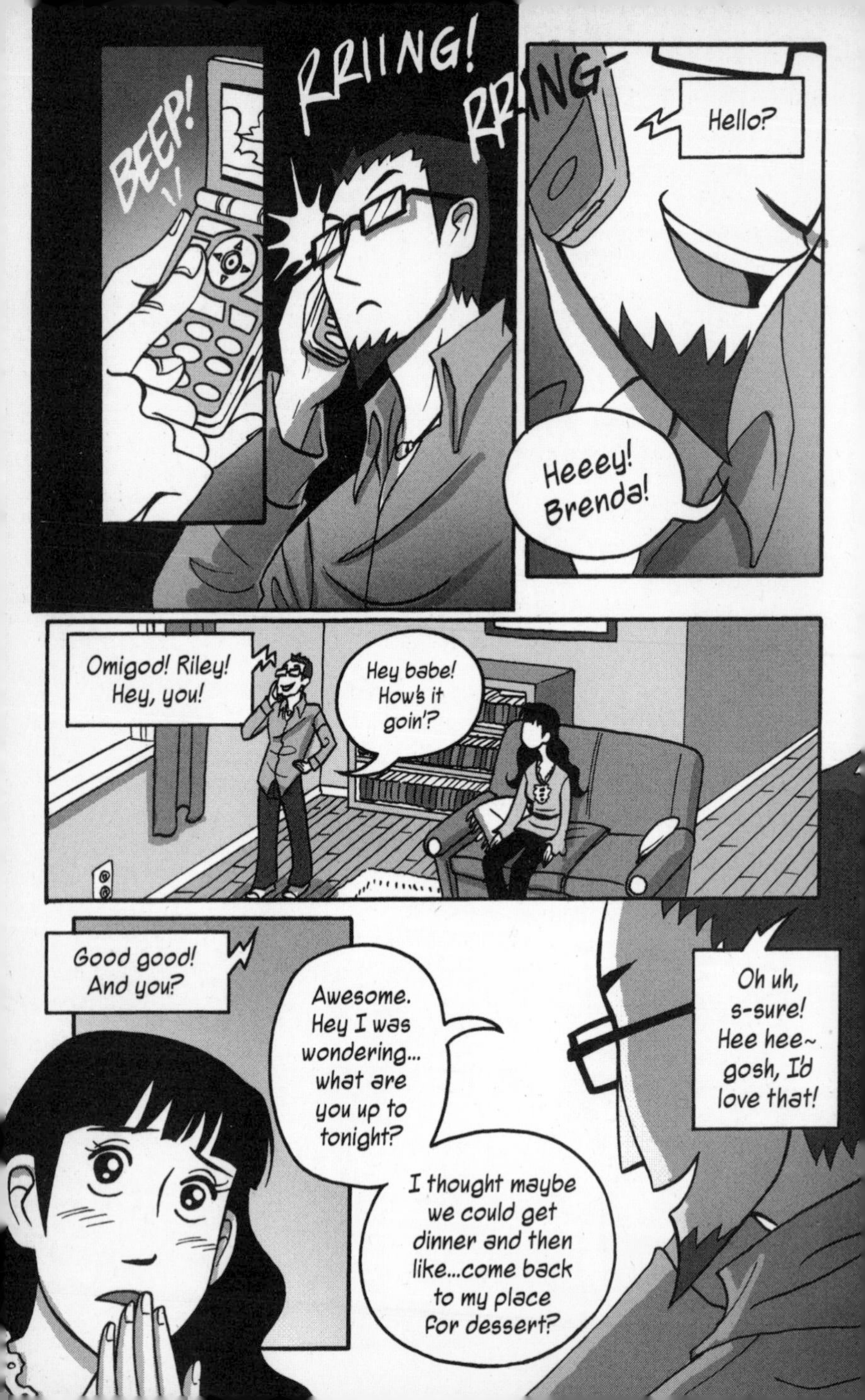
BEEP!
RRIING!
RRING-
Hello?
Heeey! Brenda!
Omigod! Riley! Hey, you!
Hey babe! How's it goin'?
Good good! And you?
Awesome. Hey I was wondering... what are you up to tonight?
I thought maybe we could get dinner and then like...come back to my place for dessert?
Oh uh, s-sure! Hee hee~ gosh, I'd love that!

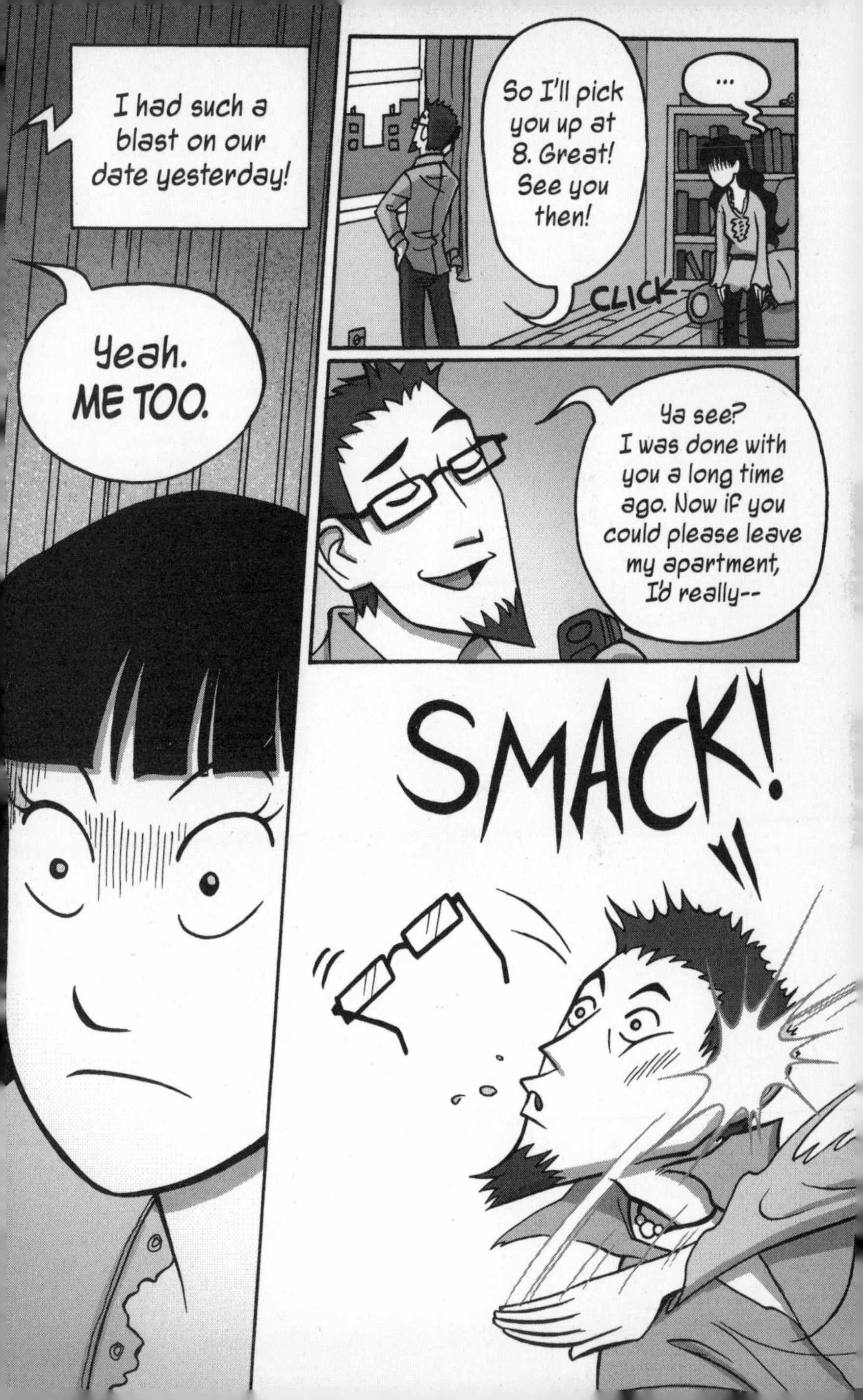
I had such a blast on our date yesterday!
Yeah. ME TOO.
So I'll pick you up at 8. Great! See you then!
...
CLICK
Ya see? I was done with you a long time ago. Now if you could please leave my apartment, I'd really--
SMACK!

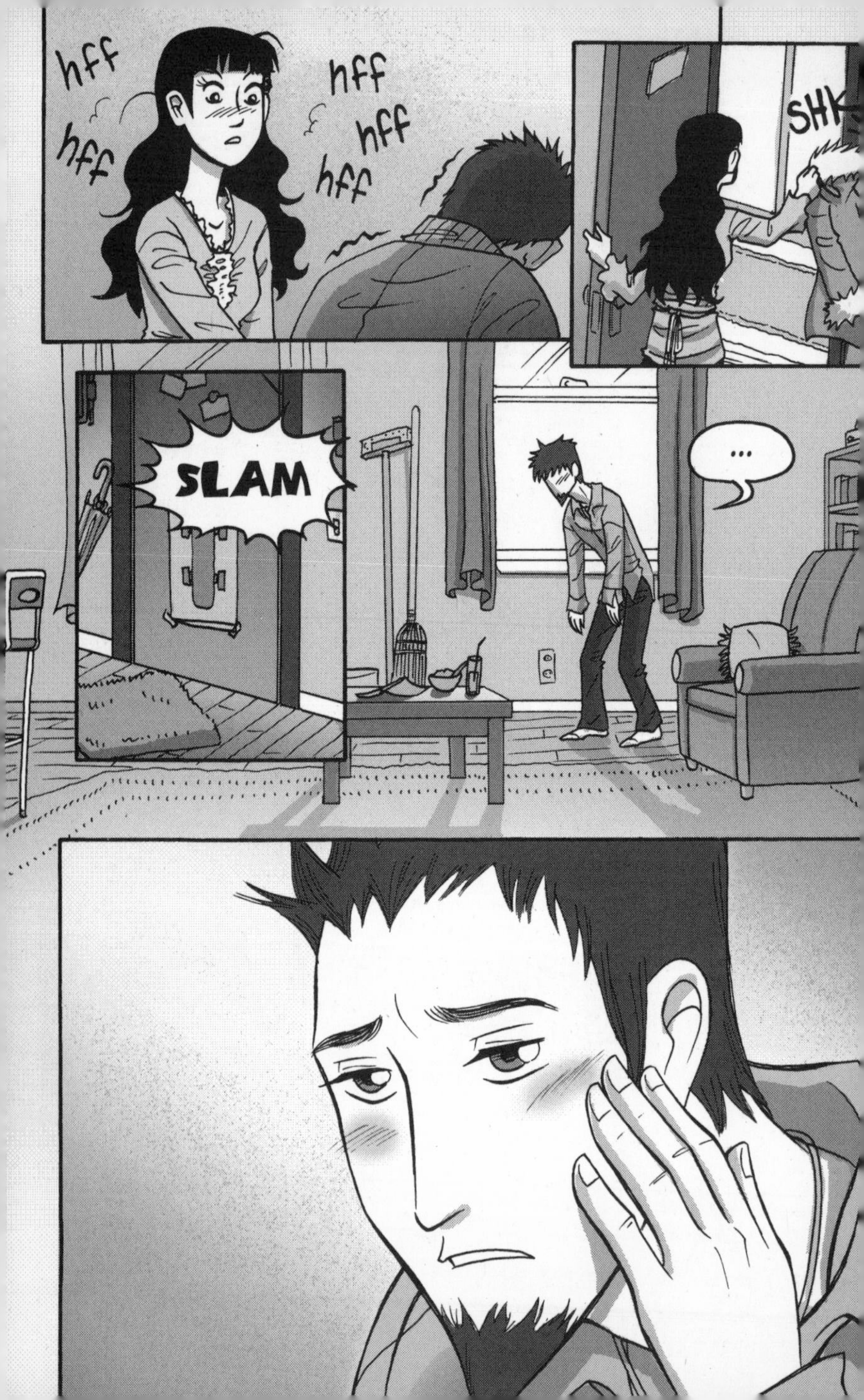
hff
hff
hff
hff
hff
SHK
SLAM
...

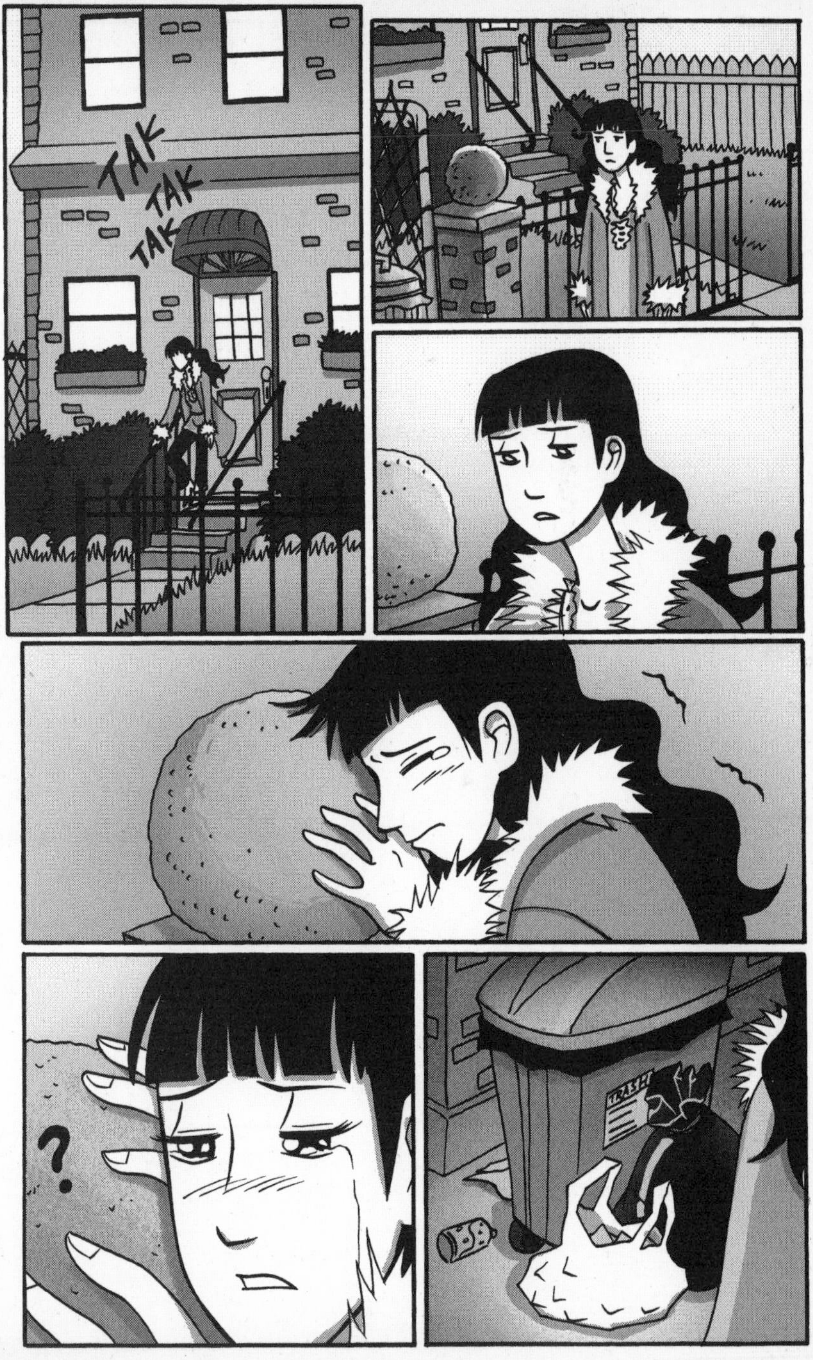
TAK
TAK
TAK
?
TRASH

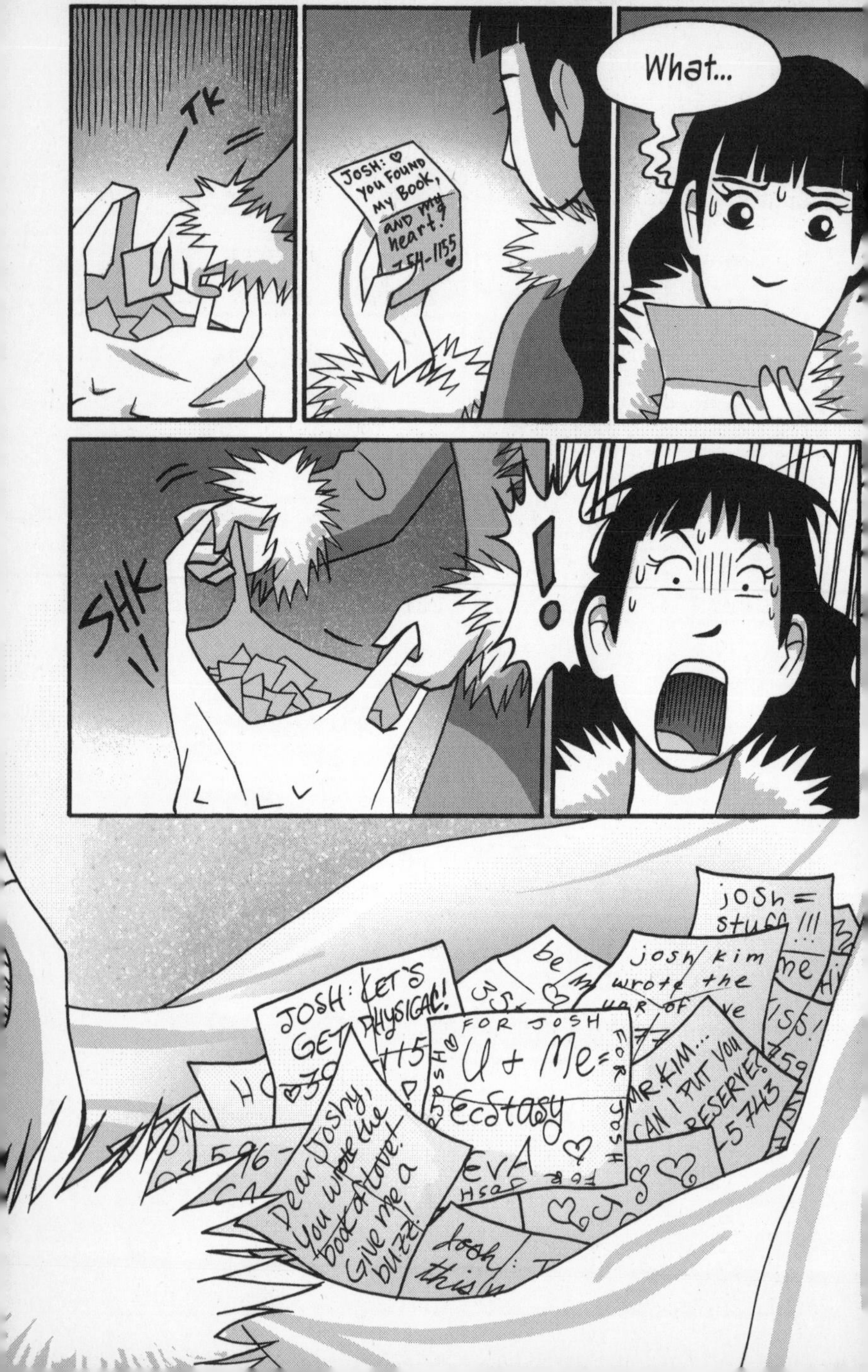
TK
JOSH: YOU FOUND MY BOOK, AND heart!
What...
SHK
!
jOSh = stuff !!!
josh kim wrote the
JOSH: LET'S GET PHYSICAL!
FOR JOSH U + Me = Ecstasy
Dear Joshy, You wrote the book of love! Give me a buzz!
MR. KIM... CAN I PUT YOU RESERVE? -5743

CHAPTER FIVE
RETURNS THE PEN

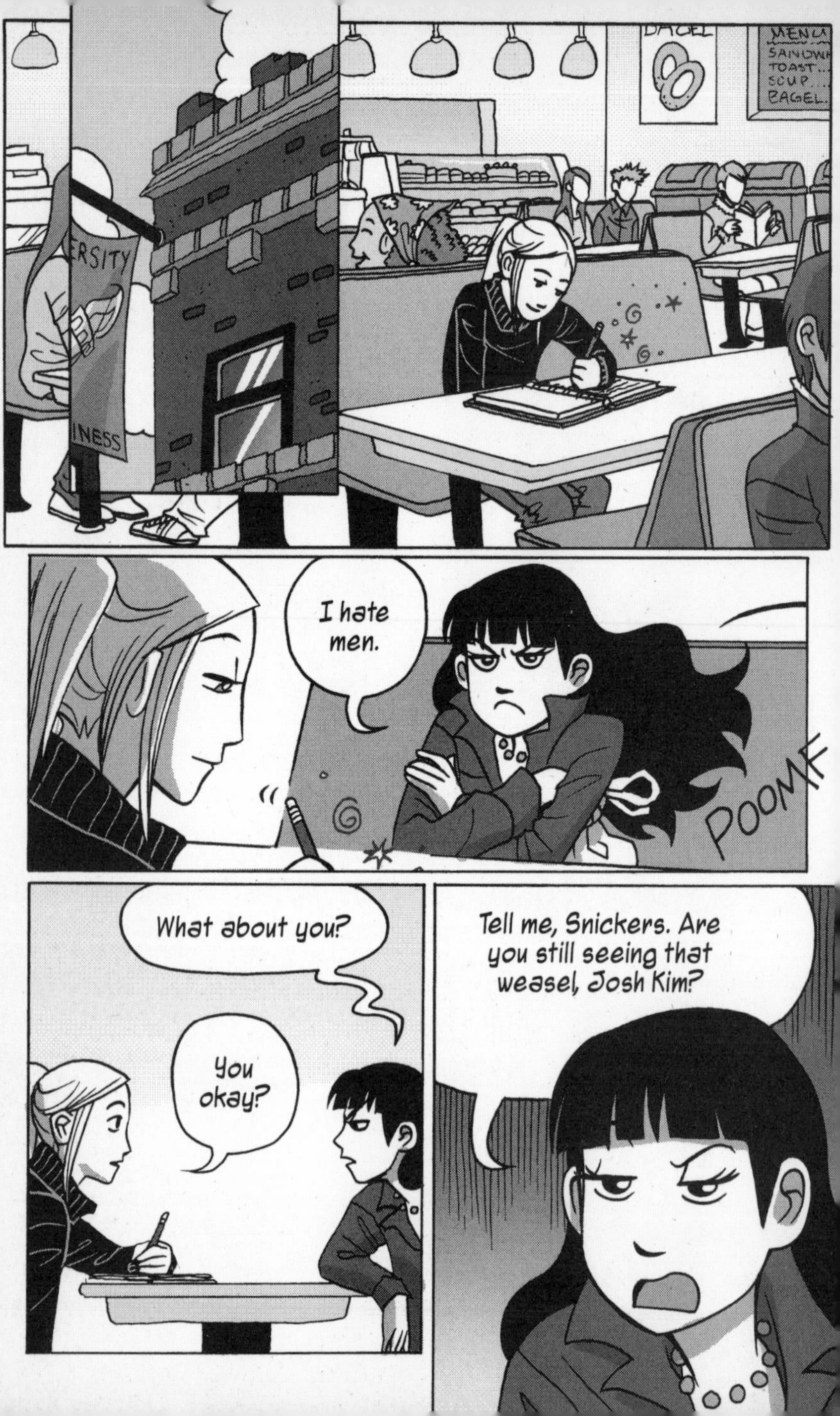
BAGEL
MENU
SANDWI
TOAST...
SOUP...
BAGEL...
ERSITY
INESS
I hate men.
POOMF
What about you?
You okay?
Tell me, Snickers. Are you still seeing that weasel, Josh Kim?

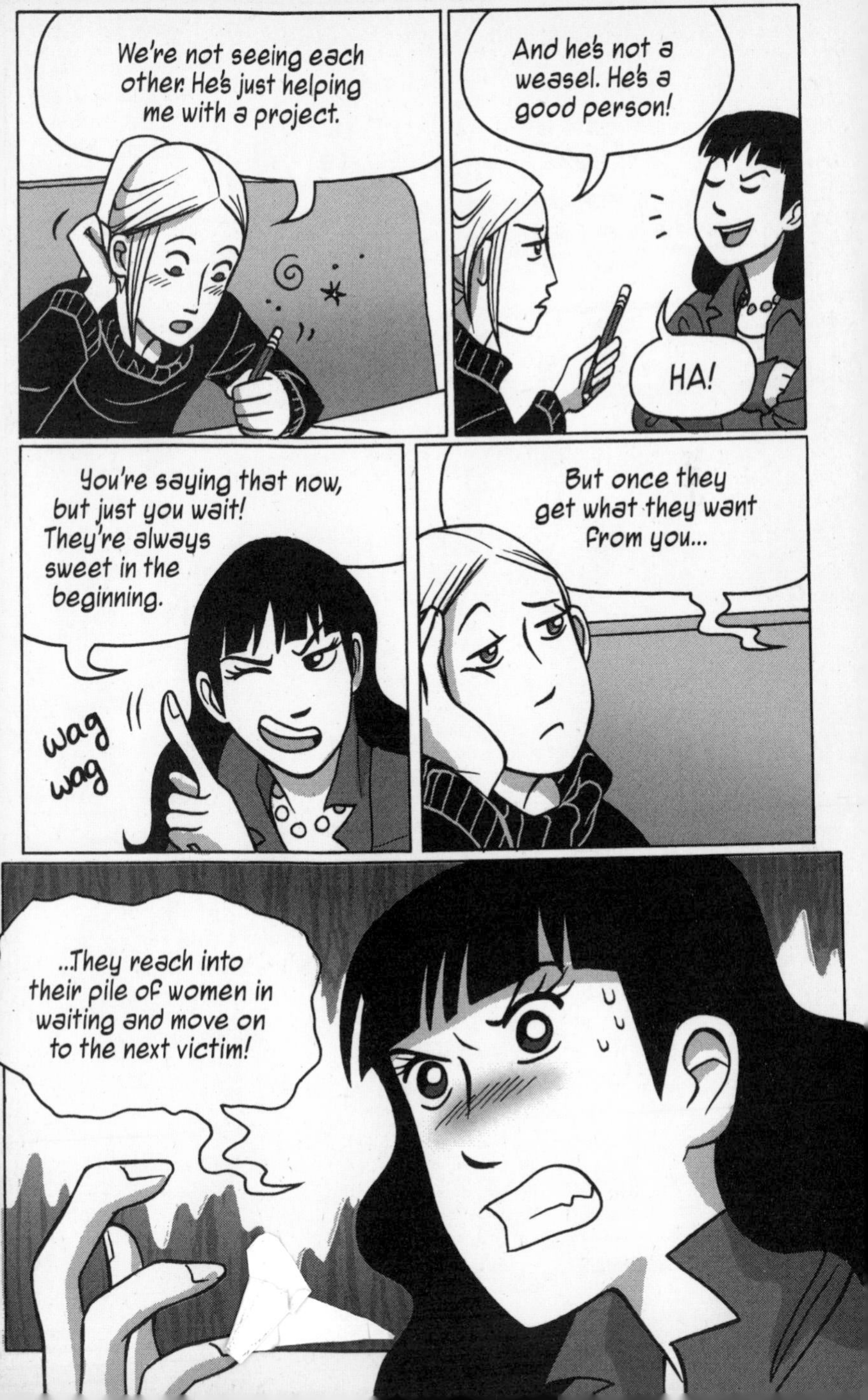
We're not seeing each other. He's just helping me with a project.
And he's not a weasel. He's a good person!
HA!
You're saying that now, but just you wait! They're always sweet in the beginning.
wag wag
But once they get what they want from you...
...They reach into their pile of women in waiting and move on to the next victim!

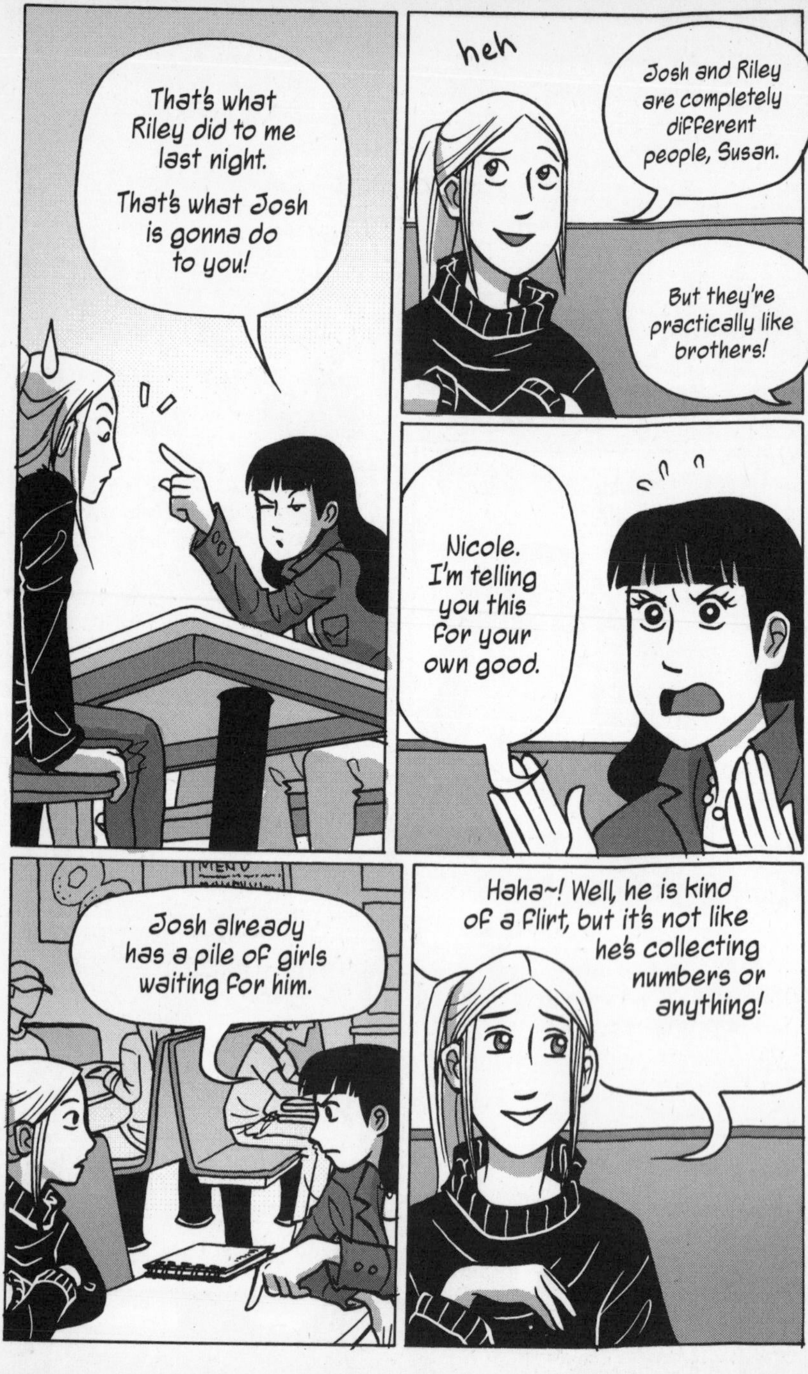
That's what Riley did to me last night.
That's what Josh is gonna do to you!
heh
Josh and Riley are completely different people, Susan.
But they're practically like brothers!
Nicole. I'm telling you this for your own good.
Josh already has a pile of girls waiting for him.
Haha~! Well, he is kind of a flirt, but it's not like he's collecting numbers or anything!

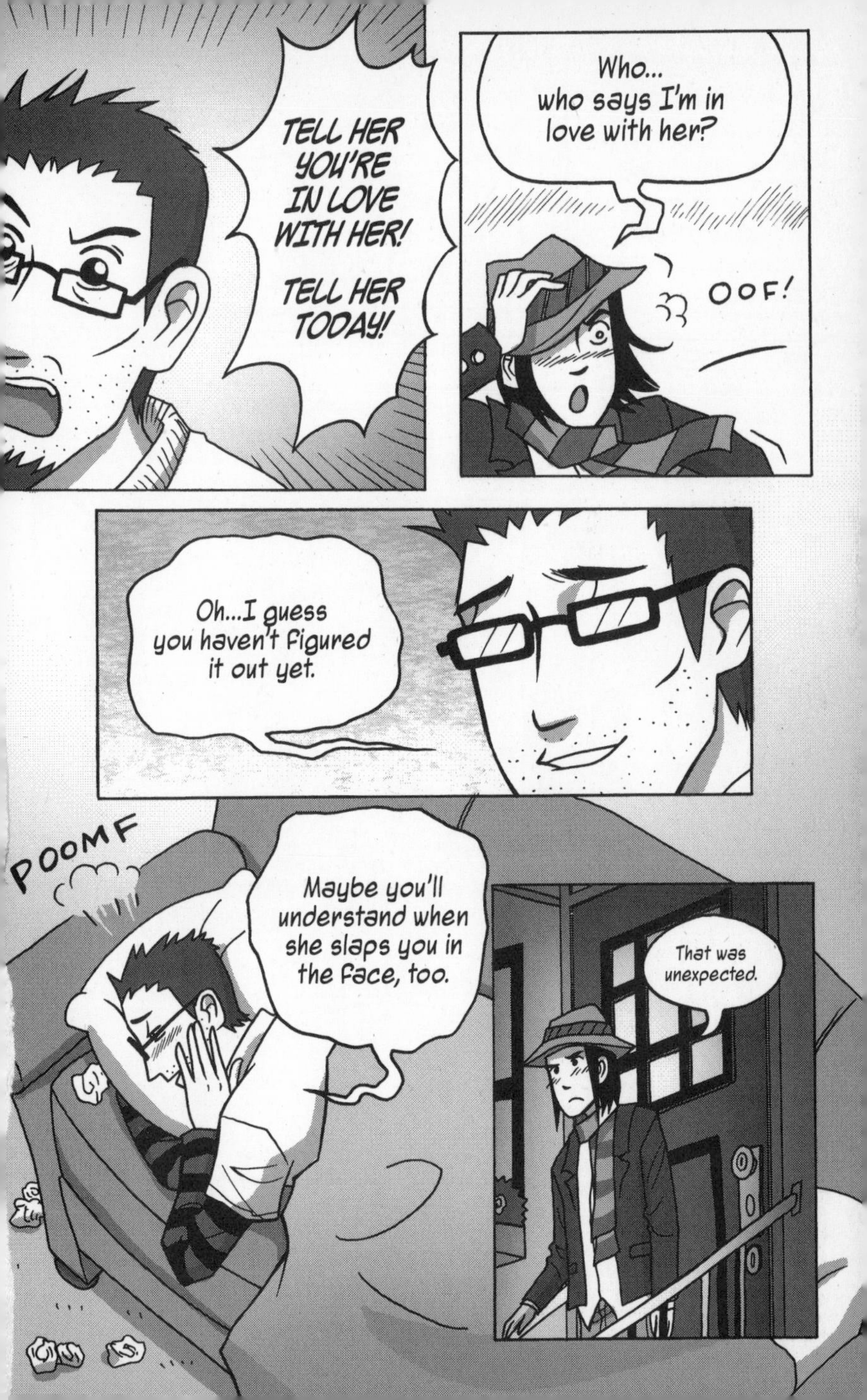
TELL HER YOU'RE IN LOVE WITH HER!
TELL HER TODAY!
Who... who says I'm in love with her?
OOF!
Oh...I guess you haven't figured it out yet.
POOMF
Maybe you'll understand when she slaps you in the face, too.
That was unexpected.

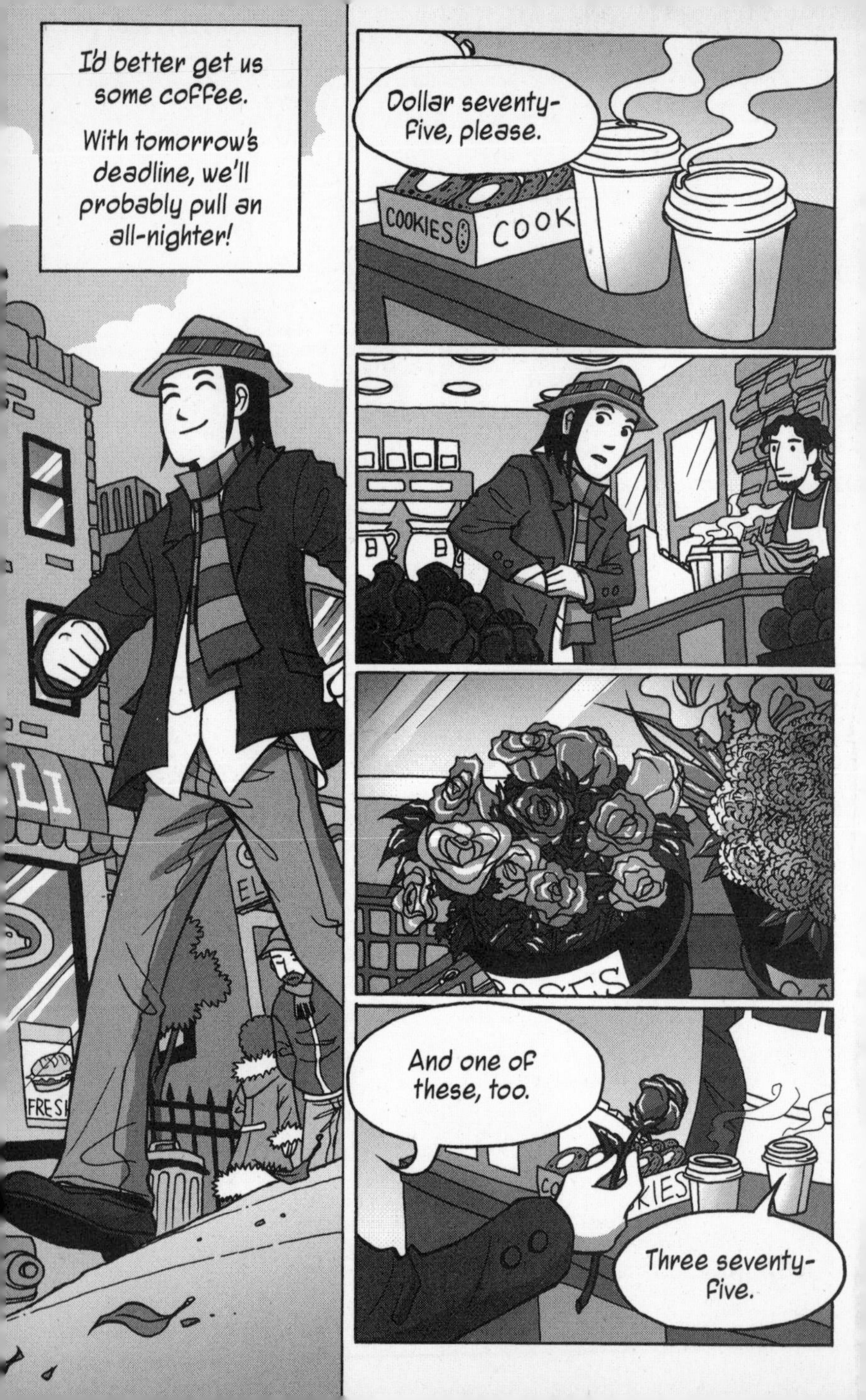
I'd better get us some coffee.
With tomorrow's deadline, we'll probably pull an all-nighter!
FRESH
Dollar seventy-five, please.
COOKIES
COOK
And one of these, too.
Three seventy-five.

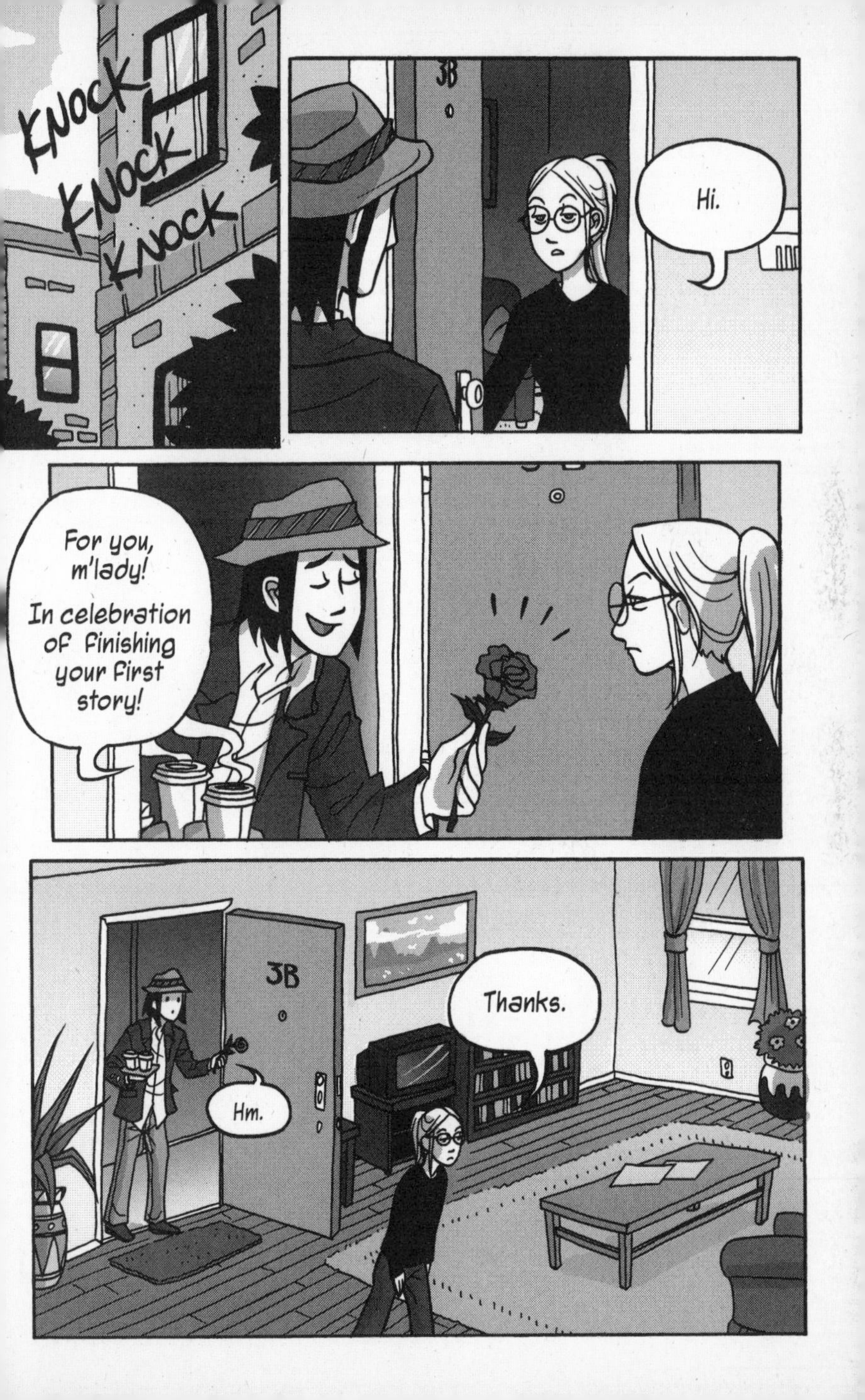
KNOCK KNOCK KNOCK
Hi.
For you, m'lady!
In celebration of finishing your first story!
3B
Hm.
Thanks.

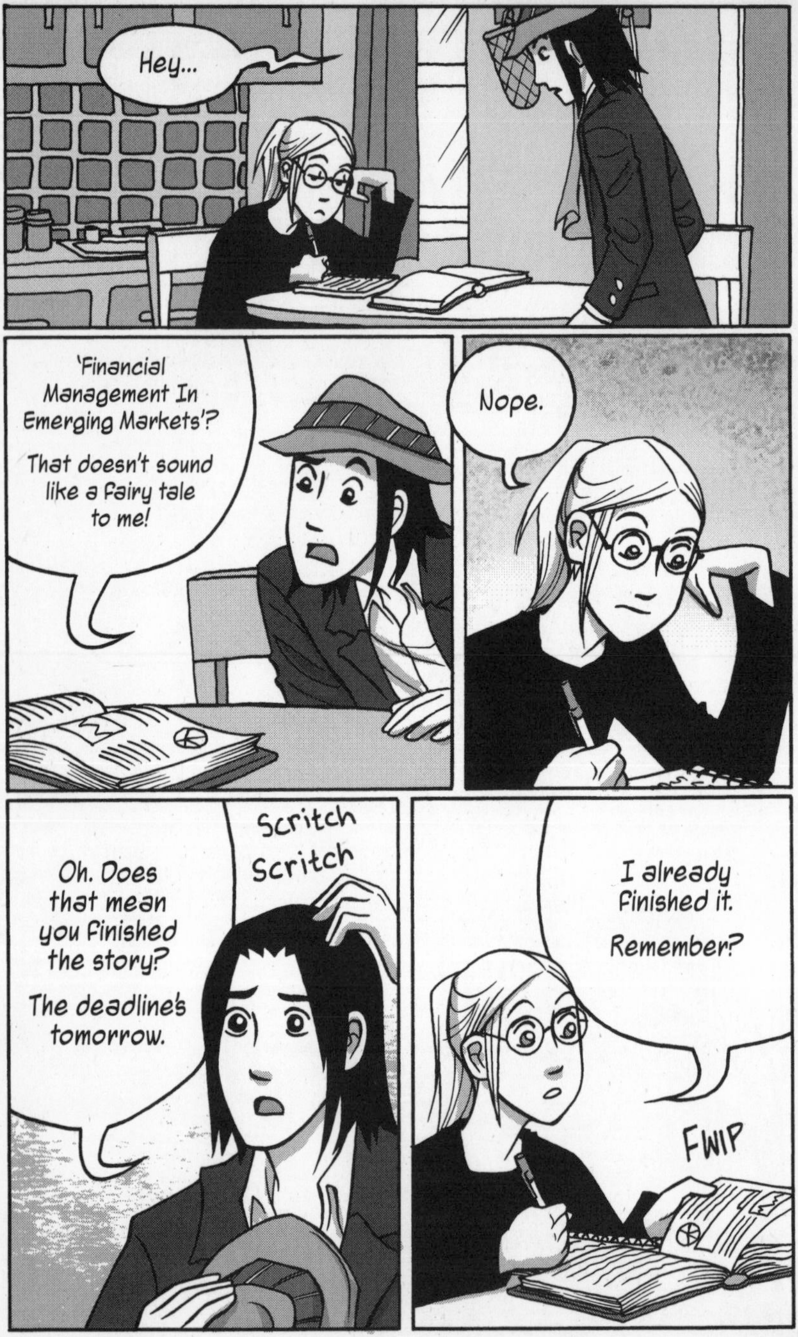
Hey...
'Financial Management In Emerging Markets'?
That doesn't sound like a fairy tale to me!
Nope.
Oh. Does that mean you finished the story?
The deadline's tomorrow.
Scritch
Scritch
I already finished it.
Remember?
FWIP

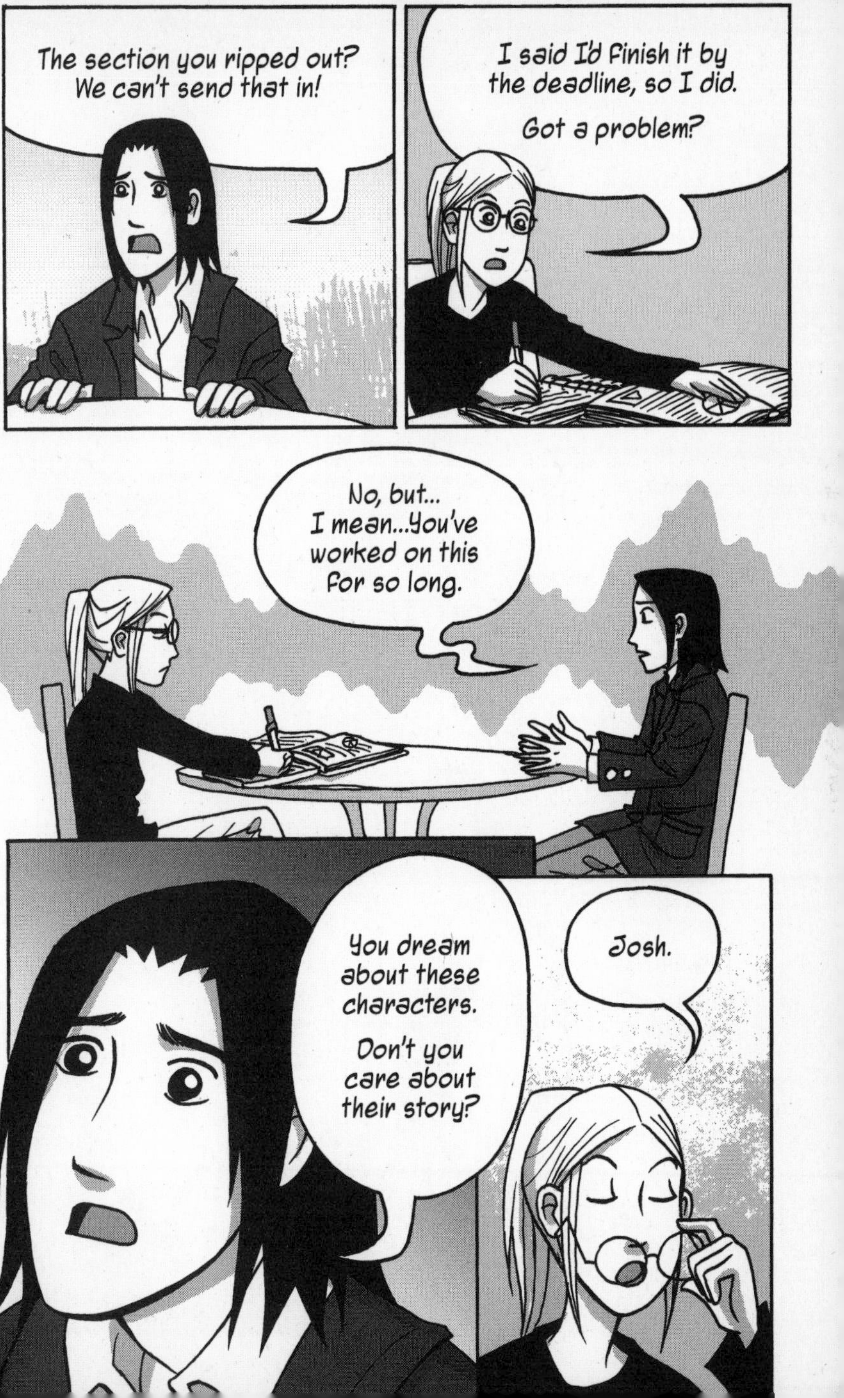
The section you ripped out? We can't send that in!
I said I'd finish it by the deadline, so I did.
Got a problem?
No, but... I mean...You've worked on this for so long.
You dream about these characters.
Don't you care about their story?
Josh.

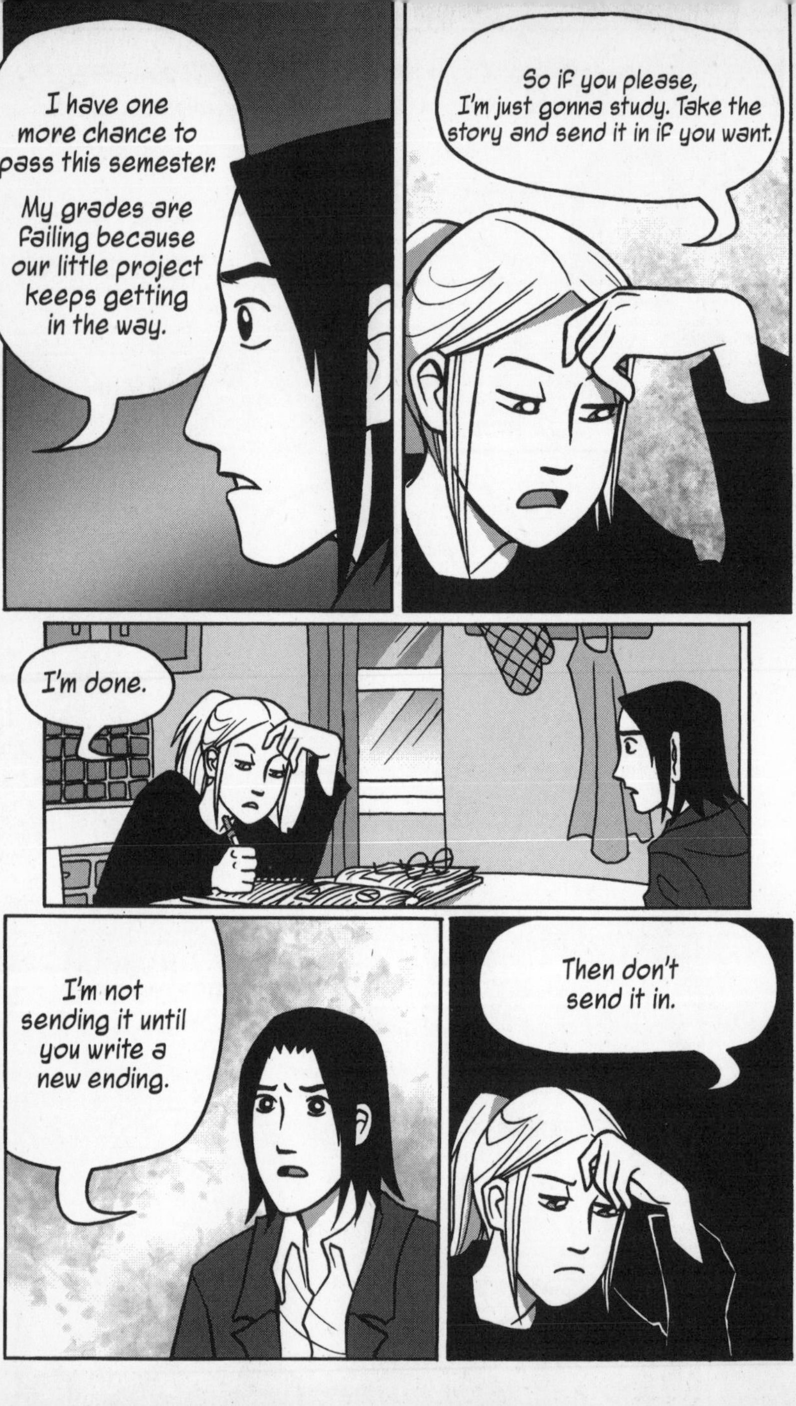
I have one more chance to pass this semester.
My grades are failing because our little project keeps getting in the way.
So if you please, I'm just gonna study. Take the story and send it in if you want.
I'm done.
I'm not sending it until you write a new ending.
Then don't send it in.

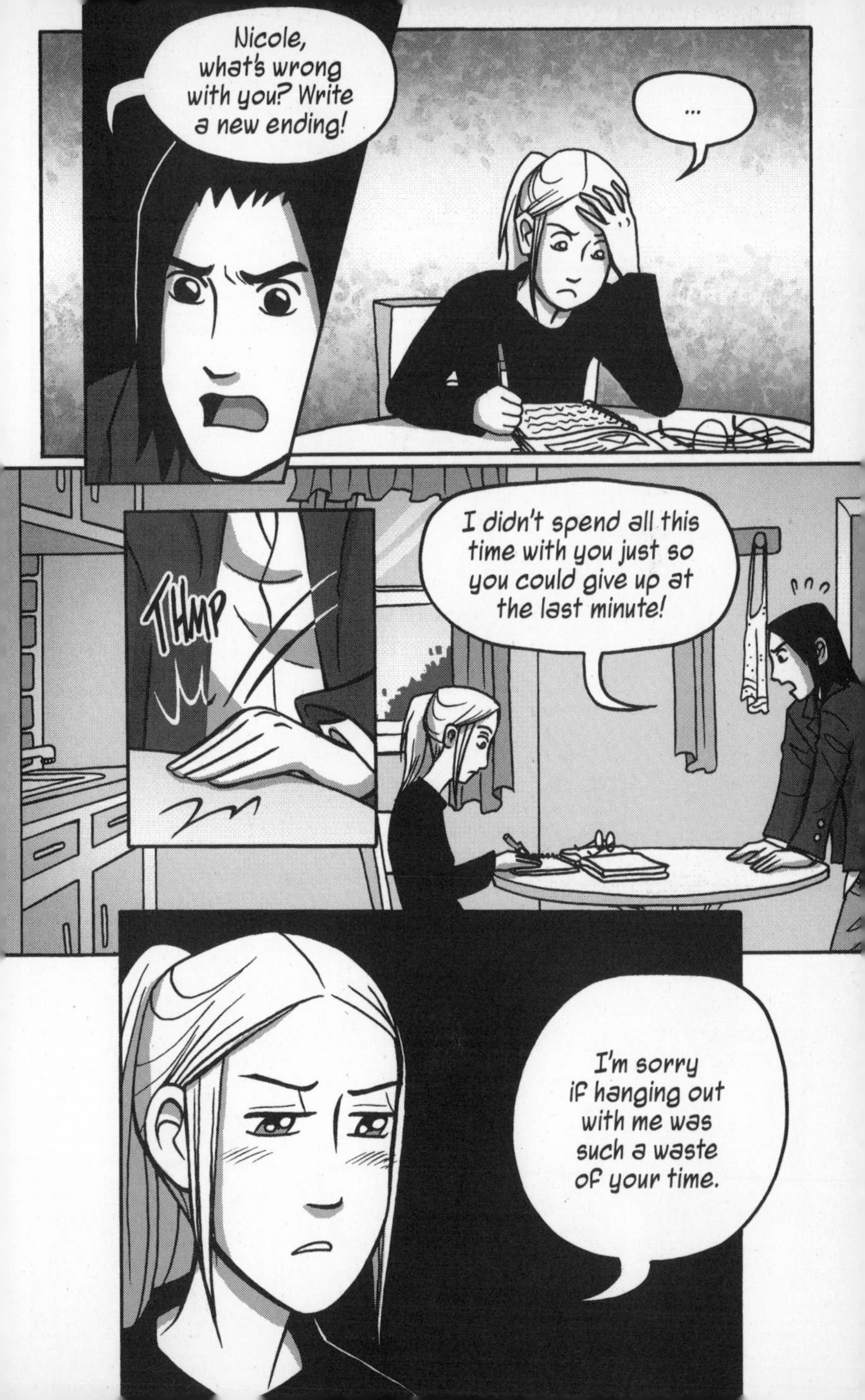
Nicole, what's wrong with you? Write a new ending!
...
THMP
I didn't spend all this time with you just so you could give up at the last minute!
I'm sorry if hanging out with me was such a waste of your time.

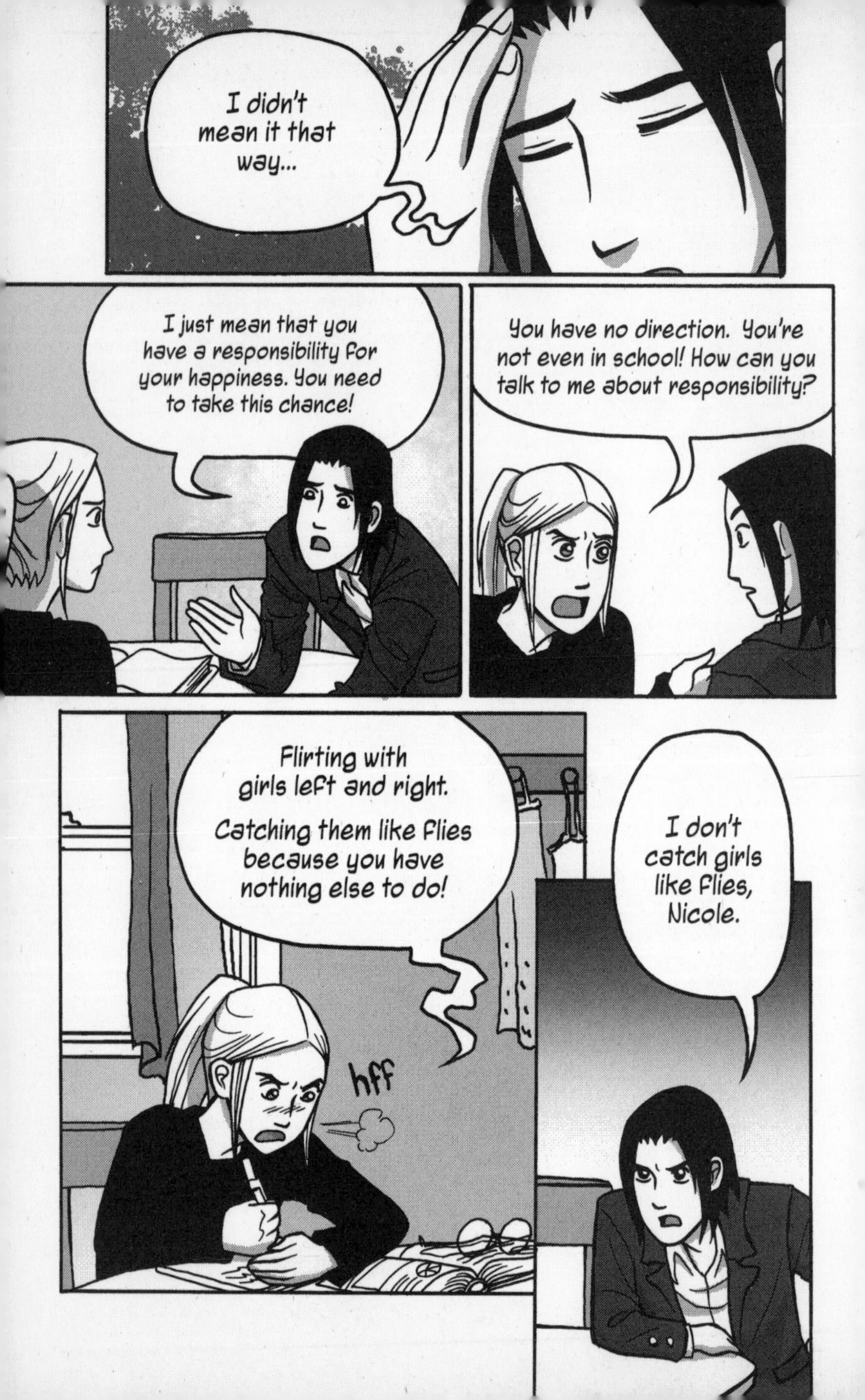
I didn't mean it that way...
I just mean that you have a responsibility for your happiness. You need to take this chance!
You have no direction. You're not even in school! How can you talk to me about responsibility?
Flirting with girls left and right.
Catching them like flies because you have nothing else to do!
hff
I don't catch girls like flies, Nicole.

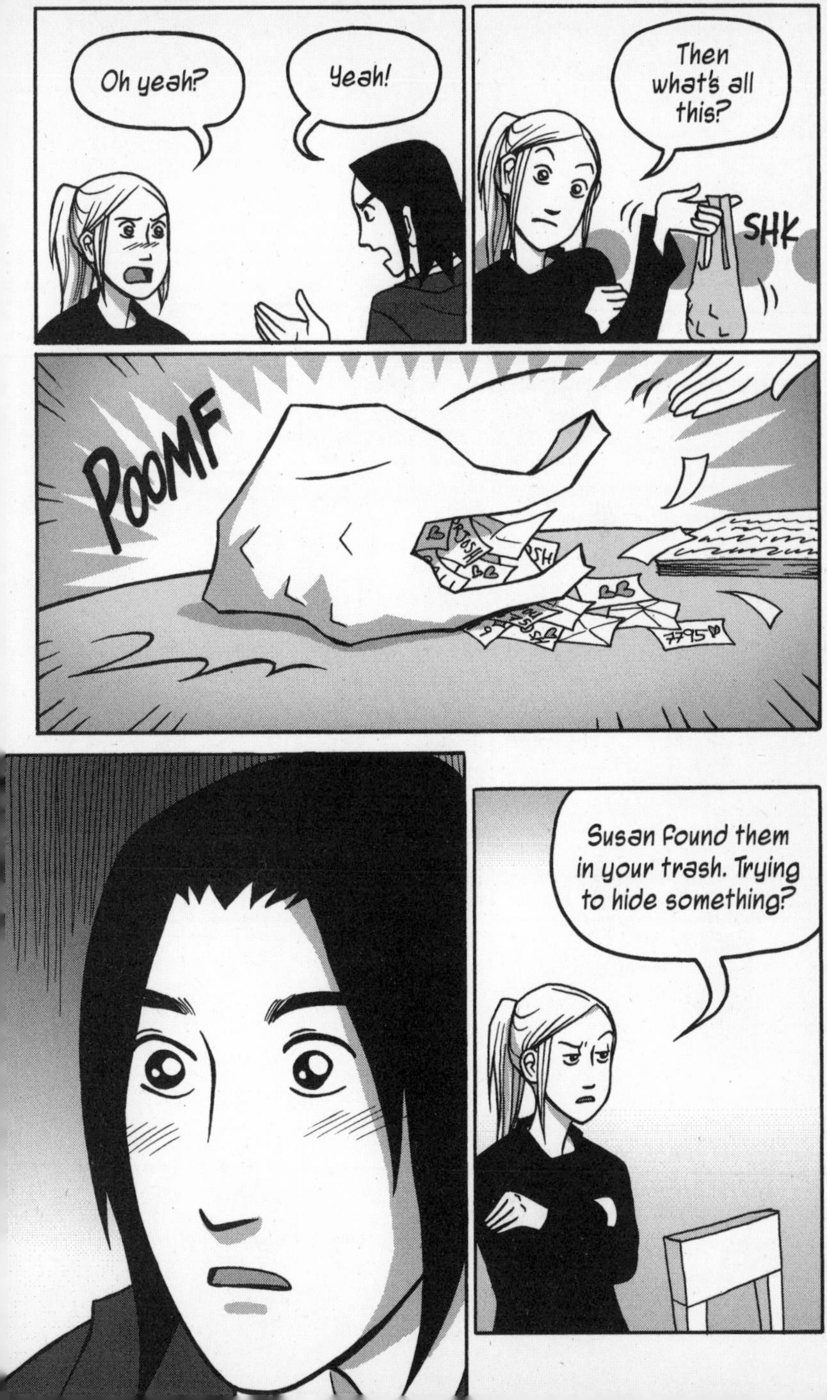
Oh yeah?
Yeah!
Then what's all this?
SHK
POOMF
Susan found them in your trash. Trying to hide something?

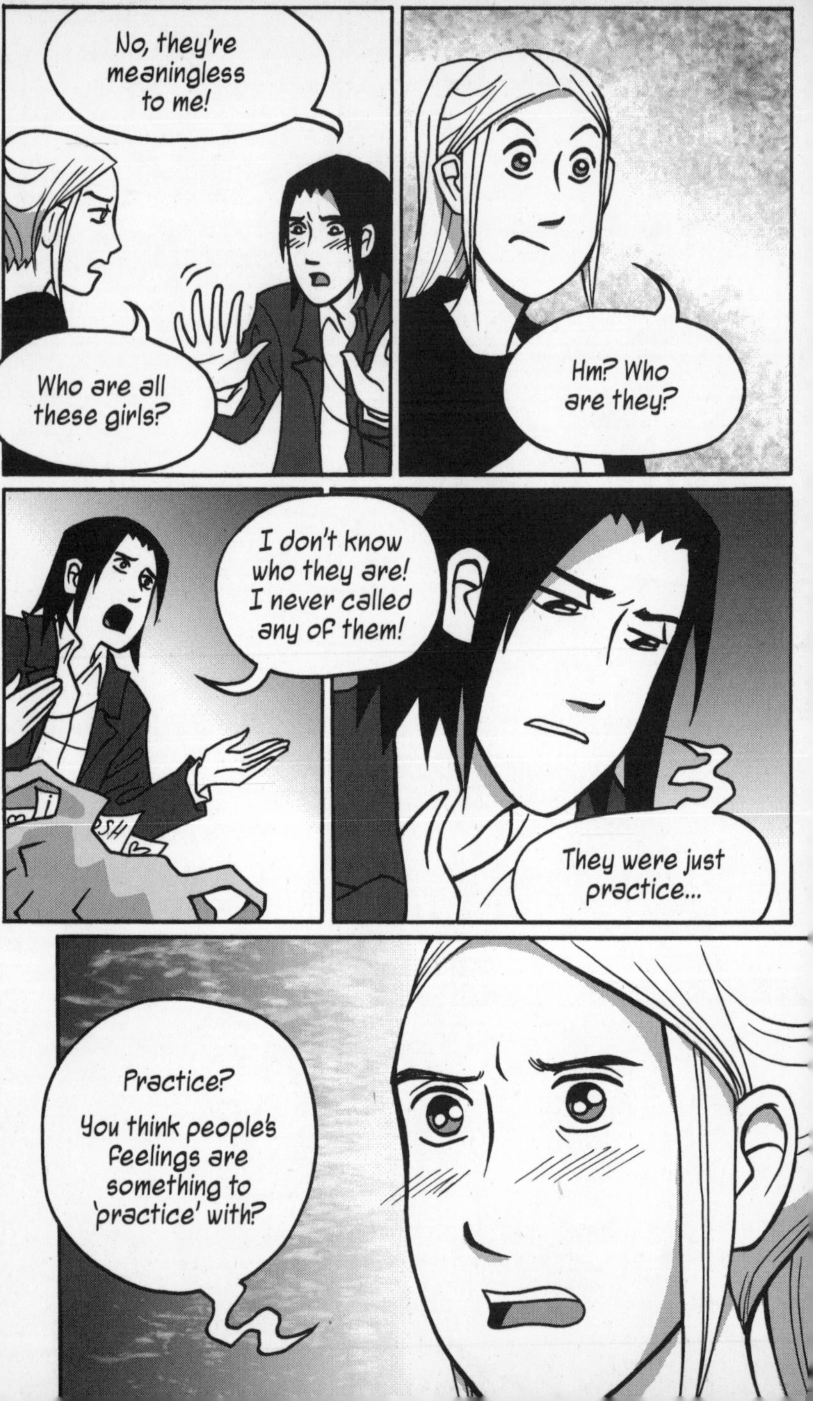
No, they're meaningless to me!
Who are all these girls?
Hm? Who are they?
I don't know who they are! I never called any of them!
They were just practice...
Practice?
You think people's feelings are something to 'practice' with?

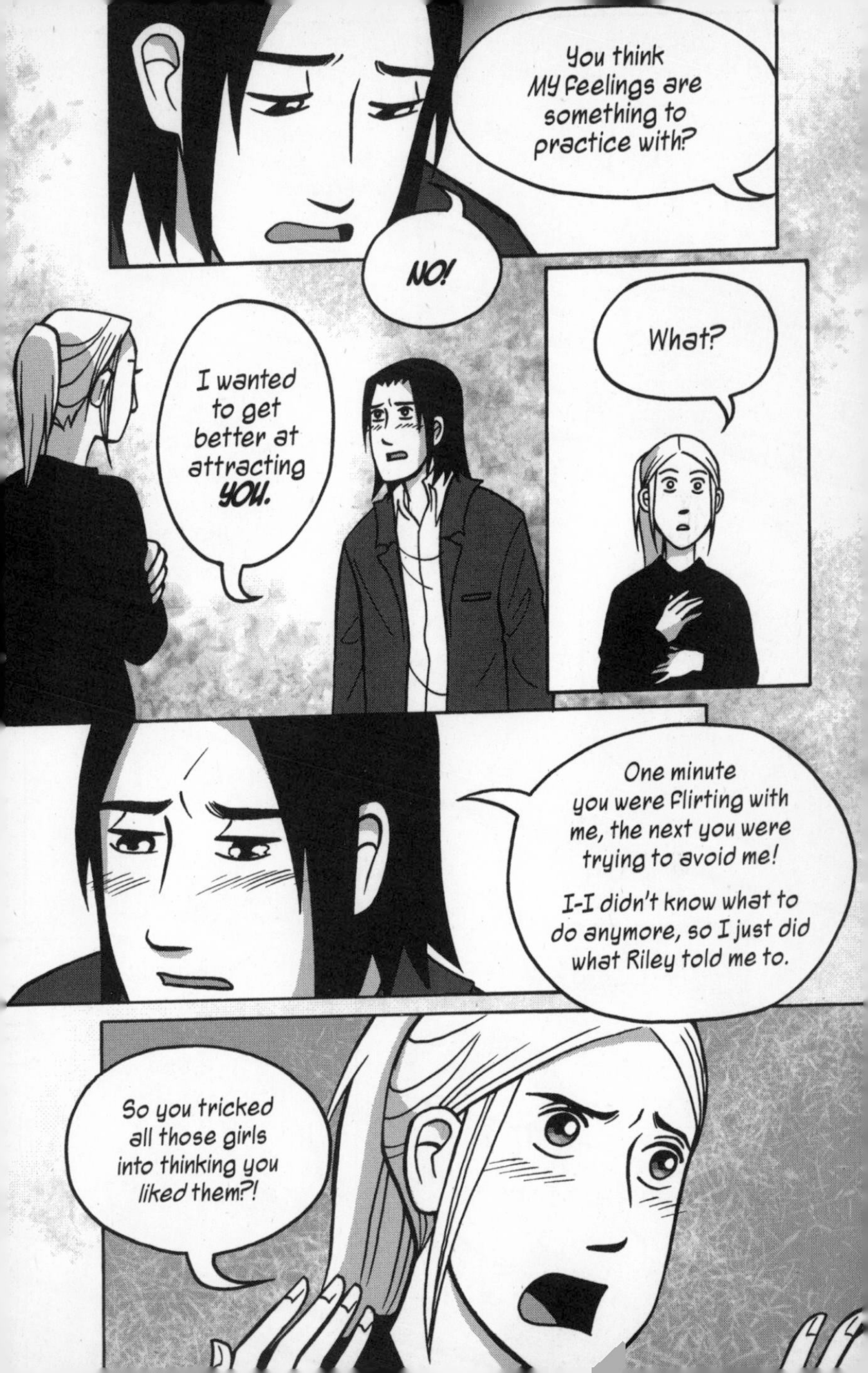
You think MY feelings are something to practice with?
NO!
I wanted to get better at attracting YOU.
What?
One minute you were flirting with me, the next you were trying to avoid me!
I-I didn't know what to do anymore, so I just did what Riley told me to.
So you tricked all those girls into thinking you liked them?!

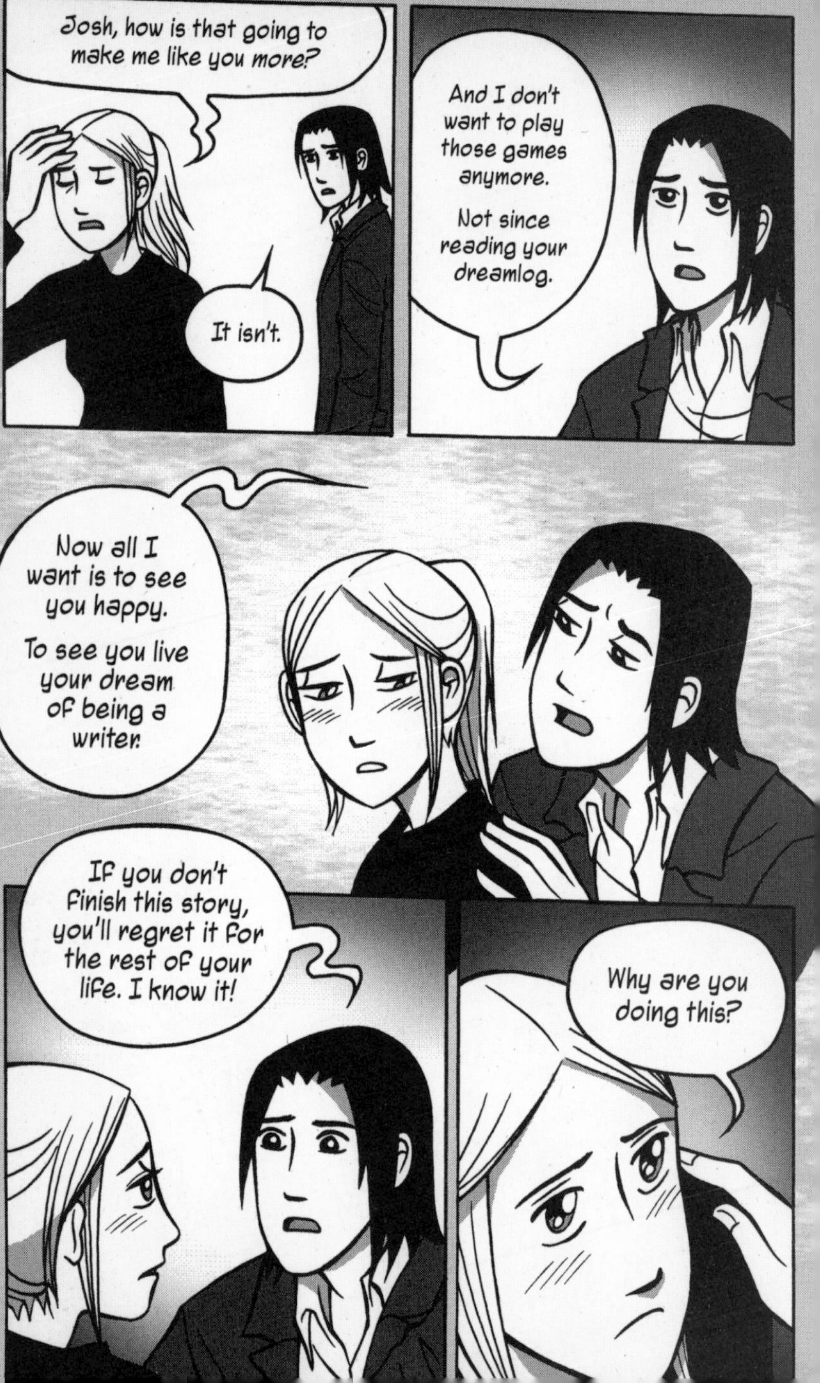
Josh, how is that going to make me like you more?
It isn't.
And I don't want to play those games anymore.
Not since reading your dreamlog.
Now all I want is to see you happy.
To see you live your dream of being a writer.
If you don't finish this story, you'll regret it for the rest of your life. I know it!
Why are you doing this?

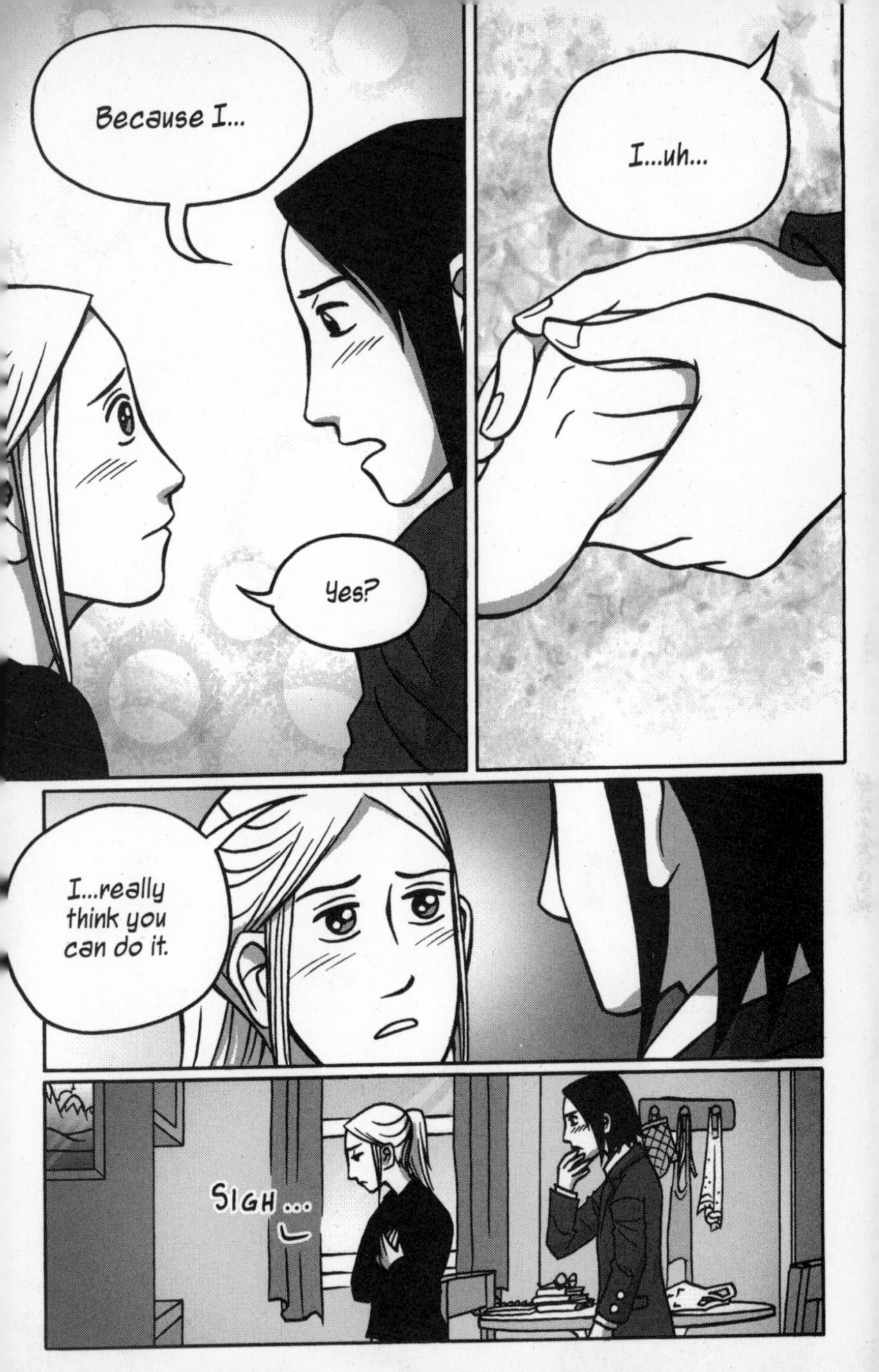
Because I...
Yes?
I...uh...
I...really think you can do it.
SIGH...

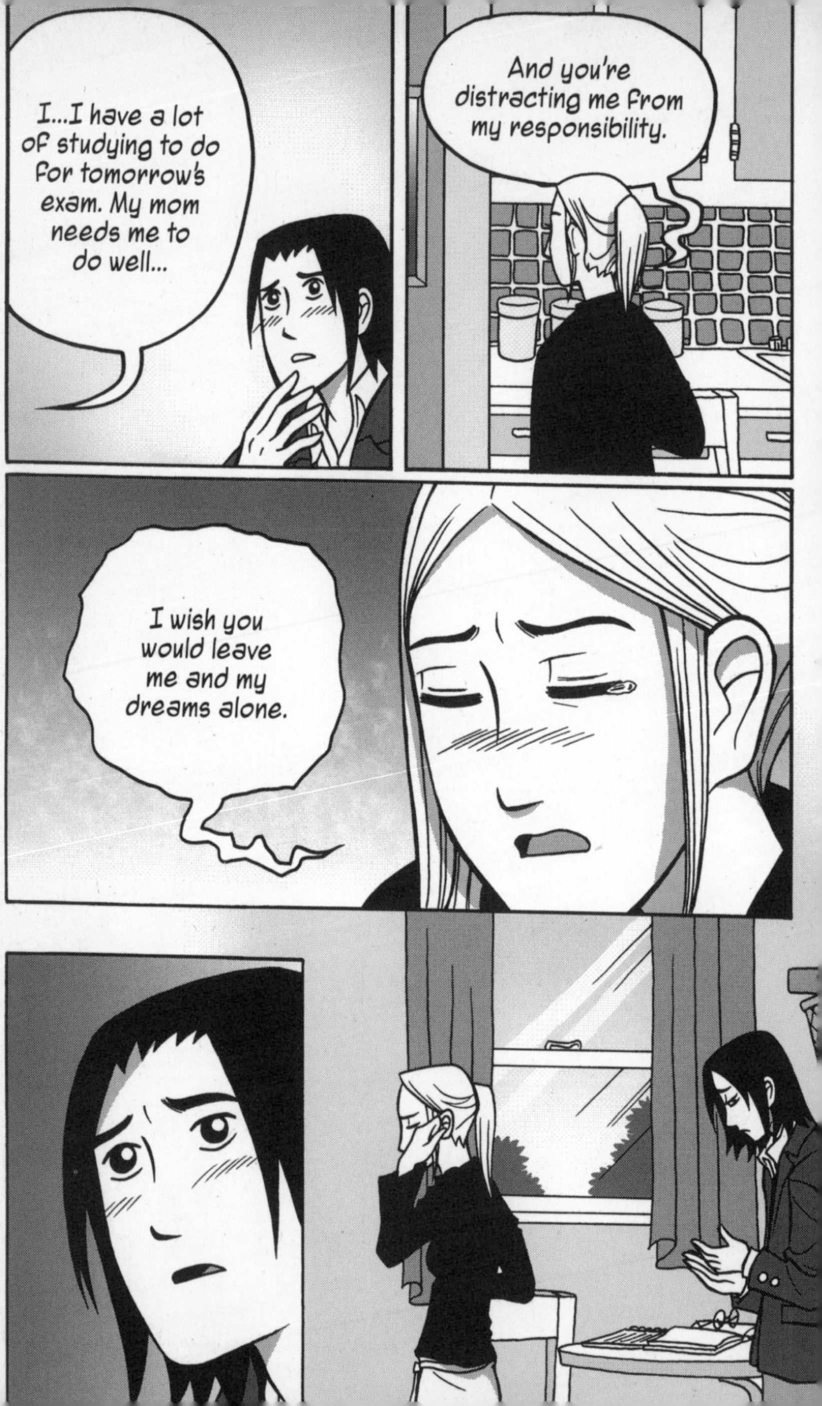
I...I have a lot of studying to do for tomorrow's exam. My mom needs me to do well...
And you're distracting me from my responsibility.
I wish you would leave me and my dreams alone.

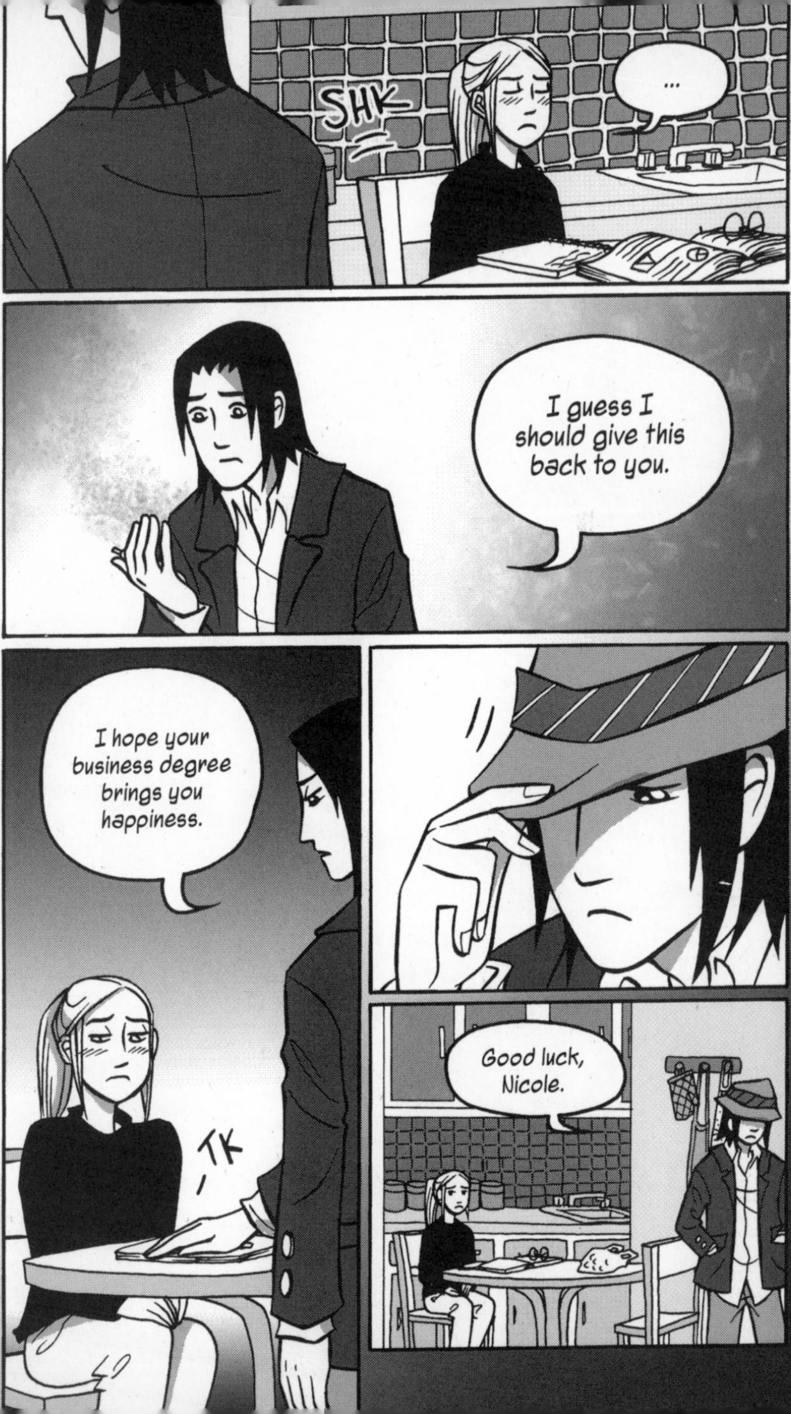
SHK
...
I guess I should give this back to you.
I hope your business degree brings you happiness.
TK
Good luck, Nicole.

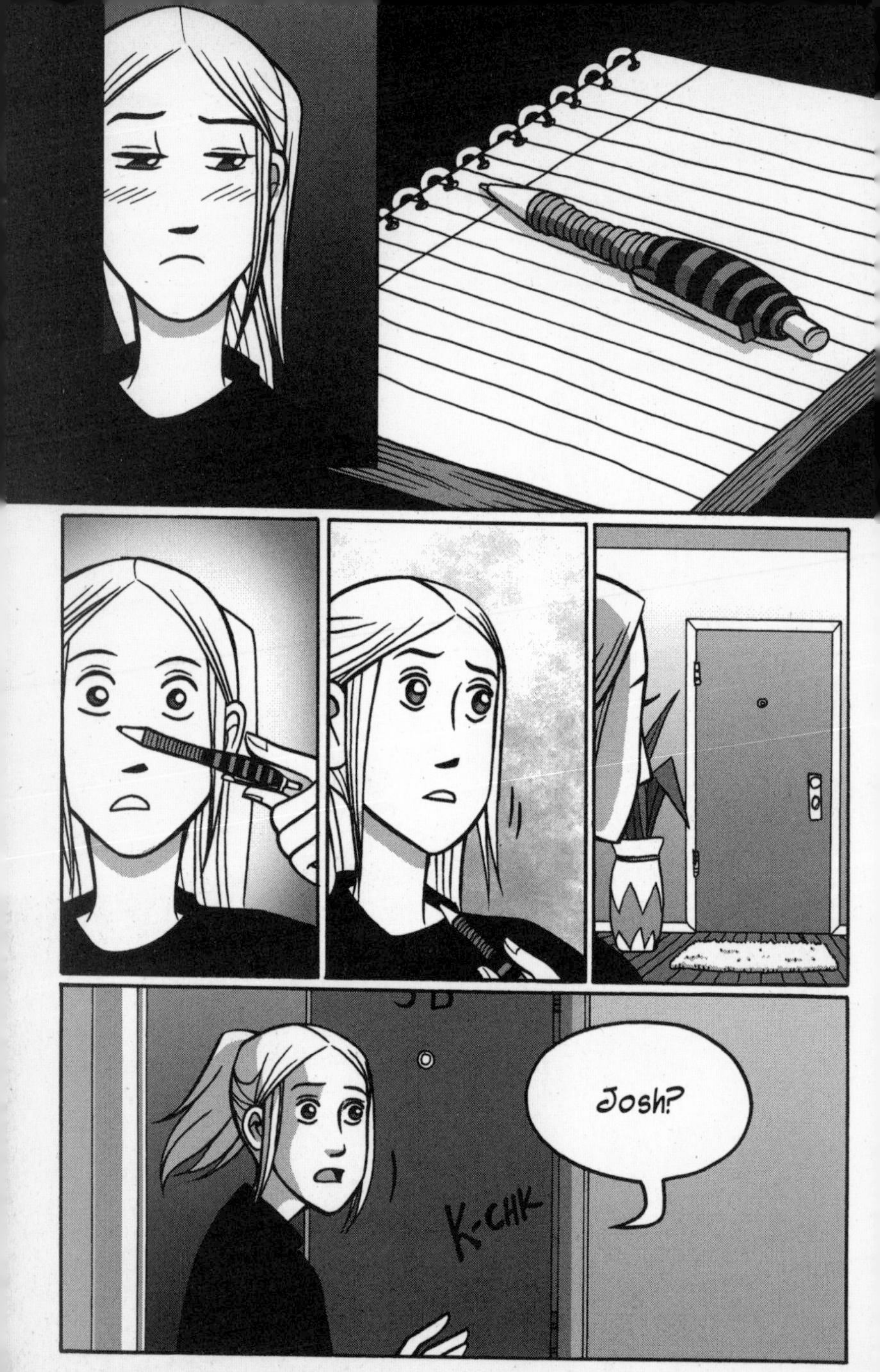
Josh?
K-CHK

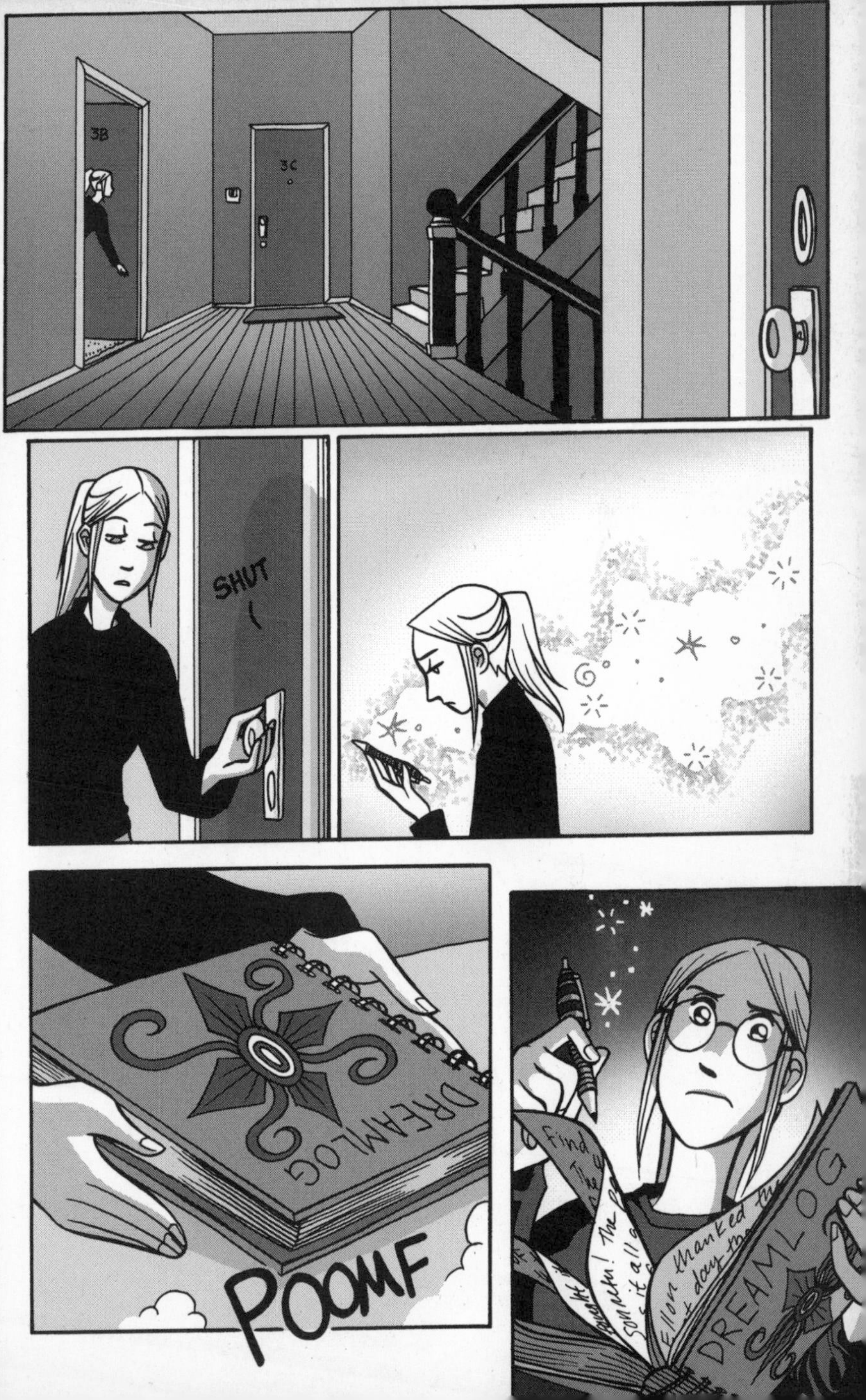
3B
3C
SHUT
DREAMLOG
POOMF
DREAMLOG

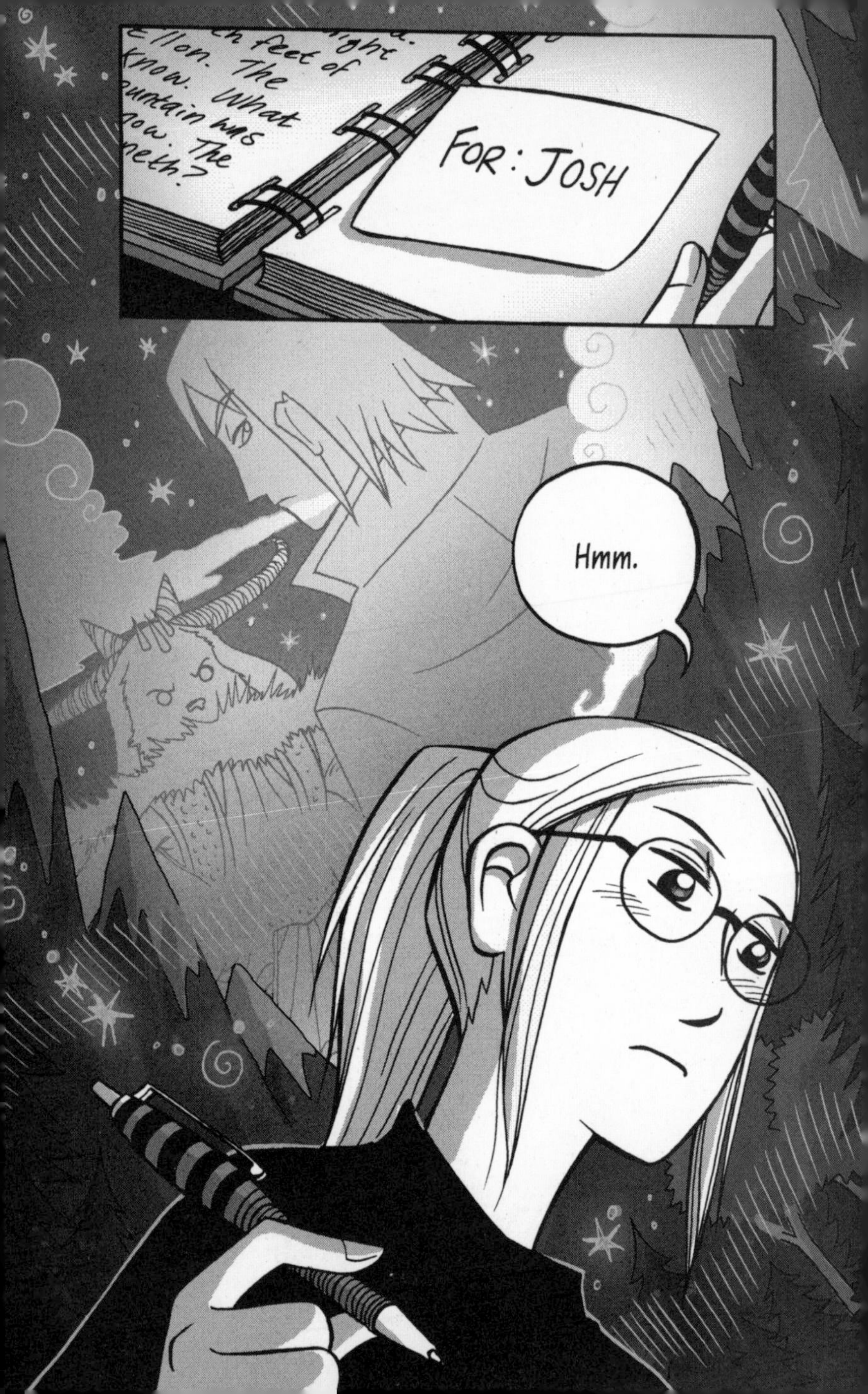
FOR : JOSH
Hmm.

Chapter Six

Ends Softly

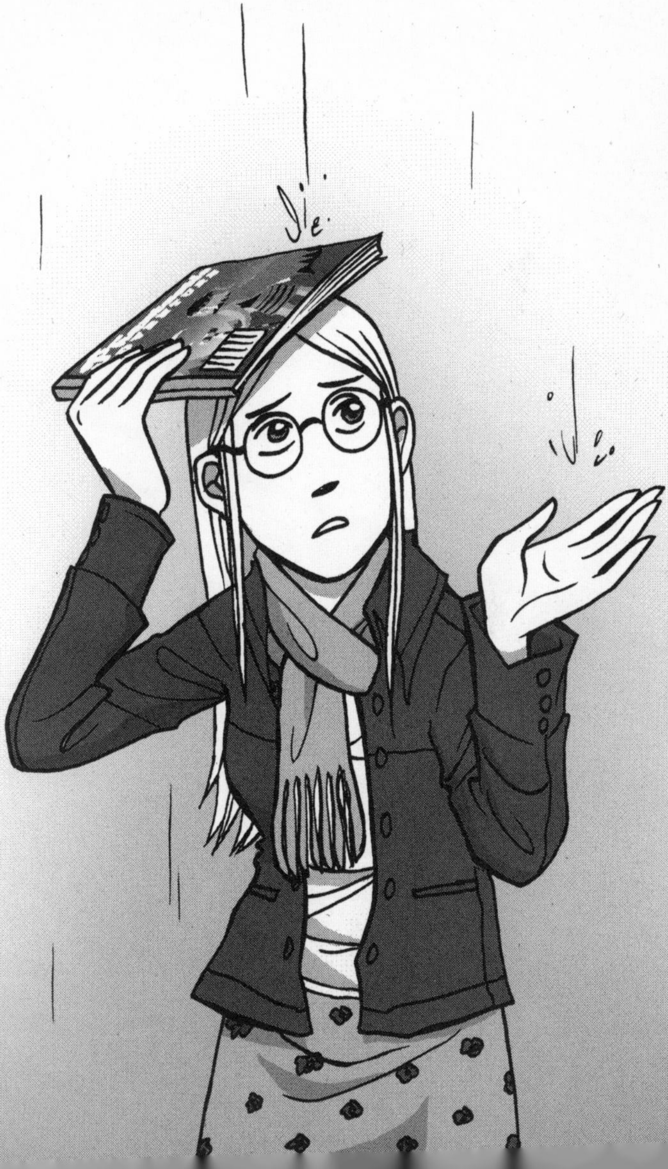

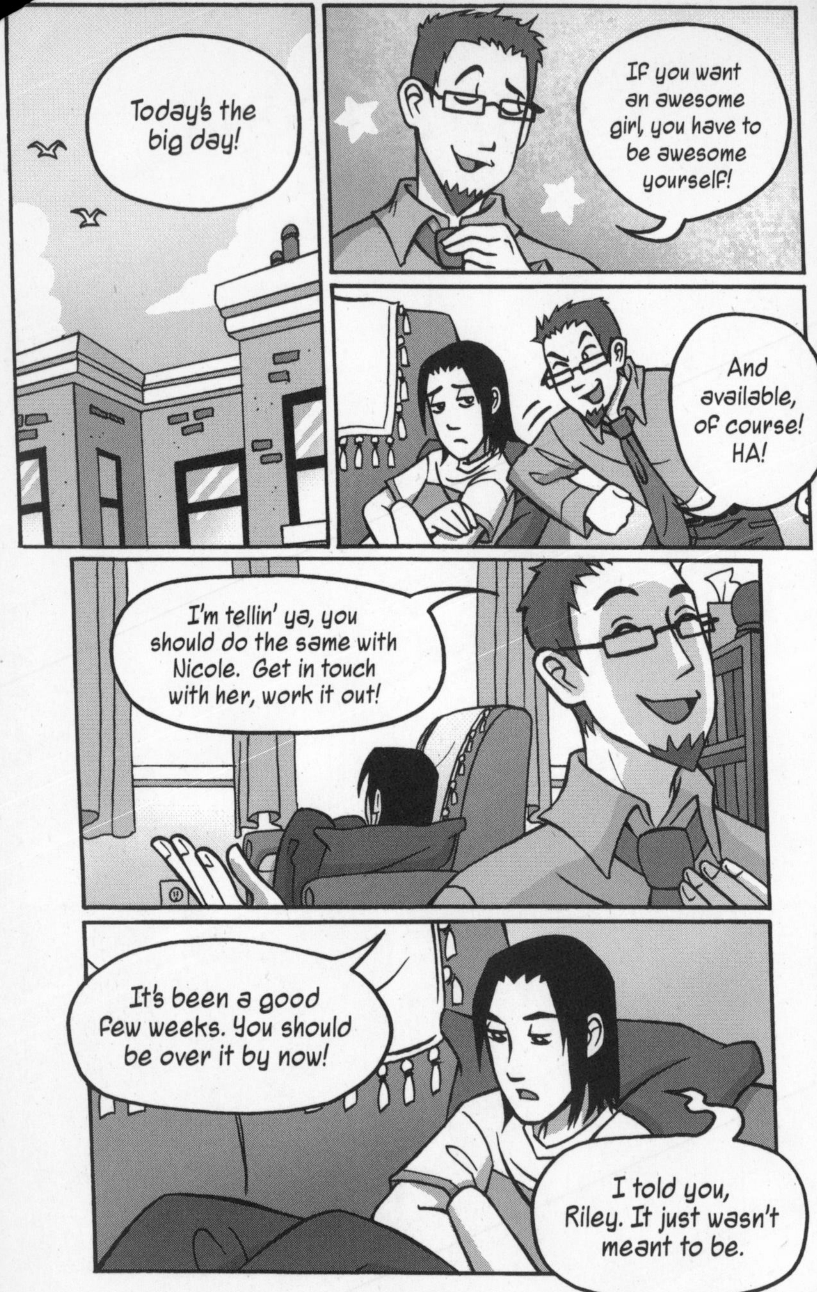
Today's the big day!
If you want an awesome girl, you have to be awesome yourself!
And available, of course! HA!
I'm tellin' ya, you should do the same with Nicole. Get in touch with her, work it out!
It's been a good few weeks. You should be over it by now!
I told you, Riley. It just wasn't meant to be.

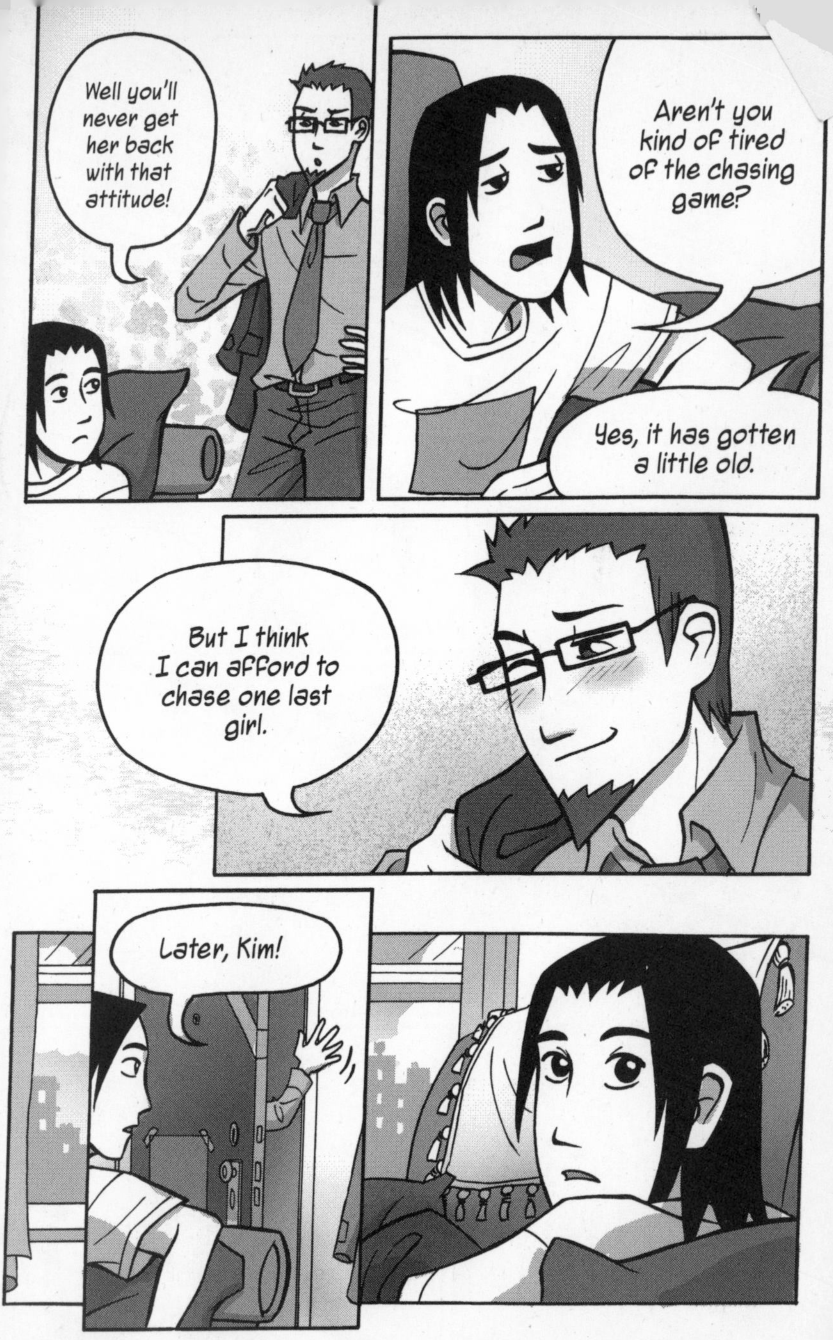
Well you'll never get her back with that attitude!
Aren't you kind of tired of the chasing game?
Yes, it has gotten a little old.
But I think I can afford to chase one last girl.
Later, Kim!

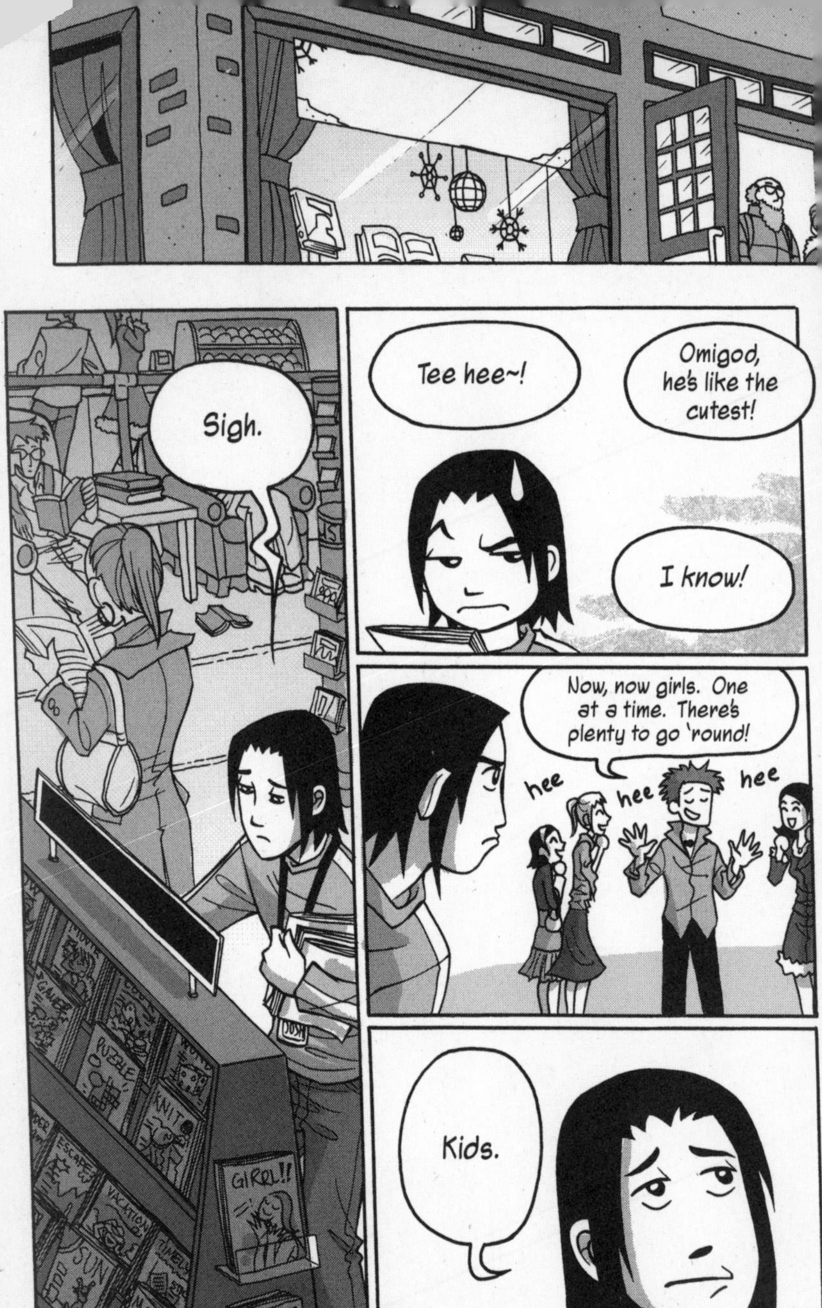
Sigh.
Tee hee~!
Omigod, he's like the cutest!
I know!
Now, now girls. One at a time. There's plenty to go 'round!
hee
hee
hee
Kids.

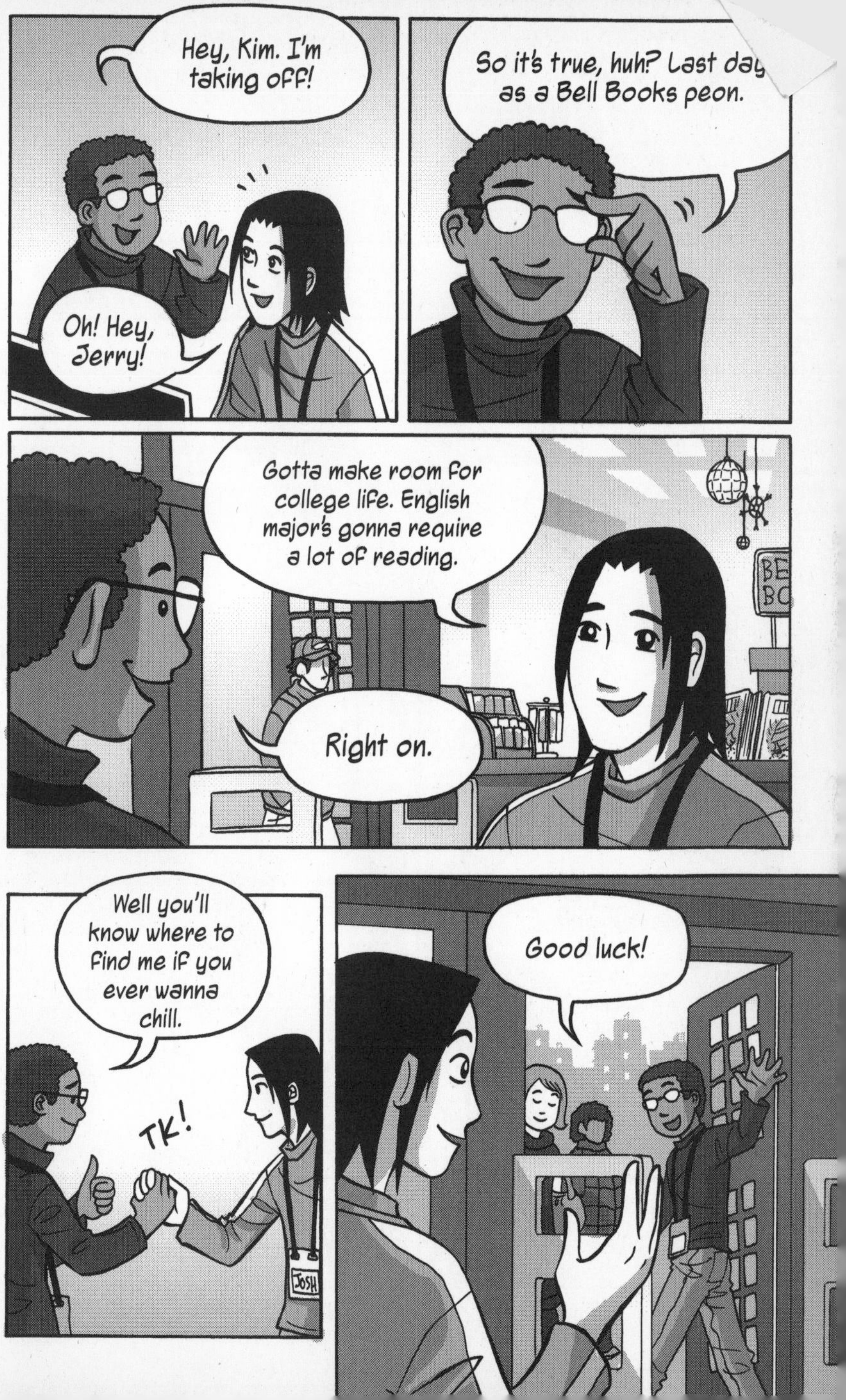

Hey, Kim. I'm taking off!
Oh! Hey, Jerry!
So it's true, huh? Last day as a Bell Books peon.
Gotta make room for college life. English major's gonna require a lot of reading.
Right on.
Well you'll know where to find me if you ever wanna chill.
TK!
JOSH
Good luck!

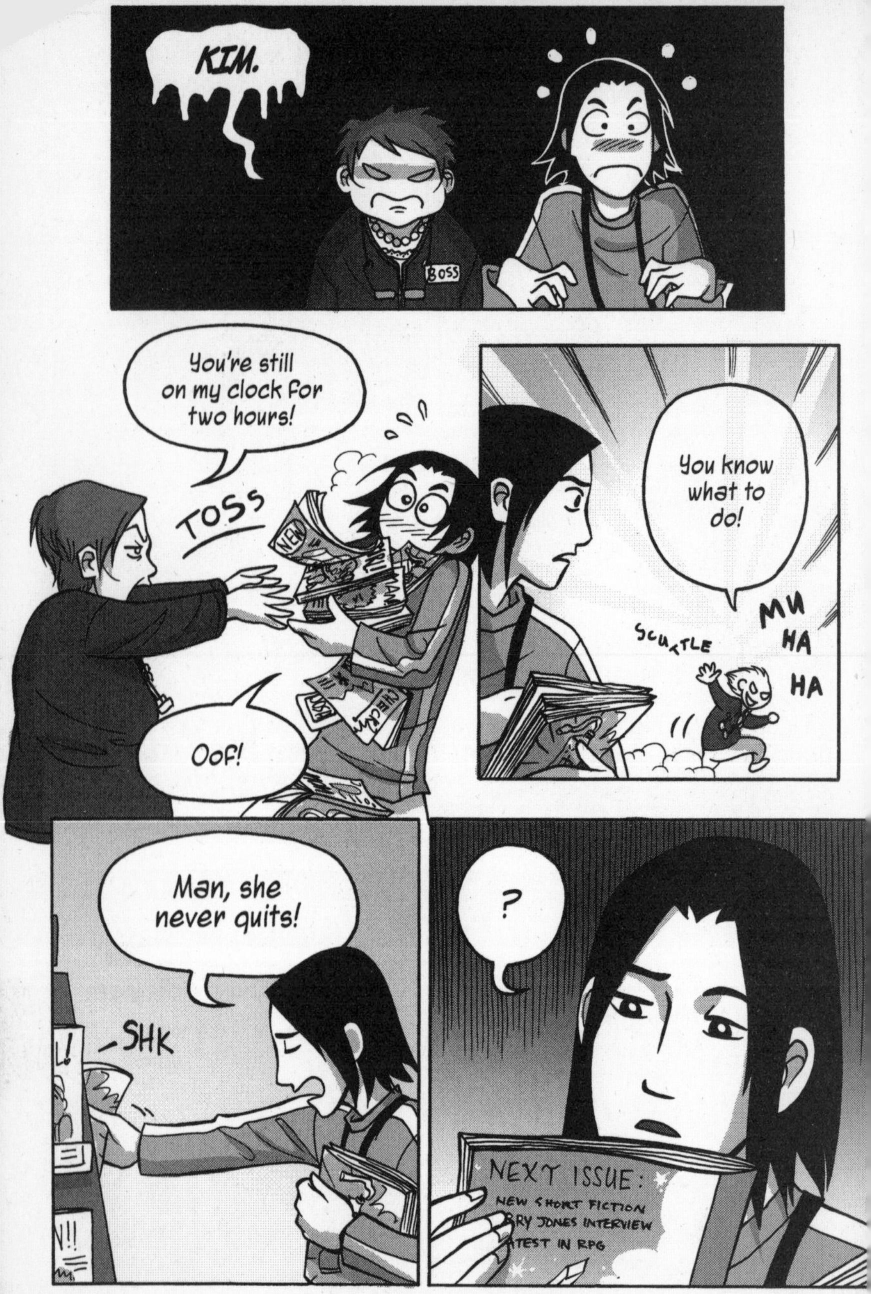
KIM.
You're still on my clock for two hours!
TOSS
Oof!
You know what to do!
SCUTTLE
MU HA HA
Man, she never quits!
SHK
?
NEXT ISSUE:
NEW SHORT FICTION

FWIP

FAMILIAR
By Nicole Hayes

FOR: JOSH

Far away in another realm there
lives a sorcerer named Ellon, and
his familiar, Sonneth. With his
piles of precious stones
his time conjuring kit
leaders for the real
by carving magica
bring them into

The sorcere
en great
's only

Ellon reached the top of
the mountain, the highest
point in the sacred realm.
Syra awaited him there.

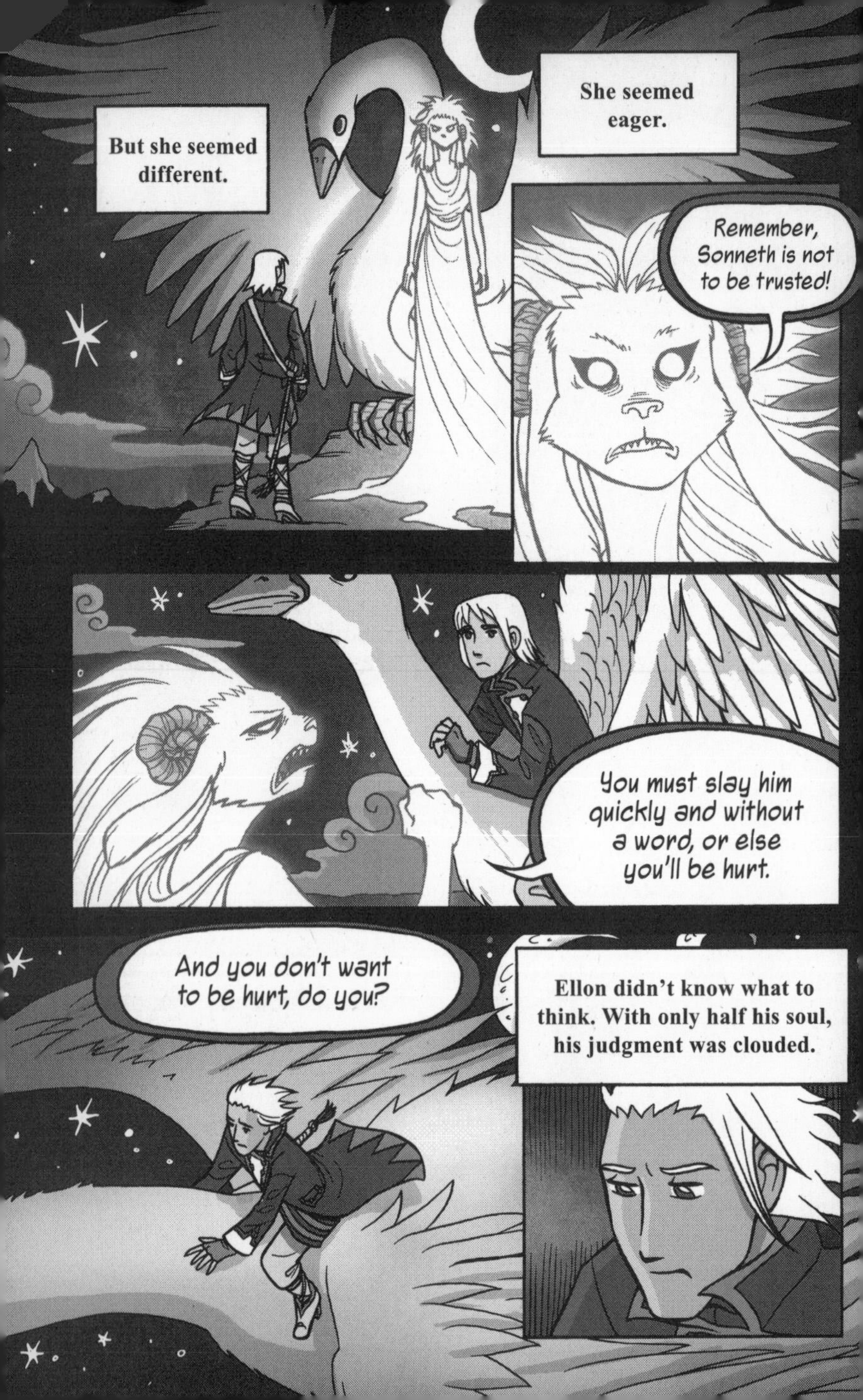
But she seemed different.
She seemed eager.
Remember, Sonneth is not to be trusted!
You must slay him quickly and without a word, or else you'll be hurt.
And you don't want to be hurt, do you?
Ellon didn't know what to think. With only half his soul, his judgment was clouded.

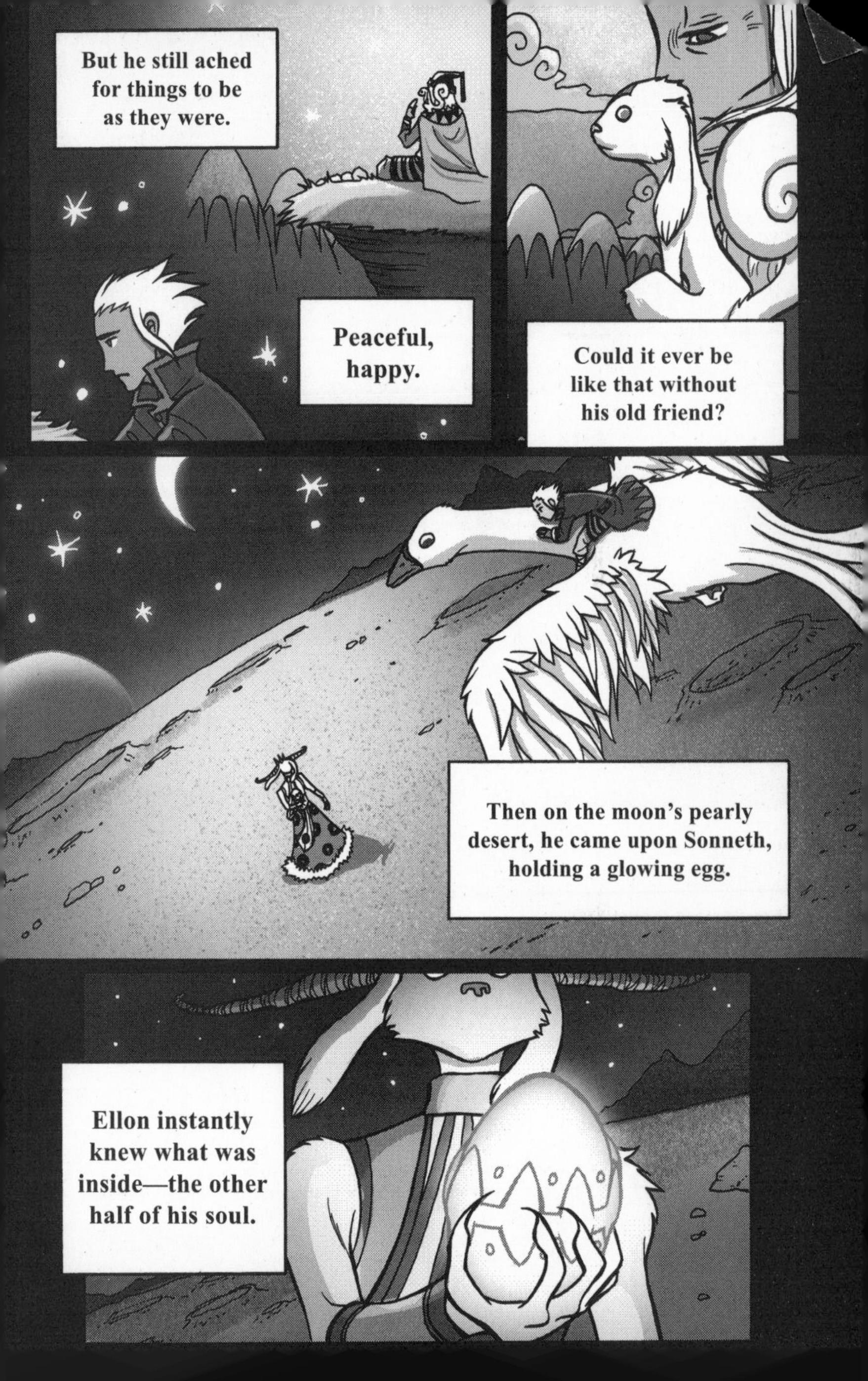
But he still ached for things to be as they were.
Peaceful, happy.
Could it ever be like that without his old friend?
Then on the moon's pearly desert, he came upon Sonneth, holding a glowing egg.
Ellon instantly knew what was inside—the other half of his soul.

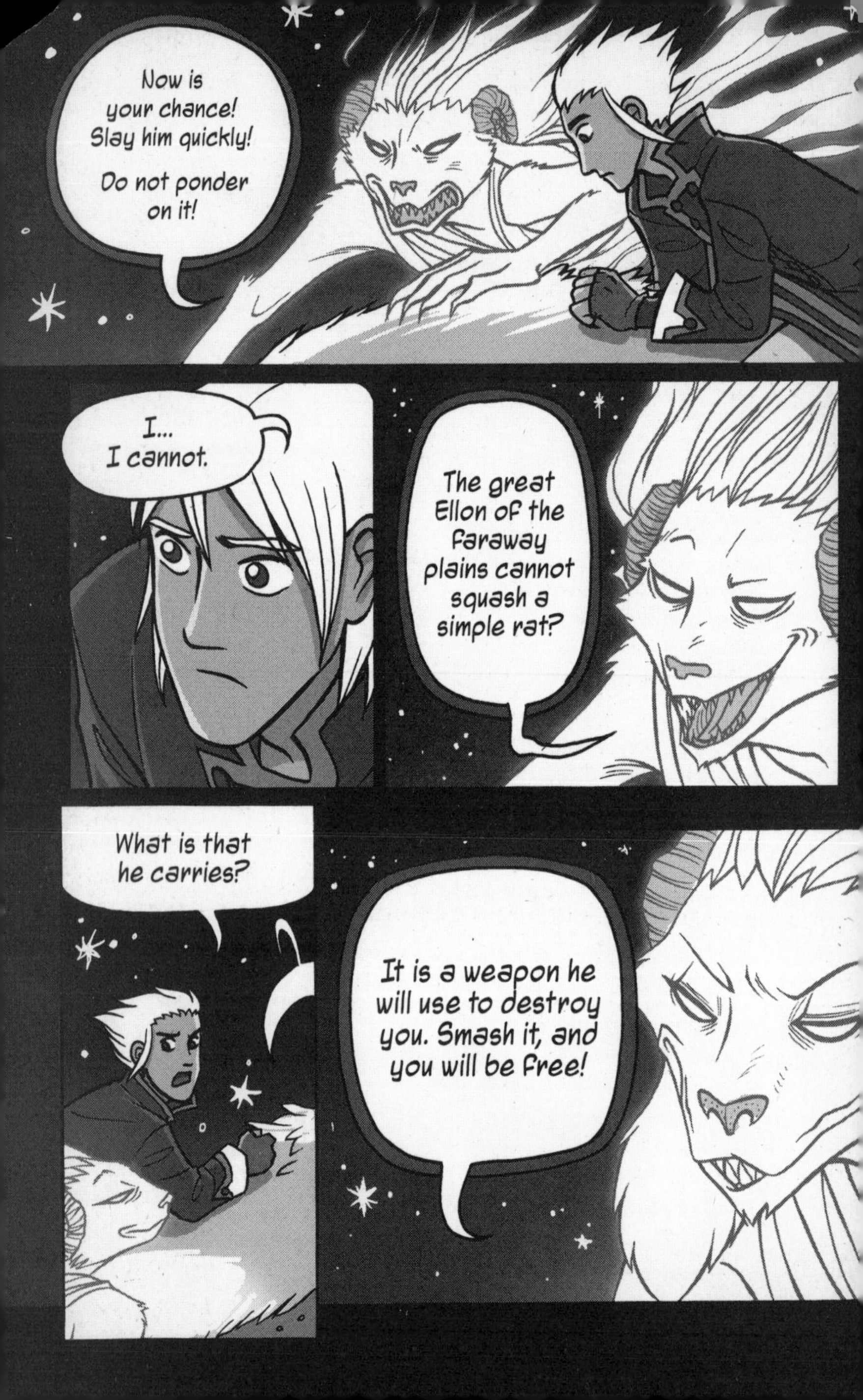
Now is your chance! Slay him quickly!
Do not ponder on it!
I... I cannot.
The great Ellon of the faraway plains cannot squash a simple rat?
What is that he carries?
It is a weapon he will use to destroy you. Smash it, and you will be free!

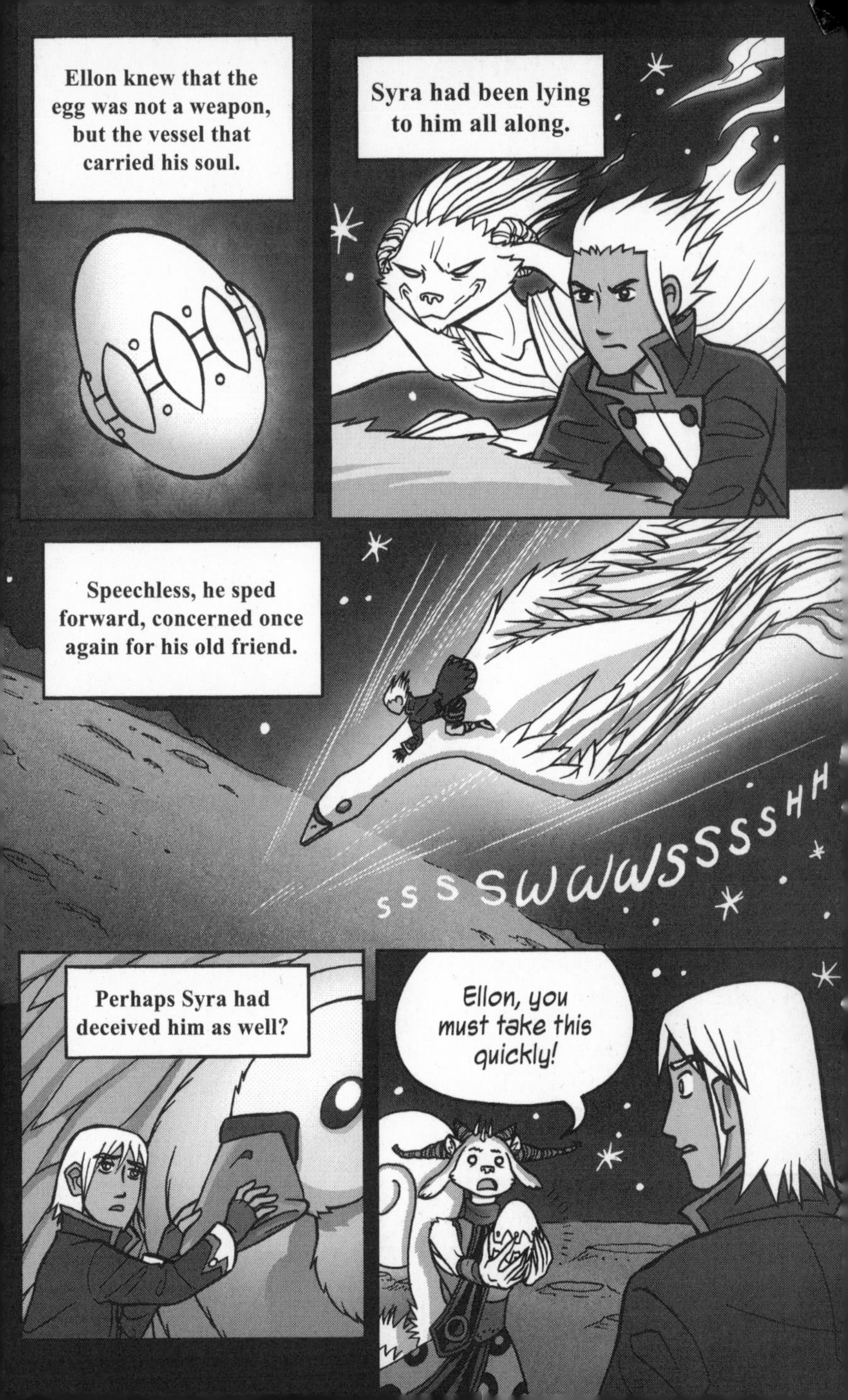
Ellon knew that the egg was not a weapon, but the vessel that carried his soul.
Syra had been lying to him all along.
Speechless, he sped forward, concerned once again for his old friend.
SSSSWWWSSSSSHH
Perhaps Syra had deceived him as well?
Ellon, you must take this quickly!

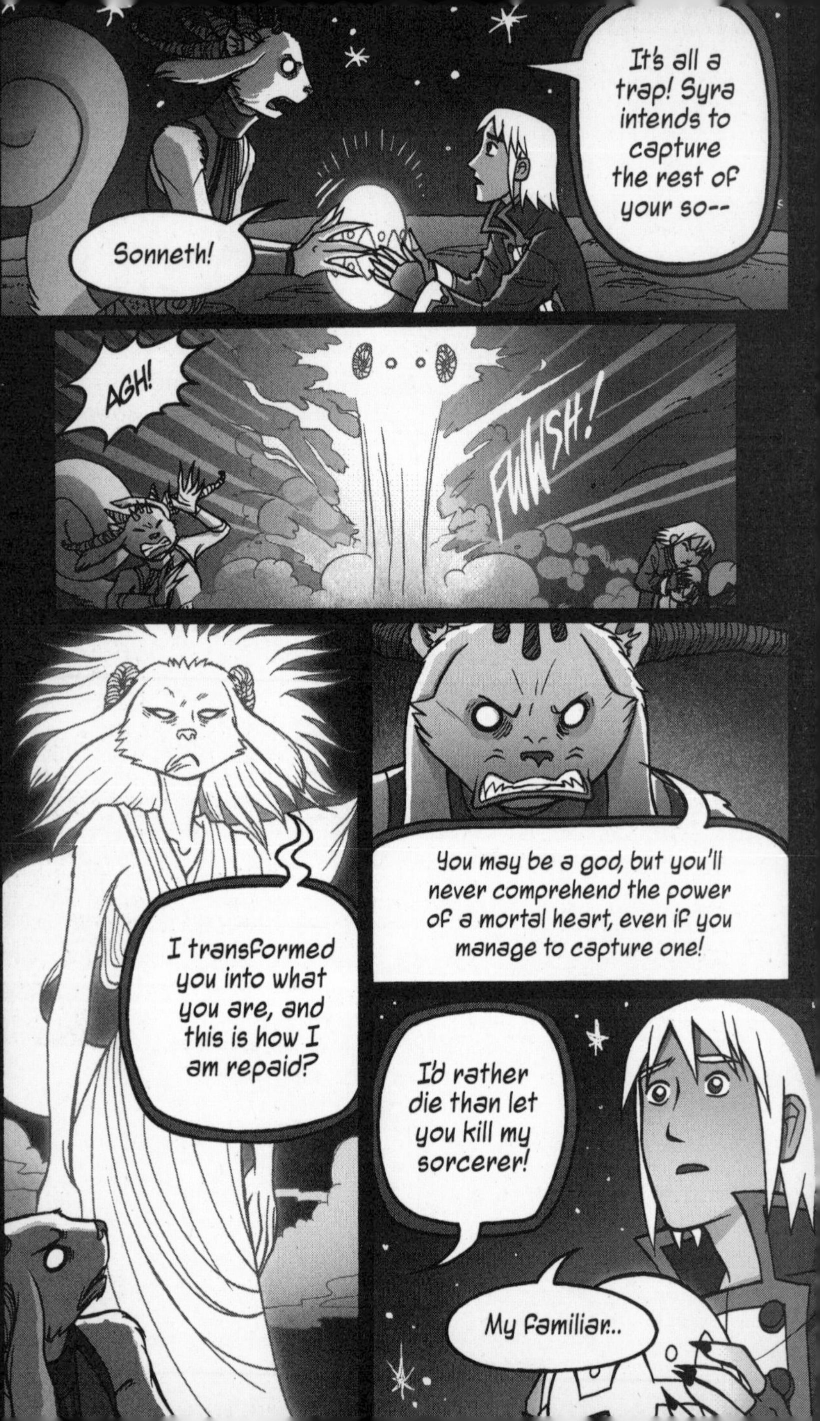
Sonneth!
It's all a trap! Syra intends to capture the rest of your so--
AGH!
FWWSH!
I transformed you into what you are, and this is how I am repaid?
You may be a god, but you'll never comprehend the power of a mortal heart, even if you manage to capture one!
I'd rather die than let you kill my sorcerer!
My familiar...

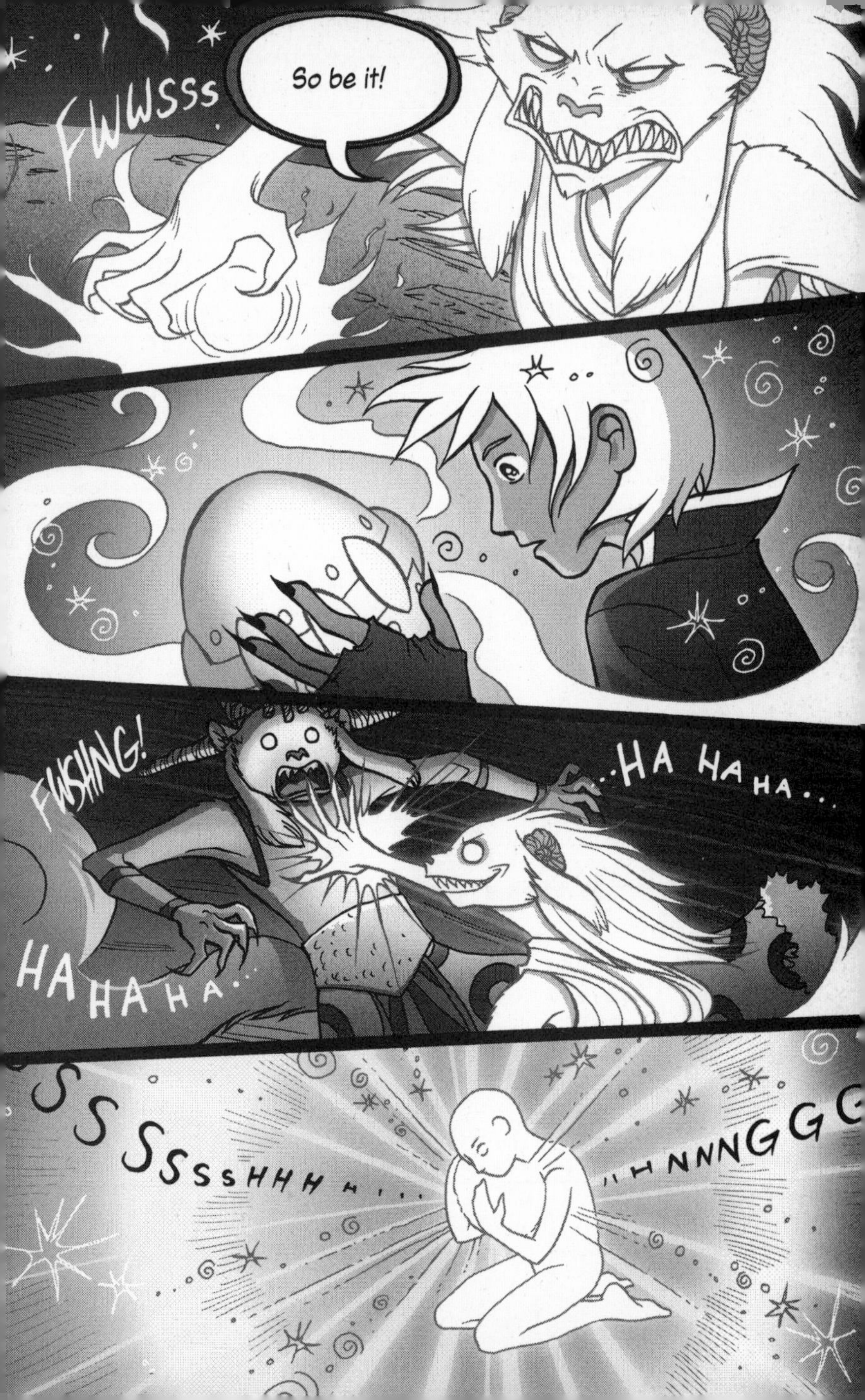
FWWSSS
So be it!
FWSHNG!
...HA HA HA...
HA HA HA HA...
SSSSSHHHH...
...HNNNGGG

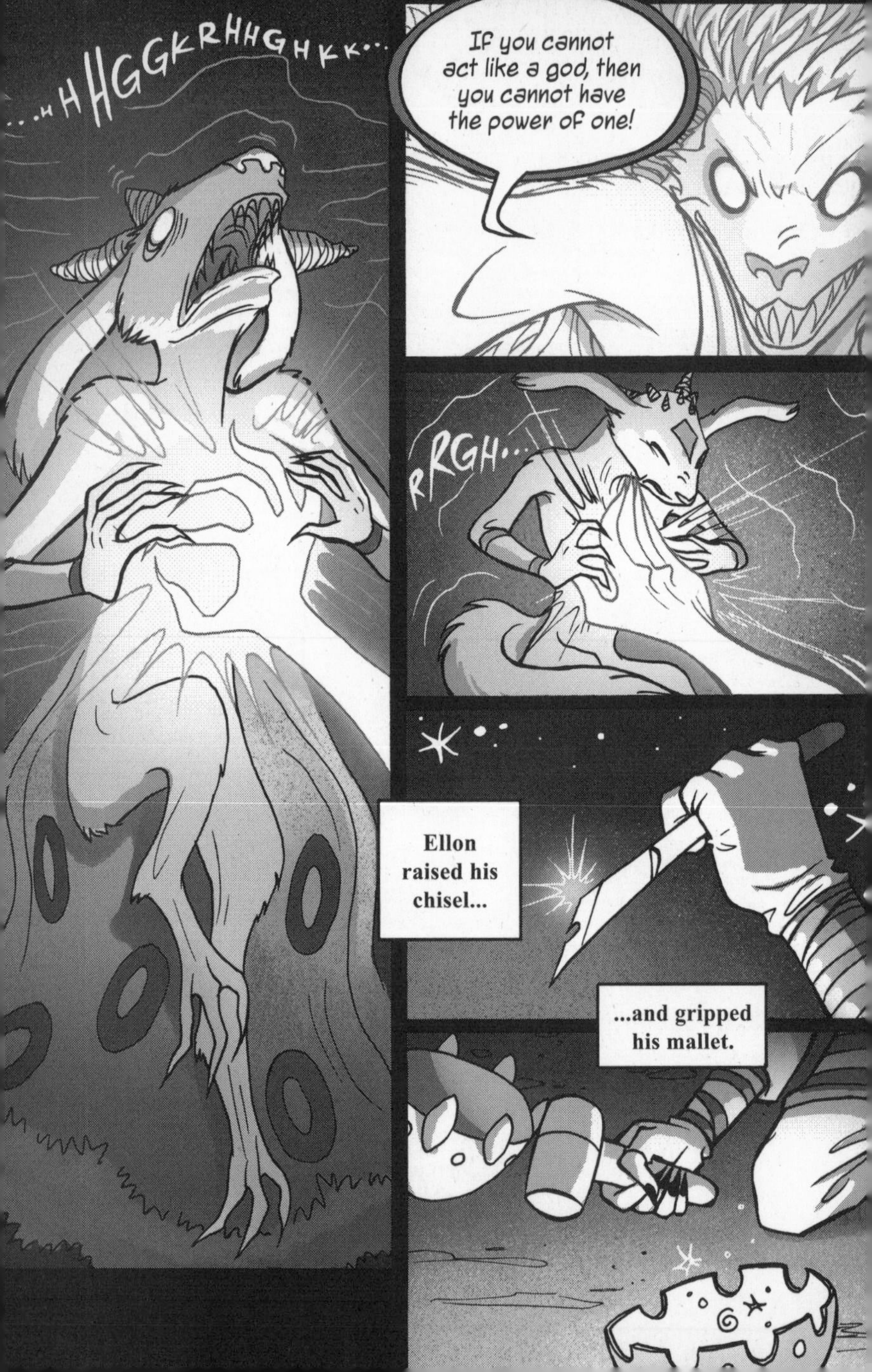
...HHHGGKRHHGHKK...
If you cannot act like a god, then you cannot have the power of one!
RRGH...
Ellon raised his chisel...
...and gripped his mallet.

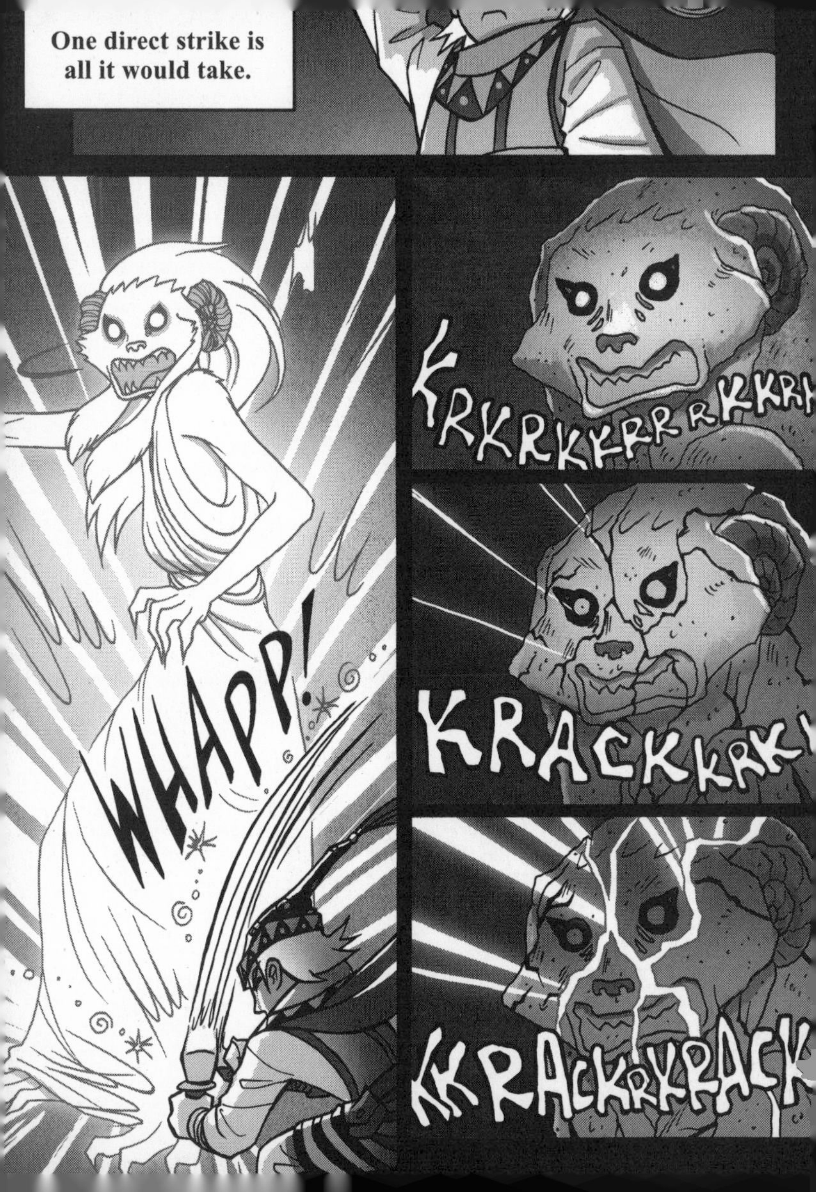

One direct strike is all it would take.
WHAPP!
KRKRKRKYRRRRKKR
KRACKKRK
KKRACKRKKRACK

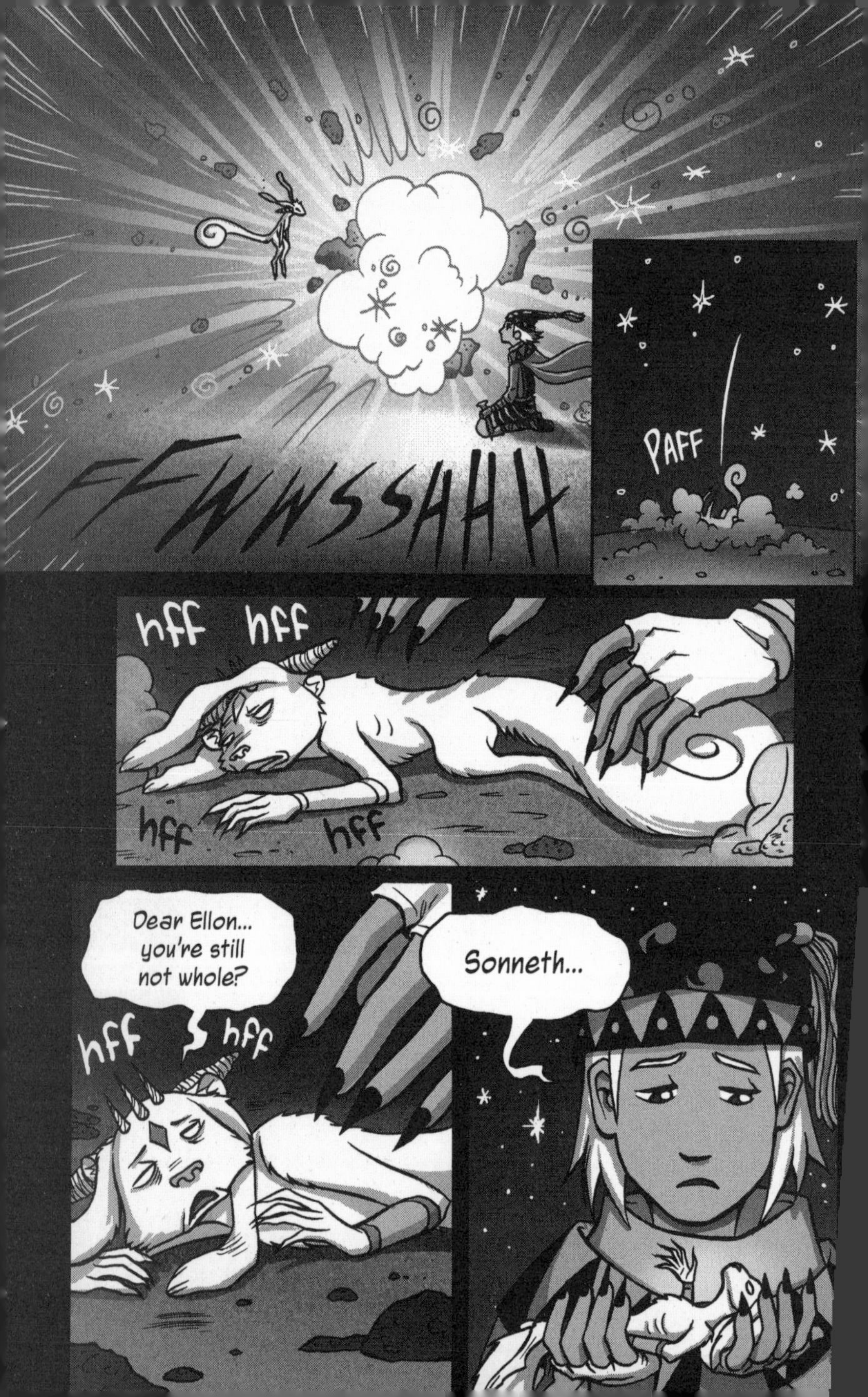
FFWWSSAHHH
PAFF
hff hff
hff hff
Dear Ellon... you're still not whole?
hff hff
Sonneth...

Both of us are broken because of me.... I am nothing.

You are still my familiar, aren't you?

After all the harm I've brought to you?

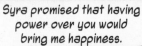

It was an adventure. We've both learned much.

Syra promised that having power over you would bring me happiness.

But how can that be, when being by your side was the happiest I've ever felt?

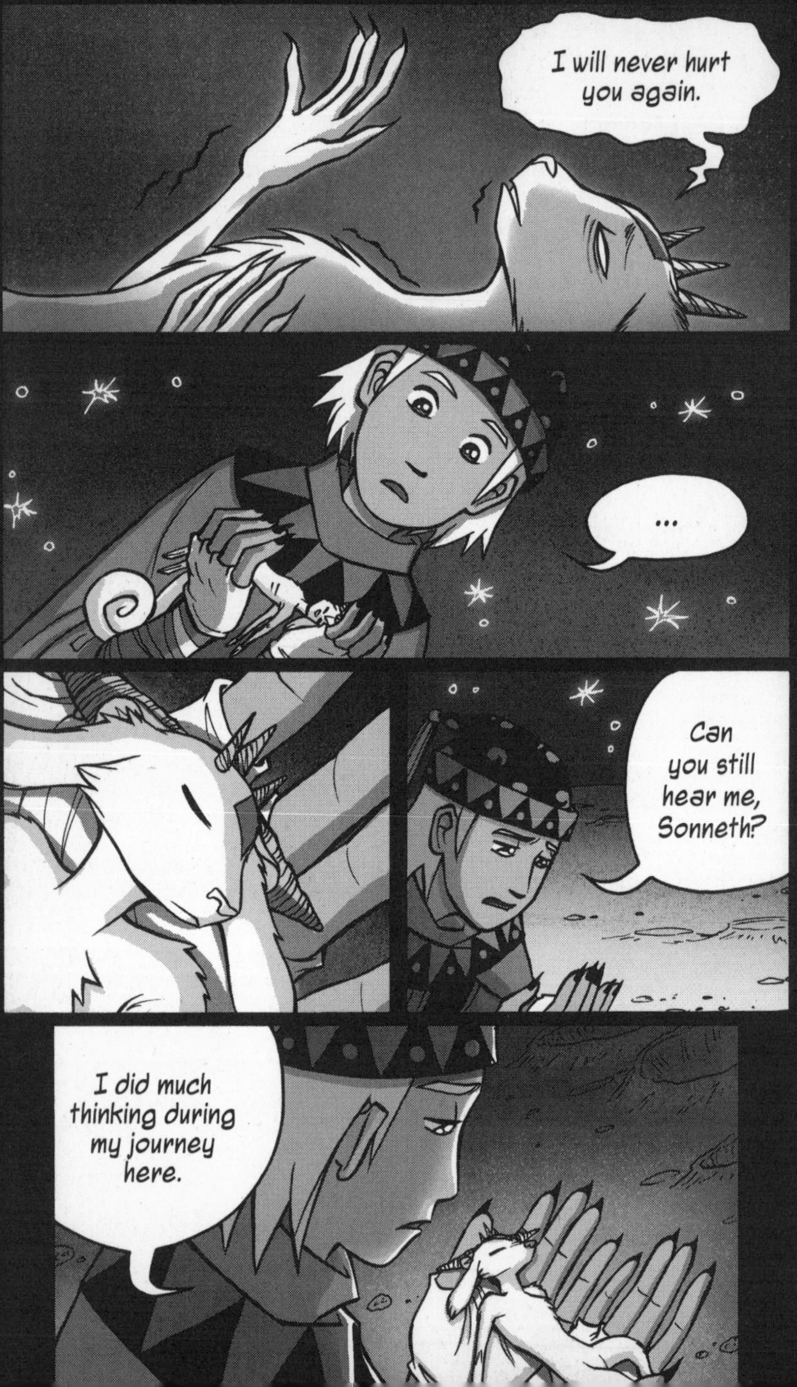
I will never hurt you again.
...
Can you still hear me, Sonneth?
I did much thinking during my journey here.

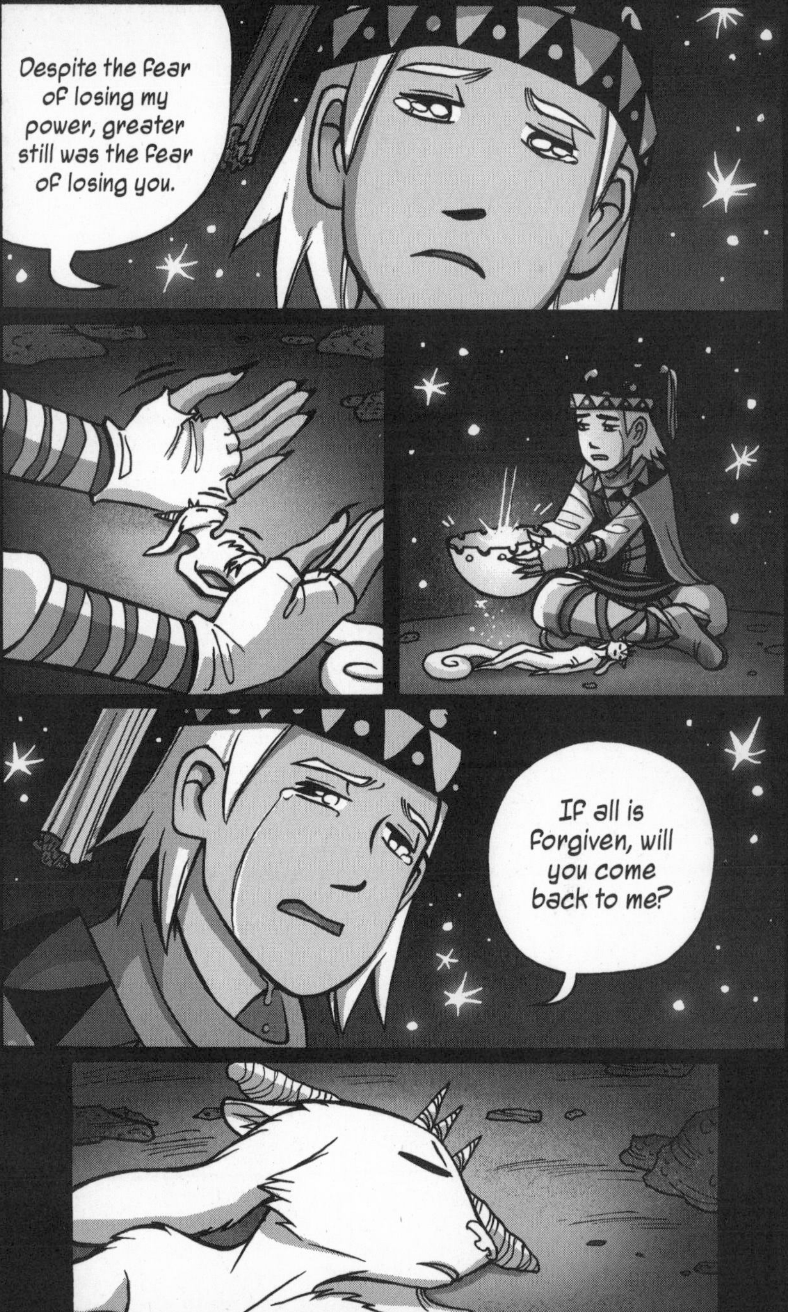
Despite the fear of losing my power, greater still was the fear of losing you.
If all is forgiven, will you come back to me?

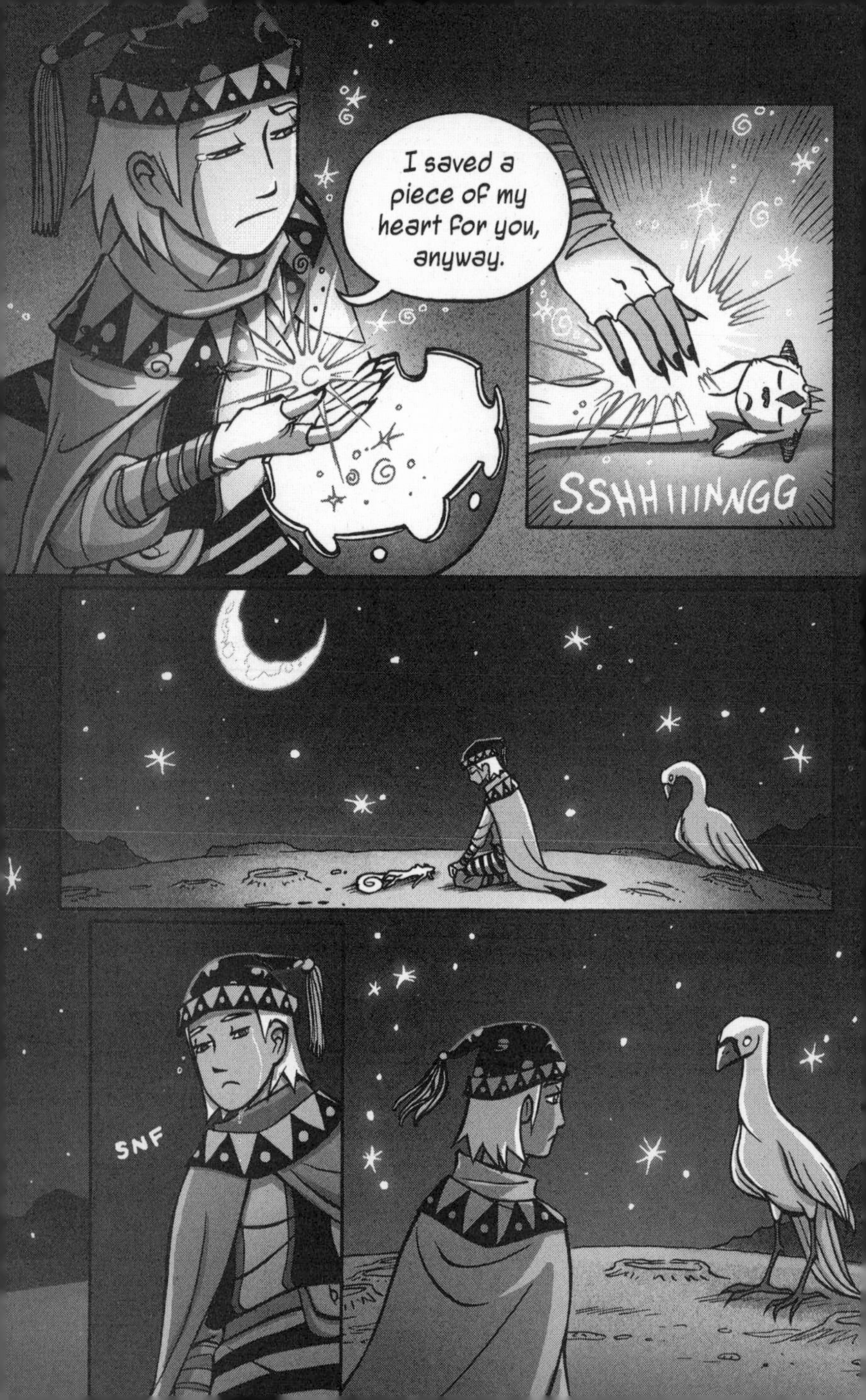
I saved a piece of my heart for you, anyway.
SSHHIIINNGG
SNF

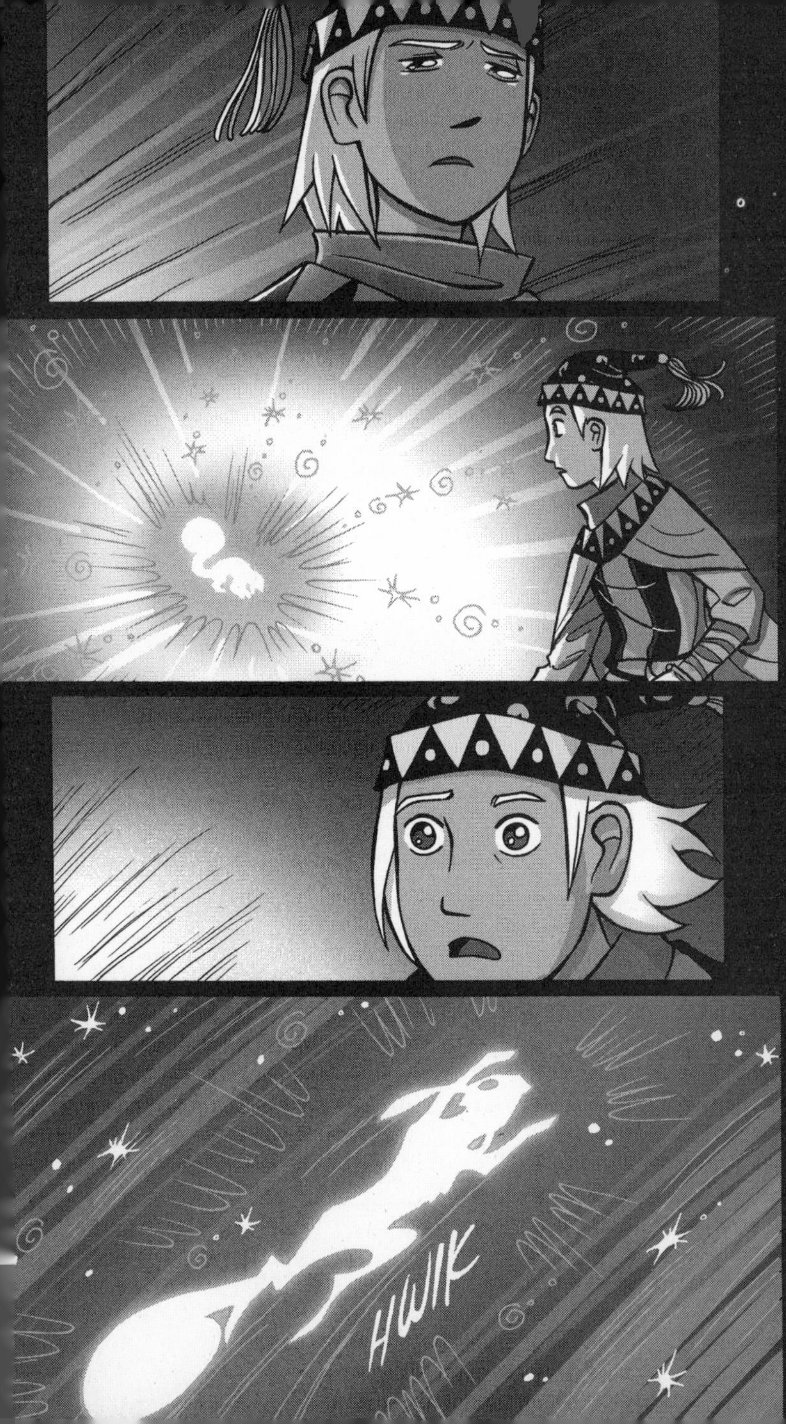
HWIK

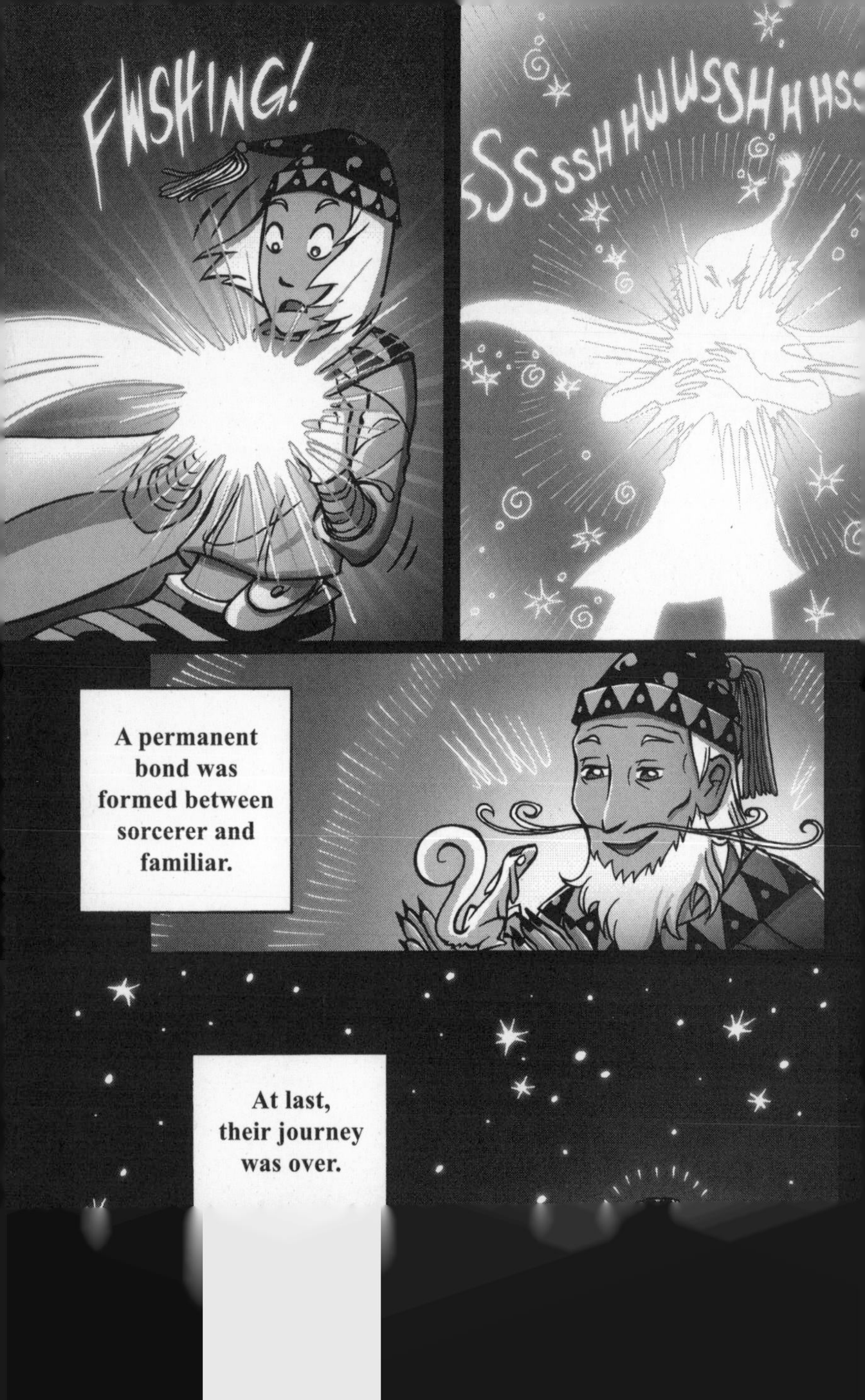
FWSHING!
SSSssSHHWWSSHHHSS
A permanent bond was formed between sorcerer and familiar.
At last, their journey was over.

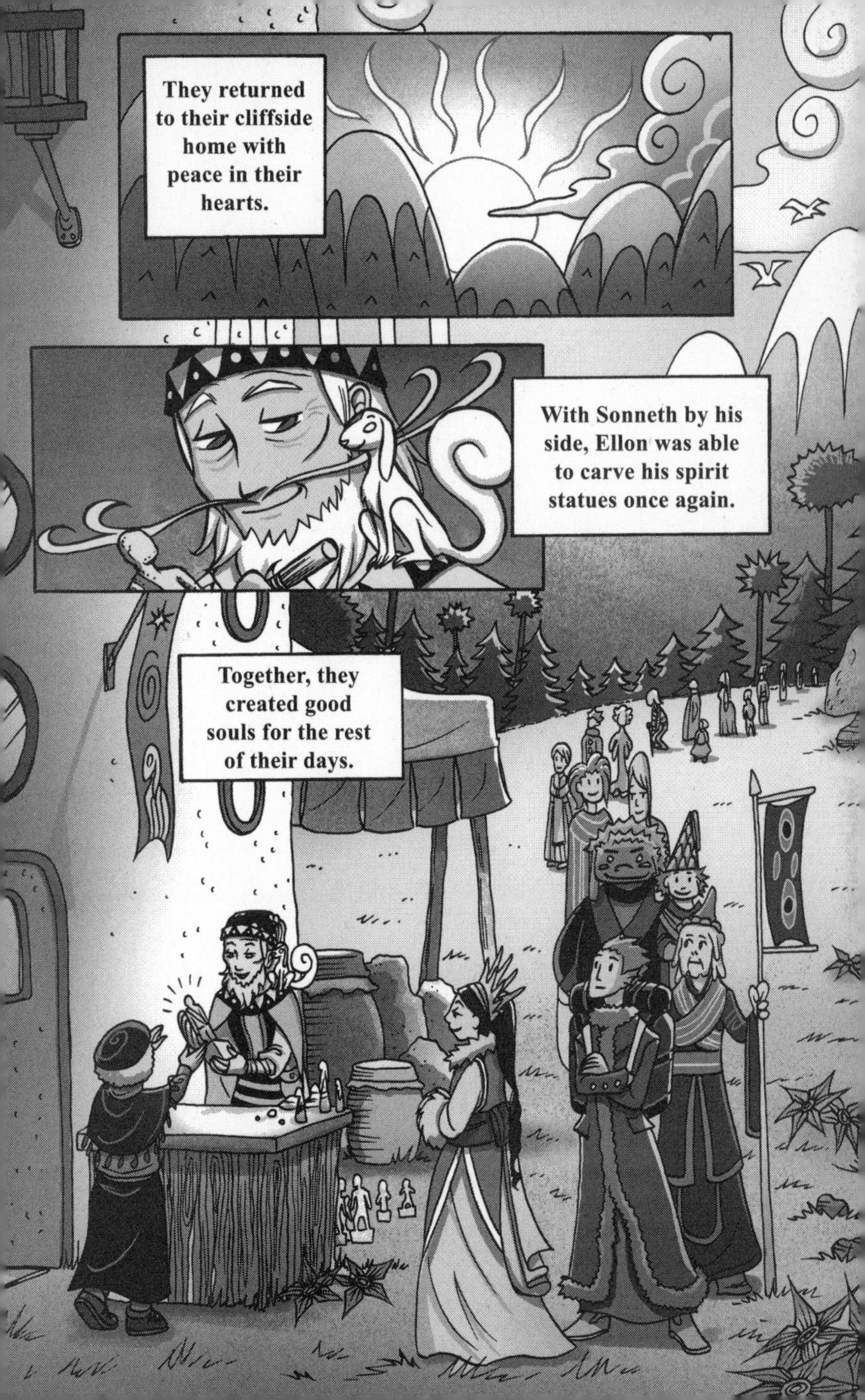
They returned to their cliffside home with peace in their hearts.
With Sonneth by his side, Ellon was able to carve his spirit statues once again.
Together, they created good souls for the rest of their days.

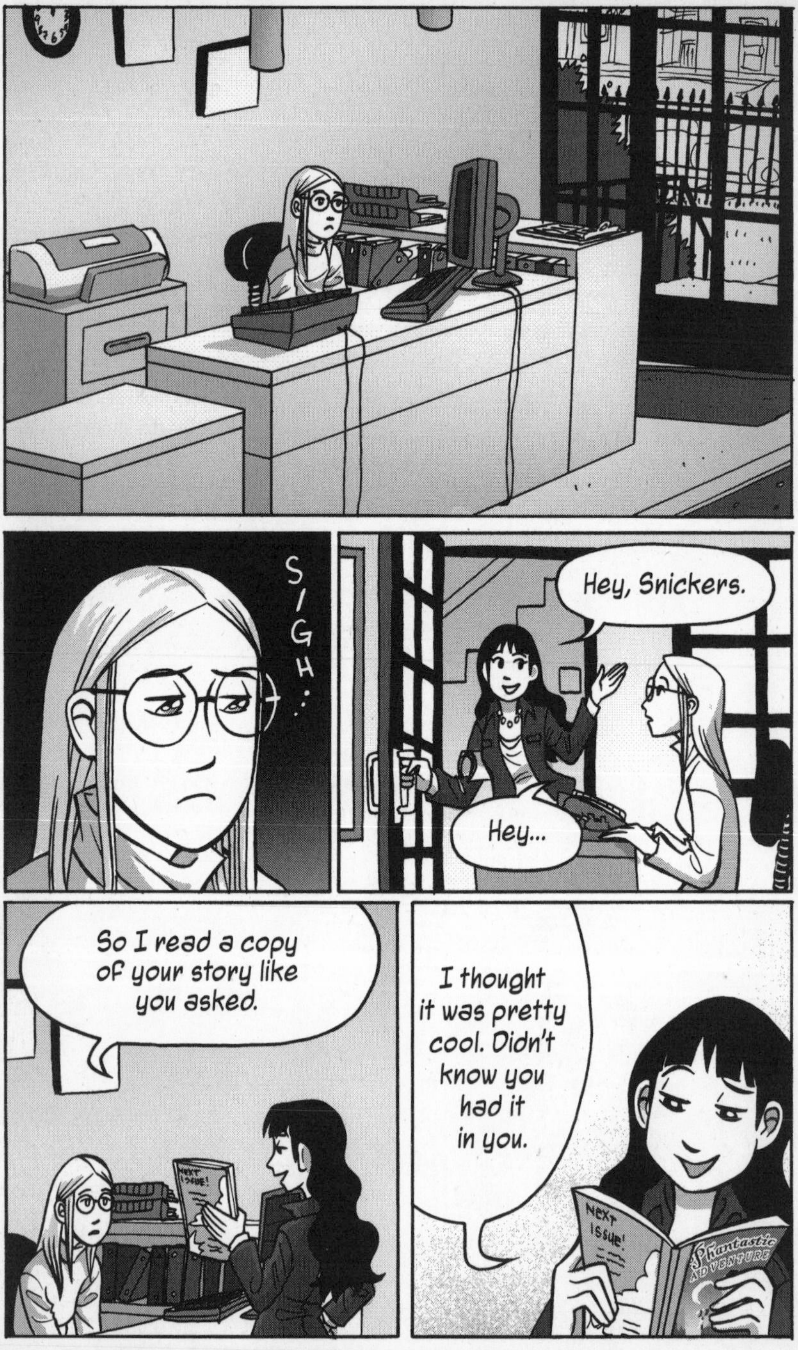
SIGH...
Hey, Snickers.
Hey...
So I read a copy of your story like you asked.
NEXT ISSUE!
I thought it was pretty cool. Didn't know you had it in you.
NEXT ISSUE!
Phantastic ADVENTURE

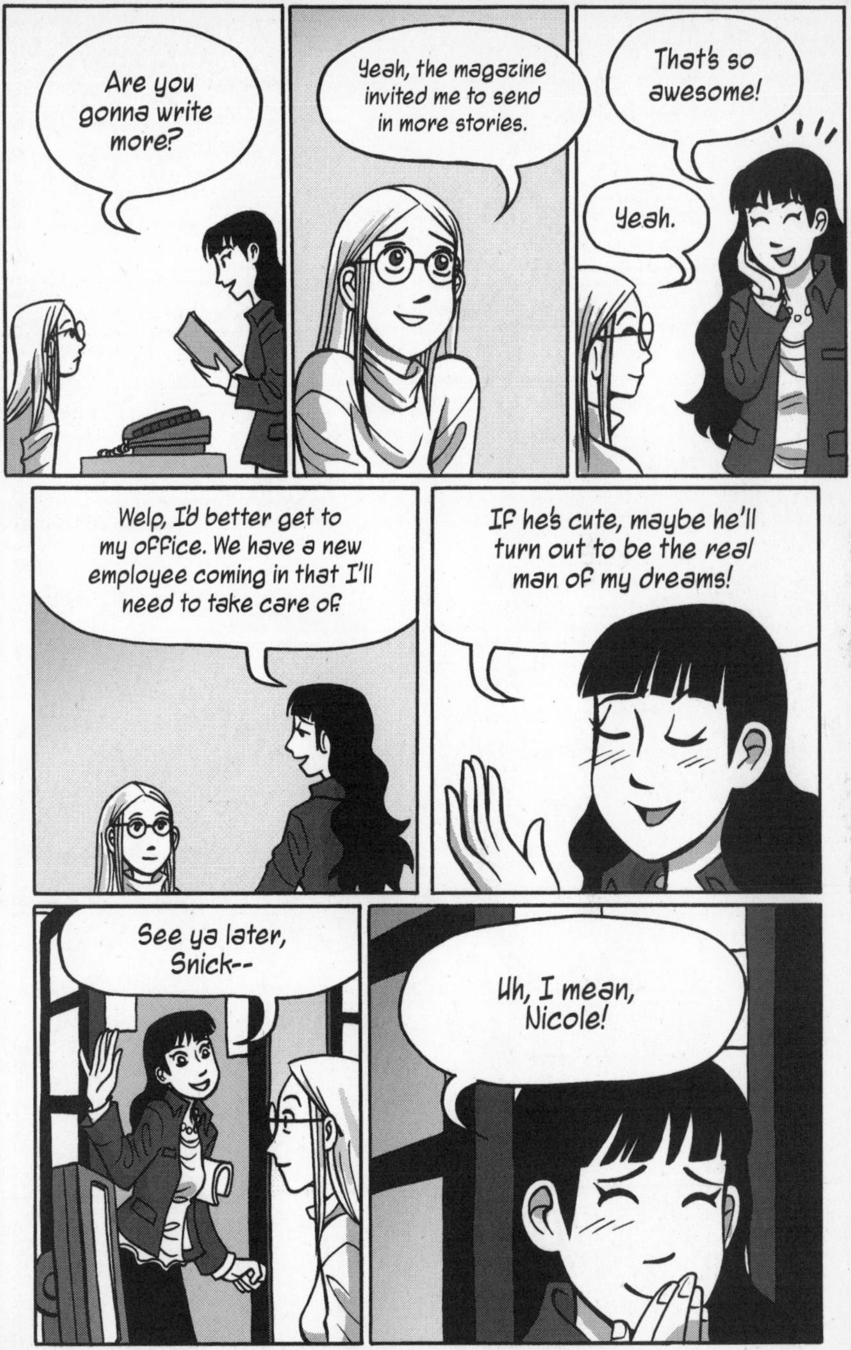
Are you gonna write more?
Yeah, the magazine invited me to send in more stories.
That's so awesome!
Yeah.
Welp, I'd better get to my office. We have a new employee coming in that I'll need to take care of.
If he's cute, maybe he'll turn out to be the *real* man of my dreams!
See ya later, Snick--
Uh, I mean, Nicole!

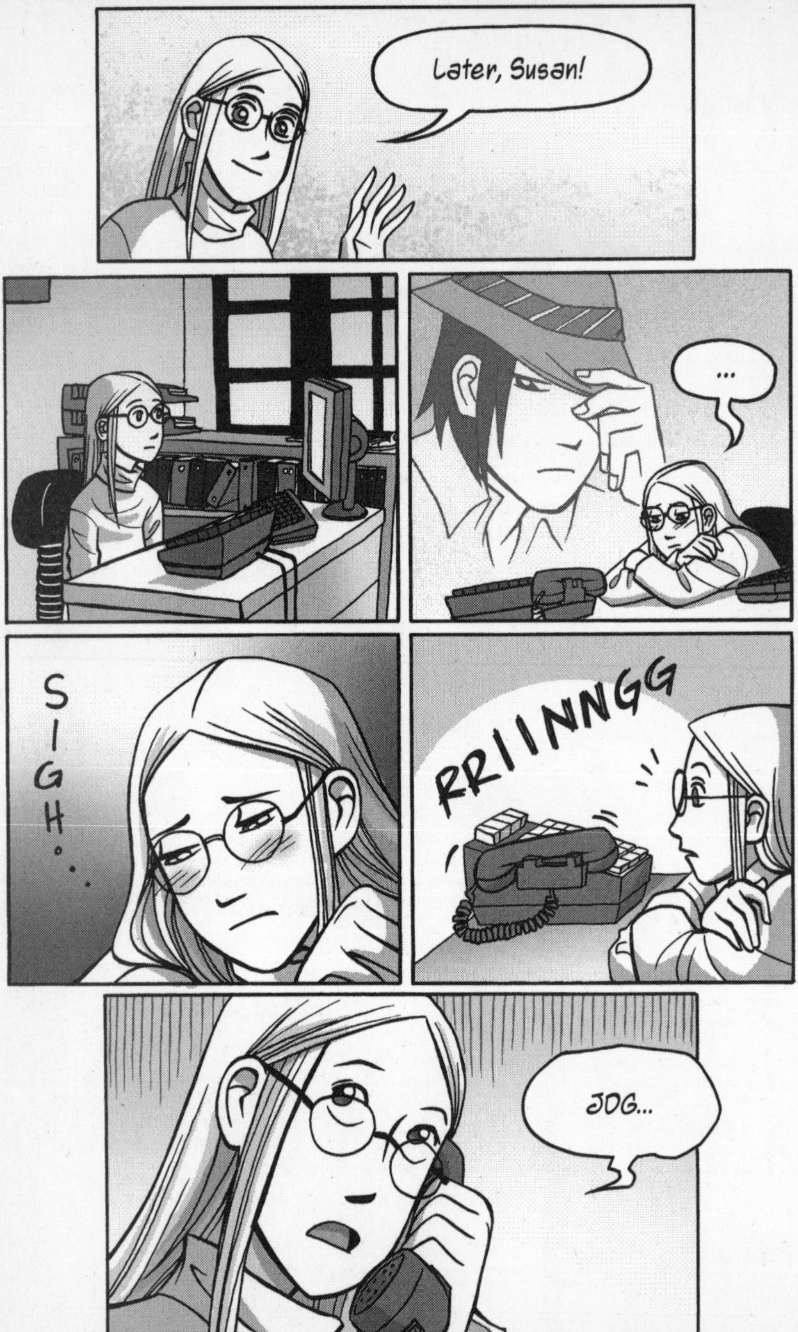
Later, Susan!
...
SIGH...
RRIINNGG
JOG...

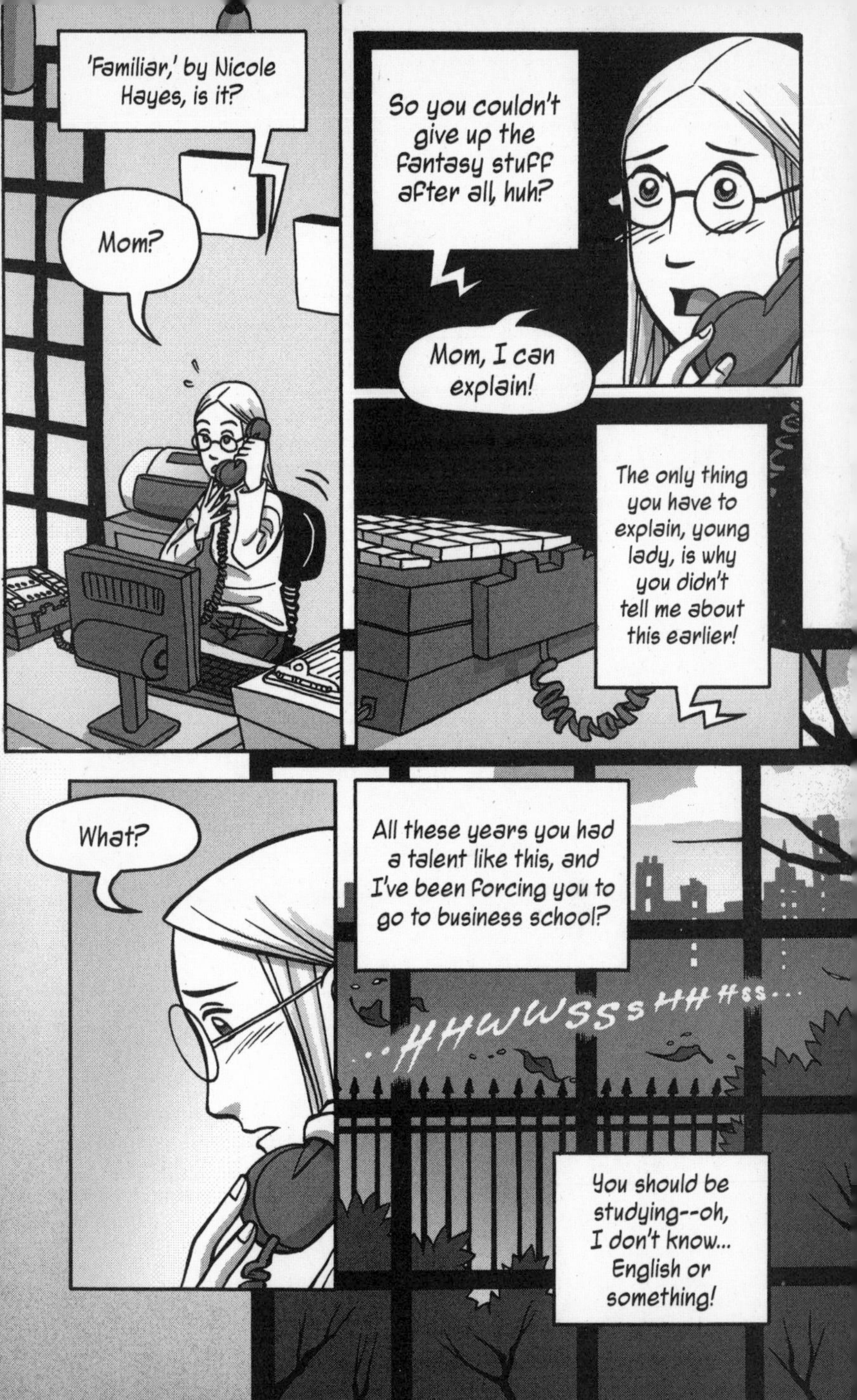
'Familiar,' by Nicole Hayes, is it?
Mom?
So you couldn't give up the fantasy stuff after all, huh?
Mom, I can explain!
The only thing you have to explain, young lady, is why you didn't tell me about this earlier!
What?
All these years you had a talent like this, and I've been forcing you to go to business school?
..HHWWSSSSHHHSS...
You should be studying--oh, I don't know... English or something!

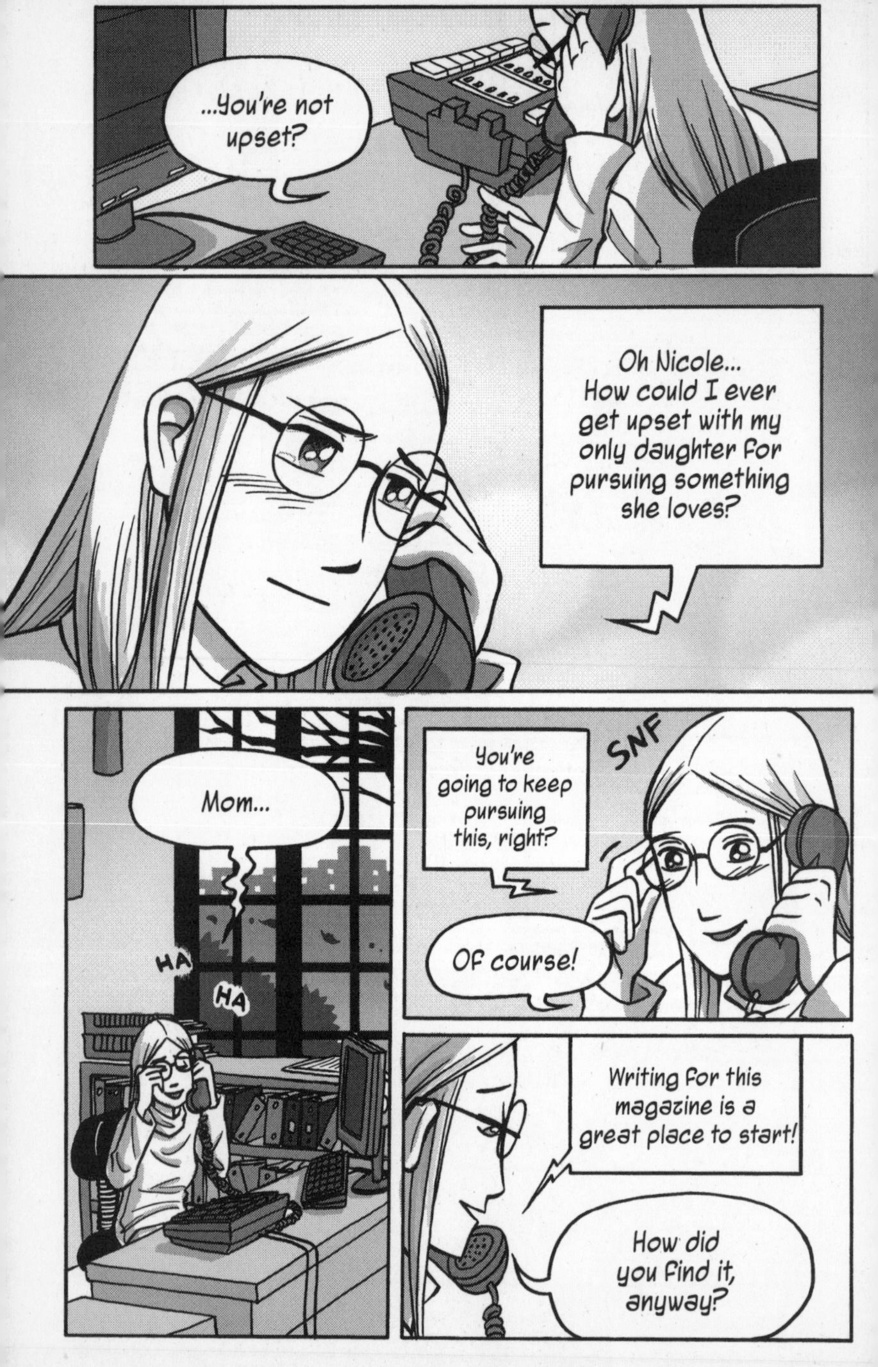
...You're not upset?
Oh Nicole... How could I ever get upset with my only daughter for pursuing something she loves?
Mom...
HA
HA
You're going to keep pursuing this, right?
SNF
Of course!
Writing for this magazine is a great place to start!
How did you find it, anyway?

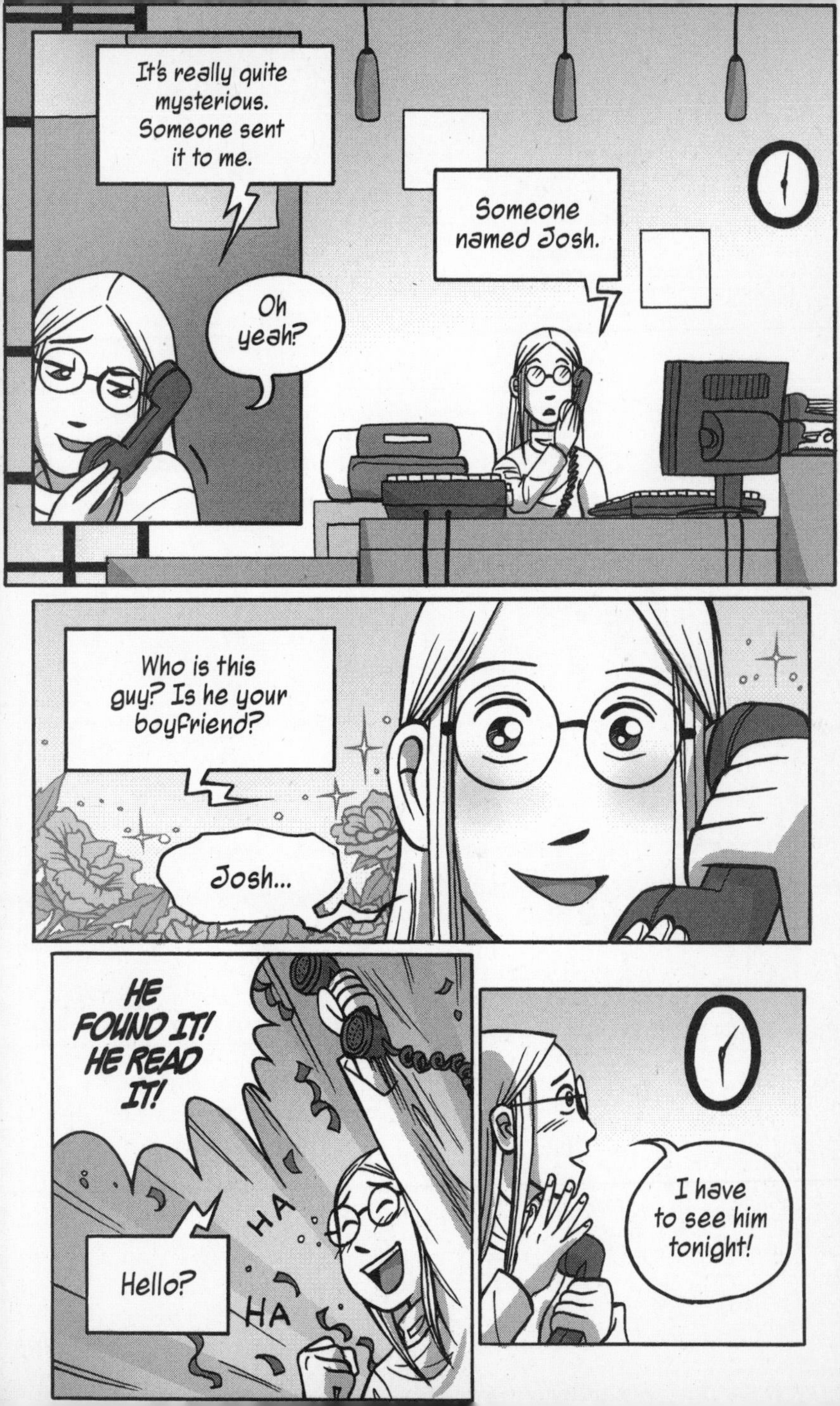
It's really quite mysterious. Someone sent it to me.
Someone named Josh.
Oh yeah?
Who is this guy? Is he your boyfriend?
Josh...
HE FOUND IT! HE READ IT!
HA
HA
Hello?
I have to see him tonight!

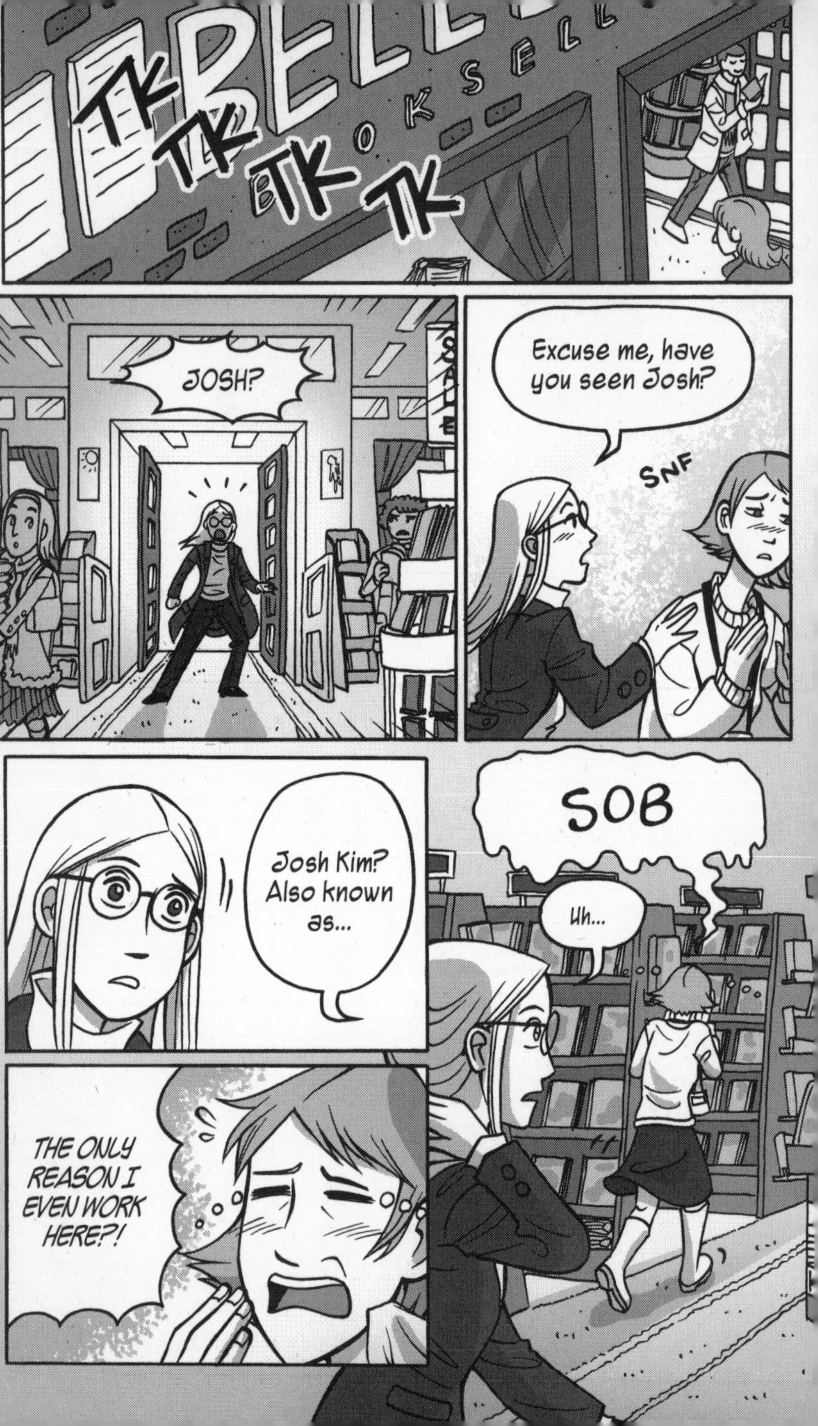

TK TK TK TK
JOSH?
Excuse me, have you seen Josh?
SNF
Josh Kim? Also known as...
THE ONLY REASON I EVEN WORK HERE?!
SOB
Uh...

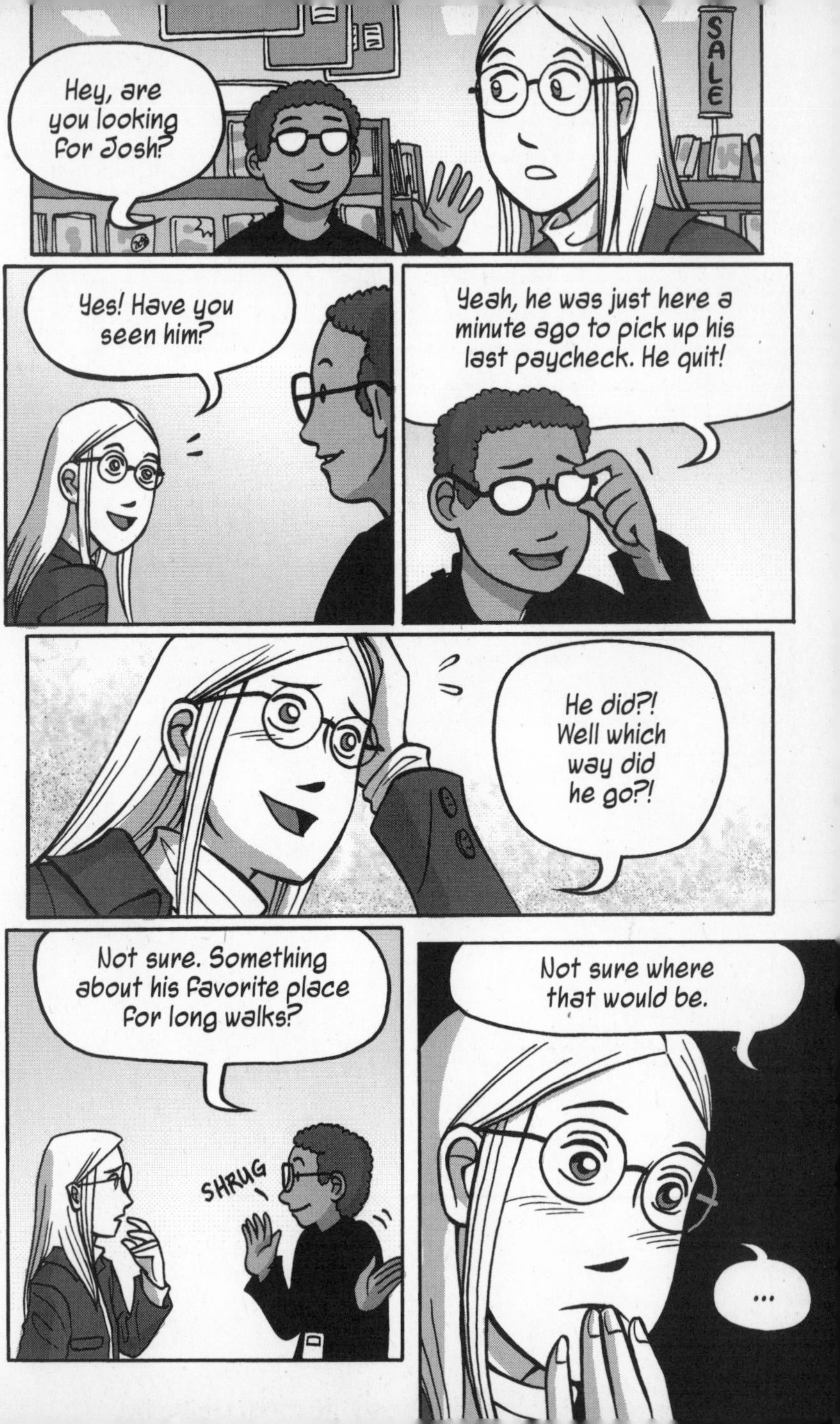
Hey, are you looking for Josh?
SALE
Yes! Have you seen him?
Yeah, he was just here a minute ago to pick up his last paycheck. He quit!
He did?! Well which way did he go?!
Not sure. Something about his favorite place for long walks?
SHRUG
Not sure where that would be.
...

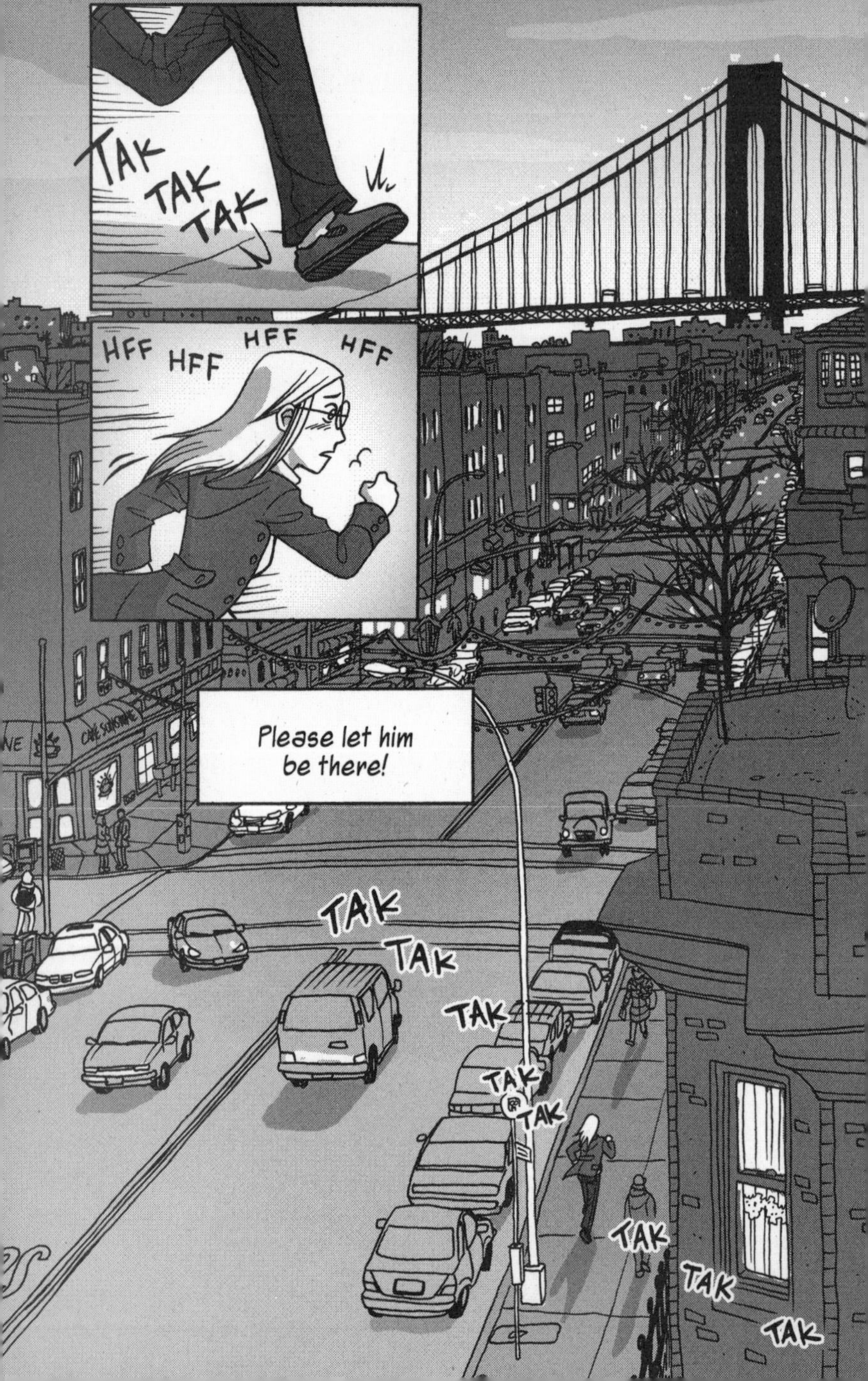
TAK
TAK
TAK
HFF
HFF
HFF
HFF
Please let him be there!
TAK
TAK
TAK
TAK
TAK
TAK
TAK
TAK

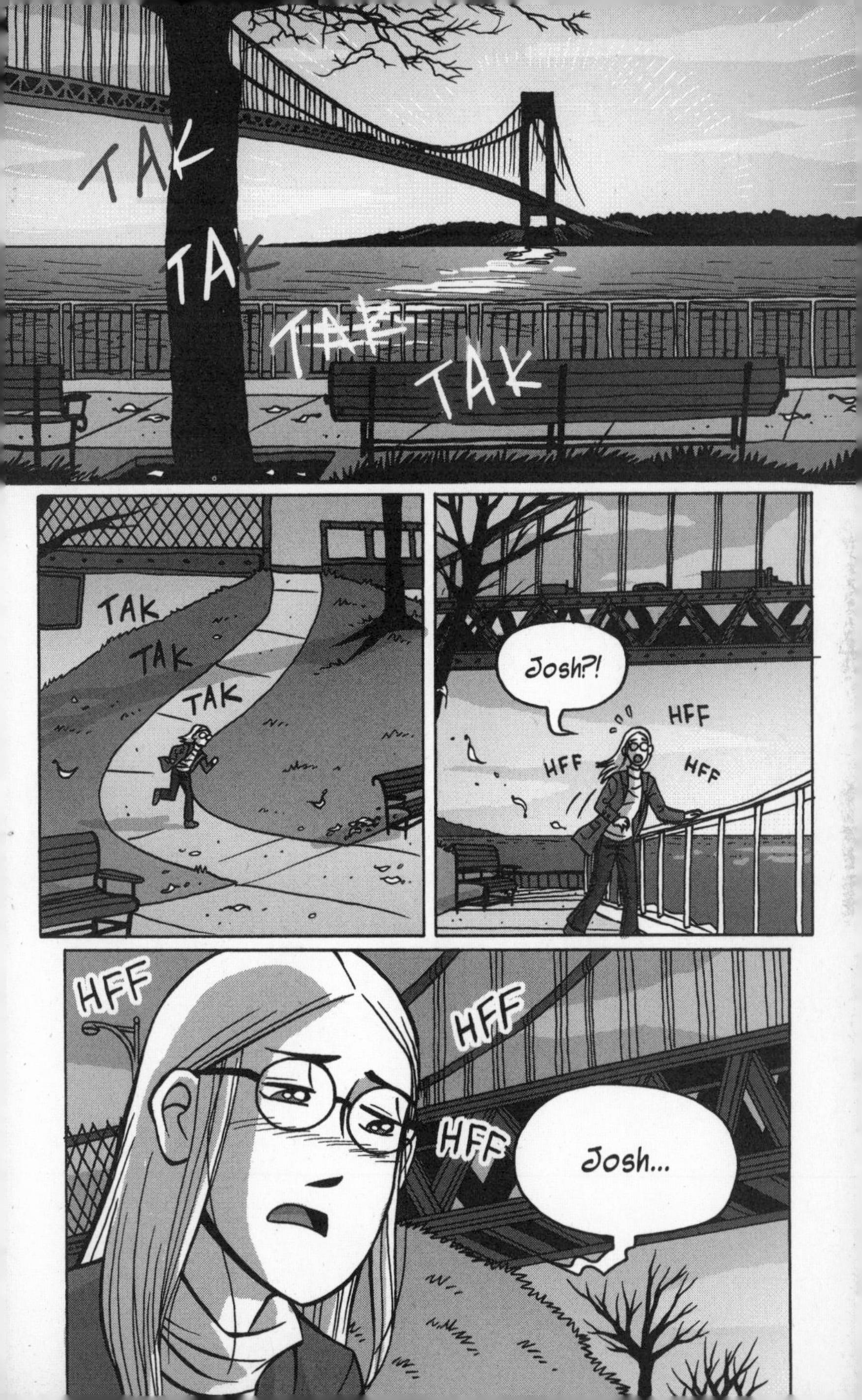
TAK
TAK
TAK
TAK
TAK
TAK
TAK
Josh?!
HFF
HFF
HFF
HFF
HFF
HFF
Josh...

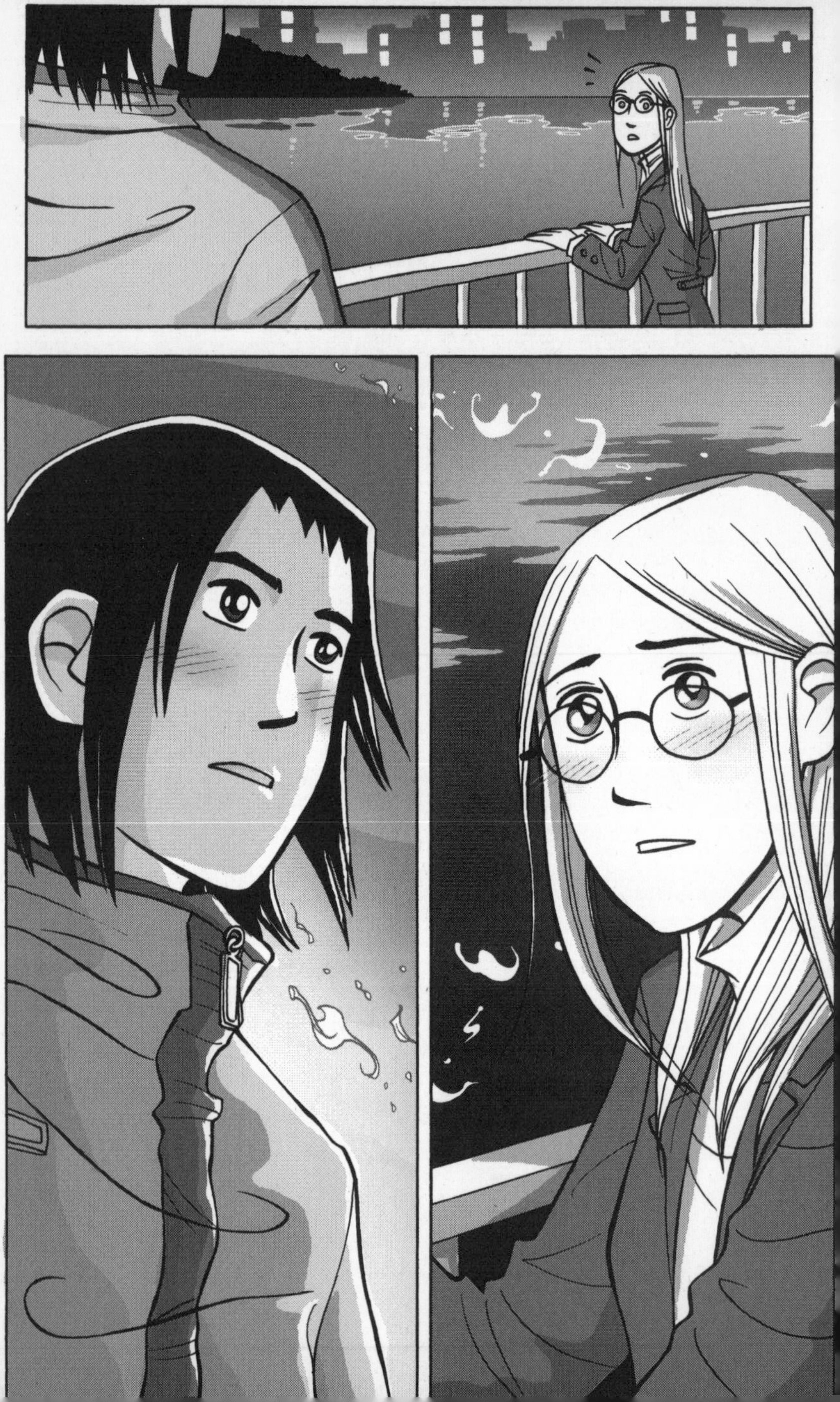

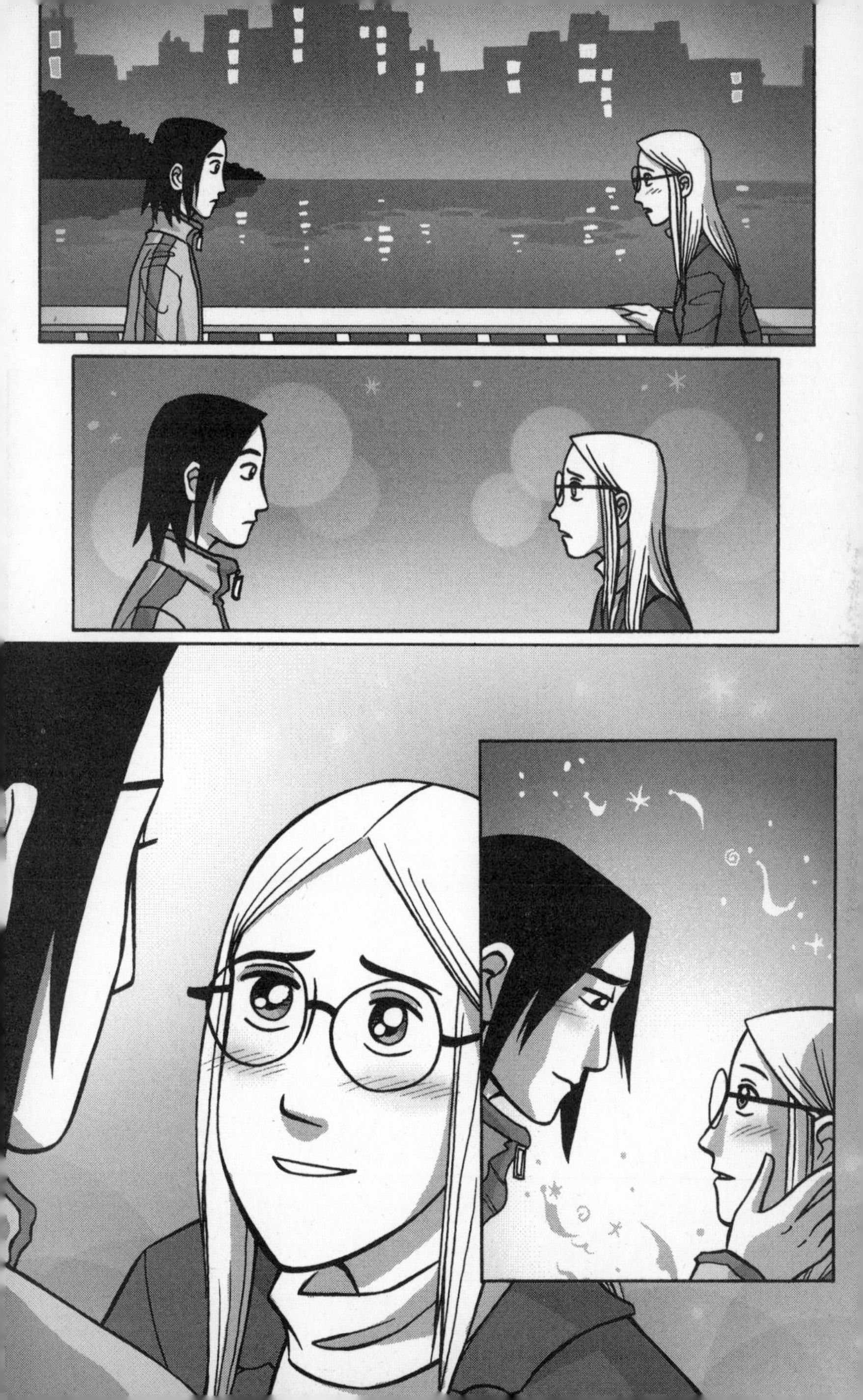

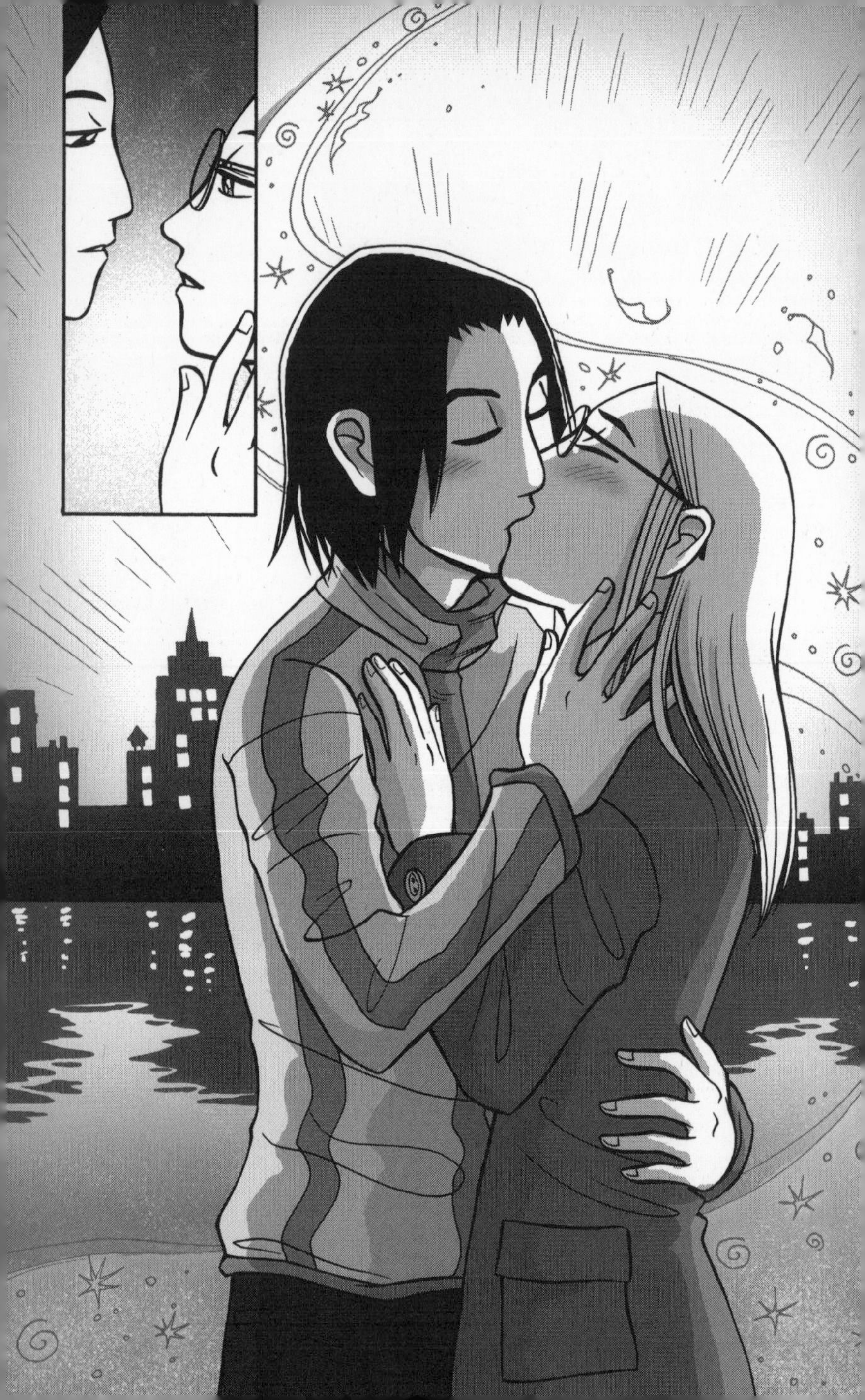

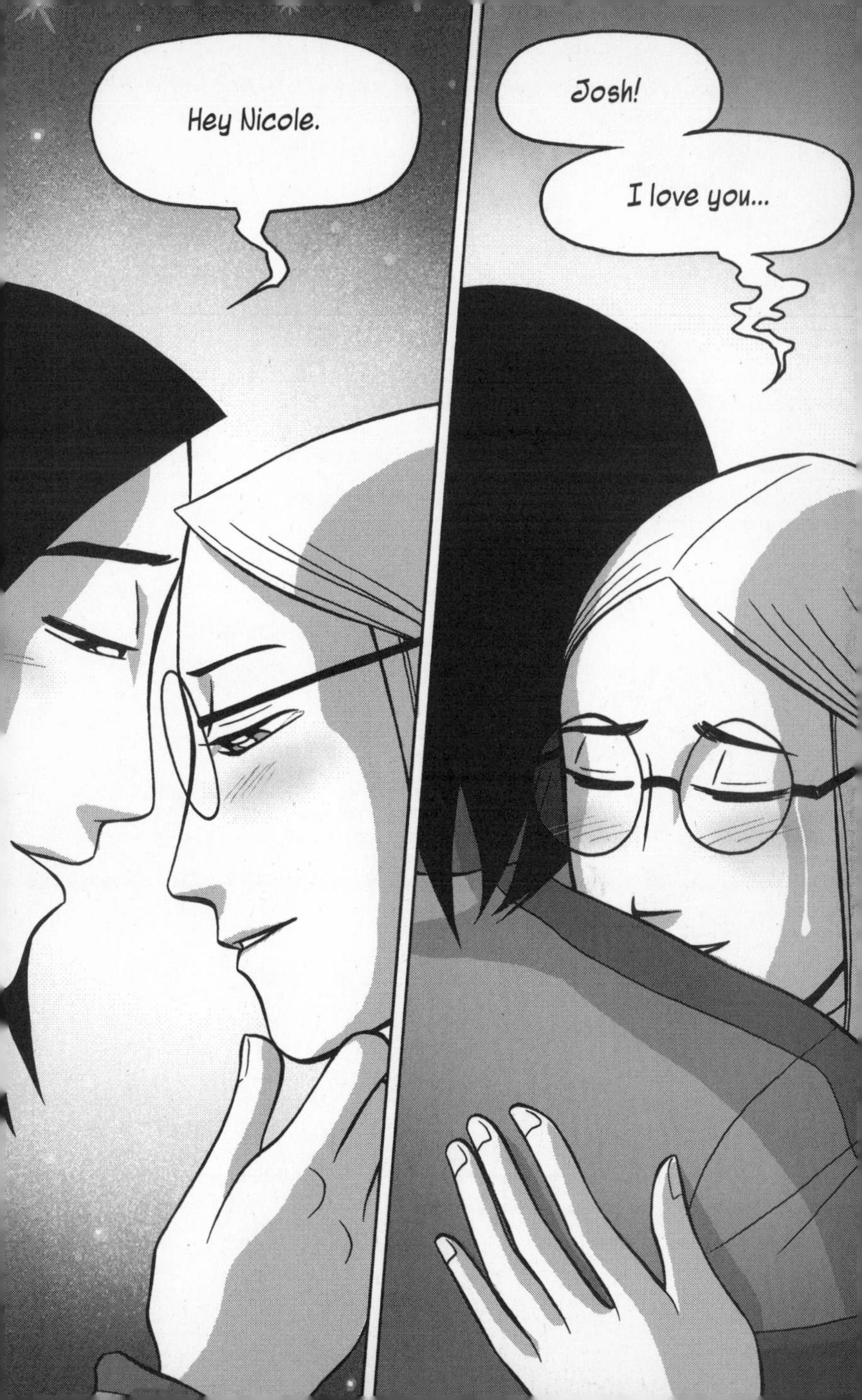
Hey Nicole.
Josh!
I love you...

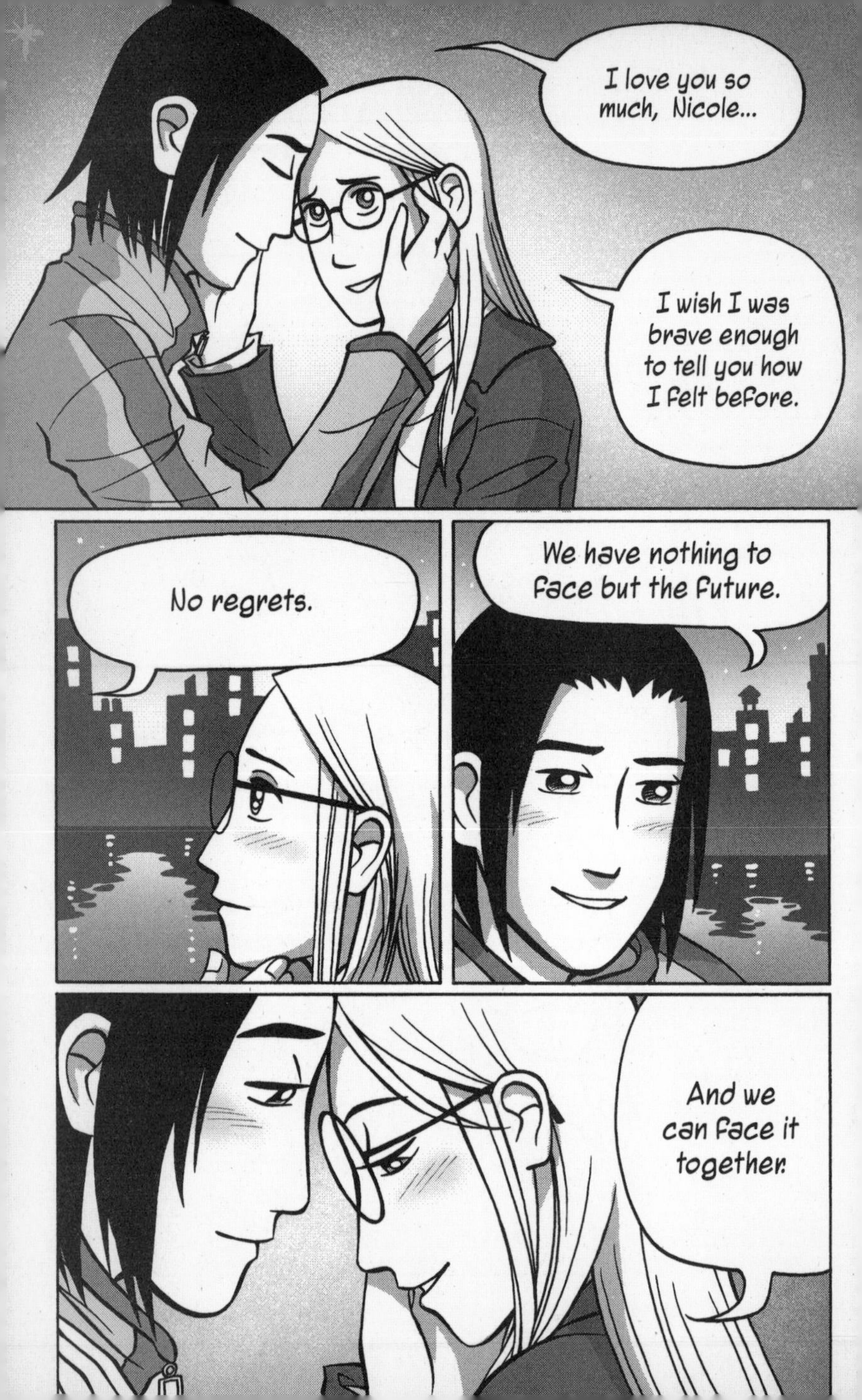
I love you so much, Nicole...
I wish I was brave enough to tell you how I felt before.
No regrets.
We have nothing to face but the future.
And we can face it together.

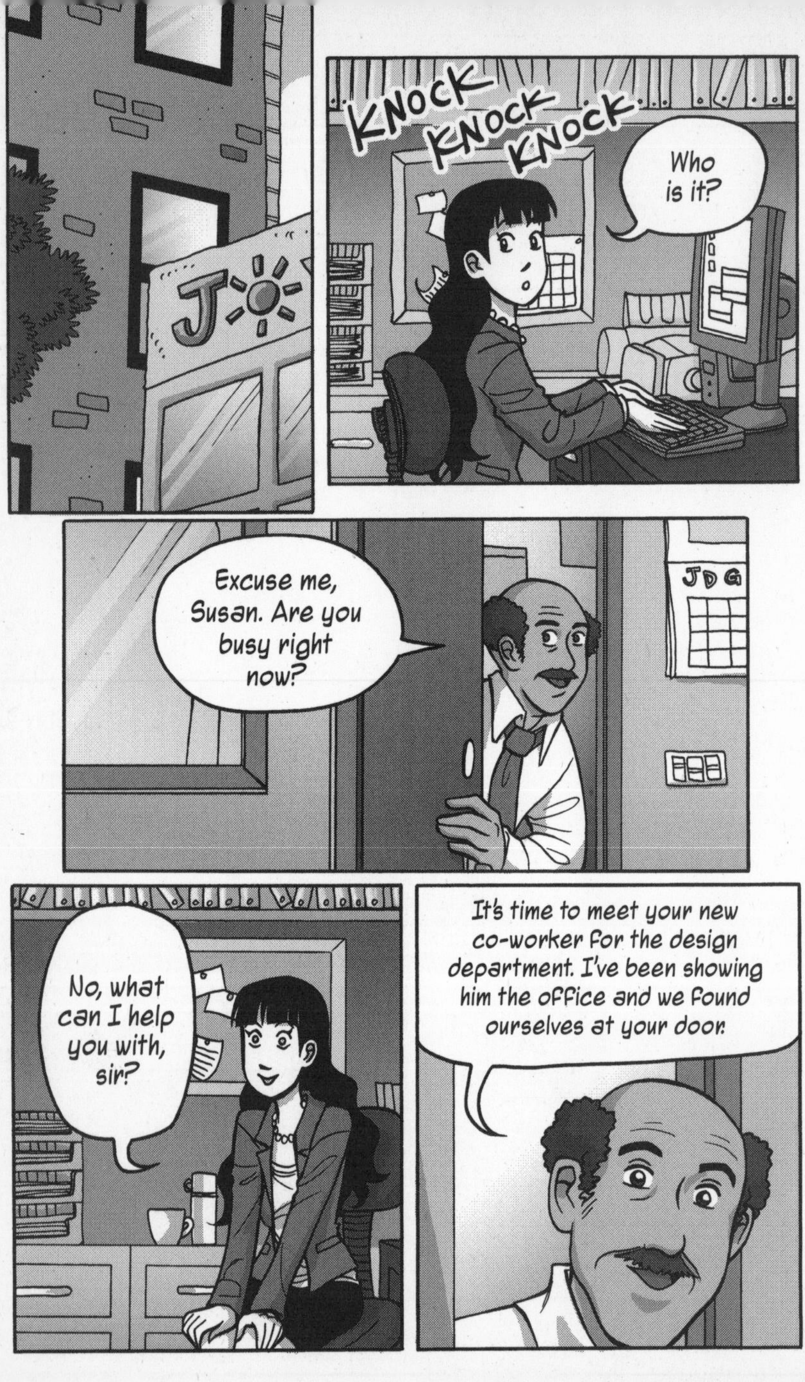
KNOCK KNOCK KNOCK
Who is it?
Excuse me, Susan. Are you busy right now?
No, what can I help you with, sir?
It's time to meet your new co-worker for the design department. I've been showing him the office and we found ourselves at your door.

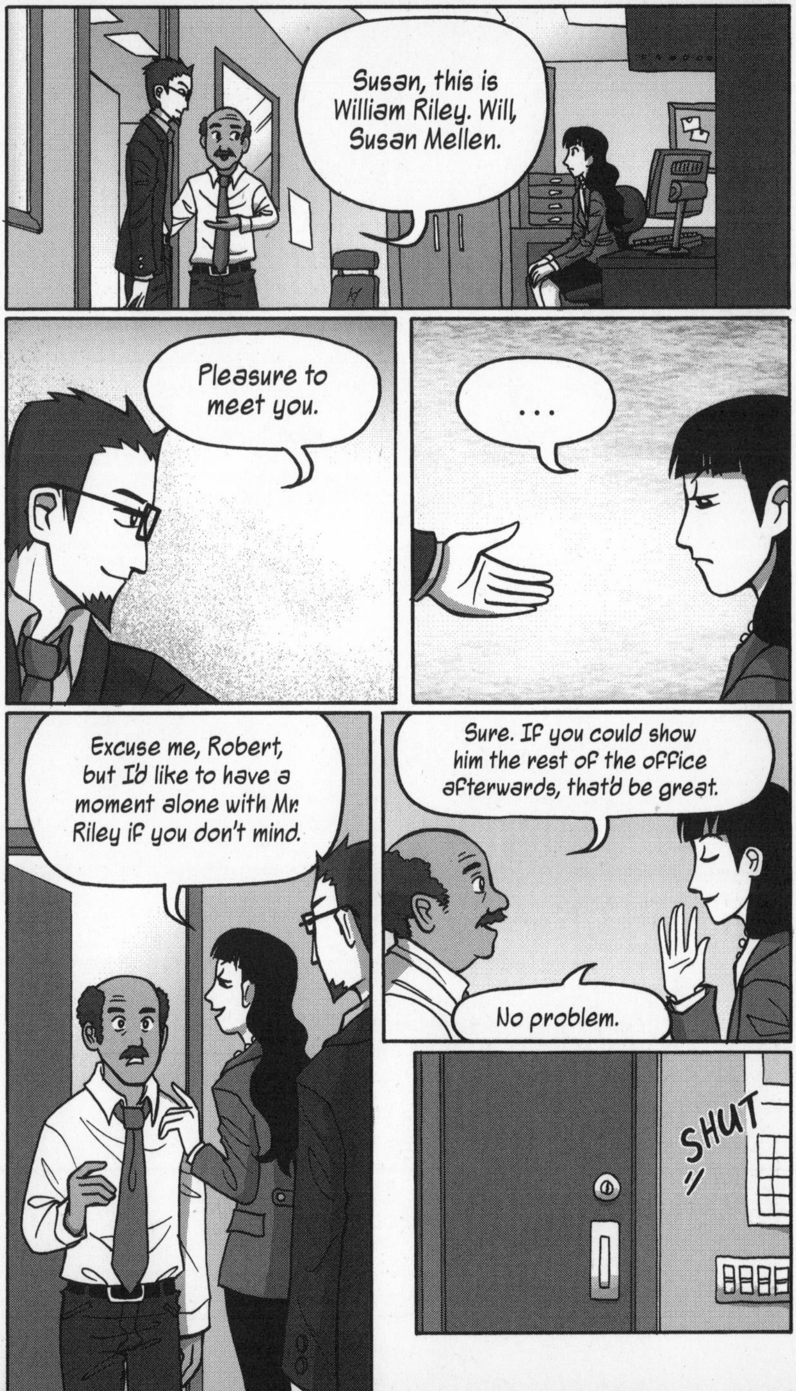
Susan, this is William Riley. Will, Susan Mellen.
Pleasure to meet you.
...
Excuse me, Robert, but I'd like to have a moment alone with Mr. Riley if you don't mind.
Sure. If you could show him the rest of the office afterwards, that'd be great.
No problem.
SHUT

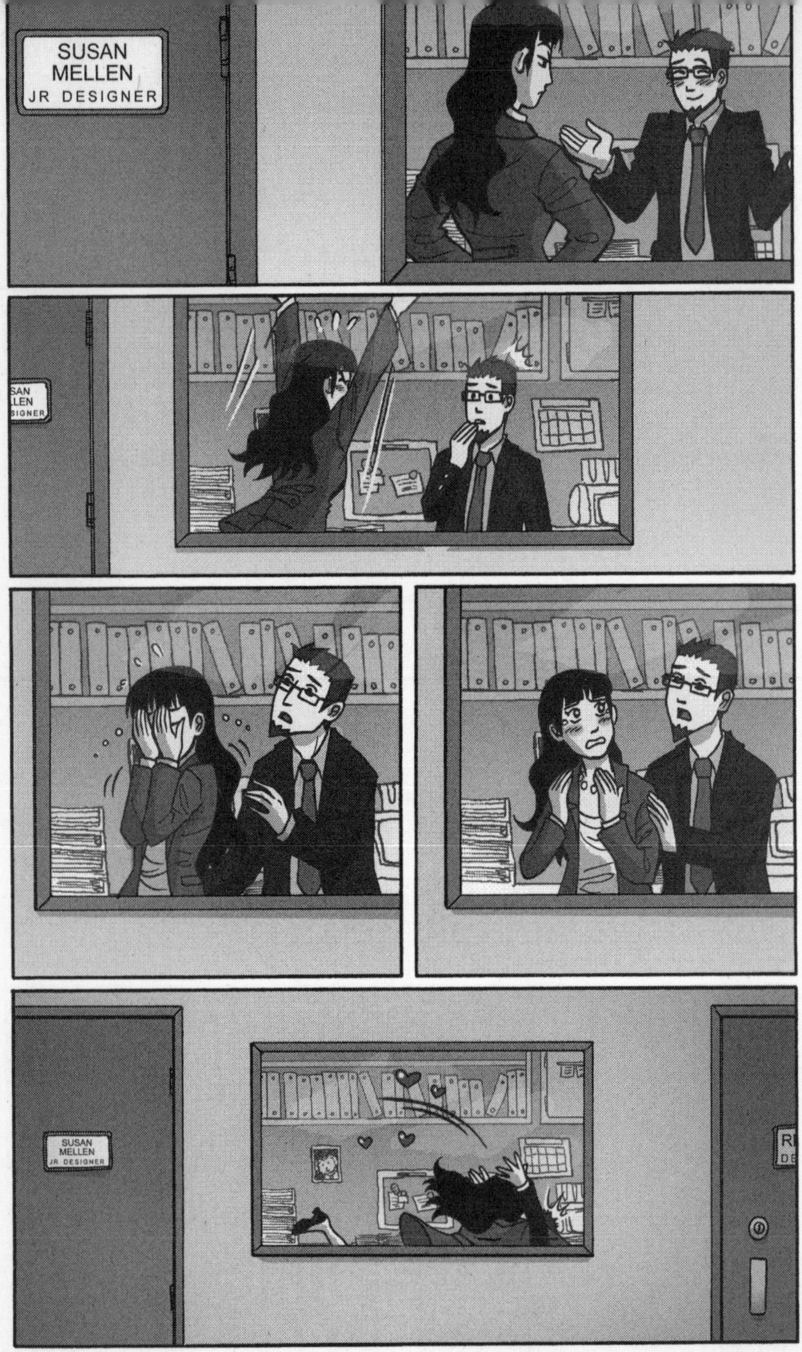
SUSAN
MELLEN
JR DESIGNER
SUSAN
MELLEN
JR DESIGNER

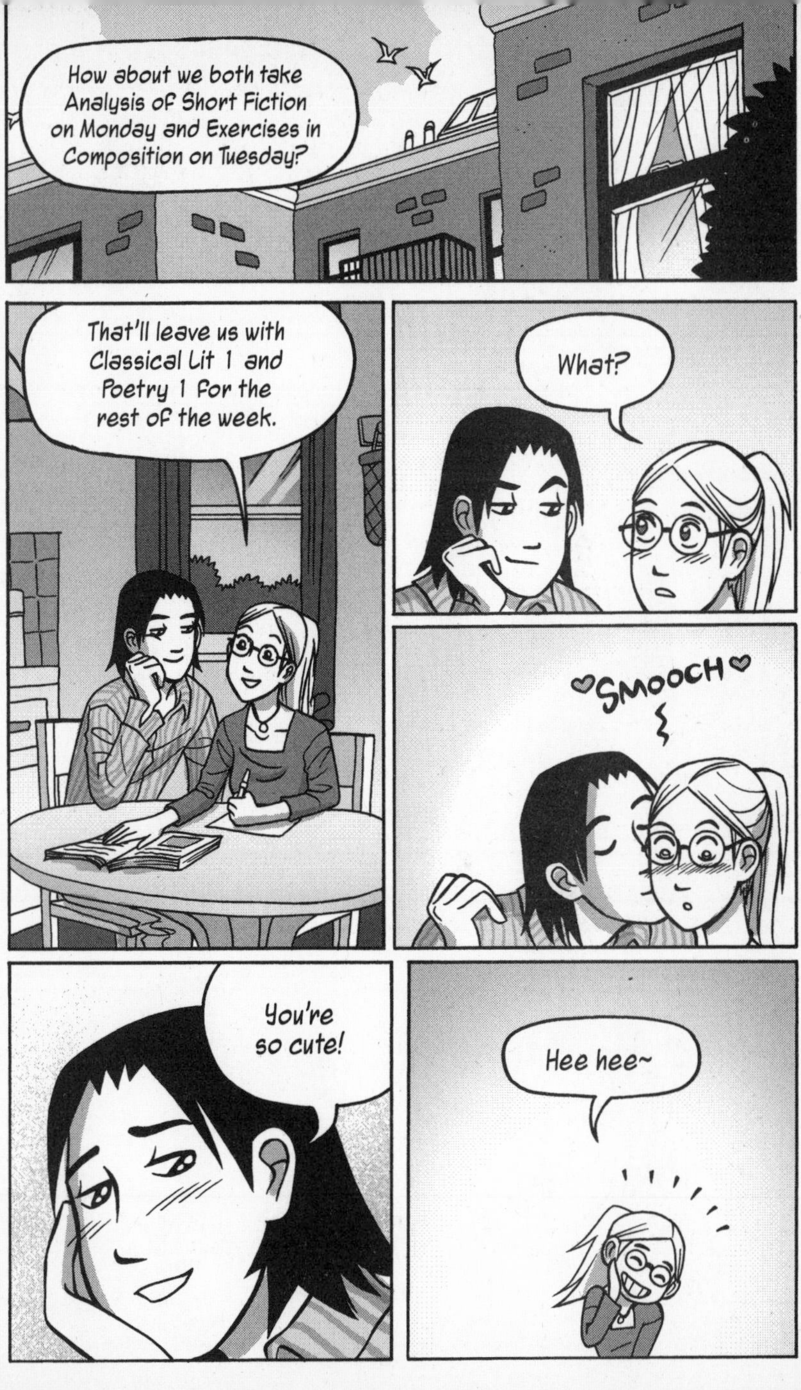
How about we both take Analysis of Short Fiction on Monday and Exercises in Composition on Tuesday?
That'll leave us with Classical Lit 1 and Poetry 1 for the rest of the week.
What?
SMOOCH
You're so cute!
Hee hee~

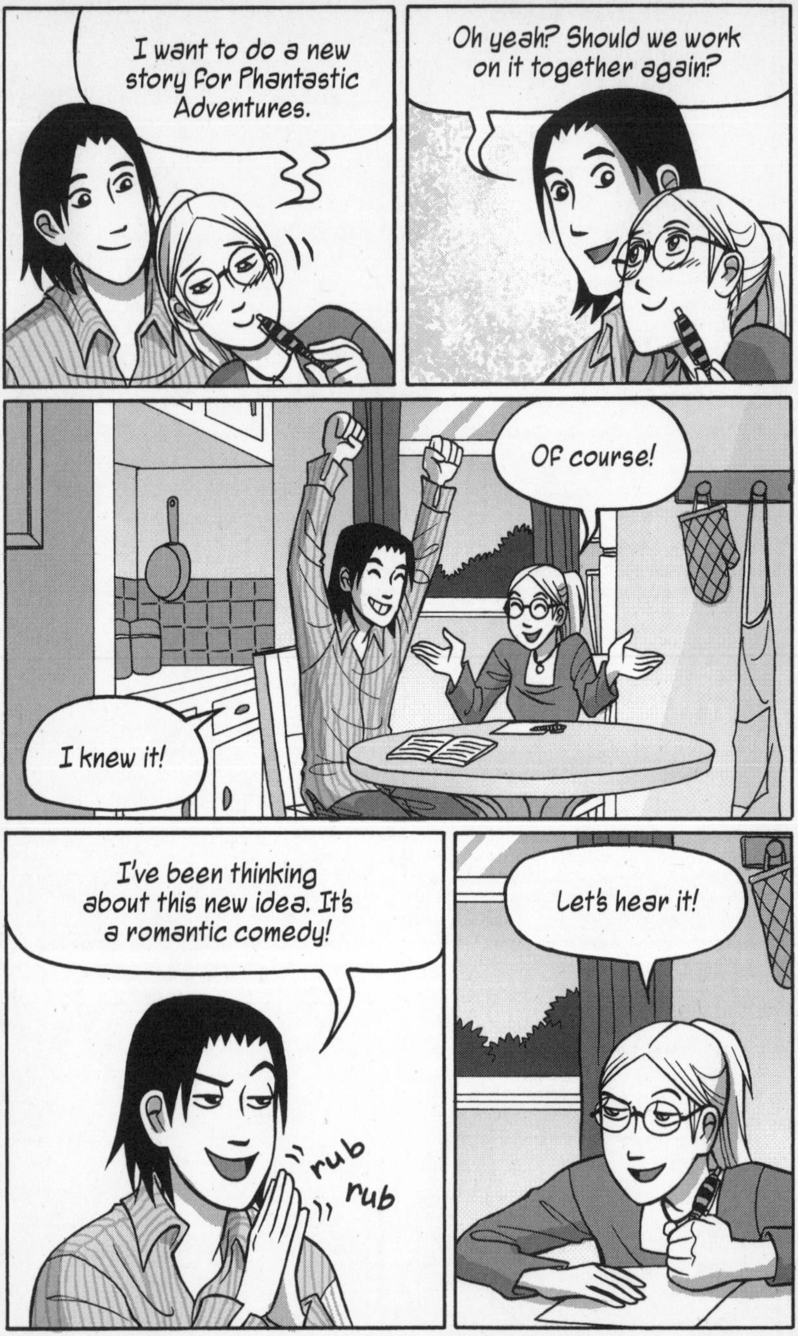
I want to do a new story for Phantastic Adventures.
Oh yeah? Should we work on it together again?
Of course!
I knew it!
I've been thinking about this new idea. It's a romantic comedy!
rub rub
Let's hear it!

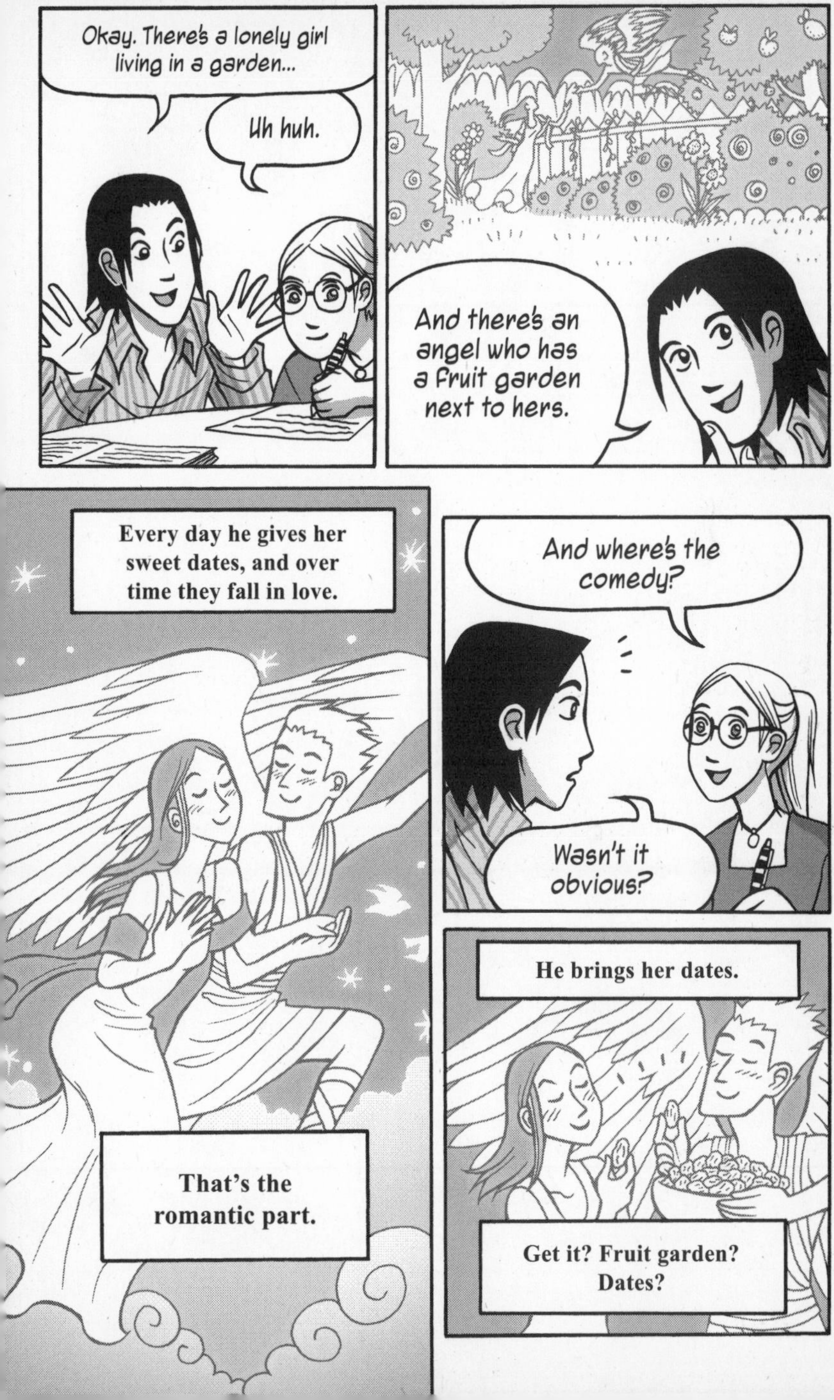
Okay. There's a lonely girl living in a garden...
Uh huh.
And there's an angel who has a fruit garden next to hers.
Every day he gives her sweet dates, and over time they fall in love.
That's the romantic part.
And where's the comedy?
Wasn't it obvious?
He brings her dates.
Get it? Fruit garden? Dates?

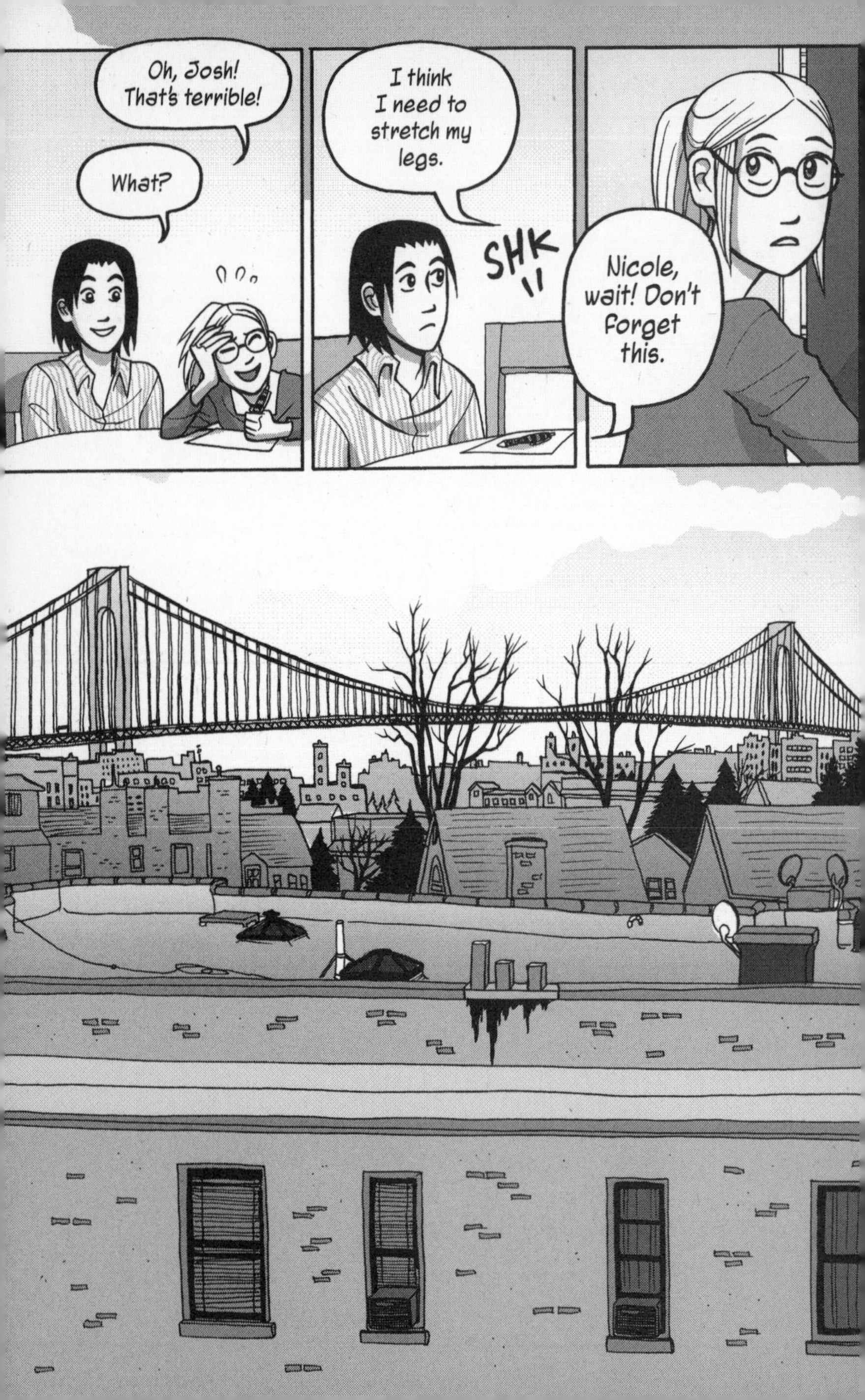
Oh, Josh! That's terrible!
What?
I think I need to stretch my legs.
SHK
Nicole, wait! Don't forget this.

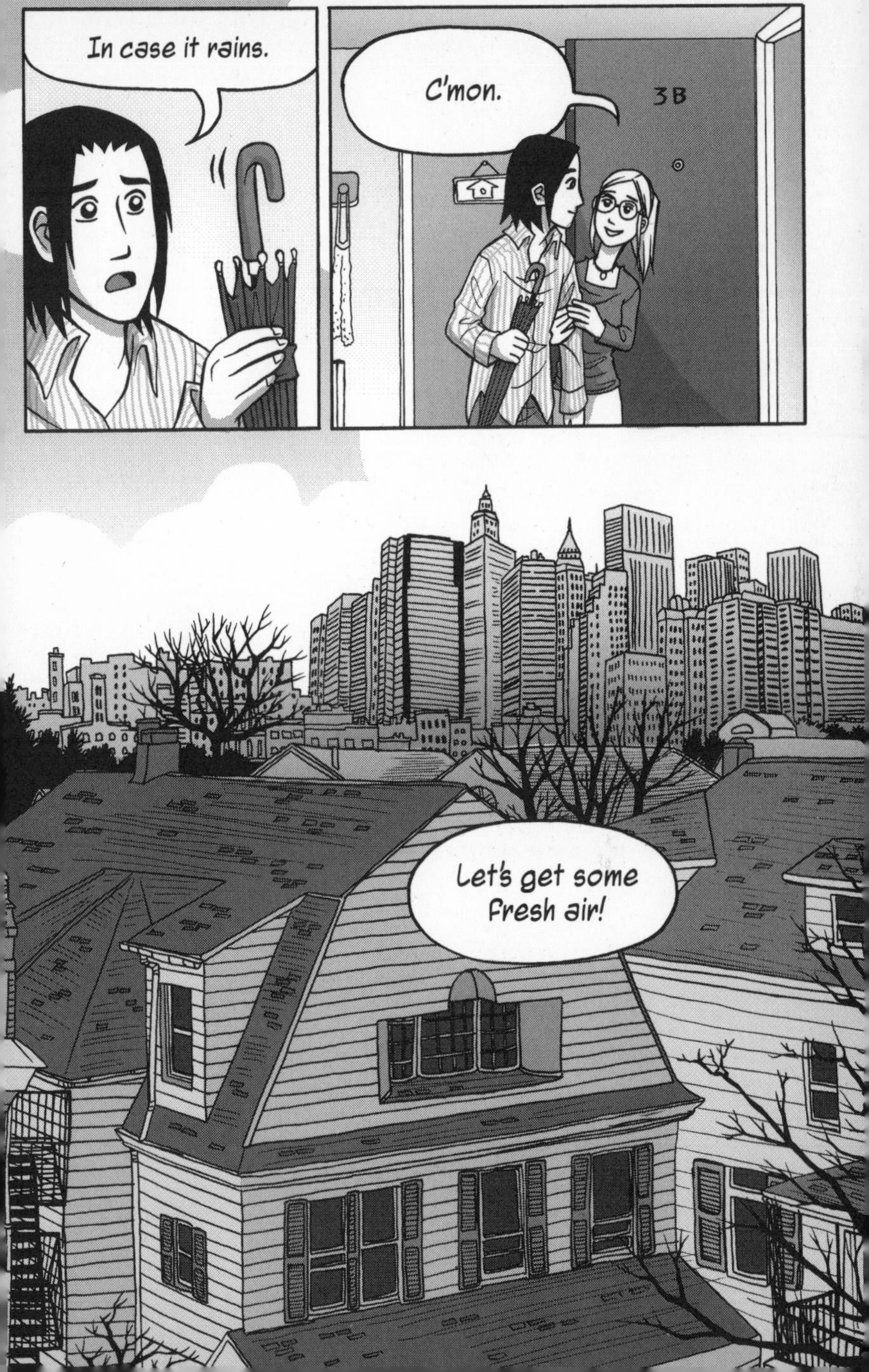
In case it rains.
C'mon.
3B
Let's get some fresh air!

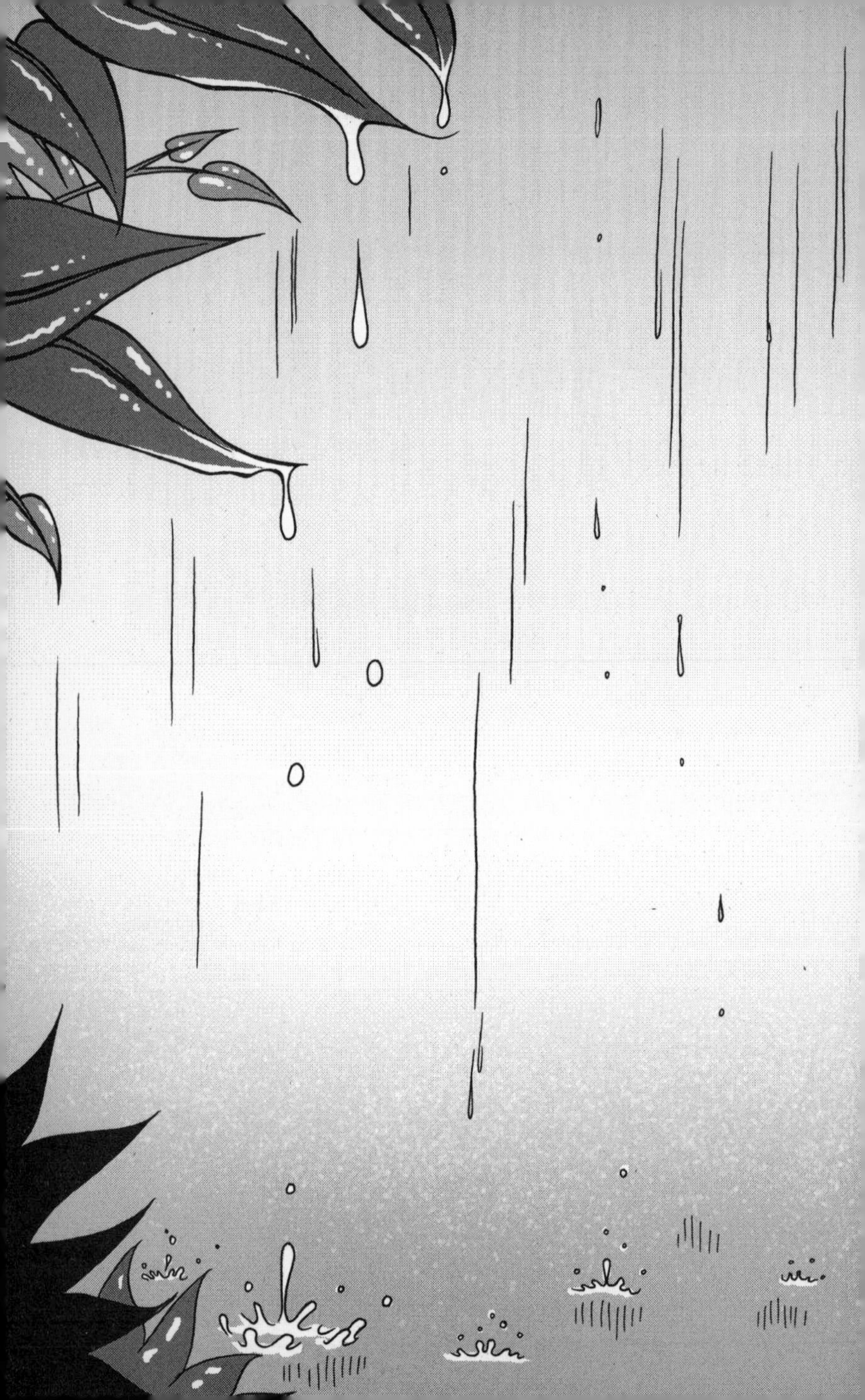

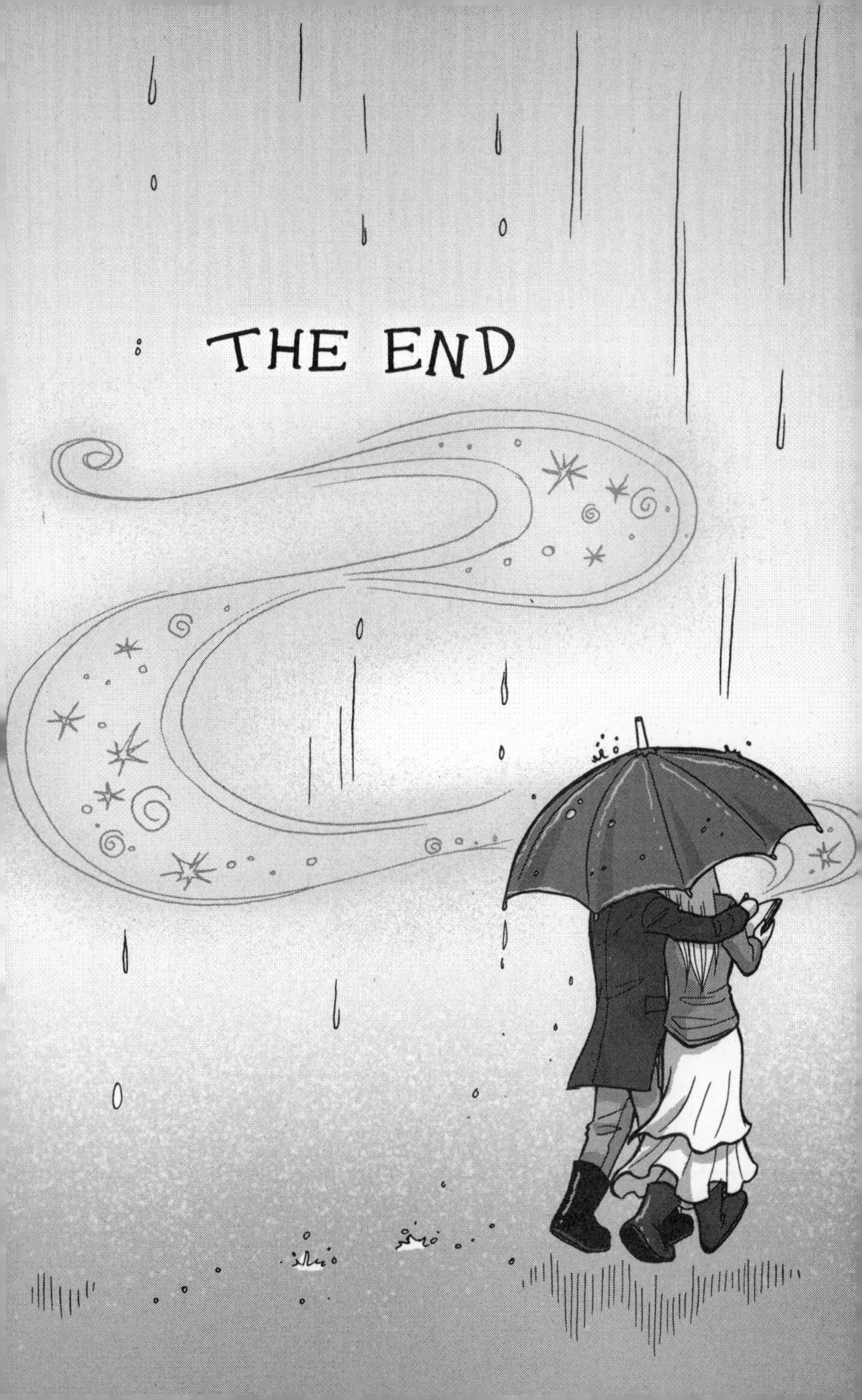
THE END

For Kazu, Mom, & Tim.

Additional thanks to:

Becky, Shadi, Ben, Alan, Judy, Kean, Christi, Cynthea, Khang, Chris, the Flight Crew, the supportive blog readers, my patient editor Lillian, and especially to my emergency toning team -- Kazu, Alan, Ben, Dee, Olga, Nicole, Laura, and Natalie. This book wouldn't exist without you.

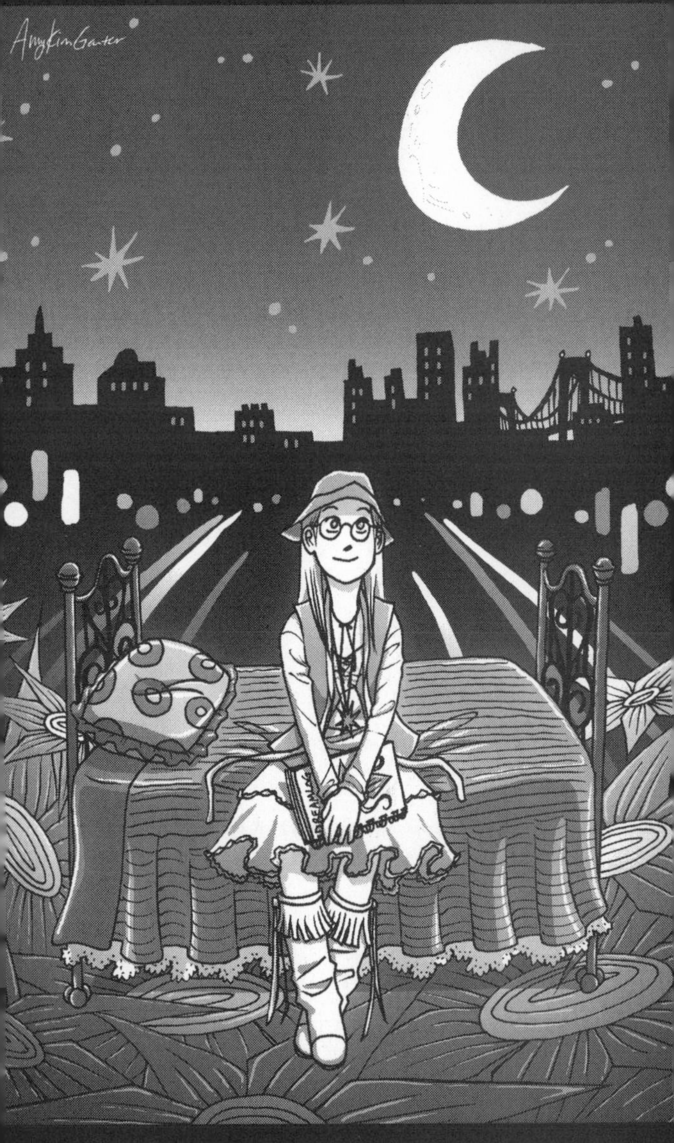

Thank you for reading!

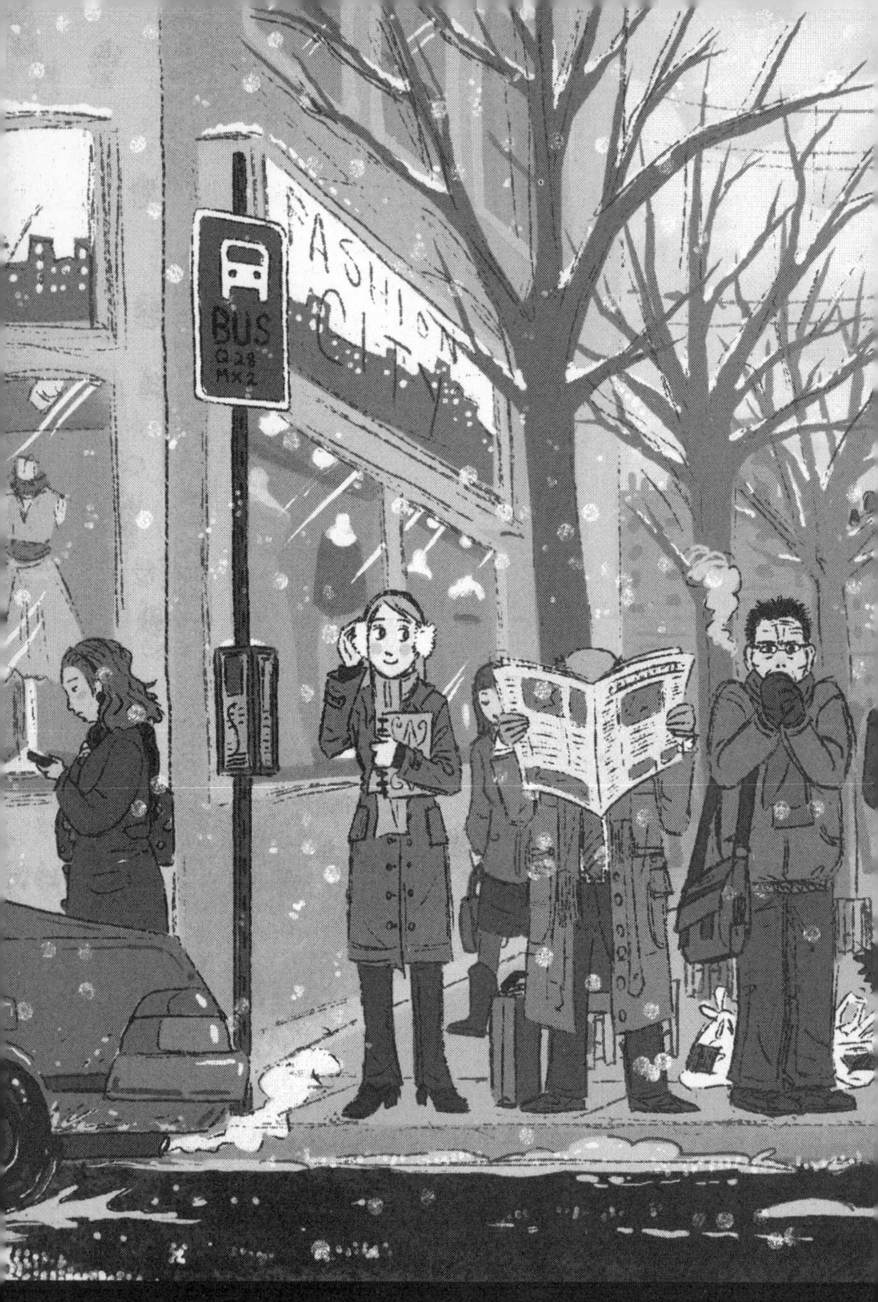
BUS
FASHION
CITY

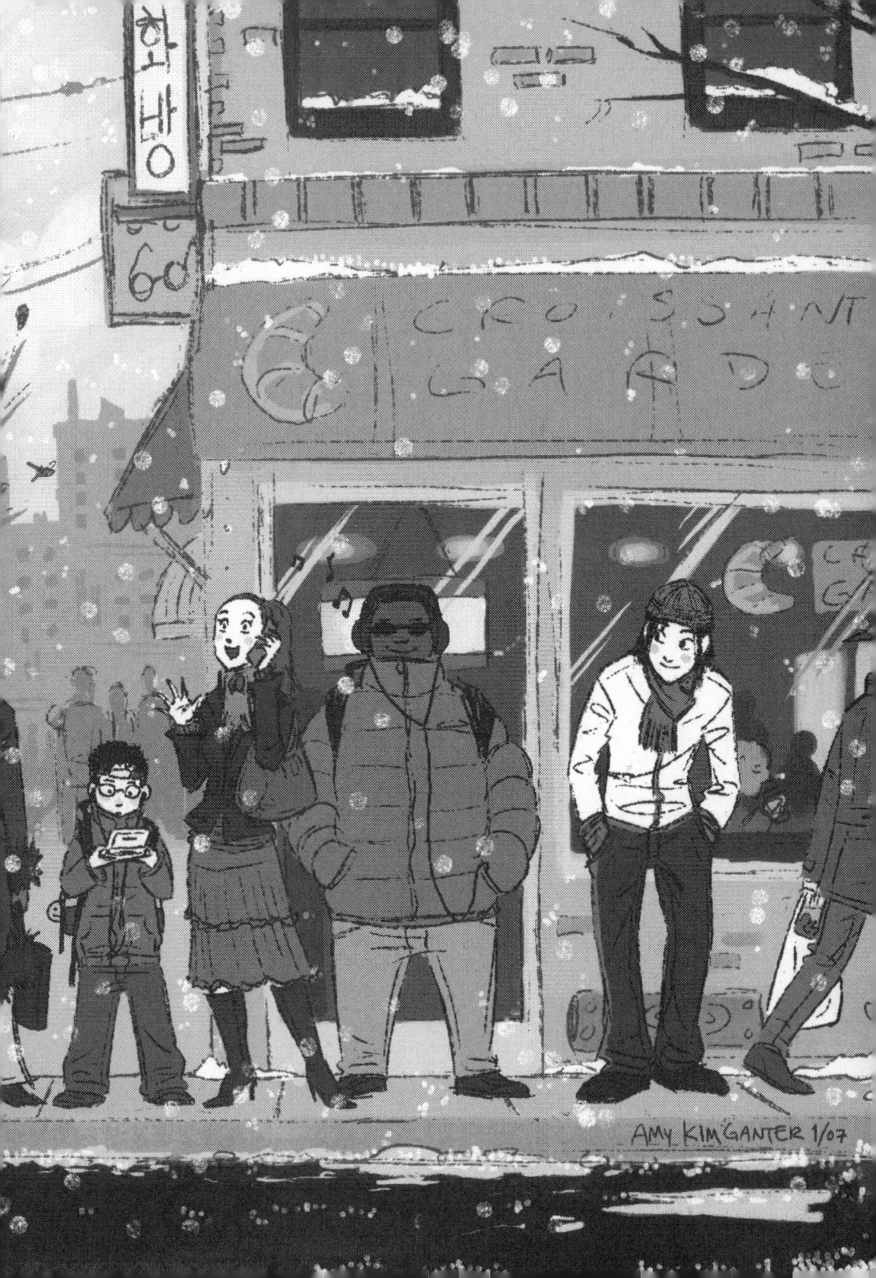
AMY KIM GANTER 1/07

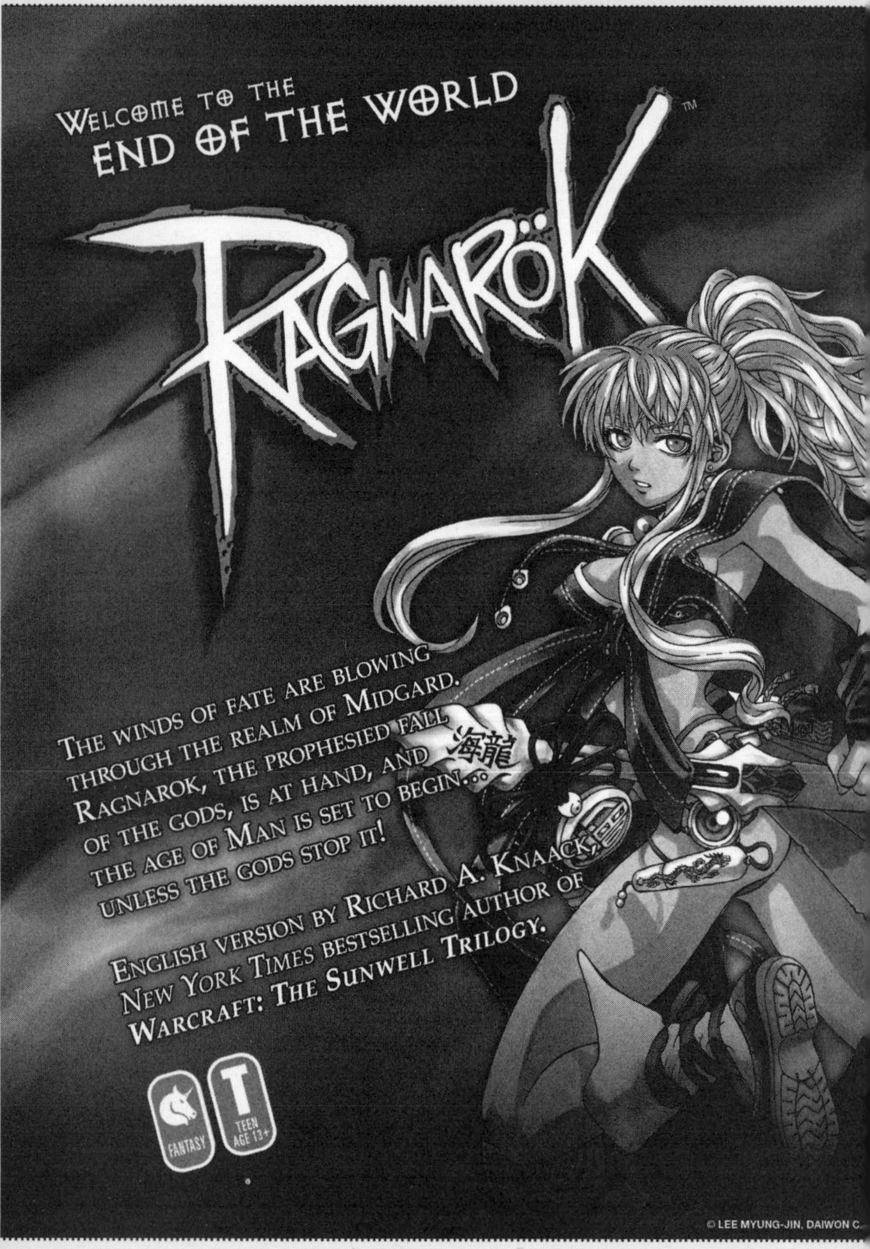
WELCOME TO THE
END OF THE WORLD
RAGNARÖK™
THE WINDS OF FATE ARE BLOWING THROUGH THE REALM OF MIDGARD. RAGNAROK, THE PROPHESIED FALL OF THE GODS, IS AT HAND, AND THE AGE OF MAN IS SET TO BEGIN... UNLESS THE GODS STOP IT!
ENGLISH VERSION BY RICHARD A. KNAACK, NEW YORK TIMES BESTSELLING AUTHOR OF WARCRAFT: THE SUNWELL TRILOGY.
海龍
FANTASY
T
TEEN AGE 13+
© LEE MYUNG-JIN, DAIWON C.

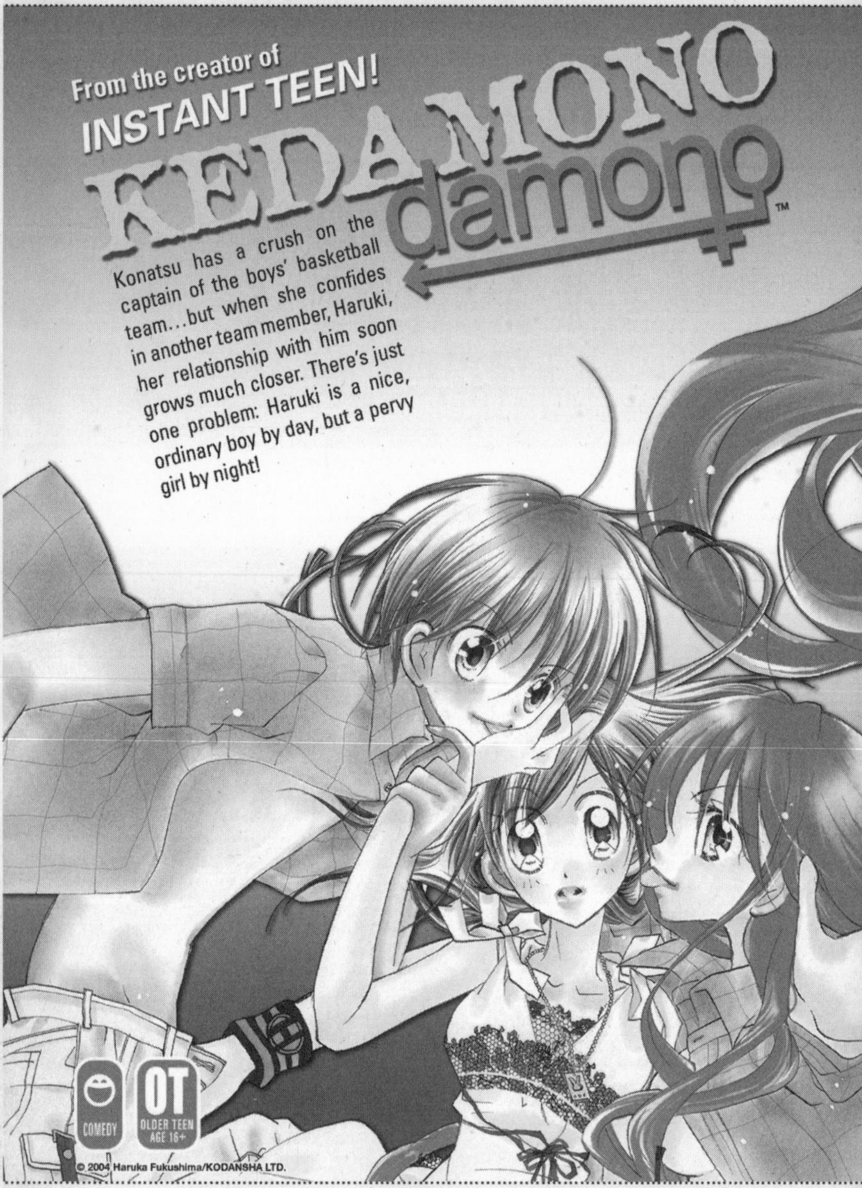
From the creator of
INSTANT TEEN!
KEDAMONO damono™
Konatsu has a crush on the captain of the boys' basketball team...but when she confides in another team member, Haruki, her relationship with him soon grows much closer. There's just one problem: Haruki is a nice, ordinary boy by day, but a pervy girl by night!
COMEDY
OT
OLDER TEEN AGE 16+
© 2004 Haruka Fukushima/KODANSHA LTD.

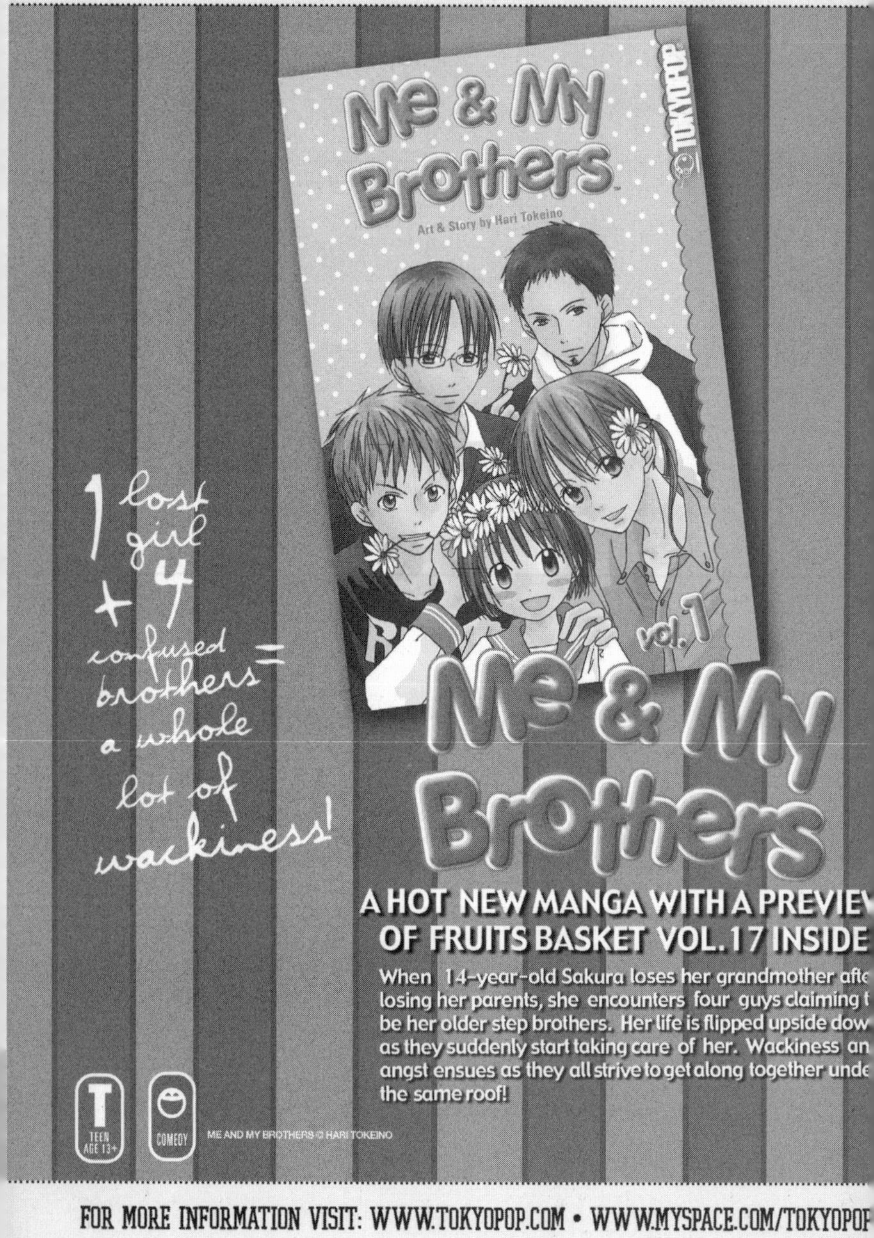
TOKYOPOP
Me & My Brothers
Art & Story by Hari Tokeino
vol. 1

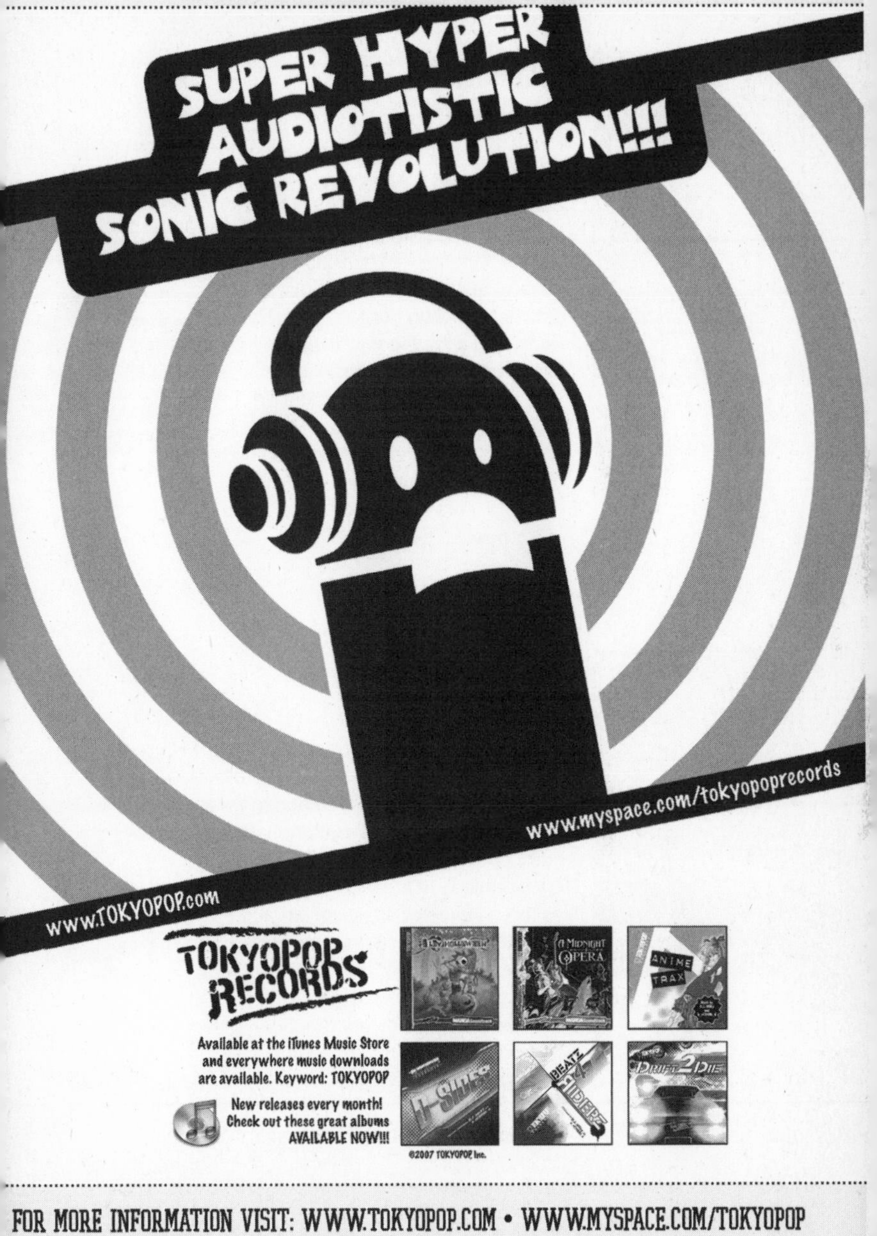
SUPER HYPER
AUDIOTISTIC
SONIC REVOLUTION!!!
www.myspace.com/tokyopoprecords
www.TOKYOPOP.com
TOKYOPOP RECORDS
Available at the iTunes Music Store
and everywhere music downloads
are available. Keyword: TOKYOPOP
New releases every month!
Check out these great albums
AVAILABLE NOW!!!
A MIDNIGHT OPERA
ANIME TRAX
©2007 TOKYOPOP Inc.

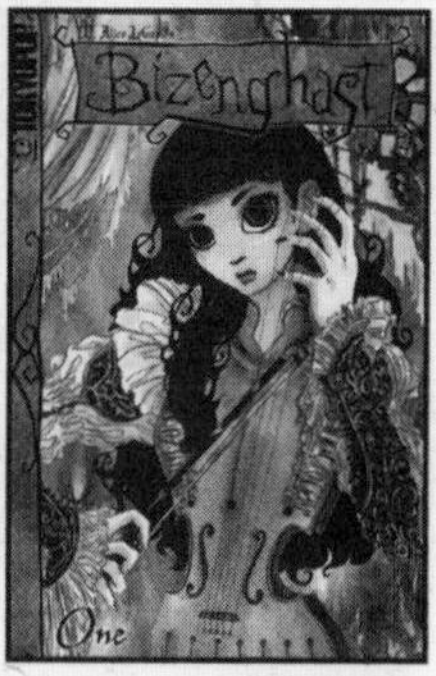
Bizenghast
One

FANTASY TEEN AGE 13+

BIZENGHAST:

BY M. ALICE LEGROW

I enjoy a good scare every now and then, and Bizenghast just has a way of getting under your skin. The best moments in M. Alice LeGrow's tale of tormented souls are the quieter ones: a prince dancing with his lover with a knife at her back, a witch quietly casting a spell on a young girl, then slowly strangling her to death. The book isn't over the top. It's just very, very creepy. It entrances you with its intricate, beautiful art, only to shock you with something unexpected and disturbing. And I, for one, can't wait for more.

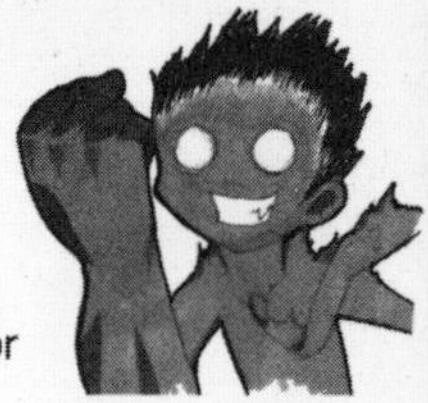

~Tim Beedle, Editor

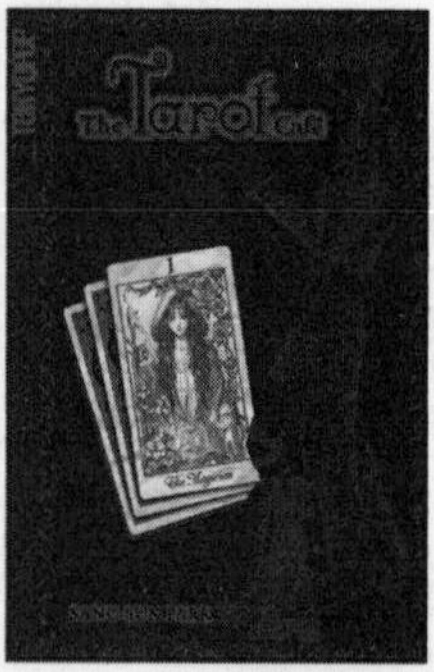

FANTASY TEEN AGE 13+

THE TAROT CAFÉ

BY SANG-SUN PARK

I was always kind of fond of Petshop of Horrors, and then along comes Tarot Cafe and blows me away. It's like Petshop, but with a bishonen factor that goes through the roof and into the stratosphere! Sang-Sung Park's art is just unreal. It's beautifully detailed, all the characters are stunning and unique, and while at first the story seems to be yet another gothy episodic piece of fluff, there is a dark side to Pamela and her powers that I can't wait to read more about. I'm a sucker for teenage werewolves, too.

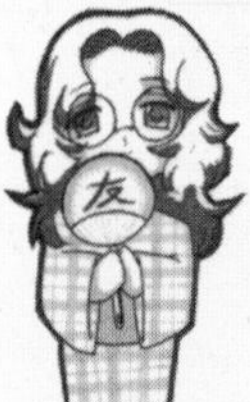

~ Lillian Diaz-Przybyl, Editor

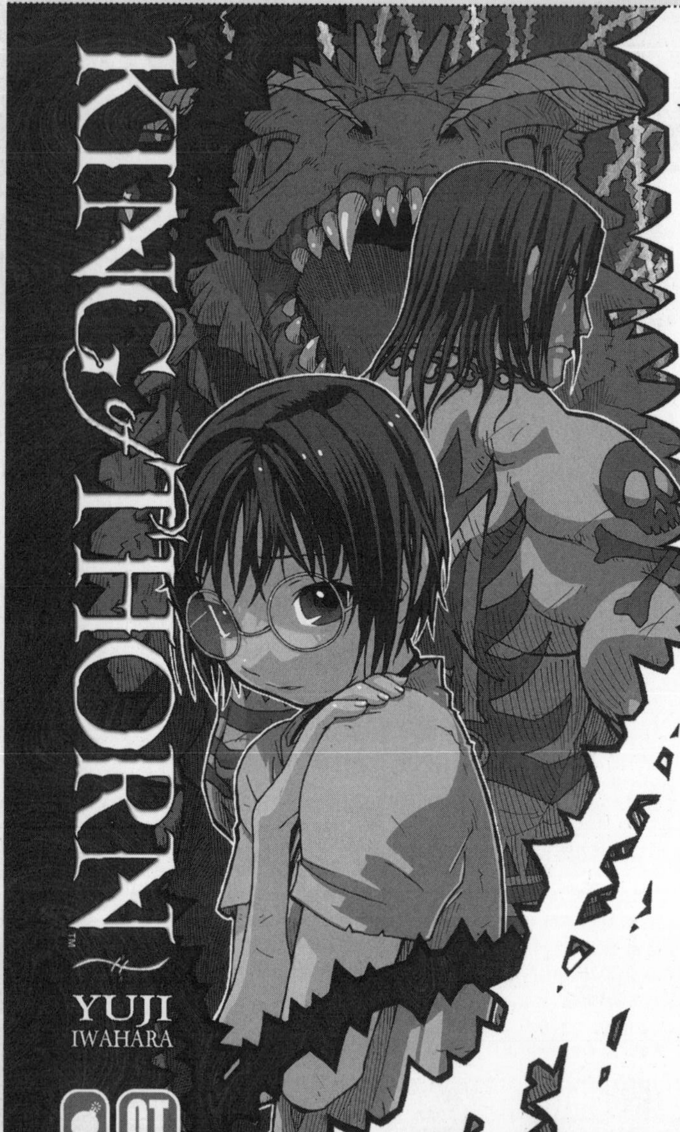
KING OF THORN™
YUJI IWAHARA
ACTION
OT
OLDER TEEN AGE 16+

0591

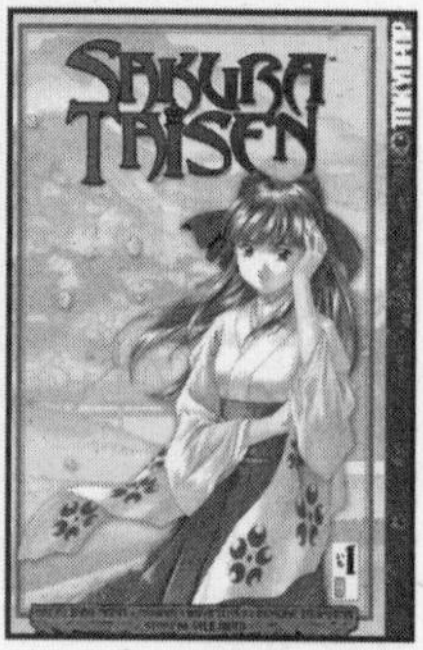
SAKURA TAISEN
TOKYOPOP

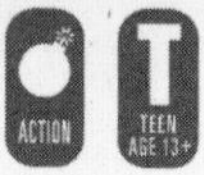
ACTION
T
TEEN AGE 13+

SAKURA TAISEN

BY OHJI HIROI, IKKU MASA AND KOSUKE FUJISHIMA

I really, really like this series. I'm a sucker for steampunk-type stories, and 1920s Japanese fashion, and throw in demon invaders, robot battles and references to Japanese popular theater? Sold! There's lots of fun tidbits for the clever reader to pick up in this series (all the characters have flower names, for one, and the fact that all the Floral Assault divisions are named after branches of the Takarazuka Review, Japan's sensational all-female theater troupe!), but the consistently stylish and clean art will appeal even to the most casual fan.

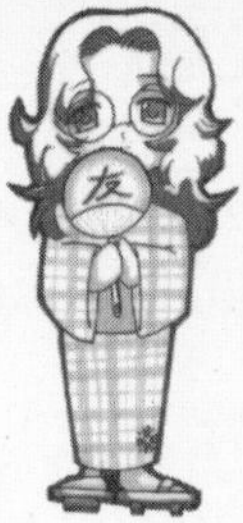

~Lillian Diaz-Przybyl, Editor

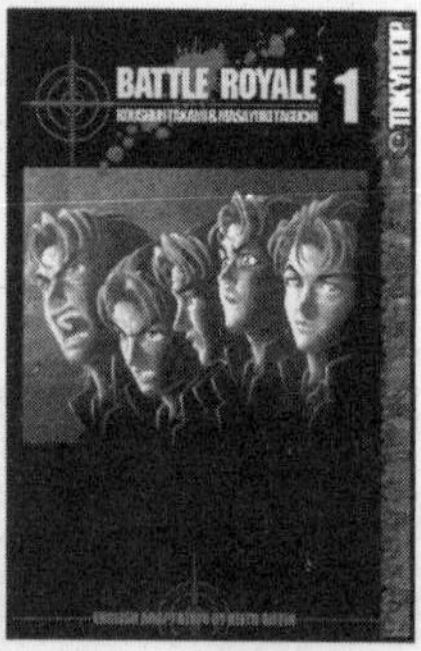
BATTLE ROYALE 1
TOKYOPOP

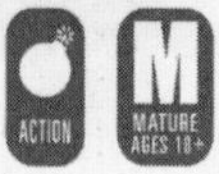
ACTION
M
MATURE AGES 18+

BATTLE ROYALE

BY KOUSHUN TAKAMI AND MASAYUKI TAGUCHI

As far as cautionary tales go, you couldn't get any timelier than *Battle Royale*. Telling the bleak story of a class of middle school students who are forced to fight each other to the death on national television, Koushun Takami and Masayuki Taguchi have created a dark satire that's sickening, yet undeniably exciting as well. And if we have that reaction reading it, it becomes alarmingly clear how the students could so easily be swayed into doing it.

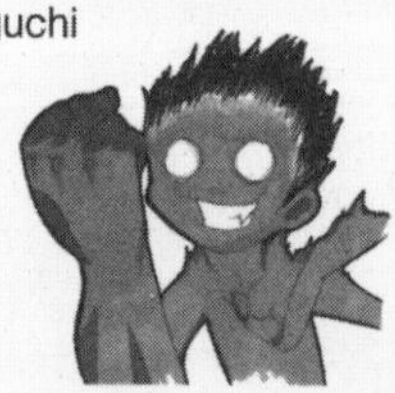

~Tim Beedle, Editor